Mastering the
Verbal SAT*1/PSAT

Building Vocabulary Skills, Critical Reading Skills, and Critical Thinking Skills for Top Performance

Second Edition

Larry S. Krieger, M.A.T.

Douglas J. Paul, Ph.D.

*SAT is a registered trademark of the College Entrance Examination B___ ___ ___ ___ which was not involved in the production of, and does not endorse, this pr___

Great Source Education Group

A Houghton Mifflin Company

Wilmington, MA

D0813499

Teacher's Edition Contents

Introduction and Schedule Options T5

SAT Pretest Explications T15

SAT Posttest Explications T23

Student Edition i

Mastering the Verbal SAT1/PSAT

 A Unique Program

Mastering the Verbal SAT1/PSAT is the only SAT preparation book specifically designed for SAT-preparation classes based in schools.

Our editorial team and program authors have taught SAT-preparation courses to thousands of students from more than 500 participating school districts. Hundreds of these students have gone on to become national merit finalists or to receive other scholarships based, in part, on SAT scores.

Over the past five years, our authors have also conducted staff-development workshops in schools around the country, training teachers to conduct their own in-school preparation classes.

The strategies and lessons in *Mastering the Verbal SAT1/PSAT* are based upon this extensive experience. Although individual score increases depend on individual student effort, classroom teachers using this program should, within a short time, compile local records showing overall significant improvement on the verbal SAT.

A Unique Organization

Mastering the Verbal SAT1/PSAT is the only major text organized to completely reflect the increasing order of difficulty of the actual test. Analogy and sentence completion questions are arranged in sets that begin with easy questions and conclude with very challenging questions. This organization is known as the "order of difficulty."

The first unit, "Building a Foundation," teaches students the vocabulary and critical thinking skills they will need to answer easy analogy, sentence completion, and critical reading questions.

After students establish a solid foundation, those who are able to move higher will tackle the second unit, "Ascending the Staircase." This unit teaches students the vocabulary and critical thinking skills they will need to answer the more challenging "middle-third" questions.

The third unit, "Rising to the Top of the Tower," teaches students the vocabulary and critical thinking skills they will need to answer the most difficult questions on the SAT.

 A Unique Instructional Program

Mastering the Verbal SAT1/PSAT is the only SAT preparation book that is organized around the principles of effective classroom teaching. Each chapter

- is divided into teachable lessons that can be used in traditional or block formats and

- concludes with a review and set of questions that enable students to apply their skills.

Each lesson

- begins with a high-interest opener that introduces a topic and serves as a springboard for the lesson,

- uses a concrete case example to illustrate a strategy or instructional point,

- contains guided practice questions that provide a detailed explanation of carefully chosen practice examples, and

- provides students with independent practice questions that give them an opportunity to practice and refine their skills.

A Unique Approach to Vocabulary Development

Mastering the Verbal SAT1/PSAT contains three vocabulary chapters. Each chapter uses prefixes, roots, and synonym clusters to teach students 400 carefully selected vocabulary words that repeatedly appear on the SAT.

The vocabulary words are then used as right and wrong answers in our sentence completion and analogy questions. As a result, students have an opportunity to practice their vocabulary in the actual formats of real SAT questions.

The Appendix provides students with specially created Word Histories that teach students the etymology of key words from ancient Greece and Rome. It also provides students with specially designed lessons on key Social Studies and Literature terms that often appear on the SAT.

Our 400 key vocabulary words are printed on flash cards that appear at the back of the student text. The flash cards are organized by prefixes, roots, and synonym clusters to aid retention.

 ## A Unique Approach to Sentence Completions

Mastering the Verbal SAT1/PSAT begins by teaching students how to find the key word or group of words in each sentence completion question.

Our research team identified four basic patterns of sentence completion questions. We call these four types *definitional*, *contrast*, *cause and effect*, and *synonym* sentences. The text provides students with a full lesson on each of these four types of sentence completion questions.

Experience gained from repeatedly taking the SAT showed that the strategy of using positive and negative words is a very effective technique for helping answer sentence completion questions. *Mastering the Verbal SAT1/PSAT* contains a full lesson (pages 196-202) on this technique.

Mastering the Verbal SAT1/PSAT provides students with a full lesson (pages 290-300) devoted to mastering the most difficult sentence completion questions used on the SAT. There is also a full lesson (pages 301-308) devoted to helping students find a comfortable pace on sentence completion questions.

A Unique Approach to Analogies

Mastering the Verbal SAT1/PSAT begins by teaching students a three-step procedure for solving analogy questions.

Our research team identified nine key types of analogies. These nine types account for over 95 percent of the analogies used on the SAT. We call these nine types *Is a Type Of, Is a Part Of, Is a Place Where, Is Used To, Relative Size, Is Characteristic Of, Antonym, Definitional*, and *Degree* analogies. *Mastering the Verbal SAT1/PSAT* provides students with a full lesson on each of these nine types of analogies.

Experience gained from repeatedly taking the SAT showed that the strategies of eliminating unrelated pairs and working in reverse are very effective techniques for helping answer analogies. *Mastering the Verbal SAT1/PSAT* contains full lessons (pages 317-329) on these techniques.

 ## A Unique Approach to Critical Reading

The critical reading passages used in *Mastering the Verbal SAT1/PSAT* are taken from books used by the SAT. For a suggested bibliography see pages 414-416.

Our research team identified five basic critical reading skills tested on the SAT. These five skills are finding the main idea, answering vocabulary-in-context questions, identifying paraphrases, recognizing inferences, and identifying the author's tone. The text provides students with a full lesson on each of these five critical reading skills.

Mastering the Verbal SAT1/PSAT provides students with two complete lessons on paired passages. The first lesson (pages 258-263) introduces students to the types of passages and questions used in paired passages. The second lesson (pages 338-351) provides a detailed discussion on the new comparison questions that conclude each paired passage.

Mastering the Verbal SAT1/PSAT provides students with a full lesson (pages 352-362) devoted to helping students find a comfortable pace on critical reading passages.

A Unique Teacher's Edition

Mastering the Verbal SAT1/PSAT is the only major preparation text that includes a complete teacher's edition to accompany the student edition.

The teacher's edition contains annotations to accompany the student edition, answers to all of the questions in the student text and item explications for all of the questions on both of the practice tests.

Mastering the Verbal SAT1/PSAT is the only SAT program that allows teachers to give homework assignments from a student text that does not contain the answers.

This program allows any competent teacher to organize and deliver a professional-quality course on the SAT or PSAT.

 ## A Unique Lasting Benefit

Mastering the Verbal SAT1/PSAT offers much more than simple preparation for the verbal SAT or PSAT. Long after the test is completed, students will realize residual benefits from improving their critical thinking skills and reading comprehension skills. Likewise, the program builds useful vocabulary, not simply for the day of the test, but for long-term retention.

The program approaches test-preparation by teaching students to think critically, to move forward with confidence, and to apply a variety of strategies for solving verbal problems.

A Wide Variety of SAT Courses

High schools across America teach SAT courses in a wide variety of ways. Many school districts report that the best results occur when they use a combination of alternatives. Here are the most popular options:

- A full year college study skills course with one semester devoted to verbal skills and one semester devoted to math skills.

- A semester college study skills course with one quarter devoted to verbal skills and one semester devoted to math skills.

- A one week before or after school "Crash Course."

- A 3-4 week before or after school SAT course.

- An evening course meeting once or twice a week for 4-6 weeks.

- A two to three week course offered in the summer.

- Special SAT units integrated into 10th grade English and math courses.

- Special SAT units integrated into 11th grade English and math courses.

- Special SAT units integrated into 12th grade English and math courses.

A Flexible Program

Mastering the Verbal SAT1/PSAT is designed to provide teachers with a flexible program that can be successfully used with any SAT course. Here are four basic options based upon how much time you have. Each option is discussed in detail on the following pages.

1. **Minimum Program:** Up to 10 Hours. Many teachers have asked us, "What do you recommend if we only have 5-10 hours and it is one week before the test?" The Minimum Program is designed to solve this problem. The Minimum Program introduces students to the SAT and familiarizes them with the three types of verbal questions used on the test. However, the program does not provide in-depth discussion or extensive practice. Needless to say, we recommend that if at all possible students spend more time preparing for the SAT.

2. **Core Program:** 10-20 Hours. The Core Program is designed to provide students with a solid overview of the SAT. Students learn about the test and practice key skills for answering sentence completion, analogy, and reading comprehension questions.

3. **Enriched Program:** 20-35 Hours. The Enriched Program is designed to provide students with a comprehensive understanding of the SAT. Students learn about the test and practice skills for answering sentence completion, analogy, and critical reading questions. In addition, students begin a vocabulary building program

4. **Advanced Program:** Over 35 Hours. The Advanced Program is designed to provide students with an in-depth course of study for the SAT. Students complete our entire program thus acquiring the vocabulary skills, critical thinking skills, and critical reading skills they will need to perform their best on the SAT. This program provides students with extensive practice and homework.

① Minimum Program 5-10 Hours

pages 1-19 Introduction

pages 21-38 SAT Pretest

page 68 Introduction to Sentence Completions

pages 69-74 Key Words and Groups of Words

pages 75-79 Definitional Sentences

pages 90-92 Introduction to Analogies

pages 228-233 *Definitional* Analogies

pages 126-134 Introduction to Critical Reading

pages 135-146 Finding the Main Idea

pages 147-153 Vocabulary-in-Context

pages 258-263 Introducing Paired Passages

② Core Program 10-20 Hours

pages 1-19 Introduction

pages 21-38 SAT Pretest

page 68 Introduction to Sentence Completions

pages 69-74 Key Words and Groups of Words

pages 75-79 Definitional Sentences

pages 80-85 Contrast Sentences

pages 86-88 Putting It All Together

pages 90-92 Introduction to Analogies

pages 93-99 *Is a Type Of* Analogies

pages 100-106 *Is a Part Of* Analogies

pages 107-114 *Is a Place Where* Analogies

pages 115-121 *Is Used To* Analogies

pages 122-124 Putting It All Together

pages 126-134 Introduction to Critical Reading

pages 135-146 Finding the Main Idea

pages 147-153 Vocabulary-in-Context

pages 154-160 Recognizing a Paraphrase

pages 161-164 Putting It All Together

pages 196-202 Using Positive and Negative Words

pages 228-233 *Definitional* Analogies

pages 258-263 Introducing Paired Passages

pages 338-351 Answering Comparison Questions

pages 370-387 SAT Posttest

③ Enriched Program 20-35 Hours

pages 1-19 Introduction

pages 21-38 SAT Pretest

pages 43-49 Words From Daily Life

pages 50-56 The Mighty Prefix

pages 57-61 Roots and Branches

pages 62-64 Synonym Clusters

pages 65-66 Using Your Vocabulary

pages 69-74 Key Words and Groups of Words

pages 75-79 Definitional Sentences

pages 80-85 Contrast Sentences

pages 86-88 Putting It All Together

pages 90-92 Introduction to Analogies

pages 93-99 *Is a Type Of* Analogies

pages 100-106 *Is a Part Of* Analogies

pages 107-114 *Is a Place Where* Analogies

pages 115-121 *Is Used To* Analogies

pages 122-124 Putting It All Together

pages 126-134 Introduction to Critical Reading

pages 135-146 Finding the Main Idea

pages 147-153 Vocabulary-in-Context

pages 154-160 Recognizing a Paraphrase

pages 161-164 Putting It All Together

pages 184-189 Cause-and-Effect Sentences

pages 190-195 Synonym Sentences

pages 196-202 Using Positive and Negative Words

pages 203-205 Putting It All Together

pages 208-214 *Relative Size* Analogies

pages 215-221 *Is Characteristic Of* Analogies

pages 222-227 *Antonym* Analogies

pages 228-233 *Definitional* Analogies

pages 234-236 Putting It All Together

pages 238-247 Making Inferences

pages 248-257 Recognizing Attitude, Mood, and Tone

pages 258-263 Introducing Paired Passages

pages 264-267 Putting It All Together

pages 338-351 Answering Comparison Questions

pages 370-387 SAT Posttest

④ Advanced Program Over 35 Hours

pages 1-19 Introduction

pages 21-38 SAT Pretest

pages 43-49 Words From Daily Life

pages 50-56 The Mighty Prefix

pages 57-61 Roots and Branches

pages 62-64 Synonym Clusters

pages 65-66 Using Your Vocabulary

pages 69-74 Key Words and Groups of Words

pages 75-79 Definitional Sentences

pages 80-85 Contrast Sentences

pages 86-88 Putting It All Together

pages 90-92 Introduction to Analogies

pages 93-99 *Is a Type Of* Analogies

pages 100-106 *Is a Part Of* Analogies

pages 107-114 *Is a Place Where* Analogies

pages 115-121 *Is Used To* Analogies

pages 122-124 Putting It All Together

pages 126-134 Introduction to Critical Reading

pages 135-146 Finding the Main Idea

pages 147-153 Vocabulary-in-Context

pages 154-160 Recognizing a Paraphrase

pages 161-164 Putting It All Together

pages 168-173 The Mighty Prefix, Part II

pages 173-177 Roots and Branches

pages 178-180 Synonym Clusters

pages 180-181 Using Your Vocabulary

pages 184-189 Cause-and-Effect Sentences

pages 190-195 Synonym Sentences

pages 196-202 Using Positive and Negative Words

pages 203-205 Putting It All Together

pages 208-214 *Relative Size* Analogies

pages 215-221 *Is Characteristic Of* Analogies

pages 222-227 *Antonym* Analogies

pages 228-233 *Definitional* Analogies

pages 234-236 Putting It All Together

pages 238-247 Making Inferences

pages 248-257 Recognizing Attitude, Mood, and Tone

pages 258-263 Introducing Paired Passages

pages 264-267 Putting It All Together

pages 272-277 The Mighty Prefix, Part III

pages 278-283 Roots and Branches

pages 284-286 Synonym Clusters

pages 287-288 Using Your Vocabulary

pages 290-300 Answering the Toughest Sentence Completion Questions

pages 301-305 Pacing Your Work on Sentence Completion Questions

pages 306-308 Putting It All Together

pages 310-316 *Degree* Analogies

pages 317-321 Eliminating Unrelated Pairs

pages 322-329 Working in Reverse

pages 330-336 Pacing Your Work on Analogies

pages 338-351 Answering Comparison Questions

pages 352-362 Pacing Your Work on Critical Reading

pages 363-368 Putting It All Together

pages 390-395 Every Word Has A History-Ancient Greece

pages 396-399 Every Word Has A History-Ancient Rome

pages 402-407 Subject Area Terms-Social Studies

pages 408-411 Subject Area Terms-Literature

pages 425-456 Vocabulary Cards

pages 370-387 SAT Posttest

Pretest Explications

Section 1: Sentence Completions

1. **E** You are looking for a word to describe Isaac Asimov. The key group of words *who wrote on a variety of topics* defines a *multifaceted* author.

2. **F** The reversal word *although* signals a contrast between how the book originated and the way the book actually reads. Since the first part of the sentence tells you that *Notes of a Native Son* originated as *a series of separate articles*, you should look for a word that best contrasts with *separate*. The only choice that contrasts with *separate* is *unified*.

3. **A** Look at the second half of the sentence first. If other countries want to *develop their own entertainment industries*, would they want to increase or decrease the number of programs coming from the United States? Decrease—so *ZAP* second blank choices *augment* (B), *enlarge* (C), and *expand* (D). Now you only have to consider (A) and (E). *Inflamed* doesn't make sense in the first blank, so the answer has to be (A).

4. **C** *Although* signals a reversal. Jessika enjoys fame, but she is described as a person *who needs quiet and repose.* These key words tell you that Jessika craves *solitude*—she needs to be left alone sometimes.

5. **D** Divide this sentence in half at the comma. The second half of the sentence needs a negative word to go with *accused*. Since the second half is negative, the first half must be positive because of the reversal word *but*. Therefore, *ZAP* all of the first blank choices that are negative—*criticized, distorted,* and *ridiculed*. Now you're left with (A) and (D). Choice (D) works best—Galileo's theories are *accepted* today, but the people of his day accused him of *heresy*.

6. **D** The faculty committee is *sympathetic*. This tells you that they care and are *concerned*. The supporting word *and* indicates that the committee will follow up their *concern* by trying to make the situation better—*to rectify the conditions* (D).

7. **B** The second half of the sentence describes what the psychologist gradually developed with years of experience. A person who is able to relate *to the feelings and frustrations* of others has *empathy*.

8. **D** The blank words have to do with learning something *new* and experiencing some type of *pleasure*, so both words need to be positive. *ZAP* all of the negative choices—*tiresome* (A), *insignificant* (C), and *banal* (E). With the choices narrowed between (B) and (D), the words *observing* and *beautiful* at the end of the sentence tell you that *aesthetic* is a better choice than *dogmatic* for the second blank.

9. **A** The second half of the sentence, *she always seems to bounce back from adversity*, describes Tawana's trait. *Resilience* means "to bounce back" and is thus the correct answer.

10. **A** Even if you're not sure of the meaning of *oasis* or *raucous*, you can still ZAP most of the choices. Would a *museum* provide *commotion*? No, ZAP (E). Would you describe *city lights* as *refined* or *sedate*? No, ZAP (B) and (C). Now you have to choose between (A) and (D). Is it more likely that the museum provided *serenity* or *dignity*; would a city known for its nightclubs more likely have *garish* or *elegant* lights? *Serenity* makes more sense in the first blank, and *garish* describes bright, glaring city lights in the second blank.

Section 1 – Analogies

11. **E** ANALOGY TYPE Is A Part Of
    SENTENCE A *link* is part of a *chain*.
    A *bone* is part of a *skeleton*.

12. **A** ANALOGY TYPE Degree
    SENTENCE *Scalding* is very *hot*.
    Glacial is very *cold*.

13. **A** ANALOGY TYPE Is Used To
    SENTENCE A *microscope* is used to see *small* things.
    A *telescope* is used to see *distant* things.

14. **D** ANALOGY TYPE Is A Type Of
    SENTENCE A *crown* is a type of *headgear*.
    A *mansion* is a type of *residence*.

15. **B** ANALOGY TYPE Definitional
    SENTENCE A *chaperone* is a person who *escorts* someone.
    A *guard* is a person who *protects* someone.

16. **A** ANALOGY TYPE Definitional
    SENTENCE A *eulogy* expresses *praise*.
    An *elegy* expresses *sorrow*.

17. **B** ANALOGY TYPE Definitional
    SENTENCE To *secede* is to withdraw from an *organization*.
    To *retreat* is to withdraw from a *position*.

18. **B** ANALOGY TYPE Is Used To
    SENTENCE An *emollient* is used to make things *soft*.
    A *desiccant* is used to make things *dry*.

19. **E** ANALOGY TYPE Definitional
    SENTENCE A *statement* that is indirect is *digressive*.
    A *route* that is indirect is *roundabout*.

20. **B** ANALOGY TYPE Is Characteristic Of
    SENTENCE Having *conceit* is characteristic of an *egoist*.
    Having *disloyalty* is characteristic of a *traitor*.

21. **C** ANALOGY TYPE Definitional
    SENTENCE To *salve* is to soothe a person's *wound*.
    To *mollify* is to soothe a person's *anger*.

22. **C** ANALOGY TYPE   Antonym
     SENTENCE   Something *impious* lacks *reverence*.
                   Something *empty* lacks *content*.

23. **B** ANALOGY TYPE   Definitional
     SENTENCE   An *intransigent* person would not allow a
                   compromise.
                   A *dogged* person would not allow a *surrender*.

Section 1 – Reading

24. **D** This is a main idea question, so eliminate choices that are too broad or too narrow in scope. Choice (E) is too broad–it goes well beyond what is discussed in the passage. Choice (A) is discussed only in the last paragraph. The *etymology of the word Bohemian* (B) is limited to lines 76-83, and the passage only alluded to a criminal life-style (C). The best choice is (D); the views of Murger, Balzac, and others were discussed at length by the author.

25. **A** The young artists were "driven by an unstinting sense of calling, enter into art . . . ." Choice (A) works best because *unstinted* means that these young artists didn't hold back at all, they gave themselves freely to art; they had a *commitment to developing their artistic talents*.

26. **C** *Zap* obviously wrong choices like (A), (D), and (E), which are in no way supported by the passage. In choice (C), *meager resources* is a paraphrase of the phrase "but without means" (lines 17-18) and is therefore the correct answer.

27. **E** Balzac obviously respects the talents of the Bohemians, so *ZAP* negative choices (B) and (D). Lines 29-31 quote Balzac as saying that these young people would probably lead their nation as "diplomats . . . writers, administrators, soldiers. . . ." You can infer from this that Balzac believes that *most Bohemians will become leaders* (E).

28. **A** This is an author's attitude question. As in the last question, *ZAP* all of the negative choices (B, C, D, and E) since Balzac cleary has respect for the Bohemians.

29. **C** Both Murger and Balzac view the Bohemians positively, so *ZAP* negative choices (A) and (B). Neither author was quoted as saying anything about *the Bohemians' ability to assimilate* (D) nor their *commitment to helping the disadvantaged* (E). Both author's are impressed with the Bohemians' way of life.

30. **B** SAT likes to test unfamiliar meanings of words in their vocabulary-in-context questions. From earlier in the passage you have a sense of the conditions in which Bohemians lived—line 38 states "Bohemia has nothing. . . ." The Bohemians were able "to make more of life than *material* (B) conditions seemed to permit."

31. **E** The statement is being declared by a "stage figure of the 1840s." Therefore, you can ZAP (A), (B), and (C). Bohemians wouldn't likely say such negative things about themselves; *ZAP* (D). The point of view reflected is that of a person who has an occupation, has an income, and is most likely part of the middle class (even if he or she is an artist).

32. **C** The only choice implied by the stage figure's quotation is (C), which can be inferred from lines 56-57 and 61-62. If the Bohemians weren't able to live honestly, they might need to resort to criminal acts.

33. **C** These lines discuss the existence of a Bohemian way of life in modern times, the eighteenth-century, and ancient times. While *Bohemianism* as a written term may only refer to ninteenth-century Bohemia, as a *way of life* it is *not unique to the nineteenth century*.

34. **D** A careless reader might pick (A) because of the line "... part of old Czechoslovakia, as the gypsies' place of origin. ..." But on the previous page it said that this was erroneous. The origin of the word "Bohemia" came from the French, who most likely used the word because of supposed similarities between the young artists and gypsies.

35. **D** If the word "bohemian" was the word used by most French people for gypsy, *common* must mean *widespread* (D).

36. **C** Nothing is mentioned about the Bohemians' actions being misleading (A), or of financial support provided by the bourgeois (B). Choice (D) can be *ZAPPED* because, although the Bohemians' struggles are mentioned earlier in the passage, they are not mentioned in this paragraph. The only statement that is supported by the last paragraph is (C). Lines 90-94 discuss that Bohemians and the bourgeoisie each have some kind of attraction to the others' way of life. Line 101 reinforces this by saying that they are "parts of a single field," indicating that they are similar.

Section 2 – Sentence Completions

1. **D** *But* indicates a reversal in the logic of the sentence. Work on the second blank first. At one time these people must have been close, so they probably *suffered* (A), *felt* (C), or *shared* (D) *each other's sorrows*. ZAP (B) and (E). Now you can more easily decide on the first blank. The reversal *but* tells you that they are no longer close, so they would not be *friends* (A) or *united* (C).

2. **D** A person who doesn't like to keep people waiting probably tries hard to be on time, or *punctual* (D). The other choices do not work in the context of the sentence.

3. **D** *Although* tells you that the scientists thought one way, but the lab tests contradicted what they thought. Since the lab tests showed no *adverse reaction* to the chemical, the scientists must have originally thought that *the chemical would be* harmful, or *toxic* (D).

4. **A** The components are described as having *parts from vacuum tubes and solid-state electronics*. The word that belongs in the blank should have a meaning similar to *containing parts from both*. *Hybrids* are things made of different or mixed parts.

5. **C** If the members of the town council are split on how they feel about the mayor, they are in disagreement. *Dissension* means "conflict or discord."

6. **A** *Although* indicates a reversal in the logic of the sentence. Feeding the animals makes them *easier to study* so ZAP *belligerent* (B), *contemptuous* (C), and *dejected* (D). Feeding them would most likely make them easier to control or *docile* (A), but it would also change, or *disrupt* (A), the way they normally behave.

7. **E** What type of manager is Amber? One who makes decisions based on facts. The correct answer is (E), *pragmatic*—meaning a practical, no-nonsense, facts-only kind of manager.

8. **B** The missing words that describe Keisha are defined in the second half—*seldom spoke out and never wasted money*. Only choices (B) *reserved*, (C) *taciturn*, and (D) *inhibited* could mean *seldom spoke out*; ZAP (A) and (E). Of the three choices left, only *frugal* (B) means *never wasted money*.

9. **E** The first part of the sentence describes Ken as *stubborn*. When he is asked to do something he doesn't want to do, he becomes even more *stubborn*. Another word for *stubborn* is *obdurate* (E).

Section 2 – Analogies

10. **E** ANALOGY TYPE   Is A Part Of
    SENTENCE   A *bird* is covered with *feathers*.
    A *fish* is covered with *scales*.

11. **D** ANALOGY TYPE   Is A Part Of
    SENTENCE   A *musician* is part of a *band*.
    A *singer* is part of a *choir*.

12. **B** ANALOGY TYPE   Is A Place Where
    SENTENCE   An *arena* is a place where a *conflict* could be held.
    A *forum* is a place where a *discussion* could be held.

13. **A** ANALOGY TYPE   Definitional
    SENTENCE   A *prologue* is an introduction to a *novel*.
    A *preamble* is an introduction to a *statute*.

14. **D** ANALOGY TYPE   Antonym
    SENTENCE   To *exonerate* is to free from *blame*.
    To *liberate* is to free from *captivity*.

15. **B** ANALOGY TYPE   Degree
    SENTENCE   *Hubris* is having great *pride*.
    Ecstasy is having great *pleasure*.

Section 2 – Reading

16. **E** This is a main idea question. Choices (A), (C), and (D) are too narrow in scope—the prominence of men in sculpture was briefly discussed in lines 6-11, Nevelson's influences were mentioned in lines 35-41, and the materials she uses were discussed only in the last paragraph. Choice (B) is too broad in scope. Glance through the passage and you'll find that Louise Nevelson and her works are mentioned or are the topic of each paragraph.

17. **D** It's important that you read the quote in the context of the whole paragraph. The author says that "Louise Nevelson . . . in the eyes of many critics is the most original female artist alive today." The author goes on to give an example of one critic's thoughts on Nevelson to back up this statement. The correct answer has to be positive, therefore (A), (B), and (C) can be ZAPPED. Choice (E) can also be ZAPPED because Kramer's quote has nothing to do with *religious intent*.

18. **D** Nevelson's theory is that "art is everywhere." The only choice that illustrates this theory is (D); she sees art in ordinary objects and uses these objects to create her sculptures.

19. **A** Remember on inference questions that your answer must be supported by facts from the passage. Choice (B) may be appealing because of lines 60-61, but it doesn't say that her works have *no qualities characteristic of sculpture*, just that some of them are closer to architecture than sculpture. *ZAP* choice (C) because the author says in line 49 that Nevelson's works are "of great beauty." Choices (D) and (E) are not supported. The best choice is (A) because of lines 55-59—even though Nevelson denies symbolic or religious intent, the author thinks her works "suggest such connotations."

20. **B** The answer is given to you in the rest of the sentence that follows "remarkable." The sentence goes on to say that " . . . the greatest resistance to women artists has been . . . in the field of sculpture." This tells you that the answer has to be (B). Lines 11-13 reinforce this by stating that women sculptors were only recently recognized as "major artists." This makes it *remarkable* that many critics believe a woman is the greatest "twentieth-century sculptor."

21. **C** Nevelson might find some of the objects that she uses outside, but the passage doesn't suggest that she displays her sculptures outside—*ZAP* (A). Lines 51-52 tell you that she only uses black, white, or gold, not several colors—*ZAP* (B). Because the passage says that Nevelson glues and nails objects together, she isn't hand carving them (D). Now that the choices are narrowed down to (C) and (E), it gets harder to decide. You must read carefully. Look at lines 45-47. In addition to wooden objects, she uses architectural ornaments. There is also nothing to suggest that she uses a central object, let alone that it is made of wood (E). However, there are facts which do suggest that her sculptures are *sometimes very large*. The author refers to them as "architectural constructions" and "ambitious works" and says they have "three-dimensional grandeur."

22. **E** Is the tone of the passage positive or negative? Positive—which tells you to *ZAP* negative choices (A), (B), (C), and (D).

23. **B** Choices (C) and (D) should be *ZAPPED* because they are not mentioned in the passage. The entire passage is a description of sea cucumbers, with background on echinoderms thrown into the first paragraph. The correct answer is (B)—the passage describes a *unique animal*, the sea cucumber. If you chose (A), the *misconception* was proven wrong in the first six lines of the passage, not the entire passage.

24. **E** The author's tone is positive, so ZAP (A), (B), (C), and (D). The author shows his amusement with statements like "one of those monstrous county-fair winners" and "Truly these guys are out in left field."

25. **C** The author is not saying that these words inaccurately describe the skin, he is just trying to give a more accurate description by comparing their skin texture to "imperfectly cooked tripe."

26. **D** You're looking for the choice that is NOT a characteristic of the echinoderm phylum. Lines 6-9 tell you that "echinoderms are distinct from other . . . animal groups . . . because they are *radially symmetrical, not bilaterally symmetrical* (D).

27. **A** Lines 76-78 state that the only living creatures at the bottom of the ocean are sea cucumbers, so ZAP (B), (C), and (D). Lines 79-81 state that they "also get along well in shallower waters," so ZAP (E). The correct answer is (A), which is supported with the information in lines 42-48—the "organic debris" is their food.

28. **A** ZAP choice (D) because it is not mentioned in the passage. "Out in left field" is an expression which in this context means that sea cucumbers are like no other animals; they are out of the ordinary, or *unorthodox*.

29. **B** Replace "equipped to" with each of the choices. Choice (B) works best in the context of the sentence. You could also reason that since other creatures are unable to live in the deepest trenches, "few other animals *would be able to* explore" them.

30. **C** You can infer from these lines that sea cucumbers are common in deep waters, but that doesn't imply that they're *the most common animal in the ocean* (A). Choices (B), (D), and (E) are not mentioned in lines 68-78; ZAP them. The main point of these lines is that sea cucumbers can live in deep water while most other living creatures can't (C).

Section 3 – Reading

1. **E** The author is extremely enthusiastic about America throughout the passage, so by line 30 it would be safe to say that the meaning of the phrase "This, then, is America!" is said in a positive sense. Therefore, ZAP (A), (B), (C), and (D).

2. **E** There is nothing in the passage to indicate that the author is writing (A), sketching (B), or on vacation (D)—ZAP these choices. The author is incredibly happy upon arriving in America, but the last paragraph voices his concern of what lies ahead of him after he leaves the safety of the ship. How will he find shelter and food? Choice (E) is a paraphrase of the author's feelings and is the reason he wants to prolong this happy moment.

3. **C** There is no mention of *relatives* in the passage (A), he is definitely not a *tourist* (B), he was not at all *disappointed by the view* (D), and he was on a ship, but that doesn't mean he became a *ferry boat captain* (E). You should have ZAPPED to the correct answer (C), which is supported by the uncertainties mentioned in lines 37-39.

4. **D** While the author does say that the woman "divides up her domain" with the sheets, it is not a description of the *best way to secure privacy*, so you can ZAP (B), even though it is appealing. Choice (A) is a false statement, and choices (C) and (E) are not mentioned in lines 42-44. The sheets are used to emphasize how cramped and small the space is, which leads you to choice (D).

5. **A** There is no hidden meaning in this question. A person who has never known waste wouldn't know what to do with it. The immigrants described came from the "Old Country" and most likely used everything they had (A). All of the other choices say something very negative about *the woman, the immigrants,* and *European cities;* SAT would not have one of these choices be the correct answer.

6. **B** The passage does not suggest that city officials went out of their way to help the immigrants, nor does it mention anything about high rents (even though this may be true)—*ZAP* (C), (D), and (E). Choice (B) is a paraphrase of lines 68-70 and is the correct answer.

7. **D** The neighborhood described is not *ordinary* (B), *fragrant* (C), or *spicy* (E). "Distinctive" in this sense means *characteristic* of, or unique.

8. **D** Which of the choices best describes "Bubbly Creek"? It's an open sewage drain (lines 111-116). Therefore, the name is incongruous (unsuitable) with what it actually is. It was jokingly named "Bubbly Creek" because it is really a *foul smelling drain* (D).

9. **A** Is the tone of the first passage positive or negative? Positive, so *ZAP* (B), (C), and (D). Passage 2 is not necessarily negative or scornful (E), but it is definitely a *realistic* account of what the immigrants faced when they came to America.

10. **A** In order to get this one correct without too much trouble, you have to carefully read the italicized introductory information. If you had read this, you would have correctly answered (A).

11. **D** The author of passage 1 is concerned with where he will find shelter. The description presented in passage 2 is that of horrible living conditions. Therefore, the author of passage 1 had good reason to worry. His concerns were *justified* (D), meaning they were warranted.

12. **C** Most of the statements in the choices are too specific to know how each author would feel about them. However, both passages do deal with immigrants coming from the "Old Country," and they both mention differences between life in Europe and America. Lines 26-27 in passage 1 and most of passage 2 tell of many differences the immigrants encountered in America. Choice (C) is a fairly general statement that both authors would most likely agree with.

Posttest Explications

Section 1 – Sentence Completions

1. **C** The signal words *as a result of* alert you to expect a cause-and-effect relationship. What impact would a conservation program have on the white rhinos of South Africa? It would protect the rhinos so they would no longer be *endangered* (C).

2. **E** If the new equipment were *insignificant* (A), *trivial* (B), or *useless* (D), the government probably wouldn't *forbid*, *ban*, or *block* anyone from taking it—ZAP (A), (B), and (D). If the new equipment were *precious* (C) the government probably wouldn't *encourage* anyone to take it, so ZAP (C). Choice (E) is the only acceptable choice—if the new equipment were *valuable*, the government would probably *prohibit* anyone from taking it.

3. **A** The two choices must agree with each other in this sentence because they both describe Matt and his skills. Therefore, ZAP (C), (D), and (E). The phrase *skills of his profession* tells you that the best answer is (A) because an *inexperienced dabbler* (B) most likely would not have a profession.

4. **B** The *but* in the middle of the sentence indicates a reversal. The first blank must be opposite in tone of the second blank. The second blank needs a word to fit with *routine*, so you should eliminate (A), (C), and (D). The first blank needs a word to fit with *interesting*, so you should eliminate (E). The correct answer is (B)—the coach's game plan looked *innovative* on paper, but the plays were usually *repetitive*.

5. **B** The sentence is contrasting people who can remain *imperturbed* (cool and calm) under trying conditions to those who cannot keep their cool. A person who cannot remain calm, cool, and collected would probably react with *agitation* to a minor problem.

6. **E** Look at the second half of the sentence. They (Copernicus and Kepler) had to endure *criticism* and *ridicule*. Now go back to the first half of the sentence. You're looking for something they *were not unfamiliar with*— *criticism* and *ridicule*. The choice that best describes *criticism and ridicule* is *adversity* (E).

7. **A** Ryan's temperament is opposite that of Sam's. Since Sam sounds like an energetic, go-getter kind of person, Ryan must be the opposite—lacking energy, not involved, and *lethargic* (A).

8. **A** Regan is NOT *argumentative* nor *supercilious*, both negative words, so you can safely ZAP all the negative choices—*arrogant* (B), *combative* and *conceited* (C), *contentious* (D), and *disagreeable* (E). Look up these words

in a dictionary and you'll find that they are similar in meaning to *argumentative* and *supercilious*. The correct answer is (A).

9. **E**   The words belonging in the blanks need to describe the General. A description of the General is given in the sentence—he *gauged the impact of every word he spoke* and he *acted with complete self-control*. The first blank has to be *succinct* (B) or *laconic* (E) because both of these words mean "concise." Between choices (B) and (E), the only word that works to describe *acted with complete self-control* is *unflappable* (E).

Section 1 – Analogies

10. **A**   ANALOGY TYPE   Is A Place Where
     SENTENCE   A *courtroom* is a place where a *lawyer* works.
     A *studio* is a place where an *artist* works.

11. **E**   ANALOGY TYPE   Is Used To
     SENTENCE   A *cot* is used to *lie* on.
     A *bench* is used to *sit* on.

12. **C**   ANALOGY TYPE   Definitional
     SENTENCE   To *schedule* is to *allocate* time.
     To *budget* is to *allocate* money.

13. **E**   ANALOGY TYPE   Is A Type Of
     SENTENCE   An *anecdote* is a type of *story*.
     A *skit* is a type of *play*.

14. **B**   ANALOGY TYPE   Is Characteristic Of
     SENTENCE   Great *skill* is characteristic of a *virtuoso*.
     Great *fervor* is characteristic of a *zealot*.

15. **B**   ANALOGY TYPE   Antonym
     SENTENCE   Being *insolent* is the opposite of having *respect*.
     Being *impulsive* is the opposite of having *restraint*.

Section 1 – Reading

16. **A**   Read the italicized introduction to the passage. Since the passage *is from a discussion of women poets*, there is a pretty good chance that the main purpose of the passage is to *describe the role and contributions of women writers* (A). Five of the seven paragraphs are mainly about women writers while the other choices are mentioned only briefly in the passage. Choice (D) is discussed in the first two paragraphs but only as background information to the main topic of discussion.

17. **D**   The author would actually *disagree* with choices (A–lines 1-3), (C–lines 9-12), and (E– lines 28-34), so *ZAP* them. Although the women wrote of "feelings of regret . . ., fickleness of love, and the ravages of age . . . ", which could be interpreted as *life's injustices* (B), you don't know that the author would agree that poetry is *most often* written about these topics. The best choice is (D), which is supported in lines 1-3.

18. **B**   This is a tough vocabulary-in-context question. It's important to remember that the Japanese men were writing in Chinese. The men who *were* writing in Japanese were doing so "under the persona of a

woman." The key phrase is in the second half of the sentence—"so long as the vernacular remained outside the realm of power and prestige." This line tells you that the women occupied an *advantageous* position in Japan as long as men thought they should be writing poetry in Chinese.

19. **D** You're looking for the choice that is NOT present in Heian literature. The passage said that the Japanese men were writing poetry in Chinese (except for the ones who were writing in Japanese under the persona of a woman), and the Japanese women were writing in Japanese. If you can keep all of this straight, you can *ZAP* choices (A), (B), and (C). Choices (D) and (E) both appear to be correct, so you have to look very closely at the passage. Lines 78-79 suggest that there were some women writing imitation Chinese poetry along with the men, therefore *ZAP* (E). The best answer is (D) because it is never suggested that Japanese women were writing under the persona of a man.

20. **E** *ZAP* (C) because the female authors discussed were writing in Japanese, not Chinese. Lines 52-57 discuss the importance of female authors—they shaped "Japanese literary tradition."

21. **C** At the time the women were writing Japanese poetry, they were not recognized (A), nor were there any military upheavals taking place (B). If you're not sure of the meaning of *melancholy*, the phrase ". . . feelings of regret about the shortness of life, the fickleness of love, and the ravages of age . . . ." tells you that it expresses some sort of *sadness*.

22. **D** Writing about *political corruption* (A) and creating *antiwar literature* (B) can both be *ZAPPED* because neither was mentioned in the passage. The only choice supported by the passage is (D). Lines 79-81 suggest that *they lost their importance*, and line 82 suggests that *their work disappeared*.

23. **C** The author's tone is very neutral. The passage is a *discussion of women poets* and does not attempt to *raise doubts* (A), *find fault* (B), *present an argument* (D), or *attack a belief* (E). The author is only trying to describe women in Japanese literature during the Heian Period, and the tone is very scholarly and matter-of-fact (C).

24. **D** The car is being compared to a snake. When you picture a snake, do you think of something *cramped* (A), *poverty* stricken (B), *dependable* (C), or *reliable* (E)? Probably not—*ZAP* all of them. A snake (especially a greased cobra) would be *fast and sleek* (D).

25. **B** The description in the third paragraph gives you the idea that Etta is a woman people look twice at because she is quite remarkable looking. Phrases like "they were rewarded by the appearance of . . . shapely legs" (lines 24-27) tell you to *ZAP* choices (D) and (E). "Race with time" (lines 29-30) tells you that this woman has aged, but still looks good.

26. **E** Notice the children's initial reaction to Etta's arrival. What did they do when her car pulled up? They ran along the sidewalks because they were very curious. Lines 19-22 tell you that, unlike the adults, they could show their curiosity freely instead of concealing it (E).

27. **D** The answer is found in the rest of the sentence—"because she knew what they thought about her." You can interpret this to mean that they *generally disapproved of her* (D). This is also supported by lines 45-47—it sounds as if they talk about her in a negative way when she's not around, even though they call her Miss Johnson to her face.

28. **B** The sunglasses are mentioned in lines 30-33 and lines 68-69. The first time they are mentioned as a means to hide weariness. The second time they are used to emphasize her relief at being able to be herself when she is alone with Mattie. The author seems to use the sunglasses to symbolize *Etta's need to shield herself* from other people (B); they are one of the "erected decoys" she uses (line 72). You could have ZAPPED (D) because it is not suggested that the sunglasses were being used for practical purposes. Choice (E) could also be ZAPPED because, while it is true that Etta seems detached from the neighbors, she is certainly not detached from Mattie—in fact, Mattie seems to be the only person she feels comfortable with.

29. **C** After you read this passage, you still don't know much about Etta Mae. For example, why did she come back to Brewster Place and why isn't she respected by the people there? The last line of the passage suggests that Etta Mae has something secretive about her life that she cannot hide from Mattie. Throughout the passage, the narrator conveys a sense of *mystery* about Etta Mae with her "erected decoys" and "secrets." The best choice is (C).

30. **C** Their relationship does not seem to be fragile (A), ordinary (D), or childlike (E) in any way—ZAP all three. Lines 69-78 talk about the relationship between Etta Mae and Mattie. Etta Mae finds freedom in Mattie's presence; she can be herself because they know almost everything about each other (lines 74-77). There are no secrets between them because they've known each other too long to deceive the other (C).

Section 2 – Sentence Completions

1. **D** The book describes a deadly insecticide. If this *deadly insecticide can persist in water and soil*, what will it most likely do to insects and wildlife? The correct answer will NOT be positive—ZAP (A), (B), and (E). The author is most likely pointing out that the deadly insecticide could *contaminate* (D) the insects and wildlife.

2. **A** *Although* is a key reversal word that indicates a contrast. The first half of the sentence is positive; therefore, the second half must be negative. Although the book is respected, *few scholars agree with its ideas today*. This means that the book's conclusions were NOT *acknowledged* (B), *acclaimed* (C), *endorsed* (D), or *authenticated* (E). The only choice that works to contrast with the first half of the sentence is *challenged* (A).

3. **D** *Despite* is another key reversal word. The first part of the sentence is positive—Amanda has a *bold plan and well thought out presentation*. *Despite* reverses the logic and tells you that both blanks will be negative. ZAP all of the positive choices—*eager* (A), *energetic* (B), *enthusiastic* (C), and *pleasant/positive* (E). The correct answer is (D).

4. **E** The word that belongs in the blank is described as a *faceless beast of prey*. ZAP (A), (B), (C), and (D) because these words are too positive to describe a *beast of prey*. *Anonymous* (E) is similar to *faceless* in describing the Board of Directors (the beast of prey).

5. **B** Look at the second blank first. Could a civilization *terminate* (A), or *perish* (D) for 700 years and then vanish? No, that doesn't make sense,

so *ZAP* both choices. Now look at the first blank. Some artifacts remain _____, but others *provide glimpses*; the *but* reverses the logic of the sentence. The opposite of artifacts that *provide glimpses* would be artifacts that *remain baffling* (B).

6. **B** Even without the first half of the sentence (which tells you there is a reversal), you can determine the correct answer. Luisa is a skillful mediator who *helped* the two sides reach a compromise. *Inflaming* (A), *magnifying* (B), *embellishing* (D), or *exaggerating* the two sides' differences would definitely not be helpful—*ZAP*. The correct answer is (B).

7. **E** College libraries are usually quiet. The reversal word *but* tells you that the blank will need a word that describes the opposite of quiet. Which word best describes the activity of a *bustling center*? Choice (E), *frenetic*.

8. **C** If you're unsure of the meaning of all of the choices, try *ZAPPING* based on positive/negative connotations. The blank needs a positive word since Taylor is admired for helping people. *ZAP* negatives (A), (D), and (E). A *philanthropist* is a person who is charitable and helps people. Therefore, (C) is the correct answer.

9. **B** The word *and* tells you that the first part of the sentence will be supported by the second part of the sentence. *Critics* would probably not *champion* (A), *applaud* (C), or *imitate* (E) *twisted arguments*—*ZAP* all three. They would either *assail* (B) or *denounce* (D) the arguments. The sentence also says that the candiate's arguments and reasoning didn't clarify the issues. Instead of being *persuasive* (D), the arguments were *convoluted* (B).

10. **C** *Marking the beginning* is the key phrase that describes the kind of event this is—a major event, one that is a turning point or *watershed* (C). You could have *ZAPPED* choices (A) and (E) because the event did not sound *trivial* or *petty*.

Section 2 – Analogies

11. **C**	ANALOGY TYPE	Is A Type Of
	SENTENCE	*Hydrogen* is a type of *gas*.
		Wool is a type of *fabric*.

12. **A**	ANALOGY TYPE	Is A Place Where
	SENTENCE	A *web* is a place where a *spider* lives.
		A *nest* is a place where a *bird* lives.

13. **C**	ANALOGY TYPE	Is A Part Of
	SENTENCE	A *singer* is part of a *choir*.
		An *actor* is part of a *cast*.

14. **A**	ANALOGY TYPE	Definitional
	SENTENCE	A *pinnacle* is the highest point of a *career*.
		A *crest* is the highest point of a *wave*.

15. **D**	ANALOGY TYPE	Definitional
	SENTENCE	A *page* is a person training to be a *knight*.
		An *apprentice* is a person training to be a *master*.

16. **B**	ANALOGY TYPE	Definitional
	SENTENCE	To *condense* a *story* is to make it shorter.
		To *abbreviate* a *word* is to make it shorter.

17. **D** ANALOGY TYPE Is Used To
    SENTENCE A *sedative* is used to *pacify*.
    An *antiseptic* is used to *sterilize*.

18. **D** ANALOGY TYPE Definitional
    SENTENCE A *misnomer* is a wrong *name*.
    A *misconception* is a wrong *idea*.

19. **B** ANALOGY TYPE Definitional
    SENTENCE A *parable* is an *illustrative* story.
    A *joke* is an *amusing* story.

20. **E** ANALOGY TYPE Definitional
    SENTENCE Something *invincible* cannot be *conquered*.
    Something *invulnerable* cannot be *subdued*.

21. **C** ANALOGY TYPE Antonym
    SENTENCE To be *unbalanced* is to lack *equilibrium*.
    To be *indifferent* is to lack *interest*.

22. **A** ANALOGY TYPE Is Characteristic Of
    SENTENCE Appreciating fine *food* is characteristic of an *epicure*.
    Appreciating fine *art* is characteristic of an *aesthete*.

23. **D** ANALOGY TYPE Is Characteristic Of
    SENTENCE *Generosity* is characteristic of a *munificent* person.
    Arrogance is characteristic of a *haughty* person.

Section 2 – Reading

24. **B** First read the meaning of "monoculture" at the end of the passage.
    Now look back at the passage. "Birds get massacred . . . " does not
    sound like something that happens from a gentle change. Choices (A),
    (D), and (E) sound a bit too gentle to describe the change involved. The
    "slide to monoculture" is a deliberate *movement* (B), not a *slip* (C).

25. **E** The author has made it fairly clear that this "slide to monoculture" is a
    bad idea and that it will not be a success, nor will it be easy—*ZAP
    fruitful* (B), *beneficial* (C), and *effortless* (D). With the choices narrowed
    between (A) and (E), look carefully at lines 4-5—" . . . these waters are
    bound to be developed." This phrase means that the development of
    the Niger flood plain is *inevitable*, thus the correct answer is (E).

26. **D** Read lines 5-12 carefully to identify the differences in the way the delta
    is viewed by each. A nomad would view the Niger delta in a *traditional*
    way, seeing the "landscape in motion," while the engineer is a scientist,
    looking at it from a *scientific* viewpoint as a "good place to build."

27. **B** According to lines 16-17, "either the technology was wrong for the
    culture, or the technology itself was faulty." Since the question says that
    the plan was *technologically sound*, then it must be wrong for the culture.
    Choice (B) is supported in lines 18-22; social hierarchies are necessary to
    run the waterworks, but the network of Sahelian relationships is
    horizontal. Choice (A) is not correct because the passage never
    discusses whether the technology was explained to local residents. It's
    tempting to pick (C), but this is *why* waterworks plans are being put in
    place—to make the soil suitable for agriculture. Choice (D) doesn't
    work because the Senegal River was only used as an example of land

resisting technology, not in relation to the design of waterworks for the Niger. Choice (E) is never mentioned in the passage.

28. **A** Lines 18-22 refer to the social difficulties of running the waterworks. The key word *also* in line 23 tells you that the author is continuing the discussion about waterworks and the problems that couldn't be predicted (A). Choice (B) is wrong because the planners *did* care about the environment and even feel guilty about it (lines 63-66). That's why they sent Jamie to set up a conservation reserve. Choices (C), (D), and (E) have nothing to do with the phrase in question.

29. **A** Lines 41-50 discuss the problems that were created by cattle-ranching and rice-growing schemes, which both require water. You can find your answer in lines 47-50 (the cattle had plenty of water but died from lack of pasture, and 20% of the grazing land—same as pasture—went to growing rice). Choice (B) is a false statement—the cattle died and the rice polders didn't produce any rice, so the schemes were not a success. Choices (C), (D), and (E) are not suggested by the passage.

30. **C** This question is difficult because you must understand the whole passage to have a sense of the author's attitude toward the World Bank in lines 51-53. The word "undaunted" is used in a critical way (C). If you rephrase the sentence, the author is basically saying that even though the World Bank's agricultural schemes have failed in the past, it hasn't scared them off from investing fifty million more. This doesn't make a lot of sense to the author, who is basically asking: "Why haven't you learned your lesson?" The author has a critical attitude and implies that he does not think very highly of the World Bank's investments. The author's attitude is not *respectful* (A), *hopeful* (B), *understanding* (D), or *indifferent* (E).

31. **E** The "onslaught" refers back to lines 53-56, which state that a "further threat to the area comes from twenty dams planned for the river . . . ." The author does not describe the waterworks in a positive light, and this phrase indicates that the plans to develop the delta are *more harmful than beneficial* (E). You can eliminate (C) because it is a positive statement. It is apparent that the author never sees the plans as victims of bad luck (D), or insignificant (B). Potential political problems are never mentioned (A).

32. **C** There is never a *misunderstanding about the effects of dam construction on waterfowl populations* (A). In fact, the planners are fully aware that more dams mean a reduction of waterfowl. There is never any mention of *a plan to encourage hunting* (B), only that hunting would be hard to stop. You can't assume that there were *large losses of waterfowl* in the 1984 drought (D), or that this triggered the original plan for a refuge. Lines 64-66 indicate that the reason Jamie is there is to ease the conscience of northern planners who know they are hurting the environment in the south. The planners know that developing the flood plain reduces waterfowl habitat, and they want to try and put a plan in place to alleviate the problems that more dams will create (C).

33. **B** There is no suggestion that Jamie believes that *saving waterfowl is not an appropriate goal for scientists* (A), only that bird reserves in the delta are not appropriate. Choice (C) is not necessarily true; European interest in waterfowl preservation is mostly well-intentioned, albeit ill-advised. Choice (D) is not a conclusion offered by Jamie. Choice (E) is never mentioned. Lines 98-101 are part of Jamie's conclusion in his report to

Switzerland: " . . . the desired reserve system exists already—it is the thousands of square kilometers of seasonally flooded pastures managed traditionally . . . ." This is saying that regular flooding *is* the best conservation practice (B).

34. **E** The passage never mentions European conservation groups (A), opposition from the local people (C), or picking another site (D). *ZAP* all three. Jamie does believe that there is a threat to waterfowl existence, so to say that no threats exist (B) is a false statement. Jamie makes several points in lines 73-86 about it being impractical, if not impossible, to set up a waterfowl reserve.

35. **D** The author's attitude is definitely one of agreement and respect for Jamie's views. Therefore, you can eliminate anything negative—(A) and (C). The author never seems to have any trouble comprehending Jamie's views, so get rid of (E). For the author to be neutral towards Jamie's views (B), there wouldn't be anything written that was critical of investors and planners of the waterworks—and there is.

Section 3 – Reading

1. **E** First *ZAP* all of the choices that don't make sense in the context of the sentence. *Innocent* (B), *credulous* (C), and *plain-spoken* (D) don't work very well to describe "mathematical relationships." With the choices narrowed between (A) and (E), it makes more sense that Mendel wanted to chart the traits in a way that would be *easily understood*. The correct answer is (E).

2. **C** You will find the answer in lines 41-43—the Brunn Society members gave his report "polite attention." Choice (C), *courteous indifference*, is another nice way of saying the same thing.

3. **D** Choice (A) would not work; lines 60-62 suggest the opposite. Choices (B), (C), and (E) should be *ZAPPED* because they were not mentioned nor were they implied by the authors. How did the "skeptical Society members" view Mendel? As undistinguished and lacking in academic credentials (lines 46-49). This implies that the members most likely would have taken Mendel's ideas more seriously if his academic credentials had been more impressive (D).

4. **D** The author doesn't really seem to have a strong opinion about *those who failed to appreciate the importance of Mendel's findings* (the Brunn Society members). Choices (B), (C), and (E) all describe strongly negative attitudes, and choice (A) is a very positive attitude. The choice that best describes the author's more neutral attitude is (D).

5. **E** Mendel's theories dealt with hereditary elements in plant traits (lines 38-39). But as the italicized intro states, he was a pioneering figure in genetic research. The results of Mendel's experiments went far beyond his data.

6. **C** Lines 73-75 present a question. The rest of the passage answers the question using Barbara McClintock as an example. Each paragraph deals with factors that could cause a scientific breakthrough to be underrated.

7. **A** This question is answered in lines 78-85. McClintock's research in 1951

was at "odds with accepted beliefs." In 1953, the "helical structure of DNA was elucidated" (made clear). If this information had been made clear before 1951, McClintock's views would have been more accepted and thus *welcomed* (A).

8. **E** " . . . the reciprocity between cognition and visual perception was so intimate . . . she knew by seeing and saw by knowing." This means that there was an interdependence between what she saw and what she knew. Something that is *intertwined* (E) is united intimately.

9. **D** Look at lines 115-119. These lines describe McClintock's analysis of the genetic patterns in maize. To McClintock, the spots on the kernels were " . . . codes in a text . . . that she could read directly and thereby infer a genetic message." The choice that is most similar to McClintock's analysis is (D).

10. **A** *ZAP* choices (B), (C), (D), and (E)—they are all factors that *hindered* other scientists' ability to understand McClintock's ideas. The correct answer is (A), which is supported in lines 124-129.

11. **B** The italicized introduction tells you that both passages discuss difficulties Mendel and McClintock had in communicating their new ideas. The correct answer is (B). None of the other statements are supported by the passages.

12. **A** The author of Passage 1 mentions in lines 60-62 that the Society members were not familiar with the way that algebra was used by Mendel to support his conclusions. This would suggest that the authors of Passage 1 would probably agree with the statement in Passage 2.

13. **C** The second passage does not support McClintock becoming an artist (A), a best selling author (B), an impoverished scientist (D), or a recluse (E). Barbara McClintock was honored with a Nobel Prize in 1984 (line 72), and the importance of Mendel's work was finally recognized.

Mastering the

Verbal SAT1/PSAT

Building Vocabulary Skills, Critical Reading Skills, and
Critical Thinking Skills
for Top Performance

About the Authors

Larry S. Krieger is the nation's leading expert on preparation for the verbal SAT. As a veteran of 25 years in the public schools, he has taught in urban, rural and suburban districts in North Carolina and New Jersey. While authoring major textbooks in American History, Sociology, and World History, he developed unique and effective methods for preparing for the verbal SAT. His program significantly raised scores in the districts where he taught and in the pilot districts for *Mastering the Verbal SAT1/PSAT*. Mr. Krieger has taught thousands of students and worked with teachers across the country, training them to integrate vocabulary development, critical reading skills, and critical thinking skills across the subject areas of language arts, science, mathematics, and social studies. He is currently the social studies supervisor in Montgomery Township, New Jersey.

Douglas J. Paul has conducted hundreds of workshops and inservice programs for students and teachers around the country. As the president of Profiles Corporation, he has also managed numerous test-development projects for large school districts and state departments of education. In the mid-1980's, his experience with test construction allowed him to develop a number of unique tutorial methods for helping students prepare for college admissions tests. He has authored several test-preparation programs, including *Inside the SAT, Buckle Down on the SAT,* and *Dr. Paul ZAPS the ACT.*

The publications department at Profiles Corporation was instrumental in polishing and completing this book. In particular, the authors wish to thank John Hansen, managing editor, Jennifer Booth, manager of design and production, and members of the publications team, including Doria Duncalf, Karen Nichols, Julia Render, Cindy Place, and Chris Wolf.

This book is the product of several years of research and development involving a large number of students, teachers, counselors, administrators, and parents. The authors gratefully acknowledge their many contributions.

The authors also wish to express appreciation for the support and contribution of Chris Johnson, Robin Herr, Sue Paro, Sandra Easton, and Richard Spencer.

Mastering the
Verbal SAT*1/PSAT

**Building Vocabulary Skills, Critical Reading Skills, and
Critical Thinking Skills
for Top Performance**

Second Edition

Larry S. Krieger, M.A.T.

Douglas J. Paul, Ph.D.

Great Source Education Group
A Houghton Mifflin Company
Wilmington, MA

Acknowledgments

Reprinted, by permission, from Paule Marshall, "The Making of the Writer: From the Poets in the Kitchen," REENA AND OTHER STORIES, (New York: The Feminist Press at The City University of New York, 1983), pp. 3–12. © 1983 Paule Marshall. All rights reserved.

From BEAUTIFUL SWIMMERS by William Warner. Copyright © 1976 by William Warner. By permission of Little, Brown and Company.

From WHEN AND WHERE I ENTER by Paula Giddings. Copyright © 1985, by Paula Giddings. By permission of William Morrow and Company, Inc.

From GEOLOGY IN THE URBAN ENVIRONMENT by Utgard, McKenzie, and Foley. Copyright © 1978, Burgess Publishing Co. Originally extracted from USGS Circular 601-K, 1975.

Acknowledgments, continued on page 452

Contents

Reviewers vii
Introduction 1
SAT Pretest 21

UNIT 1: Building a Foundation 39
CHAPTER 1: BUILDING A FOUNDATION FOR VOCABULARY 41
Lesson 1: Words From Daily Life 43
Lesson 2: The Mighty Prefix 50
Lesson 3: Roots and Branches 57
Lesson 4: Synonym Clusters 62

CHAPTER 2: BUILDING A FOUNDATION FOR SENTENCE COMPLETIONS 67
Lesson 5: Key Words and Groups of Words 69
Lesson 6: Definitional Sentences 75
Lesson 7: Contrast Sentences 80

CHAPTER 3: BUILDING A FOUNDATION FOR ANALOGIES 89
Lesson 8: "Is a Type Of" Analogies 93
Lesson 9: "Is a Part Of" Analogies 100
Lesson 10: "Is a Place Where" Analogies 107
Lesson 11: "Is Used To" Analogies 115

CHAPTER 4: BUILDING A FOUNDATION FOR CRITICAL READING 125
Lesson 12: Finding the Main Idea 135
Lesson 13: Vocabulary-in-Context 147
Lesson 14: Recognizing a Paraphrase 154

UNIT 2: Ascending the Staircase 165
CHAPTER 5: VOCABULARY FOR ASCENDING THE STAIRCASE 167
Lesson 1: The Mighty Prefix, Part II 168
Lesson 2: Roots and Branches 173
Lesson 3: Synonym Clusters 178

CHAPTER 6: SENTENCE COMPLETIONS FOR ASCENDING THE STAIRCASE 183
Lesson 4: Cause-and-Effect Sentences 184
Lesson 5: Synonym Sentences 190
Lesson 6: Using Positive and Negative Words 196

CHAPTER 7: ANALOGIES FOR ASCENDING THE STAIRCASE 207
Lesson 7: "Relative Size" Analogies 208
Lesson 8: "Is Characteristic Of" Analogies 215
Lesson 9: "Antonym" Analogies 222
Lesson 10: "Definitional" Analogies 228

CHAPTER 8: CRITICAL READING FOR ASCENDING THE STAIRCASE 237
Lesson 11: Making Inferences 238
Lesson 12: Recognizing Attitude, Mood, and Tone 248
Lesson 13: Introducing Paired Passages 258

UNIT 3: Rising to the Top of the Tower 269

CHAPTER 9: VOCABULARY FOR RISING TO THE TOP OF THE TOWER 271
Lesson 1: The Mighty Prefix, Part III 272
Lesson 2: Roots and Branches 278
Lesson 3: Synonym Clusters 284

CHAPTER 10: SENTENCE COMPLETIONS FOR RISING TO THE TOP OF THE TOWER 289
Lesson 4: Answering the Toughest Sentence Completion Questions 290
Lesson 5: Pacing Your Work on Sentence Completion Questions 301

CHAPTER 11: ANALOGIES FOR RISING TO THE TOP OF THE TOWER 309
Lesson 6: "Degree" Analogies 310
Lesson 7: Eliminating Unrelated Pairs 317
Lesson 8: Working in Reverse 322
Lesson 9: Pacing Your Work on Analogies 330

CHAPTER 12: CRITICAL READING FOR RISING TO THE TOP OF THE TOWER 337
Lesson 10: Answering Comparison Questions 338
Lesson 11: Pacing Your Work on Critical Reading 352

APPENDIX A: SAT POSTTEST 369

APPENDIX B: WORD HISTORIES 389
Lesson 1: Every Word Has a History—Ancient Greece 390
Lesson 2: Every Word Has a History—Ancient Rome 396

APPENDIX C: SUBJECT AREA VOCABULARY 401
Lesson 1: Subject Area Terms—Social Studies 402
Lesson 2: Subject Area Terms—Literature 408

APPENDIX D: READER'S GUIDE TO THE SAT I 413

APPENDIX E: THE PSAT WRITING TEST 417

APPENDIX F: PREPARING FOR THE BIG DAY 449

400 SAT Words You Absolutely Need to Learn 453

Reviewers

Dr. Penny Beers
Language Arts Supervisor
Palm Beach County Schools
West Palm Beach, Florida

Dr. Alan Brantley
Directory of Secondary Education
Rowan-Salisbury Public Schools
Salisbury, North Carolina

Maryanne Burritt
Social Studies Department Chair
Garces Memorial High
Bakersfield, California

Dr. Dana Callen
School Improvement Resource Developer
Leon County Public Schools
Tallahassee, Florida

Linda Cramer
Special Education Teacher/SAT
    Instructor
Princeton High School
Princeton, New Jersey

Victoria Ferrera
English Teacher/SAT Instructor
University High School
Newark, New Jersey

Dr. Pat Finger
Curriculum Specialist for
    English/Language Arts
Guilford County Public Schools
Greensboro, North Carolina

Joanne Francione
Director of Instructional Services
Greece Central School District
Rochester, New York

Robynn Greer
Curriculum Coordinator for Social
    Studies
Clayton County Public Schools
Morrow, Georgia

Patti Harrold
History Department Chairperson
Edmond Memorial High School
Edmond, Oklahoma

Cindy Henry
Supervisor of Educational Training
New Hanover County Public Schools
Wilmington, North Carolina

Patricia Kline Grady
Teacher, Grade 7 English, Reading
    Specialist
Brentsville District Middle/High School
Nokesville, Virginia

Patricia A. Koklnos
Supervisor of Language Arts K-12
Albany City School District
Albany, New York

Dr. Joseph Kreskey
Superintendent of Schools, Retired
Edison Public Schools
Educational Consultant
Watchung, New Jersey

Sandra Landtroop
Humble Independent School District
Kingwood High School
Humble, Texas

Ann Lawrence
Superintendent of Schools
Saddle Brook Public Schools
Saddle Brook, New Jersey

Dr. Dorothy Lloyd-Brown
Directory of Secondary Language Arts
DeKalb County Schools
Decateur, Georgia

Trudy Matthews
Language Arts Supervisor, Retired
New Hanover County Public Schools
Wilmington, North Carolina

Introduction

After completing the Introduction, you will be able to

1. identify the three types of questions used on the verbal portion of the SAT.

2. understand the SAT scoring system.

3. identify your personal starting score on the verbal SAT.

4. explain the difference between random guessing and *ZAPPING*.

INTRODUCTION

No matter what your academic level, the strategies in this book can help you improve your performance on the verbal part of the Scholastic Assessment Test (SAT) or the Preliminary Scholastic Assessment Test (PSAT). This isn't speculation. The authors have already tested and proven these strategies with thousands of students. Throughout this book, they are sharing with you more than twenty years of insights and experience in helping students raise their SAT scores.

You can take the SAT without preparation—and take whatever score you happen to get—or you can take control of the test by applying the strategies in *Mastering the Verbal SAT 1/PSAT*.

"Good morning and welcome!"

Add local information regarding test sites, dates, and numbers of students taking each test.

On seven Saturday mornings each year, a total of over 1.3 million high school juniors and seniors hear the following announcement:

> *"Good morning and welcome! The SAT I: Reasoning Test will be given this morning. Testing will begin in a few minutes. I want to tell you first that I am required to read standardized instructions and I cannot deviate from them. Pay close attention to these instructions as I read them."*

During the next three hours, students across the United States will work on one of the longest and most difficult academic tests they have ever taken—the Scholastic Assessment Test, or SAT. Each SAT contains seven sections. The three verbal sections contain 78 questions testing vocabulary, verbal reasoning, and critical reading skills. The three math sections contain 60 questions testing problem-solving skills in algebra and geometry. A seventh "experimental section," containing either math or verbal questions, looks like the other parts of the test but does not count toward your score.

After what may seem like an eternity to many students, the proctor (the person giving you the test) finally makes the announcement everyone has been longing to hear:

> *"This test administration is over. Thank you for your cooperation. Please take your belongings and leave the building quietly."*

Exhausted but relieved, you head for the nearest exit. Despite the proctor's request to leave quietly, most students eagerly exchange impressions about the test they have just taken.

Confused students may complain that the readings were "boring and hard to understand," while the analogies and sentence completions were filled with "big words nobody uses." Many students return home feeling upset and wondering why they had to take the SAT.

What Is the Purpose of the SAT?

Why do 1.3 million students sacrifice a Saturday morning taking such a tedious and difficult test? The answer to this question begins with the role of the SAT in the college admissions process.

Add recent admissions information available from local colleges and universities.

Each year, over 2 million high school seniors apply to colleges and universities across the United States. Many of these institutions don't have enough space to accept all of the qualified candidates from whom they receive applications. For example, in 1994 the University of North Carolina at Chapel Hill received applications from 15,600 high school seniors. The university, unfortunately, had space for only 3,300 incoming students. By one means or another, admissions officers had to decide who would be accepted and who would be rejected.

Consider inviting an admissions officer to your school. Many universities offer such a service.

Most admissions officers carefully examine each applicant's grade point average (GPA), class rank, extra-curricular activities, and letters of recommendation. The problem is that some high schools are better than others, so it's hard to compare grades and grade points; a GPA of 3.8 in one school may not be as good as a GPA of 3.2 in another.

Discuss the problems of comparing grade point average from one school to another or from one city to another.

The SAT provides admissions officers with a "standardized" score to help them make their selection decisions. A standardized test score makes it possible to compare applicants from widely different backgrounds, or even applicants from one year to the next.

The PSAT and College Scholarships

In addition to college admissions, the SAT is also used by students who are attempting to win valuable scholarships. The National Merit Scholarship Corporation (NMSC), for example, awards Merit Scholarships worth a total of $26 million dollars per year.

Competition for these scholarships begins with the Preliminary Scholastic Assessment Test (PSAT). The PSAT is given on two dates in October of each year. Like the SAT, it tests verbal and math skills, and it includes a third subtest on writing skills.

The NMSC recognizes about 50,000 students who attain the highest scores. This group is then reduced to 15,000 National Merit Semifinalists.

Semifinalists must complete an NMSC application and take the SAT to confirm the PSAT performance. The top 6,700 Finalists are awarded Merit Scholarships.

Distribute NMSQT information available from your guidance office.

For a detailed explanation of the process, see the PSAT/NMSQT Student Bulletin in your high school guidance office.

Using This Text

Before going into any detail on the SAT, let's briefly familiarize you with how this text is organized. Look at the table of contents on page v. As you can see, we begin with an Introductory section containing a Diagnostic Test to help measure your current level of performance. We like to think of this first test as a reality check. It will show you where you actually stand at this time, rather than where you think you stand or where you would like to stand.

Following the Introduction, this text is divided into four units. The first is "Building a Foundation." Many students believe that all of the questions on the SAT are very difficult. Nothing could be further from the truth. In fact, one-third of the questions are relatively easy. The first unit is designed to help you develop skills to ace the easy questions.

The second unit is "Ascending the Staircase." It will help you successfully tackle the middle-level questions on the SAT. Students who master this unit can expect to earn above-average scores that will help them get into most colleges and universities.

The third unit is "Top of the Tower." It will teach you the sophisticated vocabulary and skills that will enable you to earn a top verbal score.

Students who master the "Top of the Tower" can expect to earn scores that will qualify them for the United States' most selective colleges and universities.

In the appendixes we share the insights gained from working with thousands of students about how to get ready for the day of the test. We also present 400 vocabulary words that regularly appear on the SAT. Lastly, the book contains a unique list of recommended books by some of the SAT writers' favorite authors.

Format for the PSAT

Students can think of "format" as form or as shape and presentation. It will be to students' advantage to understand the form of the questions as well as the form of the test booklet.

The "format" refers to the different types of PSAT questions and how they are arranged in the test book. If you're looking at this test as a competition, as you should be doing, familiarity with the format will give you a serious advantage.

Although the questions change from one PSAT to the next, the format is always the same. Since the PSAT is made up of questions from previous SATs, every strategy that you study for the SAT also applies to the PSAT. The best way to practice for the PSAT is to study for the SAT.

Even if students take the test several times, the format will never vary.

There are 2 verbal sections, 2 math sections, and 1 writing section on the PSAT. (See Appendix E for information on the PSAT writing test.) The verbal test, made up of two sections, gives you 16 sentence completions, 12 analogies, and 20 critical reading questions.

FORMAT FOR THE PSAT VERBAL AND WRITING SECTIONS

	Number of Questions
First Verbal Section (25 minutes)	25
Analogies	6
Sentence Completions	6
Critical Reading	13
(1 passage and 1 "paired passage")	
Second Verbal Section (25 minutes)	23
Analogies	6
Sentence Completions	10
Critical Reading	7
(1 passage)	
Writing Section (30 minutes)	39
Identifying Sentence Errors	19
Improving Sentences	14
Improving Paragraphs	6
Total (80 minutes)	87

Format for the SAT

The SAT, like the PSAT, has a consistent and clearly defined format. In addition to three math sections, the SAT contains two 30-minute verbal sections and one 15-minute verbal section. The test gives you a total of 19 sentence completions, 19 analogies, and 40 reading comprehension questions based on 5 passages.

FORMAT FOR THE SAT VERBAL TEST	
	Number of Questions
First Verbal Section (30 minutes)	30-31
Sentence Completions	9
Analogies	6
Critical Reading	15-16
(2 passages)	
Second Verbal Section (30 minutes)	35-36
Sentence Completions	10
Analogies	13
Critical Reading	12-13
(1 passage or 1 paired passage)	
Third Verbal Section (15 minutes)	12-13
Critical Reading	
(1 passage or 1 paired passage)	
Total (75 minutes)	78

Stress the importance of trying hard on every section. Students who want to skip the experimental section might easily skip a scored section by mistake.

Each SAT also contains an Experimental Section that does not count toward your SAT score. This section is used to develop new questions for future tests. The Experimental Section may be either verbal or math, and it could come at any time during the test. The safest way for you to attack this section is to treat it the same as the other sections.

Order of Difficulty

Difficulty is somewhat a personal issue. If a student happens to know the meaning of a "difficult" vocabulary word, that question might appear quite easy. The "order of difficulty" refers to difficulty on the average, not for an individual student.

When you take the SAT, you will notice that the questions become much harder as the test proceeds. This is known as the "order of difficulty." The sentence completions and analogy questions are arranged in increasing order of difficulty; they start out easy and get harder as you go along.

As a general rule, the first third in each group of sentence completions and analogies are easy, the middle third are somewhat harder, and the last third are difficult.

Easy-Third Questions. The SAT writers expect students to do well on the easy-third questions. That's why they use easy vocabulary and wrong answers that are obviously incorrect. As you answer the easy questions, don't "over think" the questions by being too creative. A good rule to keep in mind is that *easy questions have easy answers*. That's why they are easy! Unit 1, our Foundation unit, is designed to help you answer the easy questions that appear in the first third of each group of questions.

Middle-Third Questions. The questions in the middle third of each group of sentence completion and analogies are more challenging. The vocabulary becomes harder, and the wrong answers (distracters) are more attractive. As a result, middle-third questions can be tricky. While it is usually possible to eliminate some obviously wrong answers, there will often be at least one distracter that is particularly tempting. Unit 2 will help you analyze and answer middle-third questions.

The Most Difficult Questions. The questions in the last third of each group of sentence completion and analogies are very difficult. The SAT writers use these questions to identify students with the best vocabulary and verbal reasoning skills. That's why these questions contain the toughest vocabulary words and the most *enticing* (very tempting) distracters. A good rule to keep in mind as you answer hard-third questions is that *hard questions usually have hard answers*. That's why they are hard! Unit 3 will provide you with a number of strategies for successfully answering the SAT's toughest sentence completion and analogy questions.

An Exception: Critical Reading Questions. The reading comprehension questions on the SAT are called "critical reading." Unlike the analogies and sentence completions, the critical reading questions are not arranged in order of difficulty. Instead, these questions are arranged in the order in which they relate to each passage. If the question relates to something in the first paragraph of the passage, it is likely to be one of the first questions to follow the passage. If it relates to the last paragraph in the passage, it will most likely fall near the end of the set of questions. Most of the questions relating to the passage as a whole, like those asking for the main idea of the passage, will be placed either at the beginning or at the end of the set of questions.

If you are having a hard time with one of the critical reading questions at the beginning of the section, don't panic. The next question may be very easy.

Reality Check: Taking the First Diagnostic Test

Depending on your schedule, you may choose to administer the test one section at a time. The most accurate estimated score is obtained by administering all three sections in one sitting.

Before we continue our discussion of the SAT, you should take the Diagnostic Test that begins on page 21. The three sections of the Diagnostic Test will familiarize you with the format and time limits of the actual SAT.

The directions for the test are presented along with the questions. After we discuss the SAT scoring system, your teacher will give you the answers and help you determine your estimated SAT verbal score. Be sure to follow the time requirements for each section.

The SAT Scoring System

How would you feel if you scored 49% on an important test in school? Chances are you'd be disappointed, since your letter grade would probably be an F. On the SAT, however, if you correctly answer 49% of the 78 verbal questions, and you leave the other questions blank, your score will be 20 points above the national average!

You need to know about two types of scores on the SAT.

1) Raw Score: This is the number of questions answered correctly minus a fraction of the number of questions answered incorrectly. Nobody cares about your raw score. It is useful ONLY to help determine your scale score.

2) Scale Score: This is what you normally think about as the SAT score. The lowest possible scale score on the verbal SAT is 200; the highest possible score is 800.

Surprisingly, even though the lowest possible score is 200, the SAT will give you 230 verbal points just for showing up! Anything more than that you have to earn.

As you know, there are 78 verbal questions on the SAT. A raw score of zero will get you 230. A perfect 78 will get you 800.

If 230 points are given for a score of zero, and 800 points are given for a perfect test, then your maximum *gain* is 570 points (800 – 230 = 570). Since there are 78 questions, each question is worth an average of 7.31 points.

Using page 38, your better math students should be able to build a table showing the average point value for each correct item at each point on the raw score scale.

If you study the score scale from a mathematical perspective, you will see that the actual value of each question depends on the total number of questions answered correctly. The average value of 7.31 points is mathematically accurate only for students with 78 correct answers. If you answer only 10 questions correctly, and you leave the other 68 questions blank, each correct answer gives you a gain of 11 SAT points— 50% more per question than if you write a perfect test. **One *implication* (implied suggestion) of this scoring system is that the lower you start, the easier it is to make a significant increase in your score.**

The SAT Raw Score

Here's how the computer determines your SAT verbal score.

STEP **1**

Each Correct Answer Gains One Point. Each correct answer gains you one raw score point, no matter whether the question was hard or easy. For example, if you correctly answer 30 questions, you gain 30 raw score points.

STEP **2**

If your students built the table referenced above, they can now build a second table taking into account the guessing penalty for wrong answers.

Each Incorrect Answer Loses .25 of a Point. What about the questions you missed? If you were blind guessing on the test, on the average you would get four out of five wrong and one out of five correct. In order to wipe out this lucky guess, SAT subtracts an extra point from your raw score for every four wrong answers. In a sense, whenever you get four wrong, they are guessing that you guessed on five problems.

If you have 4 wrong answers, you will lose 1 raw score point off the gain you made from your correct answers. If you have 28 wrong answers, you will lose 7 raw score points (28 x .25 = 7).

Using our example from Step 1, if you correctly answered 30 questions, and you incorrectly answered 28 questions, your raw score is 23 (30–7).

Most students and teachers call this adjustment "the SAT guessing penalty." After the penalty is subtracted, the resulting raw score is rounded to the nearest whole number. **It is important to point out that the guessing penalty does not apply to the questions you left blank.**

The SAT Scale Score

S T E P **3**

Raw Score Converted to Scaled Score. Your raw score is converted to the SAT scale score according to a table. The SAT scale goes from 200 to an 800. The national average verbal score is 500. It is important to *reiterate* (say again, repeat) that the SAT is a very challenging test.

The following table shows a typical conversion from raw score to SAT scale score.

Typical Raw Score to Scale Score Conversion Table

SCORE CONVERSION TABLE					
Raw Score	Verbal Scaled Score	Raw Score	Verbal Scaled Score	Raw Score	Verbal Scaled Score
78	800	51	590	24	440
77	800	50	580	23	430
76	800	49	580	22	430
75	800	48	570	21	420
74	790	47	570	20	410
73	780	46	560	19	410
72	760	45	560	18	400
71	750	44	550	17	390
70	740	43	540	16	390
69	730	42	540	15	380
68	720	41	530	14	370
67	710	40	530	13	360
66	700	39	520	12	360
65	690	38	520	11	350
64	680	37	510	10	340
63	670	36	510	9	330
62	660	35	500	8	320
61	660	34	500	7	310
60	650	33	490	6	300
59	640	32	480	5	290
58	630	31	480	4	280
57	630	30	470	3	270
56	620	29	470	2	260
55	610	28	460	1	240
54	610	27	450	0	230
53	600	26	450	−1	220
52	600	25	440	−2	200
				below	200

SAT Percentile Scores

Unlike the tests you take in school, the SAT does not assign passing or failing scores. Whether your scores are high enough or not depends upon your personal standards and the admission requirements of the colleges in which you are interested.

For some purposes, you might want to know how you did in relation to the other students who took the SAT. "Percentile scores" are given as a number between 1 and 99. This score means that you did as well as or better than that percentage of other students. For example, if your percentile rank is 71, you did as well as or better than 71% of all the students who took the SAT.

For purposes of easy reference, here is a chart showing selected scaled verbal scores and their corresponding percentile scores.

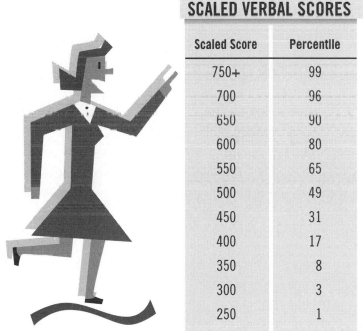

SCALED VERBAL SCORES

Scaled Score	Percentile
750+	99
700	96
650	90
600	80
550	65
500	49
450	31
400	17
350	8
300	3
250	1

Finding Your Personal SAT Verbal Score

Walk students through the worksheet on page 37.

Now that you are familiar with the SAT scoring system, we can go back to the test you already took, the Reality Check Diagnostic Test, and determine your score. Follow your teacher's directions to estimate your initial SAT verbal score.

There is an old *adage* (a saying or proverb) that no wind favors a ship without a destination. As you prepare for the SAT, it is important to have a destination or goal. Your goal may be based upon the score you need to help you gain admission to a college or university. Your goal may also be influenced by a desire to achieve a score that will make you feel good about yourself.

Before going to the next section, write down your goal for the verbal portion of the SAT.

_____

GUESSING on the SAT

Thoroughly familiarize yourself with this activity before trying it with your class. The activity works only in groups. If you are tutoring only one or two students, you should skip to page 17.

Guessing has always been a major issue on the SAT. Many students and teachers incorrectly believe that you should never guess on this test. In fact, however, guessing can significantly raise your SAT score. As an illustration of the impact of guessing, we've developed a couple of short quizzes made up of 30 of the hardest questions ever to appear on the SAT. *To make the questions even harder, we're not even going to show them to you.* Are you ready?

GUESSING QUIZ 1

DIRECTIONS: Circle the correct answer for each question.

Mention that there is no predictable pattern of answers on the SAT. There isn't any valid system for trying to discern a pattern based on the preceding answers.

1.	A	B	**C**	D	E
2.	A	B	C	**D**	E
3.	A	**B**	C	D	E
4.	**A**	B	C	D	E
5.	A	B	C	**D**	E
6.	A	B	C	**D**	E
7.	A	**B**	C	D	E
8.	A	B	C	D	**E**
9.	A	B	C	D	**E**
10.	**A**	B	C	D	E
11.	A	B	**C**	D	E
12.	A	**B**	C	D	E
13.	**A**	B	C	D	E
14.	A	B	C	D	**E**
15.	A	B	C	**D**	E
16.	A	B	**C**	D	E
17.	A	B	C	D	**E**
18.	A	**B**	C	D	E
19.	**A**	B	C	D	E
20.	A	B	C	**D**	E
21.	A	B	C	D	**E**
22.	A	B	**C**	D	E
23.	A	**B**	C	D	E
24.	**A**	B	C	D	E
25.	A	B	C	**D**	E
26.	**A**	B	C	D	E
27.	A	B	C	D	**E**
28.	A	**B**	C	D	E
29.	A	B	**C**	D	E
30.	A	B	**C**	D	E

Scoring Guessing Quiz 1

Now we'll score the quiz using the SAT Verbal Scale (start with 230). Our quiz had only 30 questions, rather than 78, so we'll make each question worth 20 SAT points. Wrong answers will cost you 5 points each, one-fourth of the value of a correct answer.

1. Start with 230 SAT Verbal points.

   (for your blank Quiz 1)   230

2. Gain 20 SAT points for every correct answer.

   (# correct _____ x 20)   _____

3. Subtotal (line 1 + line 2)   _____

4. Lose 5 points for every wrong answer.

   (# wrong _____ x 5)   _____

5. Actual gain or loss on Quiz 1

   (line 3 – line 4)   _____

6. Estimated Quiz 1 Score
   (line 5)   _____

Impact of Guessing on Quiz 1 Score

This result is true on the average for a large number of students. An individual score may be better or worse based on good or bad luck.

If one million students took Guessing Quiz 1, the average total gain would be ZERO. This is because the adjustment for wrong guesses is mathematically established to eliminate the gains from correct guesses.

Guessing Quiz 1 illustrates the impact of random guessing on the SAT Verbal test. The point is, don't bother. Depending on whether you are lucky or unlucky, random guessing might give you a small gain or loss. On the average, however, it will not make a significant difference on your score.

Does this mean you should never guess on the SAT? Not at all. It means only that you should not waste time with blind guessing. Guessing Quiz 2 illustrates the positive impact that comes from guessing after you eliminate one or more answer choices.

GUESSING QUIZ 2

In order to demonstrate the correct way to guess on the SAT, we've eliminated some of the wrong choices on Guessing Quiz 2. You will still be blind guessing, but from fewer choices. Again, you don't get to see the questions. Take Guessing Quiz 2 now.

DIRECTIONS: Circle the correct answer for each question.

Tell students they should not select choices that have been eliminated.

1.	A	~~B~~	C	D	E
2.	A	~~B~~	~~C~~	~~D~~	E
3.	A	B	C	~~D~~	E
4.	A	B	~~C~~	D	E
5.	~~A~~	~~B~~	C	D	E
6.	A	B	~~C~~	D	E
7.	~~A~~	~~B~~	C	D	~~E~~
8.	~~A~~	~~B~~	C	D	E
9.	A	B	~~C~~	~~D~~	E
10.	A	B	C	~~D~~	~~E~~
11.	A	~~B~~	C	D	E
12.	A	~~B~~	C	~~D~~	~~E~~
13.	A	B	~~C~~	D	~~E~~
14.	A	B	~~C~~	D	E
15.	~~A~~	B	C	D	E
16.	A	B	~~C~~	D	E
17.	~~A~~	~~B~~	C	D	E
18.	~~A~~	~~B~~	~~C~~	D	~~E~~
19.	A	B	~~C~~	D	~~E~~
20.	~~A~~	B	C	~~D~~	~~E~~
21.	A	~~B~~	C	~~D~~	E
22.	~~A~~	~~B~~	~~C~~	D	E
23.	~~A~~	B	C	D	~~E~~
24.	A	~~B~~	~~C~~	D	~~E~~
25.	~~A~~	B	C	D	E
26.	A	~~B~~	C	D	~~E~~
27.	~~A~~	~~B~~	~~C~~	~~D~~	E
28.	~~A~~	B	C	D	~~E~~
29.	A	B	~~C~~	D	E
30.	A	B	~~C~~	~~D~~	E

Scoring Guessing Quiz 2

We'll also score this quiz using the SAT Verbal Scale and penalty system. Each question is worth 20 points. Wrong answers will cost 5 points each.

1. Start with 230 SAT Verbal points.

   (for your blank test)   230

2. Gain 20 SAT points for every correct answer.

   (# correct _____ x 20)   _____

3. Subtotal (line 1 + line 2)   _____

4. Lose 5 points for every wrong answer.

   (# wrong _____ x 5)   _____

5. Actual gain or loss on Quiz 2

   (line 3 – line 4)   _____

6. Estimated Quiz 2 Score
   (line 5)   _____

Impact of Guessing on Quiz 2 Score

This result is true on the average for a large number of students. An individual score may be better or worse based on good or bad luck.

If one million students took Guessing Quiz 2, the average gain would be about 135 points, based on the SAT verbal score scale. In this case, the adjustment for guessing does not succeed in wiping out the impact of lucky guesses.

Guessing Quiz 2 shows dramatically the positive impact of guessing after you eliminate one or more choices. **If you can eliminate at least one choice, you should go ahead and guess, even if you don't have the slightest idea about any of the remaining choices.**

The Guessing Penalty vs. The Guessing Reward

Thinking in terms of a "guessing penalty" is a negative way of looking at the SAT. It can increase anxiety and contribute to an irrational fear of guessing on the test. Our recommendation is that you forget about it.

Instead, you should think in terms of a "guessing reward." If you want to attain your personal highest potential score, you need to be aggressive about eliminating choices and guessing from the leftovers. On Guessing Quiz 2, the average reward was 135 points. Depending on how often you need to guess, your reward on the real SAT might be even higher.

ZAPPING

Other than expanding your vocabulary, the most powerful technique you can apply on the SAT is ZAPPING. "ZAP" is an acronym for Zero-in And Pick.*

Whenever you're less than positive of an answer, you can switch to a ZAPPING strategy to improve your odds of guessing correctly. A comparison of the results of Guessing Quiz 1 and Guessing Quiz 2 illustrates the difference between ZAPPING or not ZAPPING.

Average Gain from Guessing Quiz 1, blind guessing: Zero

Average Gain from Guessing Quiz 2, after ZAPPING: 135 points

ZAPPING improves your score. At the same time, it improves the accuracy of the SAT in assessing your abilities. Why? Because you need to know something in order to ZAP. The technique of ZAPPING allows you to gain points by applying partial knowledge. Following is an example.

Can you name the capital of Burundi? Most students can't.

Now we'll try again, but this time we'll convert our question into the multiple-choice format:

The capital of Burundi is
(A) London
(B) Calcutta
(C) Moscow
(D) Bujumbura
(E) Mexico City

*ZAP, ZAPS, and ZAPPING are registered trademarks of Profiles Corporation.

Now can you name the capital of Burundi? You probably know that Mexico City is the capital of Mexico, or at least that it's in Mexico; *ZAP* (E). If you know that London is the capital of England and Moscow is the capital of Russia, you can *ZAP* (A) and (C). *ZAPPING* now leaves you with two choices—either Calcutta or Bujumbura is the capital of Burundi. Of course, if you know that Calcutta is in India, you could also *ZAP* (B).

Most multiple-choice verbal questions are *amenable* (agreeable) to *ZAPPING*. The process of *ZAPPING* allows you to use your background knowledge and reasoning ability to eliminate wrong answers. **After *ZAPPING* the answers you know are wrong, you guess from the remaining choices.**

Some students start intuitively *ZAPPING* the very first time they take a multiple-choice test. If you're in this group, you have a good head start on learning the *ZAPPING* strategies for the verbal SAT. If you've never been into *ZAPPING*, you're about to gain a whole new way of attacking standardized tests, especially the SAT.

ZAPPING doesn't give you the correct answer to every question. Rather, *ZAPPING* will increase your odds of guessing correctly whenever you aren't positive. It's like our guessing Quiz 2. Clearly you were just guessing because you didn't even get to see the questions. But your score probably went up more than 100 points.

Pacing—Working the Clock

Many students make the mistake of racing the clock in an effort to work every problem on the SAT. Your goal should be to get your personal highest score, not to be the first one finished.

If you scored under 600 on the practice test, forget about the clock. You need to focus instead on being careful, writing in the book more, checking every answer, and improving your vocabulary.

In Unit 3 we will discuss pacing so that you will have a legitimate chance at scoring points on the hardest parts of the SAT.

Building an Indomitable Will

The SAT is a challenging test. Even the best test-takers report experiencing anxious moments while they are taking the SAT. Learning how to handle these anxious moments takes mental toughness. We call this mental toughness an INDOMITABLE WILL.

Indomitable means "not easily discouraged, unconquerable." Have you ever seen an Olympic ice skater or gymnast fall down and then quickly get up and continue his/her performance? These athletes demonstrate what we mean by an indomitable will. The SAT contains some very difficult questions that may baffle you. But it is important to always remain mentally tough and push ahead. *Having an indomitable will means never giving up!*

We are not born with an indomitable will. It begins with disciplined daily practice. This text will give you an opportunity to practice your skills on hundreds of questions. As you will see, practice builds competence, competence builds confidence, and confidence builds an indomitable will that can't be beaten. Your indomitable will is the extra edge that will help you do your best!

SAT Pretest

After completing this pretest, you will be able to estimate your verbal score on the SAT.

SECTION 1

Time–30 Minutes   For each question in this section, select the best answer from among the choices
36 Questions   given.

Each sentence below has one or two blanks, each blank indicating that something has been omitted. Beneath the sentence are five words or sets of words labeled A through E. Choose the word or set of words that, when inserted in the sentence, best fits the meaning of the sentence as a whole.

Example:

Medieval kingdoms did not become constitutional republics overnight; on the contrary, the change was ----.

(A) unpopular
(B) unexpected
(C) advantageous
(D) sufficient
(●) gradual

1. Isaac Asimov was a ---- author who wrote on a variety of topics ranging from Shakespeare to science fiction.

   (A) traditional
   (B) divisive
   (C) boastful
   (D) selfish
   (●) multifaceted

2. Although it originated as a series of separate magazine articles, James Baldwin's *Notes of a Native Son* is ---- by recurring themes and by the topical arrangement of the essays.

   (A) prolonged
   (B) exalted
   (C) hindered
   (D) entangled
   (●) unified

3. Television programs produced in the United States influenced and often ---- the medium as it developed in other nations, at least until the 1970's, when African, European, and Latin American countries began to ---- the number of imported programs in an attempt to develop their own entertainment industries.

   (●) dominated . . . limit
   (B) retarded . . . augment
   (C) dwarfed . . . enlarge
   (D) fortified . . . expand
   (E) inflamed . . . curtail

4. Although she enjoys her fame, Jessika is a woman who craves ----, who needs quiet and repose.

   (A) suspense
   (B) ceremony
   (●) solitude
   (D) ferment
   (E) prosperity

5. Today, Galileo's astronomical theories are ---- by the vast majority of theologians, but religious leaders during his lifetime accused him of ----.

   (A) analyzed . . . ignorance
   (B) criticized . . . intolerance
   (C) distorted . . . deception
   (●) accepted . . . heresy
   (E) ridiculed . . . frivolity

6. Sympathetic from the start, the faculty committee listened to the students' grievances with ---- and then set out to ---- the conditions that caused them.

   (A) alarm . . . exacerbate
   (B) remorse . . . enumerate
   (C) disdain . . . improve
   (●) concern . . . rectify
   (E) enthusiasm . . . reinstate

GO ON TO THE NEXT PAGE

SECTION

7. After years of experience, the psychologist gradually developed greater ---- in her work; she relates to the feelings and frustrations of her patients with deeper insight.

   (A) skepticism
   (B) empathy
   (C) resignation
   (D) reverence
   (E) fatalism

8. For most naturalists, butterfly watching is a chance to learn something new and ----, while experiencing ---- pleasure in observing one of nature's most beautiful animals.

   (A) tiresome . . . moralistic
   (B) exhilarating . . . dogmatic
   (C) insignificant . . . pragmatic
   (D) intriguing . . . aesthetic
   (E) banal . . . simplistic

9. Tawana's distinguishing trait is her ----; she always seems to bounce back from adversity.

   (A) resilience
   (B) diffidence
   (C) ambivalence
   (D) impulsiveness
   (E) deviousness

10. The museum provided a rare oasis of ---- in a city better known for its ---- lights and raucous nightclubs.

    (A) serenity . . . garish
    (B) extravagance . . . refined
    (C) tranquillity . . . sedate
    (D) dignity . . . elegant
    (E) commotion . . . tawdry

Each question below consists of a related pair of words or phrases, followed by five pairs of words or phrases labeled A through E. Select the pair that best expresses a relationship similar to that expressed in the original pair.

Example:

   CRUMB : BREAD ::

   (A) ounce : unit
   (B) splinter : wood
   (C) water : bucket
   (D) twine : rope
   (E) cream : butter

11. LINK : CHAIN ::

    (A) wave : ocean
    (B) bandage : wound
    (C) diary : experience
    (D) frame : picture
    (E) bone : skeleton

12. SCALDING : HOT ::

    (A) glacial : cold
    (B) muffled : loud
    (C) confined : free
    (D) flatter : sincere
    (E) weary : tense

13. MICROSCOPE : SMALL ::

    (A) telescope : distant
    (B) monocle : single
    (C) lens : refracted
    (D) camera : photographic
    (E) periscope : military

14. CROWN : HEADGEAR ::

    (A) yacht : harbor
    (B) cushion : chair
    (C) leg : desk
    (D) mansion : residence
    (E) drape : window

15. CHAPERONE : ESCORTS ::

    (A) adversary : supports
    (B) guard : protects
    (C) loafer : insults
    (D) interpreter : confuses
    (E) malcontent : rewards

16. EULOGY : PRAISE ::

    (A) elegy : sorrow
    (B) epic : distress
    (C) satire : respect
    (D) rhyme : truth
    (E) fable : joy

GO ON TO THE NEXT PAGE

SECTION 1

17. SECEDE : ORGANIZATION ::

   (A) promote : job
   (B) retreat : position
   (C) retire : leisure
   (D) bankrupt : wealth
   (E) ally : country

18. EMOLLIENT : SOFT ::

   (A) lubricant : liquid
   (B) desiccant : dry
   (C) adhesive : broken
   (D) alloy : pure
   (E) toxin : fertile

19. DIGRESSIVE : STATEMENT ::

   (A) extremist : conviction
   (B) biased : opinion
   (C) creative : idea
   (D) costly : mistake
   (E) roundabout : route

20. EGOIST : CONCEIT ::

   (A) pauper : wealth
   (B) traitor : disloyalty
   (C) hedonist : denial
   (D) sage : folly
   (E) philanthropist : stinginess

21. SALVE : WOUND ::

   (A) utter : apology
   (B) exploit : weakness
   (C) mollify : anger
   (D) squander : opportunity
   (E) emulate : achievement

22. IMPIOUS : REVERENCE ::

   (A) expressive : feeling
   (B) cunning : craftiness
   (C) empty : content
   (D) precise : detail
   (E) lavish : extravagance

23. INTRANSIGENT : COMPROMISE ::

   (A) permanent : stability
   (B) dogged : surrender
   (C) disorganized : chaos
   (D) lonesome : friendship
   (E) strenuous : exercise

GO ON TO THE NEXT PAGE

SECTION

1

The passage below is followed by questions based on its content. Answer the questions on the basis of what is <u>stated</u> or <u>implied</u> in the passage and in any introductory material that may be provided.

Questions 24-36 are based on the following passage.

The word Bohemia *was coined in Paris during the 1830's to describe young artists who led unconventional lifestyles. Bohemians fascinated members of the French middle class known as the* bourgeoisie.

"Bohemia, bordered on the North by hope, work and gaiety, on the South by necessity and courage; on the West and East by slander and the hospital."

Henry Murger
Bohemian Life, 1849

For its nineteenth-century discoverers and explorers, Bohemia was an identifiable country with visible inhabitants, but one not marked on
Line any map. To trace its frontiers was to cross
(5) constantly back and forth between reality and fantasy. . . .
Explorers recognized Bohemia by signs: art, youth, the underworld, the gypsy life-style. To Henry Murger, the most influential mapper,
(10) Bohemia was the realm of young artists struggling to surmount the barriers poverty erected against their vocations, "all those who, driven by an unstinting sense of calling, enter into art with no other means of existence than art
(15) itself." They lived in Bohemia because they could not—or not yet—establish their citizenship anywhere else. Ambitious, dedicated, but without means and unrecognized, they had to turn life itself into an art: "Their everyday existence is a
(20) work of genius."
Yet even Murger admitted that not all Bohemians were future artists. Other reporters did not think even the majority were. To that sharp-eyed social anatomist Honoré de Balzac*,
(25) Bohemia was more simply the country of youth. All the most talented and promising young people lived in it, those in their twenties who had not yet made their names but who were destined eventually to lead their nation as "diplomats. . .
(30) writers, administrators, soldiers, journalists, artists! In fact all kinds of ability, of talent, are represented there. It is a microcosm. If the emperor of Russia bought up Bohemia for twenty

million—assuming it were willing to take leave
(35) of the boulevard pavements—and transferred it to Odessa, in a year Odessa would be Paris." In their genius for life, Balzac's Bohemia resembled Murger's. "Bohemia has nothing and lives from what it has. Hope is its religion, faith in itself its
(40) code, charity is all it has for a budget."
Artists and the young were not alone in their ability to make more of life than objective conditions seemed to permit. Some who were called Bohemians did so in more murky and
(45) mysterious ways, in the darker corners of society. "By Bohemians," a stage figure of the 1840's declared, "I understand that class of individuals whose existence is a problem, social condition a myth, fortune an enigma, who have no stable
(50) residence, no recognized retreat, who are located nowhere, and who one encounters everywhere! who have no single occupation and who exercise fifty professions; of whom most get up in the morning without knowing where they will dine
(55) in the evening; rich today, famished tomorrow, ready to live honestly if they can and some other way if they can't." The nature of these Bohemians was less easy to specify than either Murger's or Balzac's. They might be unrecognized geniuses
(60) or confidence men. The designation "Bohemian" located them in a twilight zone between ingenuity and criminality.
These alternative images of Bohemia are ones we still recognize when we use the term: more
(65) recent incarnations like the Beat Generation of the 1950s or the hippiedom of the 1960s contained these real or potential elements, too. Artistic, youthful, unattached, inventive, or suspect, Bohemian styles are recurring features of
(70) modern life. Have they not always existed? In a way, yes: ancient Cynics, wandering medieval poets, eighteenth-century literary hacks—all exhibit features of Bohemia. But written references to Bohemia as a special, identifiable
(75) kind of life appear only in the nineteenth century. It was in the 1830s and 1840s, to begin with in France, that the terms "Bohemia," "*la Bohème*," and "Bohemian" first appeared in this sense. The new vocabulary played on the common French
(80) word for gypsy—*bohémien*—which erroneously

GO ON TO THE NEXT PAGE

identified the province of Bohemia, which is now part of modern Czechoslovakia, as the gypsies' place of origin. . . .

(85) From the start, Bohemianism took shape by contrast with the image with which it was commonly paired: bourgeois life. The opposition is so well established and comes so easily to mind that it may mislead us, for it implies a form of separation and an intensity of hostility often (90) belied by experience. Bohemia has always exercised a powerful attraction on many solid bourgeois, matched by the deeply bourgeois instincts and aspirations of numerous Bohemians. This mysterious convergence (95) sometimes leads to accusations of insincerity, even dishonesty: "Scratch a Bohemian, find a bourgeois." But the quality revealed by scraping away that false appearance of opposition is seldom hypocrisy. Like positive and negative (100) magnetic poles, Bohemian and bourgeois were— and are—parts of a single field: they imply, require, and attract each other.

*French novelist (1799–1850)

from *Bohemian Paris: Culture, Politics, and the Boundaries of Bourgeois Life, 1830-1930* by Jerrold Seigel

24. The passage is primarily concerned with

   (A) examining the differences between Bohemians and bourgeois
   (B) describing the etymology of the word Bohemian
   (C) explaining why Bohemians were drawn to a criminal life-style
   (D) presenting alternative views of the characteristics of Bohemians
   (E) discussing the cultural contributions of nineteenth-century French Bohemians

25. In line 13, Murger uses the word "unstinting" to emphasize the Bohemians'

   (A) commitment to developing their artistic talents
   (B) dedication to a hedonistic life-style
   (C) inability to resist bourgeois values
   (D) ambition to become rich and powerful
   (E) humble origins

26. The quotation in lines 19-20 ("Their . . . genius") can best be interpreted to mean that the Bohemians

   (A) are lucky to be alive
   (B) are highly successful achievers
   (C) are spirited and creative in spite of meager resources
   (D) live at the expense of the bourgeois
   (E) live chiefly by deceit, theft, and violation of accepted social codes

27. It can be inferred that Balzac (lines 25-40) believes that most Bohemians

   (A) will become great artists
   (B) will become dangerous anarchists
   (C) would prefer to live in Odessa
   (D) lack the courage to face their problems
   (E) will become influential bourgeois leaders

28. The quotations from Balzac suggest that he viewed the Bohemians with

   (A) interest and admiration
   (B) animosity and suspicion
   (C) fear and loathing
   (D) envy and resentment
   (E) embarrassment and distress

29. Both Murger and Balzac

   (A) condemn the Bohemians for attempting to deceive the bourgeois
   (B) distrust the Bohemians because of their radical ideas
   (C) admire the Bohemians' ability to create a vibrant life-style
   (D) express reservations about the Bohemians' ability to eventually assimilate into bourgeois society
   (E) applaud the Bohemians' commitment to helping the disadvantaged

30. In line 42, "objective" most nearly means

   (A) without bias
   (B) material
   (C) impersonal
   (D) dispassionate
   (E) clearly marked

GO ON TO THE NEXT PAGE

SECTION 1

31. The quotation in lines 46-57 most probably reflects the point of view of

    (A) the gypsies
    (B) Murger
    (C) Balzac
    (D) some Bohemians
    (E) some bourgeois

32. The quotation by the stage figure implies that

    (A) Bohemians were a tiny minority who were rarely seen
    (B) most Bohemians suffered from malnutrition
    (C) some Bohemians became criminals
    (D) the presence of Bohemians in the theater district offended many bourgeois customers
    (E) Bohemians made excellent actors and actresses

33. Which statement best summarizes the point made in lines 63-73?

    (A) Bohemians have always been subjected to suspicion and scorn.
    (B) The Bohemian is an inescapable feature of urban society.
    (C) Bohemianism, as a way of life, is not unique to the nineteenth century.
    (D) Eighteenth-century Bohemia was similar to nineteenth-century Bohemia.
    (E) The province of Bohemia was home to aspiring young artists.

34. The discussion of the origins of the word "Bohemia" (lines 73-83) implies that

    (A) Czechoslovakia was the birthplace of the Bohemian life-style
    (B) Bohemians had much in common with wandering medieval poets
    (C) the French could not differentiate between Bohemian and bourgeois goals
    (D) the French believed that gypsies and Bohemians had similar life-styles
    (E) Murger's view of Bohemia was more accurate than Balzac's

35. In line 79, "common" most nearly means

    (A) unimportant
    (B) tasteless
    (C) worn-out
    (D) widespread
    (E) average

36. Which statement best summarizes the author's argument in the last paragraph?

    (A) Bohemians were purposely misleading in their actions.
    (B) Bohemians received considerable financial support from bourgeois customers.
    (C) Bohemians and bourgeois were more similar than is often realized.
    (D) Bourgeois were oblivious to the struggles of Bohemians.
    (E) Bourgeois and Bohemians inherited the same cultural traditions from their ancestors.

IF YOU FINISH BEFORE TIME IS CALLED, YOU MAY CHECK YOUR WORK ON THIS SECTION ONLY. DO NOT TURN TO ANY OTHER SECTION IN THE TEST.   **STOP**

SECTION

2

Time–30 Minutes   For each question in this section, select the best answer from among the choices
30 Questions   given.

Each sentence below has one or two blanks, each
blank indicating that something has been omitted.
Beneath the sentence are five words or sets of
words labeled A through E. Choose the word or set
of words that, when inserted in the sentence, <u>best</u>
fits the meaning of the sentence as a whole.

Example:

Medieval kingdoms did not become
constitutional republics overnight; on the
contrary, the change was ----.

(A) unpopular
(B) unexpected
(C) advantageous
(D) sufficient
(●) gradual

1. Now we are ----, but at one time we tilled
the same fields, climbed the same hills, and
----- each other's sorrows.

(A) friends . . . suffered
(B) strangers . . . ignored
(C) united . . . felt
(●) enemies . . . shared
(E) foes . . . caused

2. Adam believed in being ---- for his
appointments, saying that it was unfair to
keep people waiting.

(A) irregular
(B) guarded
(C) dignified
(●) punctual
(E) animated

3. Although the scientists thought the chemical
would be ----, laboratory tests showed that it
did not cause an adverse reaction when used
in low concentrations.

(A) invigorating
(B) profitable
(C) intricate
(●) toxic
(E) obsolete

4. Many stereo components are ----, containing
parts from both vacuum tubes and solid-
state electronics.

(●) hybrids
(B) misconceptions
(C) aesthetics
(D) frauds
(E) remotes

5. Continued ---- on the town council produced
a split between those who supported the
mayor and those who opposed her.

(A) diffidence
(B) resilience
(●) dissension
(D) consolidation
(E) speculation

6. Although providing wild animals with food
often makes them more ---- and thus easier
to study, it is also known to ---- their normal
behavioral patterns.

(●) docile . . . disrupt
(B) belligerent . . . upset
(C) contemptuous . . . reinforce
(D) dejected . . . inhibit
(E) wary . . . retard

7. Amber was a ---- manager who based all her
decisions upon a realistic appraisal of
relevant facts.

(A) romantic
(B) superficial
(C) convoluted
(D) empathetic
(●) pragmatic

8. Both ---- and ----, Keisha seldom spoke out
and never wasted money.

(A) affable . . . thrifty
(●) reserved . . . frugal
(C) taciturn . . . extravagant
(D) inhibited . . . munificent
(E) cantankerous . . . tenacious

GO ON TO THE NEXT PAGE

9. Stubborn and unyielding by nature, Ken became even more ---- when asked to perform a task he didn't want to do.

    (A) euphoric
    (B) malicious
    (C) credulous
    (D) amiable
    (●) obdurate

Each question below consists of a related pair of words or phrases, followed by five pairs of words or phrases labeled A through E. Select the pair that best expresses a relationship similar to that expressed in the original pair.

Example:

CRUMB : BREAD ::

(A) ounce : unit
(●) splinter : wood
(C) water : bucket
(D) twine : rope
(E) cream : butter

10. BIRD : FEATHERS ::

    (A) mammal : spine
    (B) hand : fingers
    (C) branch : fruit
    (D) limb : fur
    (●) fish : scales

11. BAND : MUSICIAN ::

    (A) class : lecturer
    (B) catalogue : shopper
    (C) election : voter
    (●) choir : singer
    (E) audience : entertainer

12. ARENA : CONFLICT ::

    (A) mirage : reality
    (●) forum : discussion
    (C) asylum : pursuit
    (D) utopia : place
    (E) amphitheater : stage

13. PROLOGUE : NOVEL ::

    (●) preamble : statute
    (B) sketch : drawing
    (C) movement : symphony
    (D) index : book
    (E) blueprint : building

14. EXONERATE : BLAME ::

    (A) postpone : decision
    (B) extinguish : rebellion
    (C) solve : riddle
    (●) liberate : captivity
    (E) hide : problem

15. HUBRIS : PRIDE ::

    (A) ineptness : skill
    (●) ecstasy : pleasure
    (C) abundance : value
    (D) anxiety : curiosity
    (E) obsession : nonchalance

GO ON TO THE NEXT PAGE

SECTION 2

Each passage below is followed by questions based on its content. Answer the questions following each passage on the basis of what is <u>stated</u> or <u>implied</u> in that passage and in any introductory material that may be provided

Questions 16-22 are based on the following passage.

This passage is taken from a book published in 1975.

Line
(5)
(10)
(15)
(20)
(25)
(30)
(35)
(40)

That Louise Nevelson is believed by many critics to be the greatest twentieth-century sculptor is all the more remarkable because the greatest resistance to women artists has been, until recently, in the field of sculpture. Since Neolithic times, sculpture has been considered the prerogative of men, partly, perhaps, for purely physical reasons: it was erroneously assumed that women were not suited for the hard manual labor required in sculpting stone, carving wood, or working in metal. It has been only during the twentieth century that women sculptors have been recognized as major artists, and it has been in the United States: especially since the decades of the fifties and sixties, that women sculptors have shown the greatest originality and creative power. Their rise to prominence parallels the development of sculpture itself in the United States: while there had been a few talented sculptors in the United States before the 1940's, it was only after 1945 — when New York was rapidly becoming the art capital of the world—that major sculpture was produced in the United States. Some of the best was the work of women.

By far the most outstanding of these women is Louise Nevelson, who in the eyes of many critics is the most original female artist alive today. One famous and influential critic, Hilton Kramer, said of her work, "For myself, I think Ms. Nevelson succeeds where the painters often fail."

Her works have been compared to the Cubist constructions of Picasso, the Surrealistic objects of Miro, and the Merzbau of Schwitters. Nevelson would be the first to admit that she has been influenced by all of these, as well as by African sculpture, and by Native American and pre-Columbian art, but she has absorbed all these influences and still created a distinctive art that expresses the urban landscape and the aesthetic sensibility of the twentieth century. Nevelson says, "I have always wanted to show the world

(45)
(50)
(55)
(60)

that art is everywhere, except that it has to pass through a creative mind."

Using mostly discarded wooden objects like packing crates, broken pieces of furniture, and abandoned architectural ornaments, all of which she has hoarded for years, she assembles architectural constructions of great beauty and power. Creating very freely with no sketches, she glues and nails objects together, paints them black, or more rarely white or gold, and places them in boxes. These assemblages, walls, even entire environments create a mysterious, almost awe-inspiring atmosphere. Although she has denied any symbolic or religious intent in her works, their three-dimensional grandeur and even their titles, such as *Sky Cathedral* and *Night Cathedral*, suggest such connotations. In some ways, her most ambitious works are closer to architecture than to traditional sculpture, but then neither Louise Nevelson nor her art fits into any neat category.

16. The passage is primarily concerned with

   (A) explaining why men have dominated sculpture
   (B) outlining the origins and development of sculpture in the United States
   (C) analyzing the artistic influences upon Louise Nevelson's work
   (D) evaluating the unique materials used by Louise Nevelson
   (E) describing the work and importance of Louise Nevelson

17. The quote by Hilton Kramer in lines 30-31

   (A) undermines the author's opinion of Louise Nevelson
   (B) raises doubts about Nevelson's originality
   (C) suggests that Nevelson should have studied art more carefully
   (D) corroborates the author's appraisal of Louise Nevelson
   (E) confirms the view that Nevelson's work has religious intent

GO ON TO THE NEXT PAGE

SECTION 2

18. Which of the following is one way in which Nevelson's art illustrates her theory as it is expressed in lines 42-44?

    (A) She sculpts in wood rather than in metal or stone.
    (B) She paints her sculptures and frames them in boxes.
    (C) She makes no preliminary sketches but rather allows the sculpture to develop as she works.
    (D) She puts together pieces of ordinary objects once used for different purposes to make her sculptures.
    (E) She does not deliberately attempt to convey symbolic or religious meanings through her sculpture.

19. It can be inferred from the passage that the author believes which of the following about Nevelson's sculptures?

    (A) They suggest religious and symbolic meanings.
    (B) They do not have qualities characteristic of sculpture.
    (C) They are mysterious and awe-inspiring, but not beautiful.
    (D) They are uniquely American in style and sensibility.
    (E) They show the influence of twentieth-century architecture.

20. The author regards Nevelson's stature in the art world as "remarkable" (line 3) in part because of which of the following?

    (A) Her work is currently overrated.
    (B) Women sculptors have found it especially difficult to be accepted and recognized as major artists.
    (C) Nevelson's sculptures are difficult to understand.
    (D) Many art critics have favored painting over sculpture in writing about developments in the art world.
    (E) Few of the artists prominent in the twentieth century have been sculptors.

21. Which of the following statements about Nevelson's sculptures can be inferred from the passage?

    (A) They are meant for display outdoors.
    (B) They are often painted in several colors.
    (C) They are sometimes very large.
    (D) They are hand carved by Nevelson.
    (E) They are built around a central wooden object.

22. The author's attitude toward Nevelson's work is best described as

    (A) skepticism about her enduring influence
    (B) ambivalence about her use of unconventional materials
    (C) irritation at being unable to categorize her art
    (D) confusion about her goals and ideas
    (E) admiration for her unique and inspired work

GO ON TO THE NEXT PAGE

SECTION 2

Questions 23-30 are based on the following passage.

The following passage is taken from a book about fascinating animals.

Sea cucumbers are not vegetables. They only
look and act that way. In fact they are marine
animals of the echinoderm phylum, a primitive
Line group that also includes starfish, sea urchins, and
(5) two other star-shaped members called the
feather-stars and the brittle-stars. Echinoderms
are distinct from almost all other animal groups
in being radially, rather than bilaterally
symmetrical. In other words they know top from
(10) bottom but not front from back nor left side from
right. They all share a pentamerous anatomical
organization, with most of their features
occurring in fives: five axes of symmetry, five sets
of each organ, five major arteries, and for those
(15) like the starfish and the brittle-stars, five legs.
They have a mouth hidden under the belly, and
an anus that generally marks the center of their
back. The skin of an echinoderm is often
described as "leathery" or "rubbery" but think
(20) instead of the texture of imperfectly cooked tripe.
Imbedded in that skin are calcareous plates, in
some cases quite small and with no
interconnections, constituting a minimal skeleton.
Echinoderms have been known to stay in one
(25) spot, without moving, for up to two years. They
have never heard of eyes. They developed all
these eccentric proclivities, back in the Cambrian
period a half billion years ago, before any
consensus arose as to how an animal was
(30) supposed to behave. But just as the echinoderms
are exceptional among animals, so are the sea
cucumbers exceptional among echinoderms.

They retain the five-sided symmetry on the
inside but don't give much hint of it externally.
(35) Sometime in the dim past they grew so tall and
top-heavy that they have tipped over
permanently onto one flank. The radial
symmetry is now 90 degrees off kilter.
Consequently they *do* have a discernible front:
(40) the end with the mouth, around which have been
added a ring of tentacles like the leaf ends of
celery. . . . They shuffle across the sea bottom in
worm-like fashion, by means of muscular
contractions and elongations that roll down their
(45) soft bodies in waves. Moving deliberately, they
swallow the rich benthic mixture of sand and
muck, strain the organic debris from it in their
long simple gut, and pass the sterile sand out
behind. Theoretically at least, they glide along
(50) like an open pipe while the sand, rippling faintly
as it is cleaned, remains stationary.

In sea cucumbers (again, uniquely among all
echinoderms) the skeletal plates are reduced to
microscopic size and come in delicate patterns
(55) like snowflakes, but serve who knows what use.
In overall body shape, some species resemble
Italian sausages, some are more faithful to their
garden namesake, some display the
distinguished profile of a balloon overfilled
(60) precariously with tapioca. They range from the
size of a baby gherkin to the size of a huge
zucchini, one of those monstrous county-fair
winners that gets its photo sent out on the AP
wire. They are variously decorated in swirls and
(65) mottles and stripes of lavender, orange, yellow,
parakeet green. Truly these guys are out in left
field.

But it bothers them not. In the deepest trenches
of the ocean they carry on blithely and quite
(70) successfully, working a zone that few other
animals are equipped to explore. Researchers on
the ocean abyss have discovered that, at a depth
of 13,000 feet, sea cucumbers account for half of
all the living organisms. Down at 28,000 feet, the
(75) sea cucumber majority rises to 90 percent. And at
the ocean's bottomest bottom, 33,000 feet down
in the Philippine Trench, almost no living
creatures are to be found—except sea cucumbers.

In the shallower waters, like those coral
(80) formations off the west coast of Mexico, they also
get along well. This is in part because sea
cucumbers have few natural predators, owing
presumably to the various nasty poisons
contained in the mucous secretions of their skin.
(85) Additionally, some species have developed the
useful trick of self-mutilation: If a lobster or an
otter or a snoopy human lays hold of one of this
group, the sea cucumber constricts itself
drastically at certain points along the body, and
(90) breaks into several pieces. The predator, ideally,
will be satisfied with a middle or posterior
section. All the sections are destined to die except
the front end, with the mouth and tentacles. If
this chunk is left in peace, from it will regenerate
(95) a new entire cucumber.

from *Natural Acts: A Sidelong View of Science and
Nature* by David Quammen

GO ON TO THE NEXT PAGE

SECTION 2

23. The passage is best described as
    (A) a refutation of a misconception
    (B) a description of a unique animal
    (C) a call for more research to answer the riddles posed by sea cucumbers
    (D) a plea for stricter environmental standards to protect the sea cucumber's endangered habitat
    (E) a catalog of members of the echinoderm phylum

24. The author's tone toward sea cucumbers is best described as
    (A) reserve and suspicion
    (B) concern and anxiety
    (C) mockery and scorn
    (D) confusion and frustration
    (E) amusement and fascination

25. The author implies that the description of echinoderms' skin as "leathery" and "rubbery" (line 19) is
    (A) best applied to sea urchins
    (B) completely false
    (C) close but not precisely accurate
    (D) totally correct
    (E) irrelevant

26. Which one of the following is not a characteristic of members of the echinoderm phylum?
    (A) behavioral patterns that evolved 500 million years ago
    (B) blindness
    (C) an ability to remain stationary for long periods of time
    (D) bilateral symmetry
    (E) five-sided anatomy

27. It can be inferred that the ocean bottom
    (A) provides sea cucumbers with all the nutrients they need to survive
    (B) is often too deep for sea cucumbers to survive
    (C) supports a startling variety of plant and animal life
    (D) contains numerous predators who pose a serious threat to sea cucumbers
    (E) is the only place where sea cucumbers can live

28. The author uses the sentence "Truly these guys are out in left field" (lines 66-67) to emphasize his point that sea cucumbers
    (A) are very unorthodox animals
    (B) do not belong in the echinoderm phylum
    (C) vary in size and color
    (D) are surprisingly sensitive to the reaction of other animals
    (E) resemble worms

29. In line 71, "equipped" most nearly means
    (A) outfitted for
    (B) able to
    (C) arranged for
    (D) prepared to
    (E) supplied with

30. Which statement best summarizes the point made in lines 68-78?
    (A) Sea cucumbers are the most common animal found in the world's oceans.
    (B) Very little is known about how sea cucumbers survive at great depths.
    (C) Sea cucumbers have the ability to survive in places where few other animals can.
    (D) Sea cucumbers take pride in being different from other animals.
    (E) Sea cucumbers are shy animals who resent being studied.

IF YOU FINISH BEFORE TIME IS CALLED, YOU MAY CHECK YOUR WORK ON THIS SECTION ONLY. DO NOT TURN TO ANY OTHER SECTION IN THE TEST. **STOP**

SECTION

3

Time–15 Minutes	For each question in this section, select the best answer from among the choices
12 Questions	given.

The two passages below are followed by questions based on their content and on the relationship between the two passages. Answer the questions on the basis of what is <u>stated</u> or <u>implied</u> in the passages and in any introductory material that may be provided.

Questions 1-12 are based on the following passages.

Over 20 million people immigrated to America between 1880 and 1920. These passages present two perspectives on this experience. In Passage 1, a young immigrant describes his feelings when he first arrived in America. In Passage 2, a Harvard professor of history describes the harsh realities facing the immigrants.

Passage 1

When the European discoverers of America saw land at last they fell on their knees and a hymn of thanksgiving burst from their souls. The
Line scene, which is one of the most thrilling in
(5) history, repeats itself in the heart of every immigrant as he comes in sight of the American shores. I am at a loss to convey the peculiar state of mind that the experience created in me.

When the ship reached Sandy Hook I was
(10) literally overcome with the beauty of the landscape.

The immigrant's arrival in his new home is like a second birth to him. Imagine a newborn babe in possession of a fully developed intellect. Would it
(15) ever forget its entry into the world? Neither does the immigrant ever forget his entry into a country which to him is a new world in the profoundest sense of the term and in which he expects to pass the rest of his life. I conjure up the gorgeousness
(20) of the spectacle as it appeared to me on that clear June morning: the magnificent verdure of Staten Island, the tender blue of sea and sky, the dignified bustle of passing craft—above all, those floating, squatting, multitudinously windowed
(25) palaces which I subsequently learned to call ferries. It was all so utterly unlike anything I had ever seen or dreamed of before. It unfolded itself like a divine revelation. I was in a trance or in something closely resembling one.
(30) "This, then, is America!" I exclaimed, mutely. The notion of something enchanted which the name had always evoked in me now seemed fully borne out. . . .

My transport of admiration, however, only
(35) added to my sense of helplessness and awe.

Here, on shipboard, I was sure of my shelter and food, at least. How was I going to procure my sustenance on those magic shores? I wished the remaining hour could be prolonged indefinitely.

from *The Rise of David Levinsky* by Abraham Cohan

Passage 2

(40) Here is a woman. In the Old Country she had lived much of her life, done most of her work, outdoors. In America, the flat confines her. She divides up her domain by calico sheets hung on ropes, tries to make a place for her people and
(45) possessions. But there is no place and she has not room to turn about. It is true, everything is in poor repair, the rain comes through the ceilings, the wind blows dirt through the cracks in the wall. But she does not even know how to go
(50) about restoring order, establishing cleanliness. She breaks her back to exterminate the proliferating vermin. What does she get? A dozen lice behind the collar.

The very simplest tasks become complex and
(55) disorganizing. Every day there is a family to feed. Assume she knows how to shop, and can manage the unfamiliar coal stove or gas range. But what does one do with rubbish who has never known the meaning of waste? It is not
(60) really so important to walk down the long flight of narrow stairs each time there are some scraps to be disposed of. The windows offer an easier alternative. After all, the obnoxious wooden garbage boxes that adorn the littered fronts of the
(65) houses expose their contents unashamed through

GO ON TO THE NEXT PAGE

SECTION

split sides and, rarely emptied, themselves become the nests of boldly foraging rodents.

(70) The filthy streets are seldom cleaned; the municipality is not particularly solicitous of these, the poorest quarters of the city. The alleys are altogether passed by and the larger thoroughfares receive only occasionally the services of the scavenger. The inaccessible alleys and rear yards are never touched and, to be sure,

(75) are redolent of the fact. In the hot summer months the stench of rotting things will mark these places and the stained snow of winter will not conceal what lies beneath. Here and there an unwitting newcomer tries the disastrous

(80) experiment of keeping a goat, adding thereby to the distinctive flavor of his neighborhood.

It was the same in every other encounter with the new life. Conveniences not missed in the villages became sore necessities in the city;

(85) although often the immigrants did not know their lack till dear experience taught them. Of what value were sunlight and fresh air on the farm? But how measure their worth for those who lived in the three hundred and fifty

(90) thousand dark interior rooms of New York in 1900!

There was the rude matter of what Americans called sanitation. Some of the earliest buildings had no privies at all; the residents had been

(95) expected to accommodate themselves elsewhere as best they could. Tenements from mid-century onward generally had water closets in the yards and alleys, no great comfort to the occupants of the fifth and sixth floors. The newest structures

(100) had two toilets to each floor; but these were open to the custom of all comers, charged to the care of none, and left to the neglect of all. If in winter the pipes froze in unheated hallways and the clogged contents overflowed, weeks would go by before

(105) some dilatory repairman set matters right. Months thereafter a telling odor hung along the narrow hallways.

What of it? The filth was inescapable. In these districts where the need was greatest, the

(110) sewerage systems were primitive and ineffectual. Open drains were long common; in Boston one such, for years, tumbled down the slope of Jacob's Ladder in the South Cove; and in Chicago the jocosely named Bubbly Creek wended its

(115) noisome way aboveground until well into the twentieth century.

from *The Uprooted* by Oscar Handlin

1. The phrase, "This, then, is America!" (line 30) conveys the author of Passage 1's sense of

(A) awe and revulsion
(B) relief and resignation
(C) gloom and dejection
(D) worry and dread
(E) wonder and delight

2. Why does the author of Passage 1 say (lines 38-39) that he "wished the remaining hour could be prolonged indefinitely?"

(A) Because he needed more time to write down his first impressions of America.
(B) Because he wanted to complete a sketch of New York Harbor.
(C) Because he wanted to form an indelible memory of his arrival in America.
(D) Because he knew that his vacation was over and he would soon have to begin working again.
(E) Because he understood that the security of life on the ship would soon be replaced by the uncertainties of life in America.

3. The author of Passage 1 implies that

(A) he had relatives who were going to help him adjust to life in America
(B) he was a tourist who would soon be returning to Europe
(C) he didn't know where he would live and what job he would perform
(D) he was slightly disappointed by the view as he sailed into New York Harbor
(E) he ultimately became a ferry boat captain

4. The author of Passage 2 uses the phrase "She divides up her domain by calico sheets hung on ropes" (lines 42-44) in order to

(A) reveal how spacious the flat is
(B) describe the best way to secure privacy
(C) demonstrate the most efficient way to eradicate lice
(D) show how cramped the flat is
(E) illustrate the woman's lack of knowledge of American customs

GO ON TO THE NEXT PAGE

SECTION

3

5. By asking the question, "But what does one do with rubbish who has never known the meaning of waste?" (lines 58-59) the author of Passage 2 implies that

   (A) villagers in the "Old Country" produced little waste since they fully utilized all of their household products
   (B) the woman was an inefficient housekeeper
   (C) the immigrants paid no attention to the litter and foul smells in their new neighborhoods
   (D) European cities were even filthier than American cities
   (E) the immigrants threw their waste out the windows because they were lazy

6. The author of Passage 2 implies that city officials

   (A) were unaware of the problems in the immigrant neighborhoods
   (B) neglected the impoverished sections of their cities
   (C) only helped immigrants during election years
   (D) profited from the high rents charged to immigrants
   (E) did everything in their power to help the immigrants adjust to American life

7. In line 81, "distinctive" most nearly means

   (A) different
   (B) ordinary
   (C) fragrant
   (D) characteristic
   (E) spicy

8. The name "Bubbly Creek" is incongruous because

   (A) it gave pleasure to the neighborhood children
   (B) it was a harmonious part of the neighborhood
   (C) it was out of place in an urban setting
   (D) it was a foul smelling drain
   (E) it passed through a fertile piece of land

9. The two passages differ in tone in that Passage 1 is

   (A) euphoric, whereas Passage 2 is realistic
   (B) somber, whereas Passage 2 is hysterical
   (C) cynical, whereas Passage 2 is optimistic
   (D) despondent, whereas Passage 2 is exuberant
   (E) devout, whereas Passage 2 is scornful

10. The contrast between the two passages reflects primarily the biases of

    (A) a new immigrant and a scholar
    (B) an excited tourist and a seasoned journalist
    (C) a native of Europe and a native of the United States
    (D) a passing visitor and a local resident
    (E) a passenger on a crowded ship and an overworked municipal official

11. The description of immigrant life presented in Passage 2 suggests that the author's concerns in Passage 1 (lines 37-39) are

    (A) exaggerated
    (B) irrelevant
    (C) unwarranted
    (D) justified
    (E) irrational

12. The authors of both passages would most probably agree that

    (A) urban life is better than rural life for most immigrants
    (B) many municipal governments need to be reformed
    (C) immigrants lived a different life in America than in Europe
    (D) America possesses a uniquely beautiful landscape
    (E) a lack of sanitation was the immigrant's biggest problem

IF YOU FINISH BEFORE TIME IS CALLED, YOU MAY CHECK YOUR WORK ON THIS SECTION ONLY. DO NOT TURN TO ANY OTHER SECTION IN THE TEST. **STOP**

Calculating Your Score on the Pretest

STEP **1**   **Count**

Total Number of Blanks: _____ + _____ + _____ = _____
                            Sec. 1   Sec. 2   Sec. 3

Total Number Correct: _____ + _____ + _____ = _____
                          Sec. 1   Sec. 2   Sec. 3

Total Number Incorrect: _____ + _____ + _____ = _____
                            Sec. 1   Sec. 2   Sec. 3

ADD to CHECK YOUR COUNTING. The Sum should be 78: _____

STEP **2**   **Determine Your Score Adjustment**

The Score Adjustment is:

Total Number Incorrect x .25 = _____

STEP **3**   **Determine Your RAW SCORE**

Your RAW SCORE is the Total Number Correct minus the Adjustment:

Total Correct: _____

Minus Adjustment: – _____

RAW SCORE   = _____

STEP **Convert Your RAW SCORE to an SAT Score**

SCORE CONVERSION TABLE

Raw Score	Verbal Scaled Score	Raw Score	Verbal Scaled Score	Raw Score	Verbal Scaled Score
78	800	51	590	24	440
77	800	50	580	23	430
76	800	49	580	22	430
75	800	48	570	21	420
74	790	47	570	20	410
73	780	46	560	19	410
72	760	45	560	18	400
71	750	44	550	17	390
70	740	43	540	16	390
69	730	42	540	15	380
68	720	41	530	14	370
67	710	40	530	13	360
66	700	39	520	12	360
65	690	38	520	11	350
64	680	37	510	10	340
63	670	36	510	9	330
62	660	35	500	8	320
61	660	34	500	7	310
60	650	33	490	6	300
59	640	32	480	5	290
58	630	31	480	4	280
57	630	30	470	3	270
56	620	29	470	2	260
55	610	28	460	1	240
54	610	27	450	0	230
53	600	26	450	−1	220
52	600	25	440	−2	200
				below	200

UNIT

Building a Foundation

1

CHAPTER 1
Building a Foundation for Vocabulary

CHAPTER 2
Building a Foundation for Sentence Completions

CHAPTER 3
Building a Foundation for Analogies

CHAPTER 4
Building a Foundation for Critical Reading

1

Building a Foundation for Vocabulary

After completing this chapter, you will be able to

1. explain why building a strong vocabulary is important.

2. apply the vocabulary-building strategies used in this text.

3. give examples of words that begin with the prefixes E-, A-, and RE-.

4. define the roots CORD, AMI, GREG, PATHOS, and FID and give examples of words containing them.

5. give synonyms for *enthusiasm*, *discouraged*, *stubborn*, and *secret*.

Why is vocabulary important?

Why is having a large vocabulary that includes words such as *jingoist* (a super patriot, extreme nationalist), *redoubtable* (formidable, fearsome), and *diffidence* (lacking confidence in oneself) important? Words are among our most valuable tools for learning and communication. As your vocabulary increases, you can speak, write, and absorb knowledge more effectively. Researchers have shown that a superior vocabulary is strongly associated with success in school, in business, and in the professions.

The SAT test writers recognize the importance of having a command of the English language. The analogy, sentence completion, and reading questions are in many ways a sophisticated test of your vocabulary. *Augmenting* (increasing) your vocabulary is therefore one of the best ways to raise your verbal score.

Becoming Word-Wise

A major goal of this textbook is to help you become more word-wise. Augmenting your vocabulary doesn't mean memorizing long lists of unrelated words. Instead, it means using a variety of effective strategies for learning and using new words.

This text contains three chapters devoted to helping you build a more powerful vocabulary. The words used in these chapters are all drawn from recent SATs. The vocabulary lessons focus on the following aspects of vocabulary development.

1. **Words From Daily Life** Students often complain that the SAT uses words they will never see again. This isn't true. In reality, the words used on the SAT are all around you.

2. **The Mighty Prefix** Prefixes are short but powerful word parts that appear at the beginning of many words. About one-fifth of the vocabulary words used on the SAT contain prefixes.

3. **Roots and Branches** Many words contain common roots. For example, the words *progress*, *regress*, and *digress* all contain the root *gress*, meaning "to step." Knowing that *gress* means "to step" helps you remember that *progress* means "to step forward," that *regress* means "to step backward," and that *digress* means "to step away" (and thus stray from a topic).

4. **Synonym Clusters** The English language often provides us with several words for describing the same action, behavior, or idea. For example, *amazed*, *astonished*, *astounded*, and *thunderstruck* are four different words you can use to say that you are really surprised. Learning clusters of synonyms is a particularly efficient way of augmenting your vocabulary since you often get four or five new words for just one definition.

5. **Word Histories** The English language contains an especially rich collection of words derived from legends, places, customs, and names. Knowing the story behind these words can help fix their meaning in your mind. (See Appendix B for activities.)

6. **Subject Area Terms** A surprising number of the words used on the SAT are common terms used in your history and English classes. Our content area lessons will focus upon key terms from these subjects. (See Appendix C for activities.)

Words From Daily Life

Have you ever visited a country where the people spoke a language you didn't understand? If you have had this experience, you may have vivid memories of misreading signs, ordering the wrong foods, and feeling frustrated by not understanding what is going on around you.

Many students complain that taking the SAT is like trying to understand a foreign language. The analogy, sentence completion, and reading questions all contain a number of difficult words. For example, recent SATs included such challenging words as *jingoist*, *redoubtable*, and *diffidence*.

Words and SAT Words

The English language contains over 1 million words, making it the largest vocabulary of any language in the world. Yet, the vocabulary of the average high school student includes only about 15,000 words. Does this mean that you must learn 985,000 new words to achieve a high score on the SAT? The good news is NO! While you should own a dictionary, you won't have to memorize it.

The number of words used on the SAT is surprisingly small. Although no two verbal sections are identical, the SAT writers usually use a common core vocabulary of about 2,500 words. This includes a group of about 300 high-frequency words that have each appeared as answer choices from 5 to 20 times during the past 10 years.

These special "SAT words" are not hard to find. They appear every day in newspapers and magazines. The textbooks, primary sources, and novels you read in school are *replete* (filled) with SAT words. For example, the *Declaration of Independence* contains at least 20 words that have been tested on the SAT.

The SAT Goes to the Supermarket

Supplement this activity with actual products or packaging brought by your students into the classroom. Consider a weekend scavenger hunt to find as many of the words as possible. Students can stock a small SAT supermarket, make bulletin boards, or design advertising posters.

What words come to your mind when you think of a supermarket? We typically associate a grocery store with food, pushing a shopping cart, and buying fruits, vegetables, meats, beverages and household items. But how many people associate going to the supermarket with learning new vocabulary words for the SAT? Probably few, if any. However, a trip to the supermarket can be a rewarding way to find and learn new words. The same aisles that are filled with cereals, beverages, and vegetables also contain a surprisingly large number of vocabulary words that are frequently used on the SAT. Still a little skeptical? Let's begin our special SAT tour of a large supermarket.

1. **Should we be *methodical* or *circuitous*?** Have you ever noticed how some shoppers systematically go up and down each aisle, while others dart from spot to spot? Some shoppers are *methodical*, or very systematic. They usually have a detailed shopping list and then carefully move from one part of the store to another, checking off each item. Other shoppers follow a *circuitous*, or roundabout, route. They look for one item and then push their cart to the other end of the store to locate another item they just remembered. Since we are looking for SAT words, we'll follow a more methodical strategy. A close inspection of the supermarket aisles reveals that a number of important words will play an important role in what we buy. Let's begin with the fruits and vegetables.

2. **Fruits, Vegetables, and Salad Dressings**

   - *A distinctive medley of greens* Would you buy a package containing "a distinctive medley of greens"? Our decision hinges on the meaning of the word *medley*. Since *medley* means an assortment, the label is telling us that this package includes a variety of different lettuces. Sounds perfect. Let's put a package in our cart and look for a salad dressing.

- *Salad dressing: robust or subtle flavor?* Here are the labels from two different salad dressings:
  - (1) "Delicious sauce that gives fresh vegetables a robust flavor"; and
  - (2) "Delicate spices for a subtle flavor."

What is the difference between *a robust flavor* and *a subtle flavor*? *Robust* means "vigorous, full of health and strength." In this context, a robust flavor would be strong and full-bodied. In contrast, *subtle* means "understated, light and delicate." Based upon these definitions, which type of dressing would you choose? Since we're shopping for SAT words, let's put both dressings in our shopping cart.

- *Indigenous or exotic?* What is the difference between an indigenous squash and an exotic squash? *Indigenous* and *exotic* are words that tell you where the food is grown. An *indigenous* food is native to an area and is thus grown locally. In contrast, the word *exotic* describes food grown out of the region or country and is thus imported.

- *An important warning* The packages containing ears of golden corn all contain the following warning: "Perishable, keep cool." *Perishable* means "subject to spoiling." What is the label telling us to do with our corn when we return home? Since our corn and other vegetables are *perishable*, let's hurry along and look for milk and cereal.

3. Homogenized Milk and Fortified Cereals

- *What is homogenized milk?* Each carton of milk contains a label telling us that the milk is homogenized. But what does this mean? *Homogenized* refers to a process whereby milk becomes uniform in consistency by *emulsifying,* or breaking up, the fat content.

- *What is a fortified cereal?* Now let's move up the aisle and choose from the wide selection of cereals. Many of the cereal boxes contain colorful labels insisting that the cereals are "fortified with 9 vitamins and minerals." *Fortified* is derived from the Latin word *fortis*, meaning "strong." A cereal that has been fortified has been strengthened by adding extra vitamins and minerals.

Although the authors are under constraint not to use brand names, there is no such prohibition in classroom activity. Your students will remember these words best if they are related to familiar products.

4. Soft Drinks and Cups

- *Thirst-quenching drinks* Many of the soft drink bottles and cans contain labels boasting that the drink will quench even the greatest thirst. *Quench* means "to put out or extinguish." The soft drink manufacturers are thus telling us that their drinks will quench, or satisfy, our thirst.

- *A sip or a gulp?* Cups come in a variety of sizes. The smallest hold just 5 ounces and are ideal for taking a *sip*, or small mouthful, of a drink. But what if you're really thirsty and need a big *gulp* (to swallow a large amount of liquid) to quench your thirst? The king-size 16 ounce cup is just right for guzzling down big gulps!

5. Big Words For Small Children

- *What do pacifiers and the Pacific Ocean have in common?* Crying is one of the things babies do best. Finding a pacifier is thus a top priority. The Latin word *pacificare* means "to make peace." A *pacifier* is designed to pacify or calm an infant. Can you guess how the word *pacifier* and the name *Pacific Ocean* are related? After sailing through the turbulent waters at the tip of South America, Magellan entered a broad and calm body of water. Because it seemed so tranquil, Magellan named it the *Pacific* (or peaceful) *Ocean.*

- *What to buy for sunburn?* The next item on our list is an ointment for sunburn. Read the following label: "Emollient and protective ointment for sunburn and minor skin irritations." It sounds good, but what does the word *emollient* mean? An emollient is any ointment that is used to soften or soothe the skin. The label is thus telling us that the ointment will help soothe sunburn and other skin irritations.

- *What is a non-toxic clay set?* Did you ever use clay to make animals and other toys? The clay sets on the supermarket shelf all contain a large label announcing that the clay is "non-hardening and non-toxic." Is this good or bad? Our decision hinges on the meaning of *non-toxic.* Since *toxic* means harmful and poisonous, a non-toxic substance is safe for children.

6. Pharmaceuticals

- *Stick-on bandages* Although we have all used a stick-on bandage, how many of us have read the label? Here's a label from a stick-on bandage box: "Unique, Long-Lasting Adhesive. Stays on, even in water." *Unique* means "one of a kind." But, what does *adhesive* mean? Can you think of another product that has the word adhesive in its name. How about adhesive tape? *Adhesive* means "to stick or hold fast." When you *adhere* to a diet, for example, you stick to or closely follow it.

- *Shampoo* The shampoo bottles all contain captions proclaiming how they will help your hair. Here's a label that contains a particularly good SAT word: "Our special formula rejuvenates tired hair." While everyone wants clean hair, do we also want rejuvenated hair? *Rejuvenate* means "to restore youthful vigor." So if your hair is tired or overstyled, this could be the perfect shampoo.

- *Cough-drops* The label on the cough-drop container tells us that "the cherry-flavored cough-drops are intended to relieve chest congestion and suppress the urge to cough." *Suppress* means "to hold back, to check." A cough *suppressant* is designed to check or block the urge to cough.

- *Bath tablets* Here's an interesting label: "Each effervescent tablet releases carbon dioxide into your bath. In about seven minutes the tablet dissolves, invisibly distributing natural carbonation throughout the bath water." The label goes on to explain that the carbonated water will help soothe away stress and tension. Sounds great, but what does *effervescent* mean? *Effervescent* means "to be bubbly and lively," as in an *effervescent* personality. It's been a hard day and we've been shopping for a long time, so let's treat ourselves to some effervescent tablets.

7. Don't forget the cat food!

Even though we have been methodically walking up and down each aisle, we almost forgot to buy food for our pet cat, Binky. Like most cats, Binky is very finicky, so we'd better choose carefully. The cat food cans offer a wide selection of foods. Do you think Binky would prefer *savory salmon feast* or *tender morsels of beef*? *Savory* means "very tasty, mouthwatering." Sounds perfect. But what is a morsel? A *morsel* is a small piece or bite of food. Since both sound good, let's put a can of each in our cart and head for the check-out line. We now have a cart full of groceries and new vocabulary words!

Using Your VOCABULARY

ODD WORD OUT

DIRECTIONS: Each question below consists of four words. Three of them are related in meaning. Circle the word that does not fit.

1. (fatigue)   revive   revitalize   rejuvenate

2. subdued   grave   (effervescent)   gloomy

3. emollient   soothing   calming   (irritating)

4. weaken   (fortify)   undermine   debilitate

5. (direct)   winding   roundabout   circuitous

6. obvious   direct   (subtle)   blunt

MATCHING

DIRECTIONS: Match each word in the first column with its appropriate definition in the second column.

_E_	1. methodical	A. assortment
_J_	2. morsel	B. vigorous, full of health
_G_	3. suppress	C. foreign, imported
_D_	4. gulp	D. swallow a large amount of liquid
_H_	5. quench	E. very systematic
_I_	6. indigenous	F. bubbly, lively
_A_	7. medley	G. hold back, check
_M_	8. perishable	H. satisfy or extinguish
_K_	9. sip	I. native to an area
_C_	10. exotic	J. small piece or bite of food
_B_	11. robust	K. small mouthful
_L_	12. circuitous	L. roundabout
_F_	13. effervescent	M. subject to spoiling

USING YOUR VOCABULARY

DIRECTIONS: Use your knowledge of the previously-defined words to write a definition for each undefined word.

1. If *fortified* means "to strengthen," then *fortitude* means—

   the characteristic of having strength

2. If *homogenized* means "to make uniform," then *homogeneous* means—

   the characteristic of being uniform or the same

3. If a *pacifier* is used to calm, then a *pacifist* is someone who supports—

   peace, calmness

4. If a *toxic* substance is harmful, then a *toxin* is—

   a harmful substance

5. If *adhesive* means "to stick or hold fast," then an *adherent* is something that—

   sticks or holds fast to something else

6. If *savory* means "very tasty," then *unsavory* means—

   not very tasty

The Mighty Prefix

Take a look at the following three words. What do they all have in common?

- abnormal
- submerge
- preview

If you guessed that all three words begin with a prefix, you're right. *Ab-* (away from), *sub-* (under), and *pre-* (before) are all *prefixes*. A prefix is a word part placed before a root in order to direct or change the root's meaning.

Prefixes are found in many SAT words. Excluding the prefixes discussed above, list three prefixes that you are familiar with:

Responses will vary. Possible responses are shown in the blanks.

un-_____

non-_____

ex-_____

Prefixes are short but mighty. A knowledge of prefixes will help you unlock the meaning of hundreds of words. This lesson will examine three key prefixes.

The Big E: E and EX ·····► We Are Out of Here

Take a look at the above headline. As Hurricane Felix approached the North Carolina coast, what action did thousands of coastal residents and vacationers take? They *evacuated* or got OUT! The prefixes E- and EX- mean *out*.

E- and EX- are among the most widely used prefixes on the SAT. Learning them is thus of *paramount* (very great, supreme) importance. Can you name two words that you have already learned in this text that begin with the prefix E- or EX-?

exotic

effervescent

Build a bulletin board display with headlines showing SAT words. Encourage students to search the newspaper looking for any of the SAT words presented in this book.

Here are seven words that begin with the prefixes E- or EX-:

1. *Exit* – When you head for the exit, where do you go? Out, of course!

2. *Extinguish* – What is the purpose of the fire extinguishers that you see in many buildings? The prefix EX- provides a clue telling you that the extinguisher is used to put out a fire. *Extinguish* means "to put out or wipe out." For example, "The loss *extinguished* the team's hopes of making the playoffs."

3. *Extrovert* – Some people have personalities that are outgoing, while others are shy and withdrawn. Which direction, in or out, do you think an *extrovert* would be turned? The prefix EX- tells you that an *extrovert* has an outgoing personality and enjoys being with people.

4. *Elusive* – Examine the following newspaper headline:

Based upon your knowledge of the prefix E-, what do you think *elusive* means in this headline? *Elusive* means "out of reach." The headline tells us that physicists have identified a previously hard to find atomic particle.

5. *Exorbitant* – Suppose a friend told you that a clothing store charges *exorbitant* prices for sweaters. Does this mean that the sweaters are inexpensive or high-priced? The prefix EX- tells us that *out* is involved in the definition. The word *orbit* refers to the path or track of a planet or other heavenly body. *Exorbitant* literally means "out of

orbit." *Exorbitant* prices are so unreasonably high that they are above and beyond what is normally expected. You might also say that the prices are *excessively* high.

6. *Eminent* – Suppose your English teacher told you that an *eminent* author was scheduled to visit your class. Would you guess that the author's writings were undistinguished or outstanding? Once again the prefix E- provides a valuable clue. *Eminent* is derived from the Latin word *minere* meaning "to stand." *Eminent* thus means "to stand out." An *eminent* author would therefore stand out and be very distinguished.

7. *Expound* – The word *expound* is derived from the prefix EX- meaning "out" and the Latin word *ponere* meaning "to place." To *expound* means "to put out" in the sense of setting forth a detailed view or opinion. For example, the candidate used the open forum to *expound* her views on tax reform.

A and AN ·····► The Greek Way to Say NOT!

A- and AN- are Greek prefixes meaning "not" or "without." Like E- and EX-, the prefixes A- and AN- regularly appear in many SAT words. Here are five examples:

Encourage students to write short articles or dialogues using a set of SAT words.

1. *Atypical* – If something is *typical*, it is characteristic of its kind, class, or group. Since the prefix A- means "not," *atypical* means "uncommon or unusual." For example, it would be *atypical* for the best violinist in an orchestra to go an entire week without practicing.

2. *Atheist* – *Theos* is a Greek word meaning "God." An *atheist* is literally "someone who is without God." The word *atheist* is now used to describe a person who does not believe in God.

3. *Amorphous* – *Morphous* is a Greek word meaning "shape or form." *Amorphous* means "without shape or form." For example, an *amorphous* term paper would lack shape and would appear to be disorganized. You may also be familiar with the popular horror movie *The Blob*, in which an *amorphous* gob of sticky goo rolls about the countryside devouring every living thing in its path.

4. *Atrophy* – Can you guess what the disease muscular dystrophy and the SAT word *atrophy* have in common? Both contain the Latin word *trophy* meaning "nourishment." *Muscular dystrophy* refers to a condition of irreversible muscular deterioration. *Atrophy* refers to the

general condition of wasting or withering away. For example, "The runner's once well-conditioned leg muscles *atrophied* as she recovered from an injury."

5. *Anomaly* – *Nom* is an abbreviated form of the word *norm,* meaning a standard of behavior. An *anomaly* is thus an abnormality or departure from a general rule. For example, "Lauren's mature attitude was an *anomaly* for someone so young."

RE ·····➤ Back, Again. Let me repeat, BACK, AGAIN.

RE- is a Latin prefix meaning "back" or "again." RE- can be found in many common words. List two words that are part of your everyday vocabulary that begin with the prefix RE-:

Responses will vary.

Here are six key SAT words beginning with the prefix RE-:

1. *Revoke* – Would you be pleased or displeased if your driver's license were *revoked*? Since *revoke* means "to recall or cancel" you would undoubtedly be very displeased.

2. *Revitalize* – Examine the following newspaper headline:

Based upon your knowledge of the prefix RE-, what do you think *revitalize* means in this headline? *Revitalize* means "to restore the vitality or life of, to revive."

3. *Renovate* – *Novus* is a Latin word meaning "new." *Renovate* means "to make new again." For example, "The new owners *renovated* the stadium by adding a high-tech scoreboard and more comfortable seats."

4. *Resurge* – *Resurge* can be easily divided into two parts, the prefix RE- and the word *surge*. *Surge* means "to increase suddenly." For example, bookstores report a *surge* of interest in romance novels. *Resurge* means "to rise or surge again." For example, "The interest in 1970's disco music is currently *resurging*."

5. *Redundant* – Have you ever had someone unnecessarily repeat directions that you understood the first time? If so, then that person was being *redundant*, or excessively repetitious. When you are being *redundant*, you're saying something again for the second or third time for no reason. That is to say, when you are being *redundant*, you're saying something again for the second or third time for no reason.

6. *Remuneration* – Suppose you are at an interview when the boss says, "You should be pleased with the *remuneration* this job offers." What is she talking about? *Remuneration* is derived from the Latin word *munerare*, meaning "to give." *Remuneration* literally means "to give back." Today, remuneration means "to give back" in the sense of paying or compensating someone for doing a job.

Using Your
VOCABULARY

MATCHING

DIRECTIONS: Match each word in the first column with its appropriate definition in the second column.

_D_	1. exorbitant	A.	remodel
_E_	2. anomaly	B.	explain in great detail
_A_	3. renovate	C.	outgoing personality
_H_	4. redundant	D.	unreasonable, excessive
_C_	5. extrovert	E.	irregular, not normal
_J_	6. atrophy	F.	compensation
_I_	7. eminent	G.	hard to catch
_B_	8. expound	H.	unnecessarily repetitious
_G_	9. elusive	I.	outstanding
_F_	10. remuneration	J.	wither away

RELATIONSHIPS

DIRECTIONS: For each question below, decide whether the pair of words are synonyms (S), antonyms (A), or unrelated (U) to each other.

_A_	1. atypical	representative
_S_	2. revitalize	rejuvenate
_U_	3. resurgent	savory
_S_	4. extinguish	quench
_A_	5. atheist	believer
_U_	6. renovation	effervescent
_U_	7. anomaly	emollient
_S_	8. elusive	evasive
_S_	9. expound	explicate
_U_	10. atrophy	toxic

APPLYING YOUR KNOWLEDGE

DIRECTIONS: In each of the items below, use your knowledge of the defined word or root word to write a definition for the word in italics.

1. If JECT means "to throw," what does *reject* mean?

   to throw back

2. If an EXTROVERT is a person with an outgoing personality, what is the most likely meaning of *introvert*?

   an inward personality

3. If ARCHY means "rule by," what does *anarchy* mean?

   without rule or government; chaotic

4. If CHRONOS means "time," what does *anachronism* mean?

   not within the correct time

5. If TREPIDATION means "fearful," what is the most likely meaning of *intrepid*?

   not fearful; brave

Roots and Branches

Have you noticed how often we have referred to Latin and Greek words in our definitions of modern English words? Many Latin and Greek words are *roots*. In linguistics, a root is a word or word element from which other words are formed. For example, take a close look at the following three words. What root do they all share?

- cordial
- accord
- discord

Cord is the Latin word for *heart*. Knowing what this root means gives us new insight into the word *cordial*. A *cordial* greeting is warm and friendly because it is from the heart. When two people are *in accord*, their hearts are literally joined together and in harmony. But when we add the prefix *dis-*, meaning "apart," to the root *cord*, we create the word *discord*, meaning "lack of harmony, disagreement."

As you can see, learning root families can be a very effective way to expand your vocabulary. Following are four more root families whose members regularly appear on the SAT.

Meet the AMICUS Family

They Want to Be Your Friends

Amicus is a Latin root meaning "friend." As you have probably already guessed, the French word *ami* and the Spanish word *amigo* are both derived from *amicus*. Several English words that involve friendship are also part of the AMICUS family. Here are three key members.

1. *Amicable* – *Amicable* means "characterized by or showing friendliness."

    EXAMPLE: In order to avoid fights, students must learn more *amicable* ways of settling arguments.

2. *Amity* – *Amity* means "peaceful relations," as between countries.

    EXAMPLE: A new spirit of *amity* characterizes relations between the United States and Russia now that the Cold War is over.

3. *Amiable* – *Amiable* means "good-natured, friendly, affable."

    EXAMPLE: Anita's *amiable* personality made her a welcome member of our club.

Meet the GREG Family

They Flock Together

Gregis is a Latin word for *flock* or *herd*. In English the root GREG means "group." Here are five members of the GREG family.

1. *Gregarious* – *Gregarious* means "to like groups" and the company of others.

   EXAMPLE: A *gregarious* person is very outgoing and sociable.

2. *Congregate* – *Congregate* means "to flock together in a group."

   EXAMPLE: During spring break, thousands of college students *congregate* at Daytona Beach.

3. *Segregate* – *Segregate* means "to keep apart, to separate into different groups."

   EXAMPLE: Hospitals *segregate* those patients with contagious diseases into special wards.

4. *Aggregate* – *Aggregate* means "to gather into a whole or mass" so as to constitute the sum total.

   EXAMPLE: The class treasurer announced that the *aggregate* wealth of the junior class was more than enough to pay for the prom.

5. *Egregious* – *Egregious* means "to stand out from the group" in a negative sense. *Egregious* refers to any action that is outstandingly bad.

   EXAMPLE: The home crowd complained that the referee's *egregious* call cost their team the game.

Meet the PATHOS Family

They Have Deep Feelings

Pathy comes from the Greek word *pathos*, meaning "feeling." Here are four members of the PATHOS family.

1. *Apathy* – *Apathy* means "to show or feel little or no emotions." An *apathetic* person is thus indifferent to the events and people around him or her.

   EXAMPLE: Political scientists believe that public *apathy* is one of the major causes of low voter registration.

2. *Antipathy* – The prefix *anti-* means "against." *Antipathy* refers to "strong feelings against someone or something."

   EXAMPLE: The American Civil War led to lingering *antipathy* between the nation's northern and southern citizens.

3. *Sympathy* – The prefix *sym-* means "with or together." *Sympathy* refers to "a feeling or expression of pity or sorrow" for another person.

   EXAMPLE: A seriously ill person needs *sympathy*.

4. *Empathy* – *Empathy* means "to feel as one would in another's place."

   EXAMPLE: A student who has suffered an injury can *empathize* with an athlete whose career is threatened by a severe injury.

Meet the FID Family

A Group You Can Trust

Using these "family" words, students can write a travelogue mentioning various people they met on a summer trip.

The Latin word *fidere* means "to trust, have faith." The root FID thus means "to trust." Here are four members of the FID family.

1. *Fidelity* – *Fidelity* means "a faithful devotion to duty or one's obligations."

   EXAMPLE: Sharon demonstrated her unswerving *fidelity* to the union by joining the picket line.

2. *Confidant* – Is there someone whom you trust above all others? A *confidant* is a person in whom one can trust completely.

   EXAMPLE: The Reverend Ralph Abernathy was a *confidant* of Dr. Martin Luther King, Jr., during the Montgomery Bus Boycott.

3. *Diffident* – *Diffident* means "a lack of faith or confidence in oneself."

   EXAMPLE: Brad's *diffidence* prevented him from making friends at his new school.

4. *Perfidious* – *Perfidious* means "to break faith" and thus show disloyalty or treachery.

   EXAMPLE: Benedict Arnold was a *perfidious* traitor to the colonial cause.

Using Your
VOCABULARY

MATCHING

DIRECTIONS: Match each word in the first column with its definition in the second column.

G   1. perfidious   A. faithful devotion to duty
C   2. discord   B. the ability to feel as another does
B   3. empathy   C. dispute, disagreement
H   4. egregious   D. sociable, affable
I   5. amity   E. indifference, lack of feeling
D   6. gregarious   F. without self-confidence
E   7. apathy   G. treacherous
F   8. diffident   H. flagrantly wrong
A   9. fidelity   I. peaceful friendly relations
J   10. antipathy   J. strong dislike

ODD WORD OUT

DIRECTIONS: Each question below consists of four words. Three of them are related in meaning. Circle the word that does not fit.

1. gregarious   affable   extroverted   solitary

2. belligerent   hostile   amicable   antagonistic

3. indifferent   cordial   friendly   amiable

4. unnoticeable   egregious   flagrant   glaring

5. concern   apathy   interest   attention

6. timid   shy   diffident   audacious

7. dislike   antipathy   affection   disgust

8. dependable   treacherous   traitorous   perfidious

9. congregate   disperse   scatter   separate

10. harmony   discord   accord   amity

APPLYING YOUR KNOWLEDGE

DIRECTIONS: In each of the items below, use your knowledge of the defined words to write a definition for the word in italics.

1. If FID means "faith/trust," what does *infidel* mean?

   someone who is without faith

   _____

   _____

2. If PATHY means "feeling," what does *pathos* mean?

   something that evokes feeling

   _____

   _____

3. If FID means "faith/trust," what does *infidelity* mean?

   a breaking of trust

   _____

   _____

4. If GREG means "group," what does *congregation* mean?

   a group that has come together

   _____

   _____

5. If CON is a prefix meaning "with or together" and CORD is a root meaning "heart," what does *concord* mean?

   "hearts together," or harmony

   _____

   _____

Synonym Clusters

As you have seen, roots and prefixes are important tools for building a more powerful vocabulary. Learning synonym clusters is another effective way of augmenting your vocabulary. A synonym cluster is a group of words that have similar meanings. The following four synonym clusters contain 20 vocabulary words. These 20 words have appeared in over 40 SAT questions in the last few years.

The Thrill-of-Victory Cluster

These Words Are Overflowing with Enthusiasm

Have you ever scored a high grade on a tough test, performed a flawless recital, or been part of a team that won a championship game? If you have had any of these experiences, you know what it is like to enjoy the thrill of victory. The English language provides us with a full synonym cluster of words that express excitement. Here are six key members of the Thrill-of-Victory Cluster.

1. Exuberant – overflowing with enthusiasm and excitement, full of joy

2. Ebullient – overflowing with enthusiasm and excitement

3. Exultant – overflowing with enthusiasm and excitement, triumphant

4. Elated – overflowing with enthusiasm and excitement, feeling great

5. Exhilarated – overflowing with enthusiasm and excitement, very happy

6. Ecstatic – overflowing with enthusiasm and excitement, euphoric

What did you notice about the definitions of these six words? Don't worry, you're not suffering from blurred vision. Although there are slight differences, all six words have basically the same definition. Six SAT words for just one definition! Not bad. Let's go to our next synonym cluster.

The Agony-of-Defeat Cluster

These Words Are Overwhelmed with Disappointment

If you've ever failed a big test, forgotten your lines in a play, or been part of a team that lost a consolation game, you know what it is like to feel the agony of defeat. The English language provides us with a full synonym cluster of "down" words that express the overwhelming disappointment that comes with failing to achieve your goal. Here are four key members of the Agony-of-Defeat Cluster.

1. Despondent – feeling very discouraged, downhearted

2. Dejected – feeling very discouraged, downhearted

3. Dispirited – feeling very discouraged, downhearted

4. Disconsolate – feeling very discouraged, downhearted, hopelessly sad

The Stubborn Cluster

These Words Are Hard to Budge

Do you know someone who is stubborn and just won't change? The English language provides us with several words to describe stubborn people. Here are five key words.

1. Obstinate – stubborn and unyielding

2. Obdurate – stubborn and unyielding, particularly hardhearted and callous

3. Intransigent – stubborn and unyielding, uncompromising

4. Recalcitrant – stubborn and unyielding, particularly to authority

5. Dogged – stubborn and unyielding, not easily subdued

The Secret Cluster

These Words Don't Want to Be Seen

Have you ever watched a James Bond movie? If so, you know that James Bond is a secret agent also known as 007. Here are five words that all express varieties of secrecy.

1. Clandestine – secret, hidden. Do you have a favorite spy movie? If you do, it most likely features a complex web of adventure and *clandestine* affairs.

2. Surreptitiously – secret, hidden. Have you ever done something in a concealed manner? If so, you were acting *surreptitiously*.

3. Stealthy – secret, hidden. The United States Air Force built a military plane that can travel in secret by absorbing radar waves. It is so hard to track, in fact, that they named it the *Stealth Bomber*.

4. Covert – secret, hidden. Would you like to work for a top-secret spy agency? If so, you might become a *covert* or undercover agent traveling the world on international assignments.

5. Furtive – secret, hidden. Have you ever tried to glance at someone in the hall when your teacher wasn't looking? If so, your glance was done in a *furtive* or secret manner.

Using Your VOCABULARY

ODD WORD OUT

DIRECTIONS: Each question below consists of four words. Three of them are related in meaning. Circle the word that does not fit.

1. open   public   aboveboard   (clandestine)

2. covert   (unconcealed)   cloaked   hidden

3. (revealed)   surreptitious   veiled   cloaked

4. (despair)   elation   jubilation   ecstasy

5. gloomy   (exuberant)   depressed   dispirited

6. ebullient   exhilarated   (despondent)   elated

7. inflexible   obstinate   stubborn   (docile)

8. (obedient)   intransigent   obdurate   recalcitrant

9. manageable   obedient   docile   (obstinate)

10. determined   dogged   (hesitant)   tenacious

RELATIONSHIPS

DIRECTIONS: For each question below, decide whether the pair of words are synonyms (S), antonyms (A), or unrelated (U) to each other.

<u> S </u>   1. ebullient. . . . . effervescent

<u> U </u>   2. despondent . . . . perfidious

<u> U </u>   3. elated . . . . elusive

<u> A </u>   4. obstinate . . . . docile

<u> S </u>   5. clandestine . . . . surreptitious

<u> S </u>   6. covert. . . . . furtive

<u> A </u>   7. exultant . . . . dispirited

<u> A </u>   8. dejected . . . . revitalized

<u> U </u>   9. recalcitrant. . . . . toxic

<u> U </u>   10. obdurate . . . . anomaly

COMPLETE THE HEADLINE

DIRECTIONS: Use one of the following five words to complete each headline: Elated, Clandestine, Dogged, Disconsolate, Intransigent.

1. _____Elated_____ Volleyball Team Celebrates Championship

2. Militant Rebels Remain _____Intransigent_____ , Won't Accept UN Compromise

3. _____Dogged_____ Marathon Runner's Tough Workout

4. Father _____Disconsolate_____ After Losing Pet Turtle on Camping Trip

5. MegaCorp Company Suspected of _____Clandestine_____ Plan to Build Atomic Bomb

Building a Foundation for Sentence Completions

After completing this chapter, you will be able to

1. find a key word or group of words in a sentence.

2. identify and answer definitional sentence completion questions.

3. explain what is meant by a reversal word.

4. give examples of reversal words.

5. identify and answer contrast sentence completion questions.

Introduction to Sentence Completions

Have you ever watched the television program *Wheel of Fortune*? If so, you know that the contestants try to win prizes by filling in the blanks in a saying or a group of words. For example, what letters would you use to complete this saying?

<u>D</u> A <u>W</u> N   I S   T H E   <u>B</u> E G I N N I N G   <u>O</u> F   T H E   <u>D</u> A Y

The SAT will present 19 sentence completions that are similar to playing *Wheel of Fortune*, only instead of letters, you will be plugging in one or two words. Each question consists of a sentence containing one or two blanks. Your job is to select the word or words that best complete the sentence.

To introduce this item format, you can easily make worksheets using any piece of writing where you blank out selected words. After filling in the blanks, students should discuss how they decided on each word.

One 30-minute verbal section will begin with a set of 10 sentence completions. The other 30-minute verbal section will open with a set of 9 sentence completions. Each set is arranged in order of difficulty. The first question will be relatively easy and questions will get harder as you move along.

According to the SAT people, sentence completion questions are designed to measure your vocabulary and "your ability to understand how the different parts of a sentence fit logically together." You'll find that the words you learn in our vocabulary chapters will be particularly helpful in attacking sentence completion questions.

Key Words and Groups of Words

The SAT writers can't use just any sentence and leave out any word. They have to give you enough information to make the correct choices inarguably correct and the wrong choices inarguably wrong. Otherwise, they would have a serious problem with their test. For example, read the sentence below and select the missing word.

> The general feeling in the high school was ----.
> (A) confident
> (B) confused
> (C) serious
> (D) gloomy
> (E) uncertain

Which answer did you choose? Why? Are the other answers clearly incorrect?

This situation will arise frequently during discussion of the activity suggested on page 68.

In this example, all five of the answer choices could be correct. The general feeling in the high school could have been *confident, confused, serious, gloomy,* or *uncertain*. The sentence doesn't provide us with enough information to determine what kind of feeling existed in the high school. This type of sentence could not survive on the SAT.

Now take a look at an improved version.

> The general feeling in the high school was ----, since everyone expected to win the big game.
> (A) confident
> (B) confused
> (C) serious
> (D) gloomy
> (E) uncertain

Which answer did you choose this time? Why? The additional words *since everyone expected to win the big game* tells us that the general feeling in the high school was *confident*. None of the other choices describe this feeling.

The group of words *since everyone expected to win the big game* is the key to attacking this question. Each sentence completion on the SAT will have a key word or group of words that will help lead you to the correct answer. The three lessons in this chapter will help you to identify key words and groups of words and use them to find correct answers or *ZAP* wrong choices.

A Case Example

Here are the exact directions and sample sentence completion question that will appear on your SAT. If you learn the directions now, you will save time when you take the test.

Each sentence below has one or two blanks, each blank indicating that something has been omitted. Beneath the sentence are five words or sets of words labeled A through E. Choose the word or set of words that, when inserted in the sentence, <u>best</u> fits the meaning of the sentence as a whole.

Example:

Medieval kingdoms did not become constitutional republics overnight; on the contrary, the change was ----.
(A) unpopular
(B) unexpected
(C) advantageous
(D) sufficient
(●) gradual

The semicolon following the word *overnight* divides this sentence into two parts. The first part of the sentence tells you that the medieval kingdoms did not change overnight. *Overnight* means quickly or rapidly. The second part of the sentence begins with the key group of words *on the contrary*. This key group of words tells you that the correct answer must be a word describing a change that did not happen rapidly. While all five choices could describe a change, only choice (E) describes a change that did not happen overnight.

When you attack the sentence completions, always give yourself time to carefully consider the sentence before you look at the answer choices.

DIRECTIONS: First identify the key word or group of words. Then think about a word that would fit in the blank. Mark the answer that *best* fits the meaning of the sentence as a whole.

1. The play's organization is ----; that is, each scene is presented in the order of its occurrence.

   (A) dramatic
   (B) minimal
   (C) controversial
   (D) chronological
   (E) confusing

2. Their mutual teasing seemed ----, since the two neighbors enjoyed poking fun at each other.

   (A) aimless
   (B) bitter
   (C) friendly
   (D) insincere
   (E) original

3. Although she had no prior experience as a ----, Elwell nevertheless impressed company officials with her uncanny ability to find common sense solutions to difficult human relations problems.

   (A) consultant
   (B) tourist
   (C) entertainer
   (D) customer
   (E) procrastinator

Guided PRACTICE

Discussion

1. If you read only the first part of the sentence, any of the choices would fit in the blank. However, the key group of words *in the order of its occurrence* provides a definition that leads you to choice (D). Even if you don't know the meaning of *chronological*, you should be able to ZAP (A), (B), (C), and (E).

2. Again, if you read only the first part of the sentence, choices (A), (B), (C), and (E) all work equally well. But, when you consider the key word *enjoyed*, you see that the teasing must have been *friendly*. Therefore, you can ZAP (A) and (B), leaving only (C) and (E) to think about. Since there isn't anything in the sentence to suggest that the teasing was *original*, the answer is (C).

3. What did Elwell do to impress company officials? According to the sentence, she had an *uncanny ability to find common sense solutions to difficult human relations problems*. This key group of words tells you that Elwell probably served as a *consultant*. You can ZAP (B), (C), and (D) because companies don't hire *tourists*, *entertainers*, or *customers* to find solutions to difficult human relations problems. If you're not sure what a *procrastinator* is (someone who puts everything off until later), you would need to guess between (A) and (E). In this case, (A) best fits the logic of this sentence.

Sentence Completion Practice Exercise 1 provides you with 10 sentences to practice the skill of selecting the key word or group of words.

SENTENCE COMPLETION PRACTICE EXERCISE ① "Key Words"

DIRECTIONS: For each sentence, underline the key word or group of words. Then in the space provided write a word that you feel would fit correctly in the blank.

Encourage discussion and support for words chosen as possible correct answers.

Responses will vary. Possible responses are shown in the blanks.

1. Tarantulas apparently have little sense of ----, for, no matter how hungry they are, they will ignore a loudly chirping cricket unless it happens to pass close by.

   <u>   hearing   </u>
   possible answer

2. Medwick was such an outstanding thinker that her colleagues were too often dazzled by her ---- to appreciate fully her other virtues.

   <u>   intellect   </u>
   possible answer

3. Because they hoard water in their leaves, stems, and root systems, plants that grow in the desert or on high rocky ledges can survive long periods of ----.

   <u>   drought   </u>
   possible answer

4. It may be that the students learned the material so well because the task was extremely ----: the computer program directed them to perform the same sequence over and over again.

   <u>   repetitive   </u>
   possible answer

5. A judgment made before all the facts are known must be called ----.

   <u>   ill-informed   </u>
   possible answer

6. Enamel is an extraordinarily ---- protective coating, making teeth the last part of a dead animal to decay.

_____ durable _____
possible answer

7. The agreement between the two store managers was ----: each promised to exchange with the other merchandise of comparable value.

_____ equitable _____
possible answer

8. In the late nineteenth century, scientists were mystified by the schooling behavior of certain fish; today's marine biologists are still ---- by the behavior of these fish.

_____ puzzled _____
possible answer

9. Although the critics agreed that the book was brilliant, so few copies were sold that the work brought the author little ---- reward.

_____ monetary _____
possible answer

10. The author includes very little ---- of the dragon: monsters are more fearful if pictured in the imagination.

_____ description _____
possible answer

LESSON
6

Definitional Sentences

In Lesson 5 you learned to attack each sentence completion by first looking for the key words or groups of words. Now examine the following three sentence completions.

1. These criticisms are ---- and not directed against anyone in particular.
    (A) specific
    (B) impersonal
    (C) inaccurate
    (D) cowardly
    (E) crafty

2. Studying to become a doctor can be ----, in that it often requires long hours of hard work.
    (A) arduous
    (B) effortless
    (C) irregular
    (D) elusive
    (E) extravagant

3. The Southern Stingray is ---- animal that generally avoids humans as much as possible.
    (A) a gregarious
    (B) a dangerous
    (C) a nocturnal
    (D) an apathetic
    (E) a shy

What type of pattern do you think the key words and group of words in these three sentences have in common? In each sentence the key group of words is a definition. In Sentence 1, the key group of words *not directed against anyone in particular* tells you that the answer is (B). In Sentence 2, the key group of words *often requires long hours of hard work* tells you that the answer is (A). In Sentence 3, the key group of words *avoids humans as much as possible* tells you that the answer is (E).

In these *definitional* sentences, the key word or group of words is a definition or explanation. Therefore, the answer is the word that is defined or explained in the sentence. As always, if you don't know some of the words, switch to *ZAPPING* and guess from the leftovers.

A Case Example

Read the following sentence completion question and identify the key word or group of words. It should lead you to the correct answer.

> Prehistoric hunters worked ----; they helped one another capture mammoths and other big game animals.
>
> (A) warily
> (B) quietly
> (●) cooperatively
> (D) clandestinely
> (E) passively

This question asks you to look for a word that describes how prehistoric hunters worked. The information following the semicolon tells you that the hunters *helped one another*. This key group of words provides a good definition of cooperative behavior, so the answer is (C). How would the answer have changed if the prehistoric hunters had been described as *cautiously investigating each new situation*?

Whenever you run into unknown words, apply the strategies taught in the vocabulary chapters. If that fails, *ZAP* what you can and then choose an answer. For example, in the sentence above, there is nothing to support *quietly* as the correct answer. Even if this is the only word you recognize, you could *ZAP* it and guess from the other choices.

Guided
PRACTICE

DIRECTIONS: Read each sentence and underline the key word or group of words. Then think of a word that would fit in the blank. Finally, mark the correct answer.

1. Lauren is a ---- person who has always been willing to help those in need.
   - (●) generous
   - (B) clumsy
   - (C) graceful
   - (D) attractive
   - (E) selfish

2. The queen and her more ---- counselors wished to avoid the war.
   - (A) belligerent
   - (B) reckless
   - (C) aggressive
   - (●) pacifist
   - (E) verbose

3. The philanthropist refused to identify his name and thus remained ----.
   - (A) adventurous
   - (B) notorious
   - (C) boisterous
   - (D) oblivious
   - (●) anonymous

Discussion

1. You are looking for a word to describe Lauren. The key group of words *always been willing to help those in need* defines a *generous* person. The answer is (A). How would the answer have changed if Lauren had been described as a person *who only thinks of herself*?

2. The question asks you to describe the counselors. The key group of words *wished to avoid the war* defines a *pacifist* (D). *Belligerent, reckless, aggressive,* and *verbose* counselors would all want to provoke a war. If some of these choices are unfamiliar words to you, *ZAP* the ones you do know and then consider the leftovers. If you have two or three equally unknown words, guess and move to the next question.

3. The key group of words in this sentence is *refused to identify his name*. This group of words provides a good definition of *anonymous* (E). Even if you were not sure of the answer, you should be able to *ZAP* the familiar word *adventurous*. Remember, if you can *ZAP* even one choice, you should take a guess before going to the next question.

Independent
PRACTICE

Sentence Completion Practice Exercise 2 provides you an opportunity to practice your skill of attacking definitional sentence completion questions.

SENTENCE COMPLETION PRACTICE EXERCISE 2 "Definitional"

DIRECTIONS: First identify and underline the key word or group of words in each sentence. Then mark the correct answer. Remember, the answer will be the word defined or explained by the key word or group of words.

1. The detectives conducted ---- investigation of the crime scene that left no clue unexamined.

    (A) a limited   (D) an exhaustive
    (B) a negligent   (E) a tardy
    (C) a cautious

2. Outgoing and friendly by nature, Francesca became even more ---- when talking to her close friends.

    (A) succinct   (D) stealthy
    (B) despondent   (E) extroverted
    (C) apathetic

3. Simone Bolivar came to be known as a great ---- for his role in leading the people of Latin America to victory in their wars of independence against Spain.

    (A) donor   (D) liberator
    (B) moderator   (E) orator
    (C) compromiser

4. Like a true ----, Bryan was a stingy person who wouldn't contribute a penny.

    (A) miser   (D) zealot
    (B) dolt   (E) rogue
    (C) sage

5. The Embargo Act of 1807 was one of the most ---- pieces of legislation in American history; everyone from New England merchants to Southern planters opposed it.

    (A) relevant
    (B) remarkable
    (C) disliked
    (D) flexible
    (E) elusive

6. Hannibal was ---- general, whose innovative tactics were admired by even those adversaries whom he outwitted.

   (A) a lethargic
   (B) an exorbitant
   (C) an incorrigible
   (D) an unorthodox
   (E) a conventional

7. Marine biologists have learned that salmon have a surprisingly ---- sense of smell that enables them to distinguish the odor of their own home stream.

   (A) dull
   (B) extravagant
   (C) tranquil
   (D) acute
   (E) covert

8. Sparrows are very ---- birds, often gathering into flocks and feeding together.

   (A) solitary
   (B) despondent
   (C) perfidious
   (D) furtive
   (E) gregarious

9. Until recently, anthropologists believed that Cro-Magnons were ---- who wandered from place to place in search of food.

   (A) tourists
   (B) vandals
   (C) rogues
   (D) sages
   (E) nomads

10. The convex mirror in "The Arnolfini Marriage" is painted with an almost miraculous ----, displaying Van Eyk's command of the latest techniques in oil painting.

    (A) sincerity
    (B) dexterity
    (C) energy
    (D) awkwardness
    (E) righteousness

Contrast Sentences

In Lesson 6 you learned that the key word or group of words in many sentence completion questions is a definition or explanation. Read the following three sentence completions.

1. The previous workers at the store had been rather ----, but the new owners hired employees who were unfailingly polite.

    (●) discourteous
    (B) efficient
    (C) gracious
    (D) verbose
    (E) entertaining

2. Although the professor's syllabus for the course looked very interesting, his actual lessons were quite ----.

    (A) suspicious
    (B) striking
    (C) amiable
    (D) casual
    (●) tedious

3. The players' dejected mood at the post-game news conference provided a vivid contrast to their ---- celebration at the pre-game pep rally.

    (A) gloomy
    (B) diffident
    (C) obstinate
    (●) exuberant
    (E) listless

What type of pattern do the key words and groups of words in these three sentences have in common? Each sentence contains a word or group of words that signals a change in direction. In Sentence 1, the word *but* signals a contrast between the behavior of the previous workers and the *unfailingly polite* employees hired by the new owners. In Sentence 2, the word *although* signals a contrast between a syllabus that *looked very interesting* and the professor's actual lessons. In Sentence 3, the words *contrast to* signal a change between the players' mood at the post-game news conference and the pre-game pep rally.

For purposes of strategy, think of *but*, *although*, and *in contrast with* as *reversal words*. Reversal words alert you to expect a contrast or change of direction in a sentence. The list below shows the most common reversal words and groups of words used in SAT sentence completion questions.

It does not present every possible word that can be used to express or imply a reversal.

Key Reversal Words

- BUT
- IN CONTRAST WITH
- DESPITE
- RATHER THAN
- INSTEAD OF

- ALTHOUGH
- HOWEVER
- NEVERTHELESS
- EVEN THOUGH
- YET

Students should highlight reversal words in a magazine or newspaper article.

Sentences containing reversal words are called *contrast sentences*. In this type of sentence completion, the answer will be a word that *contrasts* with the key word or group of words. For example, in the three sentences on page 60, *discourteous* contrasts with *polite*; *tedious* contrasts with *interesting*; and *exuberant* contrasts with *dejected*.

A Case Example

As you read the following sentence completion question, first identify the reversal word. Then look for the key word or group of words. Finally, select the answer that provides the best contrast with the key word or group of words.

Although computers appear to be bewilderingly complex, they operate on principles that are actually quite ----.
(A) puzzling
(B) elementary
(C) frustrating
(D) advanced
(E) amoral

The reversal word *although* signals a contrast between how computers appear and the principles upon which they operate. Since the sentence tells you that computers appear to be *bewilderingly complex* you should look for a word that best contrasts with *complex*. The answer is (B). Although the principles could have been *puzzling, frustrating, advanced,* or *amoral,* none of these choices contrast with *bewilderingly complex* and thus are not logical choices.

Whenever you see a sentence completion question with two blanks, attack the second blank first. It is usually easier to ZAP choices if you start with the second blank. This step will often eliminate three of the five choices.

Guided PRACTICE

DIRECTIONS: First circle the reversal word or group of words. Then underline the key word or group of words. Finally, mark the correct answer.

1. Some experts concluded that the diary is authentic, but skeptics still insist that it is ----.

    (A) genuine
    (B) factual
    (C) faithful
    (D) contemporary
    (E) fraudulent

2. The hotel's lobby was both spacious and luxurious; however, its guest rooms were surprisingly ---- and ----.

    (A) cramped . . . plain
    (B) ample . . . simple
    (C) small . . . lavish
    (D) large . . . ostentatious
    (E) numerous . . . extravagant

3. Political scientists agree that accurate opinion polls must be taken from a random sample of the population rather than from a ---- group of subjects.

    (A) knowledgeable
    (B) friendly
    (C) talkative
    (D) preselected
    (E) lucky

1. The reversal word *but* signals a contrast between the way experts and skeptics evaluate a diary. Since the sentence tells you that experts believe the diary is *authentic* (real), you should look for a word that best contrasts with *authentic*. The best answer is (E). Although the diary could have been *genuine, factual, faithful,* or *contemporary*, none of these choices contrast with *authentic* and thus are not logical choices.

2. The reversal word *however* signals a contrast between the hotel's lobby and its guest rooms. Since the sentence tells you that the lobby was *spacious and luxurious,* you should look for two contrasting words.

   If you look at the second blank first (see bottom of page 61), you can ZAP (C) and (E) because neither *lavish* nor *extravagant* contrast with *luxurious*. (If you don't know what *ostentatious* means, you should leave it for now.) By ZAPPING the second blank first, you now have to think about only three pairs of words, instead of five pairs.

   When you look at the first words for (A), (B), and (D), both (B) and (D) can be ZAPPED because neither *ample* nor *large* contrast with *spacious*. Since (C) and (E) are already ZAPPED, the answer must be (A).

   Notice that we arrived at the correct answer even without necessarily knowing the meaning of *ostentatious*.

3. The reversal expression *rather than* signals a contrast between two ways of selecting subjects for an opinion poll. Since the sentence tells you that accurate results must be taken from a *random sample of the population,* you should look for an answer that contrasts with *random*. The best choice is (D). Although the subjects could be *knowledgeable, friendly, talkative,* and *lucky,* none of these words contrast with *random* and thus are not logical choices.

Independent PRACTICE

Sentence Completion Practice Exercise 3 provides you with an opportunity to practice your skill of attacking contrast sentences.

SENTENCE COMPLETION PRACTICE EXERCISE 3 "Contrast"

DIRECTIONS: First circle the reversal word in each sentence. Then underline the key word or group of words. Finally, mark the correct answer. Remember, the answer will be the word or words that best contrast with the key word or group of words.

1. Although stingrays look ----, they are, in fact, playful creatures that are beautifully soft and smooth to touch.
   - (A) beneficial
   - (B) amiable
   - (C) menacing
   - (D) exuberant
   - (E) silky

2. Doctors warned that the new medication would create new problems, some of them ---- but others totally unexpected.
   - (A) unanticipated
   - (B) accidental
   - (C) predictable
   - (D) expensive
   - (E) unhealthy

3. The significance of Hammurabi's Code lies not in its 282 ---- laws, but in its broader impact of establishing the principle that government had a responsibility for what occurred in a society.
   - (A) unproved
   - (B) specific
   - (C) debatable
   - (D) conservative
   - (E) strict

4. Although art critics ---- the exhibit as a tired collection of clichés, audiences around the country praised the art for its wholesome portrayal of daily life.
   - (A) suppressed
   - (B) valued
   - (C) applauded
   - (D) romanticized
   - (E) denounced

5. In Japan, his incredible skill as an actor in Kabuki plays is widely
   ----, but he is almost unknown in the rest of the world.

   (A) ignored   (D) emotional
   (B) disdained   (●) admired
   (C) misunderstood

6. On first glance the financial section of a newspaper may seem ----,
   yet the persistent reader soon finds the charts and tables easy to
   understand.

   (A) inviting
   (●) baffling
   (C) organized
   (D) stubborn
   (E) exclusive

7. Chris was amazed to hear that his sister, whom he knew to be ----,
   was nevertheless described as quite chatty by her friends.

   (A) garrulous
   (B) obstinate
   (C) pious
   (D) miserly
   (●) taciturn

8. Although they may seem tame, the birds feeding in our backyards
   never lose a natural ----.

   (A) warmth
   (●) wariness
   (C) trust
   (D) wastefulness
   (E) optimism

9. Shahenaz was neither lonely nor argumentative but was as ---- and
   as ---- a person as I have ever met.

   (●) gregarious . . . gentle
   (B) solitary . . . belligerent
   (C) withdrawn . . . quarrelsome
   (D) popular . . . contentious
   (E) depressed . . . amiable

10. Unlike today, few people were neutral about modern art when it
    first appeared; it inspired either uncritical praise or extreme ----.

    (●) antipathy
    (B) acclaim
    (C) sympathy
    (D) attachment
    (E) renown

Putting It All
TOGETHER

1 There will be 19 sentence completion questions on your SAT. Each question consists of a sentence containing one or two blanks. Your job is to select the one or two words that best complete the sentence.

2 Each sentence completion question has a key word or group of words that will help guide you to the correct answer.

3 The key word or group of words is sometimes a definition or explanation. The missing word is defined or explained in the sentence.

4 Sentences containing reversal words are called contrast sentences. In this type of sentence, the answer will be a word or group of words that contrasts with the key word or group of words. The contrast will be signalled by reversal words such as *but*, *although*, *however*, or *in contrast with*.

5 Before looking at the answer choices, give yourself a chance to try to mentally fill in the blank. Then you will have an idea of the kind of word you're looking for.

Attacking Definition and Contrast Sentences

DIRECTIONS: Read each sentence and underline the key word or group of words. If the sentence contains a contrast, circle its reversal word. Finally, mark the correct answer.

1. Heavily perfumed white flowers, such as gardenias, were favorites with collectors in the eighteenth century, when ---- was valued much more highly than it is today.

   (A) scent
   (B) beauty
   (C) elegance
   (D) color
   (E) variety

2. The ---- of St. Francis of Assisi deeply impressed his contemporaries; he always behaved modestly and never displayed any pride.

   (A) arrogance
   (B) prominence
   (C) humility
   (D) cleverness
   (E) industriousness

3. Louis XIV spared no expense when he built the Versailles Palace, turning a modest hunting lodge into ---- monument to his power and glory.

   (A) a frugal
   (B) a restrained
   (C) a humble
   (D) a popular
   (E) an extravagant

4. As ---- as she is ----, Jackie Joyner-Kersy combined a rigorous conditioning program with a natural talent to become one of the world's most celebrated female athletes.

   (A) earnest . . . inept
   (B) apathetic . . . talented
   (C) quick . . . careless
   (D) inconsistent . . . proficient
   (E) hardworking . . . gifted

5. Kavita's feelings about going to college were ----; although eager to begin a new phase in life, she was nonetheless anxious about leaving home for the first time.

(A) immutable   (●) ambivalent
(B) impulsive   (E) ambitious
(C) unwavering

6. Peter the Great was a ruler of incredible contrasts; periods of ---- and generosity alternated with periods of heartless ----.

(A) tenderness . . . generosity
(B) empathy . . . benevolence
(●) compassion . . . cruelty
(D) selfishness . . . extravagance
(E) despondence . . . tranquility

7. Although a cantankerous bully, the starling is surprisingly ---- when handled.

(A) recalcitrant   (●) docile
(B) wild   (E) irritable
(C) obstinate

8. Some physicists declared that the discovery marked ---- event in modern science, but others argued just as persuasively that it was ---- finding that would have little lasting importance.

(●) a watershed . . . an insignificant
(B) a trivial . . . a momentous
(C) a decisive . . . a distinctive
(D) an improbable . . . a remarkable
(E) a weighty . . . a notable

9. Like a true ----, Colleen believed that all people are motivated by greed and selfishness.

(A) patriot
(B) hedonist
(C) stoic
(D) anarchist
(●) cynic

10. Dr. Errington achieved complete authority over the hospital by stern discipline, by rigid attention to detail, and by ceaseless labor; in short, he exerted the fixed determination of an ---- will.

(A) unwarranted
(●) indomitable
(C) impious
(D) inflated
(E) inopportune

3

Building a Foundation for Analogies

After completing this chapter, you will be able to

1. apply the three-step procedure for solving an analogy.

2. identify and solve *Is a Type Of* analogies.

3. identify and solve *Is a Part Of* analogies.

4. identify and solve *Is a Place Where* analogies.

5. identify and solve *Is Used To* analogies.

Introduction to Analogies

What do a dam and a roadblock have in common? On the basis of appearance, they would seem to have little in common. The dam is a large concrete structure that is many stories high. In contrast, the roadblock consists of small wooden barricades. But first impressions can sometimes be superficial. A closer consideration of the two structures reveals that the dam and the roadblock perform similar functions. Think for a moment about how you would describe the function of a dam. Can you describe in similar terms what a roadblock does?

A dam is used to hold back water and a roadblock is used to hold back traffic. This gives us the foundation for an *analogy*: Dam is to Water as Roadblock is to Traffic.

An analogy refers to a similarity between two things that are otherwise not alike. For example, your family doctor will urge you to eat a well-balanced diet and exercise regularly, arguing that your heart should be properly maintained just like a well-maintained electric pump.

Your teachers often use analogies to help you understand important concepts. A world history teacher explaining the concept of *excommunication* might say, "Being excommunicated from the Church is like being expelled from school." A science teacher explaining how a geyser works might say, "Steam is to a geyser as lava is to a volcano." And a literature teacher introducing an epic poem could point out, "An epic is to literature as a symphony is to music."

Forming analogies is an important and ongoing aspect of how we view and interpret the world around us. The SAT test writers have long recognized the value of using analogies to test students' vocabulary, ability to see relationships, and knowledge of subject matter and everyday affairs. As a result, analogies have always been an important part of the verbal portion of the SAT. Your SAT will have 19 analogies – 13 on one 30-minute verbal section and 6 on the other 30-minute verbal section.

These 19 analogies are the best known and most challenging questions on the SAT. Attacking the analogies correctly can be a stimulating challenge, producing big increases in your verbal score. Of the three types of verbal questions (sentence completion, analogy, and reading comprehension), analogies are the easiest to teach and practice. This part of the SAT offers the fastest way to raise your verbal score.

A Case Example

Analogies are designed to test your verbal reasoning by asking you first to establish a relationship between a pair of words and then to recognize a similar relationship between another pair of words. To illustrate this, let's take a look at an example of an SAT analogy.

Here are the directions and sample analogy that you will find on the SAT. Reading these directions now will save you time when you take the test.

> Each question below consists of a related pair of words or phrases, followed by five pairs of words or phrases labeled A through E. Select the pair that <u>best</u> expresses a relationship similar to that expressed in the original pair.
>
> Example:
>
>   CRUMB : BREAD ::
>   (A) ounce : unit
>   (●) splinter : wood
>   (C) water : bucket
>   (D) twine : rope
>   (E) cream : butter

Solving Analogies

Analogies are like verbal riddles. Here is a three-step procedure for solving them.

STEP **1**   **Relate** CRUMB and BREAD. These words are called the stem words. Begin by establishing a clear relationship between these two words. The best way to do this is to form a sentence connecting them. In the example above, the relationship between CRUMB and BREAD can best be stated as *A CRUMB is a small piece of BREAD.* Note that our sentence is short and specific. Avoid long sentences. They usually mean you are off the track.

This first step is fairly quick after you get good at it. You need to practice because not every sentence is going to be helpful. For example: *There was a CRUMB on the plate next to the BREAD.* This sentence does not clearly express any relationship between *CRUMB* and *BREAD*. The first suggested sentence, *A CRUMB is a small piece of BREAD*, gives you something tangible (solid) to look for when you move to Step Two.

STEP **2**   **Apply** your sentence to each of the answer choices.

(A)	ounce : unit	Is an ounce a small piece of a unit? No. *ZAP* (A).
(B)	splinter : wood	Is a splinter a small piece of wood? Yes. (B) is a possible answer.
(C)	water : bucket	Is water a small piece of bucket? No. *ZAP* (C).
(D)	twine : rope	Is twine a small piece of rope? Not exactly, but you might think of twine as a small rope, so leave it for now.
(E)	cream : butter	Is cream a small piece of butter? No. *ZAP* (E).

STEP **3**   **Select** the answer that best matches the relationship between the original pair of words. In this example, the answer is (B) since "A CRUMB is a small piece of BREAD in the same way as a SPLINTER is a small piece of WOOD."

Notice that after *ZAPPING* you only had to think hard about two choices, (B) and (D). It is important to note that you did not need to waste time thinking about the relationship between OUNCE and UNIT. All you needed to do was ask yourself if this pair of words fit your sentence. Since the answer was "No," you could *ZAP* it and move to the next choice.

"Is a Type Of" Analogies

Analogy Relationship 1

When you first begin working with analogies, stating a relationship between the two stem words can be a challenging task. After all, there appear to be an unlimited number of relationships that could occur between the stem words. Fortunately, about 90 percent of all SAT analogies can be grouped into eight basic types of relationships. In this lesson we'll begin by examining *Is a Type Of* analogies.

Identifying *IS A TYPE OF* Analogies

Take a close look at the following six analogies.

- silver : metal
- whale : mammal
- sonnet : poem
- cinnamon : spice
- ballad : song
- evergreen : tree

What type of relationship do these six analogies have in common? All six illustrate a type of analogy called *Is a Type Of*. If you know the words, this type of relationship is the easiest to identify. The SAT writers provide you with a category such as *metal*, *mammal*, or *poem* and then a member of that category. *Is a Type Of* can be used to connect these words and solve each of the six analogies.

- silver *is a type of* metal
- a whale *is a type of* mammal
- a sonnet *is a type of* poem
- cinnamon *is a type of* spice
- a ballad *is a type of* song
- an evergreen *is a type of* tree

A Case Example

Let's apply our basic three-step procedure to the following analogy.

BRONZE : METAL ::

(A) iron : tin
(B) oxygen : water
(C) bead : necklace
(D) weed : garden
(E) hydrogen : gas

STEP **1**   **Relate** the stem words and then form a sentence connecting them. BRONZE : METAL is a good example of an *Is a Type Of* analogy. Using this phrase, we can form a sentence relating BRONZE and METAL by saying, "BRONZE is a type of METAL."

STEP **2**   **Apply** this sentence to each of the answer choices and *ZAP* the choices that clearly don't fit. Don't waste time thinking about the relationship between the two words in any choice that you *ZAPPED*. All you need to consider is whether or not the words might fit the relationship you already identified for the stem.

(A) iron : tin	Is iron a type of tin? No. *ZAP* it.
(B) oxygen : water	Is oxygen a type of water? No. *ZAP* it.
(C) bead : necklace	Is a bead a type of necklace? This one is tricky because you might think of a bead as a part of a necklace. You might want to leave it for now, but it seems fairly weak.
(D) weed : garden	Is a weed a type of garden? No. *ZAP* it.
(E) hydrogen : gas	Is hydrogen a type of gas? Yes. This looks good.

STEP **3**   **Select** the answer that best matches your original sentence. In this case, you need only to think about (C) and (E). The answer is clearly (E) since "BRONZE is a type of METAL in the same way as HYDROGEN is a type of GAS."

Guided
PRACTICE

DIRECTIONS: Here are three more *Is a Type Of* analogies. Let's use our three-step process to find the correct answer. On the writing lines, write a sentence connecting the capitalized words. Then apply the sentence to each answer choice. Finally, mark the correct answer.

1. WATCH : TIMEPIECE :: ___A watch is a type of timepiece.___

    (A) sneaker : shoe
    (B) vault : money
    (C) chariot : wheel
    (D) blanket : bed
    (E) hat : coat

2. MAMMAL : ELEPHANT :: ___An elephant is a type of mammal.___

    (A) branch : tree
    (B) insect : mosquito
    (C) circus : clown
    (D) seal : pup
    (E) fruit : jam

3. MAHOGANY : WOOD :: ___Mahogany is a type of wood.___

    (A) pencil : paper
    (B) bark : tree
    (C) alloy : element
    (D) marble : stone
    (E) flour : bread

Analogy 1

Relate the stem words and then form a sentence connecting them. WATCH : TIMEPIECE is an example of an *Is a Type Of* analogy. Using this phrase, we can form a sentence connecting WATCH and TIMEPIECE by saying, "A WATCH is a type of TIMEPIECE."

Apply this sentence to each of the answer choices.

(A)	sneaker : shoe	Is a sneaker a type of shoe? Yes. But, let's check the other choices.
(B)	vault : money	Is a vault a type of money? No. *ZAP* it.
(C)	chariot : wheel	Is a chariot a type of wheel? No. *ZAP* it.
(D)	blanket : bed	Is a blanket a type of bed? No. *ZAP* it.
(E)	hat : coat	Is a hat a type of coat. No. *ZAP* it.

Select the answer that best matches your original sentence. In this example, you already *ZAPPED* four choices. The answer is (A) since a WATCH is a type of TIMEPIECE in the same way as a SNEAKER is a type of SHOE.

Discussion

Analogy 2

Relate the stem words and then form a sentence connecting them. So far we have read each analogy from left to right. However, it is sometimes better to read an analogy from right to left. Once you choose a direction, you must consistently apply it to all of the answer choices. In this example, MAMMAL : ELEPHANT is an *Is a Type Of* analogy. In this case, it is more effective to read the analogy from right to left by saying, "An ELEPHANT is a type of MAMMAL."

Apply this sentence to each of the answer choices.

(A)	branch : tree	Is a tree a type of branch? No. *ZAP* it.
(B)	insect : mosquito	Is a mosquito a type of insect? Yes. As always, check the other answers.
(C)	circus : clown	Is a clown a type of circus? No. *ZAP* it.
(D)	seal : pup	Is a pup a type of seal? In a way, depending on how you look at it. A pup is a young seal.
(E)	fruit : jam	Is jam a type of fruit? No. *ZAP* it.

Select the answer that best matches your original sentence. In this example, you need to think about (B) and (D). The best answer is (B) since "An ELEPHANT is a type of MAMMAL in the same way as a MOSQUITO is a type of INSECT."

Analogy 3

Relate the stem words and then form a sentence connecting them. MAHOGANY : WOOD is an example of an *Is a Type Of* analogy. Using this phrase, we can form a sentence connecting MAHOGANY and WOOD by saying, "MAHOGANY is a type of WOOD."

Apply this sentence to each of the answer choices.

(A)	pencil : paper	Is a pencil a type of paper? No. *ZAP* it.
(B)	bark : tree	Is bark a type of tree? No. *ZAP* it.
(C)	alloy : element	Is an alloy a type of element? If you know what an alloy is, you can *ZAP* this choice. If you're not sure, leave it for now.
(D)	marble : stone	Is marble a type of stone? Yes. But let's check the remaining answer.
(E)	flour : bread	Is flour a type of bread? No. *ZAP* it.

Select the answer that best matches your original sentence. In this example, you might have trouble if you don't know the meanings of *alloy* or *element*. In that case, you would need to guess between (C) and (D). The answer is (D) since "MAHOGANY is a type of WOOD in the same way as MARBLE is a type of STONE."

Developing an Extra Edge

1. *Is a Type Of* analogies are relatively easy. SAT writers expect over 90 percent of students to correctly answer this type of analogy. It is therefore important to remember that *Is a Type Of* analogies have easy and obvious answers. Don't try to be creative. Always keep in mind that easy questions count just as much as the most difficult questions.

2. Recently, typical categories used in *Is a Type Of* analogies have included metals (gold, silver, copper), joints (elbow, knee, knuckle), organs (heart, kidney, lung) and trees (pine, oak, maple).

Independent PRACTICE

Analogy Practice Exercise 1 provides you with 10 *Is a Type Of* analogies. Use the three-step process to answer each one. Remember, you will not increase your score without serious, attentive practice.

ANALOGY PRACTICE EXERCISE 1 "Is a Type Of"

DIRECTIONS: For each question, first write a sentence linking the stem words. Then mark the correct answer.

1. LIVER : ORGAN ::

   (A) skull : brain
   (B) muscle : bone
   (C) shoulder : neck
   (D) toe : foot
   (●) arm : limb

   Liver is a type of organ.

2. PASTEL : COLOR ::

   (●) vanilla : flavor
   (B) shadow : silhouette
   (C) twig : tree
   (D) dressing : salad
   (E) blouse : pattern

   Pastel is a type of color.

3. BEAN : LEGUME ::

   (A) grass : blade
   (B) citrus : lemon
   (C) frog : pond
   (●) cantaloupe : melon
   (E) cub : bear

   A bean is a type of legume.

4. EAGLE : BIRD ::

   (A) caterpillar : moth
   (B) gosling : goose
   (●) leopard : cat
   (D) reptile : crocodile
   (E) tadpole : frog

   An eagle is a type of bird.

5. FORK : UTENSIL ::

   (A) wool : winter
   (●) hammer : tool
   (C) foot : sock
   (D) fish : ocean
   (E) belt : waist

   A fork is a type of utensil.

6. ORANGE : FRUIT ::

    (A) crust : pie
    (B) wheat : grain
    (C) watermelon : seed
    (D) root : tree
    (E) apple : core

An orange is a type of fruit. _____

_____

_____

_____

7. KNEE : JOINT ::

    (A) molar : tooth
    (B) cell : tissue
    (C) rib cage : lung
    (D) link : chain
    (E) finger : hand

A knee is a type of joint. _____

_____

_____

_____

8. BALLAD : SONG ::

    (A) comedy : tragedy
    (B) act : play
    (C) fiction : biography
    (D) rhyme : legend
    (E) sonnet : poem

A ballad is a type of song. _____

_____

_____

_____

9. SUITCASE : LUGGAGE ::

    (A) lemon : orange
    (B) landscape : meadow
    (C) sofa : furniture
    (D) reservoir : water
    (E) itinerary : trip

A suitcase is a type of luggage. _____

_____

_____

_____

10. WOOL : FABRIC ::

    (A) bone : skeleton
    (B) orange : pear
    (C) reef : waves
    (D) shell : egg
    (E) oil : fuel

Wool is a type of fabric. _____

_____

_____

_____

LESSON

9

"Is a Part Of" Analogies

Identifying *IS A PART OF* Analogies

Analogy Relationship 2

Take a look at the following six analogies.

- letter : alphabet
- suit : wardrobe
- element : compound

- link : chain
- card : deck
- word : vocabulary

What type of relationship do these six analogies have in common? All six illustrate a type of relationship where one word *Is a Part Of* the other word. This relationship is almost as easy to spot as the *Is a Kind Of* relationship. SAT writers give you one word representing the whole and another word representing a part of that whole.

Is a Part Of is the connection that solves each of these six analogies.

- a letter *is a part of* an alphabet
- a suit *is a part of* a wardrobe
- an element *is a part of* a compound
- a link *is a part of* a chain
- a card *is a part of* a deck
- a word *is a part of* a vocabulary

A Case Example

Let's apply our three-step procedure to the following analogy.

TREE : FOREST ::

(A) hill : valley
(B) leaf : bark
(C) cat : animal
(D) shoe : sock
(E) flower : bouquet

STEP **1**

Relate the stem words and then form a sentence connecting them. TREE : FOREST is a good example of an *Is a Part Of* analogy. Using this phrase, we can form a sentence connecting TREE and FOREST by saying, "A TREE is a part of a FOREST."

STEP **2**

Apply this sentence to each of the answer choices.

(A) hill : valley	Is a hill a part of a valley? No. *ZAP* it.
(B) leaf : bark	Is a leaf a part of a bark? No. *ZAP* it.
(C) cat : animal	Is a cat a part of an animal? No. A cat is a type of animal, but not a part of an animal. *ZAP*.
(D) shoe : sock	Is a shoe a part of a sock? No. *ZAP* away.
(E) flower : bouquet	Is a flower a part of a bouquet? Yes. This is by far the best choice.

STEP **3**

Select the answer that best matches your original sentence. In this example, the answer is (E) since "A TREE is a part of a FOREST in the same way as a FLOWER is a part of a BOUQUET."

DIRECTIONS: Here are three more *Is a Part Of* analogies. Use the three-step process to find the correct answers.

1. SHIP : FLEET ::

   (A) crew : airplane
   (B) star : galaxy
   (C) planet : orbit
   (D) parrot : jungle
   (E) view : skyscraper

   A ship is a part of a fleet.
   _____
   _____
   _____

2. ACTOR : CAST ::

   (A) entertainer : audience
   (B) voter : candidate
   (C) patient : physician
   (D) student : faculty
   (E) singer : choir

   An actor is a part of a cast.
   _____
   _____
   _____

3. STANZA : SONG ::

   (A) census : population
   (B) dance : ballroom
   (C) verse : poem
   (D) lyric : melody
   (E) computer : book

   A stanza is a part of a song.
   _____
   _____
   _____

Analogy 1

Relate the stem words and then form a sentence connecting them. SHIP : FLEET is an example of an *Is a Part Of* analogy. Using this phrase we can form a sentence connecting SHIP and FLEET by saying, "A SHIP is a part of a FLEET."

Apply this sentence to each of the answer choices.

Discussion

(A) crew : airplane	Is a crew a part of an airplane? This may be attractive because you might think of a crew as being necessary to the flight of the plane. Even though it's weak, you could leave it for now.
(B) star : galaxy	Is a star a part of a galaxy? Yes. This is a very attractive choice, but, as always, let's check the other answers.
(C) planet : orbit	Is a planet a part of an orbit? No. ZAP it.
(D) parrot : jungle	Is a parrot a part of a jungle? This choice would attract many students because a jungle includes, in a sense, all of its flora (plant life) and fauna (animal life). It is possible to think of a parrot as part of the jungle.
(E) view : skyscraper	Is a view a part of a skyscraper? No. ZAP it.

Select the answer that best matches your original sentence. In this example, we first ZAPPED (C) and (E). You would need to think about (A), (B), and (D). The answer is (B) since "A SHIP is a part of a FLEET in the same way as a STAR is a part of a GALAXY."

Analogy 2

Relate the stem words and then form a sentence connecting them. ACTOR : CAST is an example of an *Is a Part Of* analogy. Using this phrase, we can form a sentence connecting ACTOR and CAST by saying, "An ACTOR is a part of a CAST."

Apply this sentence to each of the answer choices.

(A) entertainer : audience	Is an entertainer a part of an audience? No. ZAP it. An entertainer might be sitting in the audience of a particular performance, but this possibility does not establish a clear *is a part of* relationship.
(B) voter : candidate	Is a voter a part of a candidate? No. ZAP it.
(C) patient : physician	Is a patient a part of a physician? No. ZAP it.

(D) student : faculty	Is a student a part of a faculty? No. *ZAP* it. (The faculty is composed of teachers.)
(E) singer : choir	Is a singer a part of a choir? Yes.

Select the answer that best matches your original sentence. In this example, the answer is (E) since "An ACTOR is a part of a CAST in the same way as a SINGER is a part of a CHOIR."

Analogy 3

Relate the stem words and then form a sentence connecting them. STANZA : SONG is an example of an *Is a Part Of* analogy. Using this phrase, we can form a sentence connecting STANZA and SONG by saying, "A STANZA is a part of a SONG."

Apply this sentence to each of the answer choices.

(A) census : population	Is a census a part of a population? No. These words are strongly related in another way. A census is used to count the population. You can *ZAP* (A).
(B) dance : ballroom	Is a dance a part of a ballroom? No. *ZAP* it.
(C) verse : poem	Is a verse a part of a poem? Yes. This is an attractive choice.
(D) lyric : melody	Is a lyric a part of a melody? If you're not sure what a *lyric* is, leave this for now. Otherwise, you can *ZAP* it because *lyric* refers to the words and a melody is the tune.
(E) computer : book	Is a computer a part of a book? No. *ZAP* it.

Select the answer that best matches your original sentence. In this example, the answer is (C) since "A STANZA is a part of a SONG in the same way as a VERSE is a part of a POEM."

Developing an Extra Edge

1. *Is a Part Of* analogies are easy to identify and answer. Like *Is a Type Of* analogies, they have easy answers.

2. SAT writers like to mix *Is a Part Of* analogies from music and dance. For example, MUSICIAN is to ORCHESTRA as ACTOR is to CAST, or SINGER is to CHOIR as ACTOR is to TROUPE.

Independent
PRACTICE

Analogy Practice Exercise 2 provides you with 10 more *Is a Part Of* analogies. Use the three-step process to answer each one. Remember, practice is the first step in building competence.

ANALOGY PRACTICE EXERCISE 2 "Is a Part Of"

DIRECTIONS: For each question, first write a sentence linking the stem words. Then circle the correct answer.

1. STORY : ANTHOLOGY ::

   (A) jacket : book
   (B) dictionary : language
   (C) song : medley
   (D) writer : editor
   (E) itinerary : trip

   A story is a part of an anthology.

2. ACTOR : TROUPE ::

   (A) director : chorus
   (B) dancer : ensemble
   (C) apprentice : master
   (D) applicant : job
   (E) investor : banker

   An actor is a part of a troupe.

3. CHAPTER : BOOK ::

   (A) act : play
   (B) teacher : exam
   (C) ink : paper
   (D) reviewer : film
   (E) editor : text

   A chapter is a part of a book.

4. STAR : GALAXY ::

   (A) silo : corn
   (B) mist : rain
   (C) grade : teacher
   (D) tree : forest
   (E) mirror : light

   A star is a part of a galaxy.

5. MUSICIAN : BAND ::

   (A) student : faculty
   (B) umpire : game
   (C) clarinet : melody
   (D) speaker : audience
   (E) actor : cast

   A musician is a part of a band.

6. BEAD : NECKLACE ::

    (A) ring : finger
    (●) link : chain
    (C) beret : cap
    (D) ruby : gemstone
    (E) nail : hammer

A bead is a part of a necklace.

7. TREE : GROVE ::

    (A) hive : honey
    (B) farm : orchard
    (C) bell : cow
    (●) bush : thicket
    (E) tank : fuel

A tree is a part of a grove.

8. ISLAND : ARCHIPELAGO ::

    (●) star : constellation
    (B) ranger : forest
    (C) nail : wall
    (D) number : calculator
    (E) school : principal

An island is a part of an archipelago.

9. MONTAGE : PICTURE ::

    (A) nation : flag
    (B) broadcast : listener
    (C) film : review
    (●) mosaic : tile
    (E) team : visitor

A picture is a part of a montage.

10. LINE : STANZA ::

    (A) intermission : performance
    (●) scene : act
    (C) cure : disease
    (D) rhyme : poem
    (E) glue : page

A line is a part of a stanza.

LESSON 10

"Is a Place Where" Analogies

Analogy Relationship 3

Identifying *IS A PLACE WHERE* Analogies

So far, you have learned attack strategies for *Is a Type Of* and *Is a Part Of* analogies. Now take a look at the following six analogies.

- coop : chickens
- zoo : animals
- judge : courthouse
- camel : desert
- ranch : livestock
- laboratory : experiments

What type of relationship do these six analogies have in common? All six illustrate a type of analogy called *Is a Place Where*. The SAT gives you one word that is a place and another word that is an animal, person, or action associated with that place, as in the following examples.

- a coop *is a place where* people keep chickens
- a zoo *is a place where* animals are displayed
- a courthouse *is a place where* a judge works
- a desert *is a place where* a camel lives
- a ranch *is a place where* livestock are raised
- a laboratory *is a place where* experiments are conducted

When you formulate a sentence relating the words in one of these analogies, you usually need to add an extra defining word to clarify the type of place or the nature of the place. For example, hospitals are places where surgeons *work* in the same way that offices are places where administrators *work*. The practice problems on the following pages will show how this tip will help you.

A Case Example

Let's apply our three-step procedure to the following analogy. Pay close attention to the special problem we encounter in forming a sentence.

ANIMALS : ZOO ::

(A) earthworms : soil
(B) artists : studio
(C) bees : honey
(●) fish : aquarium
(E) skiers : lodge

STEP **1**   **Relate** the stem words and then form a sentence connecting them. ANIMALS : ZOO is a good example of an *Is a Place Where* analogy. Using this phrase, we can form a sentence connecting ANIMALS and ZOO by saying, "A ZOO is a place where ANIMALS live."

STEP **2**   **Apply** this sentence to each of the answer choices.

(A) earthworms : soil	Is soil a place where earthworms live? Yes. Let's keep (A) for now.
(B) artists : studio	Is a studio a place where artists live? Could be. We should also keep (B) for now.
(C) bees : honey	Is honey a place where bees live? No. *ZAP* (C).
(D) fish : aquarium	Is an aquarium a place where fish live? Yes. We'll also keep (D) for now.
(E) skiers : lodge	Is a lodge a place where skiers live? The main relationship between skiers and lodges is that skiers go to the lodge to warm up, eat, and rest a while. *ZAP* (E).

STEP **3**   **Select** the answer that best matches your original sentence. This example presents a common problem. After one round of *ZAPPING*, you're left with three choices that all fit your sentence. The solution is to go back to Step One and improve on your original sentence. You need to tighten it up. Is a zoo a natural habitat for animals? No. It's a place where people display animals. Add this clarification to the original sentence: "A ZOO is a place where people display ANIMALS."

Now run through Step Two again. On this second pass, you can *ZAP* (A) and (B). You already *ZAPPED* (C) and (E), so the correct answer is (D).

Guided PRACTICE

DIRECTIONS: Here are three more *Is a Place Where* analogies. Let's use our three-step process to find the correct answers.

1. STY : PIGS ::

   (A) corral : horses
   (B) litter : dogs
   (C) garden : bees
   (D) field : rabbits
   (E) desert : camels

   A sty is a place where people keep pigs.

   _____

   _____

   _____

2. CLASSROOM : TEACHER ::

   (A) freezer : meat
   (B) museum : artifacts
   (C) hospital : physician
   (D) supermarket : shopper
   (E) courtroom : defendant

   A classroom is a place where a teacher works.

   _____

   _____

3. PHARMACY : DRUGS ::

   (A) highway : traffic
   (B) barn : tractors
   (C) forest : woods
   (D) cemetery : coffins
   (E) box office : tickets

   A pharmacy is a place where drugs are sold.

   _____

   _____

Analogy 1

Discussion

Relate the stem words and then form a sentence connecting them. STY : PIGS is an example of an *Is a Place Where* analogy. Using this phrase, we can form a sentence connecting STY and PIGS by saying, "A STY is a place where people keep PIGS."

The SAT writers know that the word *sty* is unfamiliar to many students. If you don't know what *sty* means, you can try different types of analogies.

Is a sty a type of pig?

Is a sty a part of a pig?

Is a sty a place where a pig does something?

A quick check of the answers tells you that none of the choices are *a type of* or *a part of*, so you can experiment with *a place where*.

When you don't know one of the stem words, you should do whatever you can to *ZAP* at least one choice before guessing. In this case, if all you suspect is that a sty is a place where pigs do something, you could still *ZAP* (B) and guess from the other choices. Now let's go back to our original sentence, "A STY is a place where people keep PIGS."

Apply your sentence to each of the answer choices.

(A)	corral : horses	Is a corral a place where humans keep horses? Yes. This choice is very attractive.
(B)	litter : dogs	Is a litter a place where humans keep dogs? No. *ZAP* it.
(C)	garden : bees	Is a garden a place where humans keep bees? This may be tempting because bees are attracted to gardens, and you might think of a beekeeper standing on the edge of a garden collecting honey from an apiary (a beehive made by people).
(D)	field : rabbits	Is a field a place where humans keep rabbits? No. *ZAP* it.
(E)	desert : camels	Is a desert a place where humans keep camels? No. *ZAP* it.

Select the answer that best matches your original sentence. You've already *ZAPPED* (B), (D), and (E), so you need to think hard about (A) and (C). The answer is (A).

Analogy 2

Relate the stem words and then form a sentence connecting them. CLASSROOM : TEACHER is an example of an *Is a Place Where* analogy. Using this sentence, we can form a sentence connecting CLASSROOM and TEACHER by saying, "A CLASSROOM is a place where a TEACHER works."

Apply this sentence to each of the answer choices.

(A)	freezer : meat	Is a freezer a place where meat works? Of course not. Easy *ZAP*.
(B)	museum: artifacts	Is a museum a place where artifacts work? No. *ZAP* it.
(C)	hospital : physician	Is a hospital a place where a physician works? Yes. As always, let's check the remaining answers.
(D)	supermarket : shopper	Is a supermarket a place where a shopper works? This will trap students who are thinking, "A teacher goes to a classroom and a shopper goes to a supermarket." If your original sentence clearly defines the relationship, you won't get caught in this trap.
(E)	courtroom : defendant	Is a courtroom a place where a defendant works? If you know that the defendant is the person accused of a crime, you would be able to *ZAP* this choice. Otherwise, you should leave it. If all of the other choices were weak, you could guess this answer even without knowing both of the words.

Select the answer that best matches your original sentence. In this example, the answer is (C) since "A CLASSROOM is a place where a TEACHER works in the same way that a HOSPITAL is a place where a PHYSICIAN works."

Analogy 3

Relate the stem words and then form a sentence connecting them. PHARMACY : DRUGS is an example of an *Is a Place Where* analogy. Using this phrase, we can form a sentence connecting PHARMACY and DRUGS by saying, "A PHARMACY is a place where DRUGS are sold."

Apply this sentence to each of the answer choices.

(A)	highway : traffic	Is a highway a place where traffic is sold? No. *ZAP* it.
(B)	barn : tractors	Is a barn a place where tractors are sold? No. *ZAP* it.
(C)	forest : woods	Is a forest a place where woods are sold? No. *ZAP* it.
(D)	cemetery : coffins	Is a cemetery a place where coffins are sold? No. A cemetery is a place where coffins are buried. *ZAP* it.
(E)	box office : tickets	Is a box office a place where tickets are sold? Yes. This is a case where, even if you aren't sure of the meaning of box office, you can safely pick this answer because all of the other choices have been *ZAPPED*.

Select the answer that best matches your original sentence. In this example, the answer is (E) since "A PHARMACY is a place where DRUGS are sold in the same way that a BOX OFFICE is a place where TICKETS are sold."

Developing an Extra Edge

1. *Is a Place Where* Analogies are easy to identify and answer, just like *Is a Type Of* and *Is a Part Of* analogies. Most of the vocabulary will be on the easy side, but you might run into a few unknown words.

2. *Is a Place Where* analogies tend to cluster into very distinctive groups. For example, STY is part of a large cluster based on places that humans have built to keep animals. Other places include a *coop* (chickens), *aviary* (birds), *corral* (horses), and *apiary* (bees). In contrast, animals live naturally in an *aerie* (eagle's nest) and a *lair* (bed or resting place of a wild animal).

3. A suffix is a word part that is attached to the end of a root. When you spot the suffixes -ARY and -ORY at the end of a word, it is a good bet that the word refers to a place where people do something. For example, a *conservatory* is a place where plants are displayed, a *laboratory* is a place where experiments are conducted, and a *seminary* is a place where priests are trained.

Independent PRACTICE

nalogy Practice Exercise 3 provides you with 10 more *Is a Place Where* analogies. Use the three-step process to answer each one. Remember, practice is the first step in building competence.

ANALOGY PRACTICE EXERCISE 3 "Is a Place Where"

DIRECTIONS: For each question, first write a sentence linking the stem words. Then circle the correct answer.

1. STUDENTS : DORMITORY ::   A dormitory is a place where students live.

   (A) spectators : stadium
   (B) soldiers : barracks
   (C) actors : theater
   (D) doctors : hospital
   (E) commuters : train

2. TERMINAL : AIRPLANE ::   A terminal is a place where an airplane is kept.

   (A) lake : ferry
   (B) sidewalk : pedestrian
   (C) bridge : barge
   (D) wharf : boat
   (E) lodge : skier

3. GALLERY : PAINTINGS ::   A gallery is a place where paintings are displayed.

   (A) showcase : trophies
   (B) checkbook : money
   (C) board : directors
   (D) church : worshippers
   (E) vault : jewels

4. AVIARY : BIRDS ::   An aviary is a place where birds are kept in captivity.

   (A) kennel : dogs
   (B) tree : squirrels
   (C) refuge : wildlife
   (D) field : wheat
   (E) planetarium : stars

5. LABORATORY : CHEMIST ::   A laboratory is a place where a chemist works.

   (A) lodge : guest
   (B) computer : program
   (C) stadium : spectator
   (D) play : invitation
   (E) kitchen : chef

6. TUNDRA : REINDEER ::

   (A) aquarium : dolphin
   (B) corral : pony
   (●) jungle : parrot
   (D) wall : fly
   (E) sled : dogs

The tundra is a place where reindeer live in the wild.

_____

_____

_____

7. LIBRARY : RESEARCH ::

   (A) armory : defense
   (B) hospital : grief
   (●) laboratory : experimentation
   (D) palace : intrigue
   (E) stadium : applause

A library is a place where research is done.

_____

_____

_____

8. ARMORY : WEAPONS ::

   (A) meadow : grass
   (B) building : stone
   (C) lake : river
   (●) reservoir : water
   (E) band : instruments

An armory is a place where weapons are stored.

_____

_____

_____

9. OFFICE : WORK ::

   (A) library : publish
   (B) orchestra : perform
   (C) landscape : paint
   (D) jail : escape
   (●) classroom : learn

An office is a place where people go to work.

_____

_____

_____

10. WAREHOUSE : GOODS ::

   (A) novel : quotations
   (B) board : directors
   (C) swamp : mosquitoes
   (D) courthouse : sentences
   (●) shed : tools

A warehouse is used to store goods.

_____

_____

_____

"Is Used To" Analogies

Identifying *IS USED TO* Analogies

Analogy Relationship 4

In Lessons 8, 9, and 10, you learned how to attack *Is a Type Of*, *Is a Part Of*, and *Is a Place Where* analogies. Now take a look at the following six analogies.

- scissors : cut
- bottle : liquid
- apron : clothes
- thesaurus : synonym
- analgesic : pain
- scale : weight

What type of relationship do these six analogies have in common? All six illustrate a type of analogy called *Is Used To*. An *Is Used To* analogy is easy to spot. In the pair of related words, SAT writers include a tool, a reference source, or a type of medication and a word describing its use or function.

Is Used To is the connecting phrase that solves each of these six analogies.

- a scissors *is used to* cut   (tool)
- a bottle *is used to* hold a liquid   (tool)
- an apron *is used to* protect clothes   (tool)
- a thesaurus *is used to* find a synonym   (reference source)
- an analgesic *is used to* lessen pain   (type of medication)
- a scale *is used to* measure weight   (tool)

A Case Example

Let's apply our three-step procedure to the following analogy.

COMPASS : DIRECTION ::

(A) skyscraper : height
(B) thermometer : mercury
(C) speedometer : route
(D) radio : listeners
(E) watch : time

STEP **1**   **Relate** the stem words and then form a sentence connecting them. COMPASS : DIRECTION is a good example of an *Is Used To* analogy. Using this phrase, we can form a sentence connecting COMPASS and DIRECTION by saying, "A COMPASS is used to determine DIRECTION."

STEP **2**   **Apply** this sentence to each of the answer choices.

(A) skyscraper : height	Is a skyscraper used to determine height? No. *ZAP* it.
(B) thermometer : mercury	Is a thermometer used to determine mercury? No. *ZAP* it.
(C) speedometer : route	Is a speedometer used to determine a route? No. *ZAP* it.
(D) radio : listeners	Is a radio used to determine listeners? No. *ZAP* it.
(E) watch : time	Is a watch used to determine time? Yes.

STEP **3**   **Select** the answer that best matches your original sentence. In this example, the answer is (E) since "A COMPASS is used to determine direction in the same way as a WATCH is used to determine TIME."

Guided PRACTICE

DIRECTIONS: Here are three more *Is Used To* analogies. Use our three-step process to find the correct answer. On the writing lines, write a sentence connecting the capitalized words. Then apply the sentence to each answer choice. Finally, circle the correct answer.

1. TRACTOR : PLOW ::

   (A) airplane : runway
   (B) pole : tent
   (C) elephant : circus
   (D) confectionery : candy
   (E) tugboat : barge

   A tractor is used to pull a plow.

2. ODOMETER : DISTANCE ::

   (A) kettle : steam
   (B) scale : weight
   (C) lamp : light
   (D) engine : fuel
   (E) trumpet : brass

   An odometer is used to measure distance.

3. ALMANAC : FACTS ::

   (A) skit : jokes
   (B) diary : quotes
   (C) novel : facts
   (D) map : definitions
   (E) atlas : maps

   An almanac is a reference used to find facts.

Analogy 1

Relate the stem words and then form a sentence connecting them. TRACTOR : PLOW is an example of an *Is Used To* analogy. Using this phrase, we can form a sentence connecting TRACTOR and PLOW by saying, "A TRACTOR is used to pull a PLOW."

Apply this sentence to each of the answer choices.

Discussion

(A)	airplane : runway	Is a runway used to pull an airplane? No. *ZAP* it.
(B)	pole : tent	Is a pole used to pull a tent? A pole is used to hold up a tent, but it doesn't pull a tent. Maybe leave it for now.
(C)	elephant : circus	Is an elephant used to pull a circus? No. *ZAP* it.
(D)	confectionery : candy	Is a confectionery used to pull candy? If you're not sure what *confectionery* means, leave this one for now.
(E)	tugboat : barge	Is a tugboat used to pull a barge? Yes. Excellent choice.

Select the answer that best matches your original sentence. In this example, we found one fuzzy choice (B) and one choice with an unknown word (D). We also found an excellent choice (E). Without further ado, you could answer (E) because "A TRACTOR is used to pull a PLOW in the same way that a TUGBOAT is used to pull a BARGE." (By the way, a *confectionery* is a candy store, *a place where* candy is sold.)

Analogy 2

Relate the stem words and then form a sentence connecting them. ODOMETER : DISTANCE is an example of an *Is Used To* analogy. Using this phrase, we can form a sentence connecting ODOMETER and DISTANCE by saying, "An ODOMETER is used to measure DISTANCE."

Apply this sentence to each of the answer choices.

(A)	kettle : steam	Is a kettle used to measure steam? No. *ZAP* it.
(B)	scale : weight	Is a scale used to measure weight? Yes.
(C)	lamp : light	Is a lamp used to measure light? No. *ZAP* it.
(D)	engine : fuel	Is an engine used to measure fuel? No. *ZAP* it.
(E)	trumpet : brass	Is a trumpet used to measure brass? No. *ZAP* it.

Select the answer that best matches your original sentence. In this example, the answer is (B) since "An ODOMETER is used to measure DISTANCE in the same way as a SCALE is used to measure WEIGHT."

Analogy 3

Relate the stem words and then form a sentence connecting them. ALMANAC : FACTS is an example of an *Is Used To* analogy. Using this phrase we can form a sentence connecting ALMANAC and FACTS by saying, "An ALMANAC is a reference used to find FACTS."

Apply this sentence to each of the answer choices.

(A)	skit : jokes	Is a skit a reference used to find jokes? No. *ZAP* it.
(B)	diary : quotes	Is a diary a reference used to find quotes? No. A diary is a record of someone's life. It may contain quotes, but that is not its primary function. *ZAP* it.
(C)	novel : facts	Is a novel a reference used to find facts? No. *ZAP* it.
(D)	map : definitions	Is a map a reference used to find definitions? No. *ZAP* it.
(E)	atlas : maps	Is an atlas a reference used to find maps? Yes.

Select the answer that best matches your original sentence. In this example, the answer is (E) since "An ALMANAC is a reference used to find FACTS in the same way as an ATLAS is a reference used to find MAPS."

Developing an Extra Edge

1. *Is Used To* analogies are usually in the easy section of the SAT because they are relatively easy to identify and answer.

2. *Is Used To* analogies are becoming more and more popular with SAT writers. At the present time, they show up about 1 in 10 times.

3. SAT writers often use reference sources in their *Is Used To* analogies. It is important to remember that *glossaries* are used to find terms, *directories* are used to find names, and *manuals* are used to find instructions.

Independent PRACTICE

Analogy Practice Exercise 4 provides you with 10 more *Is Used To* analogies. Use the three-step process to answer each one. Remember, practice is the first step in building competence.

ANALOGY PRACTICE EXERCISE 4 "Is Used To"

DIRECTIONS: For each question, first write a sentence linking the stem words. Then circle the correct answer.

1. AQUEDUCT : WATER ::

   (A) runway : airplane
   (B) sewer : plumbing
   (C) quarry : slate
   (D) horse : carriage
   (E) pipeline : gas

   An aqueduct is used to carry water.

2. TELESCOPE : DISTANT ::

   (A) monocle : single
   (B) microscope : tiny
   (C) drill : depth
   (D) elevator : height
   (E) horoscope : truth

   A telescope is used to see things that are distant.

3. QUILT : BED ::

   (A) coat : hanger
   (B) bandage : wound
   (C) harbor : boat
   (D) tent : ground
   (E) frame : picture

   A quilt is used to cover a bed.

4. SPONGE : ABSORB ::

   (A) jack : raise
   (B) towel : drip
   (C) bottle : cap
   (D) glass : polish
   (E) eye : blink

   A sponge is used to absorb something.

5. CAST : MOVEMENT ::

   (A) bars : jail
   (B) amplifier : sound
   (C) cane : support
   (D) blinder : vision
   (E) buttress : support

   A cast is used to hinder movement.

6. HELMET : HEAD ::

    (A) ice pack : swelling
    (B) splint : movement
    (C) thimble : finger
    (D) bracelet : wrist
    (E) napkin : table

A helmet is used to protect the head.

7. ANTISEPTIC : STERILIZE ::

    (A) stimulant : pacify
    (B) fertilizer : shrink
    (C) sedative : calm
    (D) lubricant : enlarge
    (E) detergent : soil

An antiseptic is used to sterilize something.

8. BLANKET : COLD ::

    (A) towel : bath
    (B) uniform : team
    (C) pick : lock
    (D) staple : paper
    (E) pot holder : burn

A blanket is used to protect from cold.

9. TRANQUILIZER : TENSION ::

    (A) analgesic : pain
    (B) vaccine : immunity
    (C) anesthetic : sleep
    (D) pollen : sneeze
    (E) shield : protection

A tranquilizer is used to lessen tension.

10. GLOSSARY : DEFINITIONS ::

    (A) bank : deposits
    (B) guidebook : souvenirs
    (C) novel : pages
    (D) debate : ideas
    (E) bibliography : sources

A glossary is used to look up definitions.

Putting It All

TOGETHER

1 There will be 19 analogies on your SAT. One 30-minute section will have a set of 13 analogies and one 30-minute section will have a set of 6 analogies.

2 Each analogy consists of a pair of stem words and five pairs of answer choices.

3 . Begin each analogy by establishing a clear relationship between the two stem words. Then form a short, specific sentence connecting the stem words.

4 Apply your sentence to each of the answer choices. Analogies can be read from left to right or from right to left. But once you choose a direction, you must consistently apply it to all of the answer choices. If you use the words in reverse direction (the second word first), make a mark in your test book to remind you to reverse all of the choices.

5 Select the answer that best matches your sentence.

6 In *Is a Type Of* analogies, SAT writers provide you with a category, (e.g. fuel) and a member of that category (e.g. oil).

7 In *Is a Part Of* analogies, SAT writers provide you with a whole (e.g. chain) and a member of that whole (e.g. link).

8 In *Is a Place Where* analogies, SAT writers provide you with a place (e.g. office) and an animal, person, or action (e.g. work) associated with it.

9 In *Is Used To* analogies, SAT writers provide you with a tool or type of product (e.g. sedative) and a word related to its use or function (e.g. calm).

10 *Is a Type Of*, *Is a Part Of*, *Is a Place Where*, and *Is Used To* analogies are almost always found in the easy third of each analogy set. Remember, easy analogies have easy answers.

Answering "Is a Type Of," "Is a Part Of," "Is a Place Where," and "Is Used To" Analogies

DIRECTIONS: Fill in the blank with a short specific sentence connecting the stem words. Then circle the answer that best matches your sentence.

1. FROG : AMPHIBIAN ::

   (A) elephant : invertebrate
   (B) hummingbird : eagle
   (C) snake : reptile
   (D) stem : flower
   (E) branch : tree

   A frog is a type of amphibian.

2. ACTOR : COMPANY ::

   (A) frame : canvas
   (B) gift : package
   (C) belt : waist
   (D) tango : dance
   (E) musician : orchestra

   An actor is a part of a company.

3. GYMNASIUM : EXERCISE ::

   (A) blackboard : screen
   (B) pool : swim
   (C) cathedral : build
   (D) picture : see
   (E) stage : improvise

   A gymnasium is a place where people go for exercise.

4. WIRE : ELECTRICITY ::

   (A) tape : adhesive
   (B) flare : light
   (C) hose : water
   (D) umbrella : rain
   (E) refinery : gas

   A wire is used to carry electricity.

5. BANANA : BUNCH ::

   (A) grape : cluster
   (B) pig : pen
   (C) tomato : ketchup
   (D) pea : legume
   (E) remnant : fabric

   A banana is part of a bunch.

6. THESAURUS : SYNONYM ::   A thesaurus is used to find a synonym.

   (A) deck : card
   (B) timetable : date
   (C) play : quote
   (D) diary : page
   (E) novel : theme

7. NOTE : SCALE ::   A note is part of a scale.

   (A) duo : number
   (B) dance : auditorium
   (C) color : spectrum
   (D) flute : melody
   (E) clock : time

8. SWEEP : BROOM ::   A broom is used to sweep.

   (A) pay : receipt
   (B) worship : organ
   (C) hit : nail
   (D) restrain : leash
   (E) compress : saw

9. FIELD : WHEAT ::   A field is where wheat is grown.

   (A) forest : weeds
   (B) oven : bread
   (C) house : furniture
   (D) orchard : oranges
   (E) grocery : cereal

10. BLUEPRINT : BUILD ::   A blueprint is used to build.

   (A) map : navigate
   (B) table : rest
   (C) song : soothe
   (D) calculator : entertain
   (E) ring : marry

4

Building a Foundation for Critical Reading

After completing this chapter, you will be able to

1. apply seven basic principles of active reading.

2. use topic sentences to find the main idea in a critical reading passage.

3. recognize the four typical answer choices in a main idea question.

4. use a procedure for answering a vocabulary-in-context question.

5. use paraphrasing to answer critical reading questions.

Introduction to Critical Reading

What academic activity do you spend the most time doing? As high school students, you devote hours to reading textbooks, novels, and many other written sources. Within a short time, you will be attending college classes in which much of your success will depend on your ability to read and understand written material.

The reading passages and questions on the SAT are designed to measure your abilities as a critical reader. It is important to remember that good readers, like good athletes, actors, and musicians, get that way through practice. You probably know that the "best" approach to reading any material depends partly on the purpose for which you are reading it. When you take the SAT, you are reading strictly for the purpose of answering a few multiple-choice questions. This special purpose requires a variety of unique strategies, regardless of your reading ability.

This section will explain basic facts about SAT reading passages and questions, and it will illustrate a strategy of active, aggressive critical reading. Lessons 12-14 will then explain and illustrate specific skills that will help you become a better reader for the purpose of taking the SAT.

The Passages

Number and length Each SAT will contain four reading passages. On other tests you may have taken, this section would be called the *Reading Comprehension Test*. On the SAT, it's called *Critical Reading*. The SAT passages range in length from 400 words (1 column) to 850 words (2 columns).

Types of passages Most passages are drawn from the following four basic categories.

- **Social Sciences** These passages deal with topics drawn from history, sociology, and government. Recent examples include articles about the emergence of women artists during the Renaissance and differing views on the value of public opinion polls.
- **Natural Sciences** These passages deal with topics drawn from botany, geology, and astronomy. Recent examples include articles about meteors and the relationships between plants.

- **Narrative** These passages contain excerpts from novels, short stories, and memoirs. Recent examples include excerpts from *Sula* by Toni Morrison and *Efforts of Affection: A Memoir of Marianne Moore* by Elizabeth Bishop.
- **Humanities** These passages are typically essays dealing with topics drawn from art, literature, music, philosophy, and folklore. Recent examples include articles about jazz and the characteristics of Bohemians.

You should note that at least one of the four passages on each SAT will reflect the concerns or accomplishments of a particular ethnic group.

Where do the passages come from? Many students complain that SAT passages come from obscure sources no one could possibly find. This is not true, however. The SAT test writers choose passages from highly regarded books. Most of the selections come from paperback books that can be found in any good college book store. For a list of recommended books, see page 413 in the Appendix.

The Questions

Number of questions Each passage will be followed by 5 to 13 questions. In all, the SAT contains 40 critical reading questions.

Types of questions Most SAT critical reading questions can be assigned to one of the following three categories.

1. **General questions** General questions test your overall understanding of a passage. They usually ask you to
   - identify the main idea, theme, or purpose of a passage.
   - distinguish the author's tone, mood, or attitude.

2. **Vocabulary-in-context questions** These questions ask you to infer the meaning of a word or phrase from its context. As you will see in Lesson 13, vocabulary-in-context questions are much like sentence completions. You can expect to have 4 to 7 vocabulary-in-context questions on the SAT.

3. **Specific questions** These questions ask you about a specific paragraph, sentence, or phrase. Specific questions comprise about two-thirds of all critical reading questions. There are two basic types of specific questions.

- **Literal comprehension questions** Literal comprehension questions ask about facts or points directly stated in the passage. The correct answer is usually a restatement or paraphrasing of words found in the text of the passage.
- **Extended reasoning questions** Extended reasoning questions ask you to draw inferences or conclusions from information stated in the passage. Typical extended reasoning questions ask you to understand the implications of what is stated, follow the logic of an argument, and evaluate the author's assumptions.

Order of Difficulty

As you have seen, analogy and sentence completion questions are presented in order of difficulty. Critical reading questions are the only questions on the SAT that are NOT presented in order of difficulty. As a result, you may find that the first two questions are very difficult. Don't despair.

Passages, like the questions, will also vary in difficulty. As a general rule, one of the four passages will be relatively easy, two will be medium, and one will be difficult. However, the degree of difficulty of a passage is subjective and will vary from reader to reader. For example, students who enjoy science may find a difficult science passage easy and an easy social science passage quite challenging.

Time

The reading passages require a lot of time and concentration. Since they are so time consuming, it is wise to do the sentence completions and analogies first. As a general rule, you should try to allow 10 minutes for each of the passages in the two-passage section and 15 minutes for the passage in the single-passage section. If you are struggling with the verbal test, forget about the time limits and concentrate instead on being as careful as you need to be on the portion of the test that you do have time to attack.

Basic Principles of Active, Aggressive Critical Reading

Many students expect to read a passage and then quickly answer all of the questions. They then become frustrated and confused when this strategy doesn't work. Don't be frustrated. Reading the passages and identifying the correct answers require concentration and careful thought.

You might find it useful to imagine this part of the SAT as a sort of treasure hunt. The reading passages are your maps and the 40 correct answers are your buried treasure. The passages contain all the clues you need to cash in on the treasure for a potential gain of about 300 points. It's not easy because it's not supposed to be easy.

The three critical reading chapters in this text are designed to help you become a successful treasure hunter. On the SAT, this means being an active reader. It means being alert and aggressive, rather than passive. Active readers ask mental questions, know how to find main ideas, and make an effort to understand the overall structure of each passage. Here are seven key principles for active reading on the SAT.

1. **Read the passage first and then answer the questions.** On some reading tests, it might be a good idea to read the questions first, but not on the SAT. Reading the questions first really means that you have to read the questions twice, which would take way too much time. There are 40 critical reading questions on the SAT. Don't turn it into 80.

2. **Don't study the passage.** SAT passages are not homework assignments. The passage will not be snatched away from you when you get to the questions, so don't try to memorize facts and dates. Remember, the questions only draw from about 25 percent of the information in a typical passage.

3. **Form a mental map of the passage.** As you read a passage for the first time, try to form a mental map or outline of the key points in the article. A mental outline shouldn't be too detailed. It should just be a mental list of the sequence of topics and key ideas contained in the passage. By forming a mental outline of the passage, you gain a feel for the author's main idea and attitude toward his/her subject.

4. **Expect to refer back to the article.** Since SAT critical reading passages and questions are both very challenging, it will usually be necessary to read a question and then refer back to the passage. Fortunately, the SAT writers make this search-and-find process much easier by frequently including a line or paragraph reference with the questions.

5. **Correct answers must be supported by evidence from the passage.** Critical reading questions frequently contain very tempting answer choices. For example, the SAT writers often include choices that seem to make perfect sense even though there was never any mention of it in the passage. That's why it is very important to remember that correct answers must be supported by evidence from the passage. Most of the time, you should be able to draw a line from your answer to the supporting evidence in the passage.

6. **Underline as you read.** It is a good idea to underline key points as you read through the passage. These marks will then serve as handy guideposts to help you locate information when you answer the questions.

7. **Don't give up.** Many students often report feeling lost and bored as they work on critical reading passages. Don't expect to enjoy each SAT passage. The passages are not intended to entertain you; they are designed to evaluate your critical reading skills. The critical reading passages are the ultimate test of your indomitable will. Stay mentally alert and don't quit. Remember, your job is to get a feel for the passage so you can answer the questions and earn points.

Active Reading—A Case Example

Like any other skill, active reading requires practice. The left column below contains a passage from a short story by Paule Marshall. The right column contains examples of the kinds of mental notes that an active reader would make. For purposes of illustration, we've also underlined key phrases and words in the passage.

The basement kitchen of the brownstone house where my family lived was the usual gathering place. *Line* Once inside the warm safety of its (5) walls the women threw off the drab coats and hats, seated themselves at the large center table, drank their cups of tea or cocoa, and talked. While my sister and I sat at a smaller table over (10) in a corner doing our homework, they talked—endlessly, passionately, poetically, and with impressive range. No subject was beyond them. True, they would indulge in the usual (15) gossip. . . . But they also tackled the great issues of the time. They were always, for example, discussing the state of the economy. It was the mid and late 30's then, and the aftershock (20) of the Depression, with its soup lines and suicides on Wall Street, was still being felt. . . .

This paragraph tells me about the setting. But who are these women and why are they talking so much? Maybe the next paragraph will answer these questions.

There was no way for me to understand it at the time, but the talk (25) that filled the kitchen those afternoons was highly functional. It served as therapy, the cheapest kind available to my mother and her friends. Not only did it help them recover from the long (30) wait on the corner that morning and the bargaining over their labor, it restored them to a sense of themselves and reaffirmed their self-worth. Through language they were able to (35) overcome the humiliations of the work-day.

Main idea: "the talk that filled the kitchen those afternoons was highly functional." This passage is going to describe some of the functions of their talk. Here's the first— "therapy."

But more than therapy, that freewheeling, wide-ranging, exuberant talk functioned as an outlet for the (40) tremendous creative energy they possessed. They were women in

This paragraph deals with a second function. The talk was an "outlet." It looks like each paragraph will discuss a function of the talk.

whom the need for self-expression was
strong, and since language was the
only vehicle readily available to them
(45) they made of it an art form that—in
keeping with the African tradition in
which art and life are one—was an
integral part of their lives.

    And their talk was a refuge. They
(50) never really ceased being baffled and
overwhelmed by America—its
vastness, complexity and power. Its
strange customs and laws. At a level
beyond words they remained fearful
(55) and in awe. Their uneasiness and fear
were even reflected in their attitude
toward the children they had given
birth to in this country. They referred
to those like myself, the little
(60) Brooklyn-born Bajans (Barbadians), as
"these New York children."

    Confronted therefore by a world
they could not encompass, . . . and at
the same time finding themselves
(65) permanently separated from the world
they had known, they took refuge in
language. "Language is the only
homeland," Czeslaw Milosz, the
émigré Polish writer and Nobel
(70) Laureate, has said. This is what it
became for the women at the kitchen
table.

    It served another purpose also, I
suspect. My mother and her friends
(75) were after all the female counterpart of
Ralph Ellison's invisible man. Indeed,
you might say they suffered a triple
invisibility, being black, female, and
foreigners. They didn't count in
(80) American society except as a source of
cheap labor. But given the kind of
women they were, they couldn't
tolerate the fact of their invisibility,
their powerlessness. And they fought
(85) back, using the only weapon at their
command: the spoken word.

from *Reena and Other Stories* by Paule Marshall

*As expected, here's the third
function—the talk was a
"refuge."*

*The quote looks important.
Better underline it. The
women are from Barbados and
the narrator was born in
Brooklyn.*

*The phrase, "It served another
purpose also" indicates the
author is going to provide a
final function. The women
used the "spoken word" to
fight against a feeling of
invisibility.*

Our notes and speculations may not all appear important to answering the actual questions. Even so, they help us concentrate while we are reading. This passage could generate a variety of general and specific questions. Since this chapter will discuss how to find main ideas, answer vocabulary-in-context questions, and recognize paraphrases, let's examine three questions that illustrate each of these skills.

Main Idea

1. The main focus of the passage is on the

    (A) situation encountered by immigrants in a new country
    (B) isolation felt by a particular group of women
    (C) difference between the author's generation and that of her mother
    (D) benefits of language for a group of women
    (E) contrast between New York and Barbados

This question asks you to identify the *main focus* of the passage. The author states her main idea in lines 24-26 when she states that "the talk that filled the kitchen those afternoons was highly functional." The passage then discusses four benefits of language for the group of women. The best answer is (D). Because the other choices are mentioned briefly in the fourth paragraph, these choices will attract many careless readers, especially those who don't read the entire passage.

Vocabulary-in-Context

2. In line 14, "indulge" most nearly means

    (A) spoiled completely
    (B) engage in
    (C) humor to excess
    (D) luxuriate in
    (E) forbid entirely

Indulge means to allow oneself a special pleasure. The author tells us that "No subject was beyond them." The women talked about the "great issues of the time," such as "the state of the economy." They also would "indulge in the usual gossip." In this context, *indulge* means "to allow or to engage in." Choice (E) is clearly wrong. Choices (A), (C), and (D) refer to other possible meanings of *indulge*, but are not supported by the passage. The correct answer is (B).

Recognizing a Paraphrase

3. The third paragraph serves to show
   (●) that the women used language as an artistic process that became an essential component of their lives
   (B) how African tradition enabled the women to understand their lives
   (C) how the women used language as therapy to alleviate the difficulties of their lives
   (D) how the women tried to learn a new language
   (E) how the women used language to protest the state of the economy

Paragraph 3 states that the women turned language into "an art form that . . . was an integral part of their lives." None of the choices specifically repeat this answer. However, choice (A) does provide a paraphrase or rewording of this answer. "Art form" becomes *artistic process* and "integral part of their lives" becomes *essential component of their lives*. None of the other answer choices are supported by the facts in paragraph 3. Lesson 14 will provide a detailed discussion on how to recognize and use paraphrases.

Finding the Main Idea

Has your family ever become lost while driving in an unfamiliar city? If so, you are not alone. Most travelers have had this frustrating experience. Similarly, many students often report "getting lost" while reading about an unfamiliar topic. These students are so overwhelmed by details that they miss the author's main idea.

Like drivers in an unfamiliar city, good readers need signs to help them find their way through a difficult passage. The signs provided on the SAT are called topic sentences. These key sentences or phrases present the author's main ideas.

Learning how to find topic sentences is a valuable critical reading skill. This section will begin by helping you find topic sentences in paragraphs and passages. We will then describe ways to use the characteristics of main idea questions to *ZAP* wrong answers and find the right answers.

Finding Topic Sentences in Paragraphs

Paragraphs are the building blocks of a well-constructed passage. In general, well-written paragraphs contain one sentence or phrase that is more important than the other sentences. This sentence expresses the paragraph's central idea.

The following paragraph is from a chapter about the Chesapeake Bay. Read the paragraph and underline the sentence that best expresses the paragraph's main idea.

> The Bay has other treasures, not all at the head of lists. Enormous herring runs, sufficient to support a sizable canning industry and provide the herring roe Virginians like to eat for breakfast with scrambled eggs. Mink, muskrat, nutria and otter, sad to include, trapped in the lovely marshes of Maryland's Dorchester County, in numbers second only to Louisiana. Sky-darkening flocks of migrating and wintering waterfowl, in the thickest concentrations on the Atlantic flyway.
>
> from *Beautiful Swimmers* by William Warner

The topic sentence often expresses the point of a series of details or examples. Why does the author of this paragraph tell us about the "enormous herring runs," "the mink, muskrat, nutria, and otter, . . .

trapped in the lovely marshes of Maryland's Dorchester County," and the "sky-darkening flocks of migrating and wintering waterfowl"? Each of these three details illustrates the Bay's "other treasures."

In this selection, the main idea of the paragraph is presented in the first sentence: "The Bay has other treasures, not all at the head of lists." The sentence that tells the main idea is called the *topic sentence*. In this case, the topic sentence is the first sentence. Often, it will appear in the middle or at the end of a paragraph. Read the following selection and circle the sentence that expresses the main idea of the paragraph.

> Any survey of medieval town life delights in the color of guild organizations: the broiders and glovers, the hatters and scriveners, the shipwrights and upholsterers, each with its guild hall, its distinctive livery, and its elaborate set of rules. But if life in the guilds and at the fairs provides a sharp contrast with the stodgy life on the manor, we must not be misled by surface resemblances into thinking that it represented a foretaste of modern life in medieval dress. It is a long distance from guilds to the modern business firm, and it is well to fix in mind some of the differences.
>
> from *The Making of Economic Society* by Robert Heilbroner

The topic sentence often provides a concise statement of the author's purpose. Based upon this paragraph, what subject do you think the rest of the passage will address? The author's intention is clearly stated in the final sentence. By saying, "It is a long distance from guilds to the modern business firm, and it is well to fix in mind some of the differences," the author tells us that this passage will discuss some of the differences between medieval and modern business practices.

Finding the Main Idea in a Passage

The previous discussion related to finding the main idea of a single paragraph. The selections on the SAT are much longer and are composed of several paragraphs. Each paragraph will have a main idea and the entire SAT reading selection will also have an overall main idea. This overall main idea defines what the entire passage is all about. Authors usually provide descriptive details and illustrative examples to support their main ideas.

Finding the main idea is one of the keys to successfully attacking an SAT reading section. SAT passages usually present the main idea early and then follow with the supporting details. This is especially true of the easy passages.

The main idea of an easy passage is typically found in the first paragraph—that's one of the things that makes it easy. The main idea of a hard passage is often found in the last paragraph—that's one of the things that makes it hard!

Use the following three-step approach to find the main idea of each reading passage.

1. Begin by carefully reading the first paragraph, paying particular attention to the first two sentences.

2. Read the first two sentences of each additional paragraph.

3. And finally, read the last paragraph, paying special attention to the last sentence.

Use this three-step approach as you read the following passage. Then answer the main idea question.

> The Crusades failed to accomplish their primary objective of conquering and holding the Holy Land. Like many great movements, however, the Crusades produced a number of
> *Line* additional and unexpected results. First, the Crusades weakened the
> (5) feudal nobility. Thousands of knights died in battle or lost their lives from disease. In addition, many knights had sold or mortgaged their properties to finance their expeditions. Led by France, European monarchs successfully took advantage of the nobles' misfortune by strengthening royal power.
> (10) Second, two centuries of religious warfare not only promoted hostility between Christians and Muslims but also increased tensions between Christians and Jews. Angry mobs attacked Jewish communities that were often used as scapegoats for social problems.
> Third, the Fourth Crusade dealt a serious blow to the Byzantine
> (15) Empire. Although Constantinople regained its independence, it never recovered its former power or prestige.
> And finally, the Crusades played a major role in stimulating trade between Europe and the Middle East. While living in the Holy Land, the crusaders acquired a taste for new spices, foods, and
> (20) clothes they purchased in Arab markets. Many crusaders brought home samples of these products.

1. The major purpose of the passage is to
   (A) assess the impact of increased trade upon European life
   (B) explain why nobility lost power
   (C) evaluate how the Fourth Crusade affected the Byzantine Empire
   (D) show how the Crusades promoted understanding between Christians and Jews
   (E) discuss the long-term effects of the Crusades

The second sentence of the passage states that "the Crusades produced a number of additional and unexpected results." The author then discusses four consequences of the Crusades. Choice (A) goes well beyond the scope of the passage. *ZAP* it. Choices (B) and (C) apply only to the first and third paragraphs. *ZAP* them both. At this point, you need to give careful consideration only to (D) and (E). Choice (D) is an inaccurate statement and can thus be *ZAPPED*. Choice (E) best summarizes the major purpose of the passage.

Identifying Main Idea Questions

Main idea questions are easy to spot. The question specifically asks you to identify the *primary focus* or *major purpose* of the passage. Here are examples of the formats used on recent main idea questions.

- The major purpose of the passage is to . . .
- The primary purpose of the passage is to . . .
- The passage is primarily concerned with . . .
- Which of the following statements best represents a major idea of the passage?
- The main focus of the passage is on the . . .
- The passage is best described as . . .
- Which of the following titles best summarizes the content of the passage?

ZAPPING Main Idea Questions

Remind students that ***ZAPPING*** doesn't always provide the correct answer. It simply improves the odds of guessing correctly.

Suppose that you were asked to write a main idea question for an SAT passage. Writing the question is easy. All you have to do is choose one of the seven main idea formats used above. Writing the correct answer is also fairly simple. All you have to do is clearly summarize the topic sentence. But, your job is still not finished. The hard part is to write the four other choices that are attractive but still inarguably wrong.

At first glance, writing the incorrect choices would appear to be a very *arduous* (very hard, difficult) task. As you might have already guessed, appearances are once again deceiving. In fact, the SAT writers follow a recognizable pattern when they design the incorrect choices for main idea questions. Knowing this pattern will help you *ZAP* the distracters and find the correct answer.

1. **One or more answers are too broad.** A broad answer goes well beyond the facts provided in the passage. In the Crusades question, choice (A) (*assess the impact of increased trade upon European life*) goes well beyond the scope of what is discussed in the passage.

2. **One or more answers are too narrow.** A narrow answer only covers a small portion of the passage. Narrow responses may be true, but they only apply to a paragraph or a sentence. Choices (B) and (C) in the Crusades question are both too narrow since they only apply to single paragraphs.

3. **One or more answers will be inaccurate.** Inaccurate answers are tempting because they often use actual words from the passage. However, the statement contradicts or is not supported by information in the passage. In the Crusades question, choice (D) (*show how the Crusades promoted understanding between Christians and Jews*) is inaccurate. According to the passage, the Crusades "increased tensions between Christians and Jews."

These three patterns are one reason why teachers and test-takers find the SAT so frustrating. They often approach the test with the misconception that the wrong answers should be obvious.

Identifying broad, narrow, and inaccurate answer choices will help you *ZAP* wrong answer choices and zero-in on the correct answer. It is important to point out that the SAT writers do not have to include a broad, narrow, and inaccurate choice in every main idea question. A question could include one broad choice and three narrow ones. The most important point always to keep in mind is that the correct answer will summarize the main idea and embrace the passage as a whole.

Throughout this program, encourage students to write in the margins and directly on each passage.

DIRECTIONS: The following passage and question gives you an opportunity to apply our strategies for finding the main idea and *ZAPPING* the wrong answer choices. Read the passage and then answer the main idea question below.

Crete lies across the southern end of the Aegean Sea, between Greece and Egypt. From the beginning of the island's settlement, the Cretans found the soil too poor for growing crops. To survive,
Line they had to turn their geographic location into an economic
(5) advantage. During the peak centuries of their prosperity, the Cretans became the earliest people to use seafaring and trade to establish a commercial economy.

Crete's thriving commercial activities supported a comfortable lifestyle. Evidence from archaeological digs provides a picture of
(10) Cretan life. Wall paintings in the king's palace-city at Knossos show a lively people with a zest for athletic contests, festivals, and stylish dress. Clad in ruffled gowns, women of the court wore delicate gold jewelry and styled their hair into long, graceful coils. They took part in activities ranging from dancing to strenuous
(15) sports. This evidence suggests that the Cretan women enjoyed a level of social equality rarely found in the ancient world.

The many flowers, fish, and animals in Cretan paintings reveal that people also delighted in the beauty of nature. Another remarkable aspect of Cretan life was its plumbing. The joys of
(20) Crete appear to have ended abruptly some time between 1400 and 1200 B.C. Historians do not know whether the cause was a natural disaster or human conquest. Did a nearby volcanic eruption, with an earthquake and tidal wave, destroy the Cretans' world? Were they overrun by invaders? Evidence shows that the Minoans
(25) attempted to rebuild but soon fell to invaders from mainland Greece.

1. The primary purpose of the passage is to
   (A) discuss the advantages and disadvantages of a commercial economy
   (B) describe an early culture
   (C) describe the role of women in Cretan society
   (D) prove that the Cretan kings were unpopular
   (E) speculate on reasons why Cretan civilization collapsed

Guided PRACTICE

Discussion

This example illustrates the four types of answer choices typically found in a main idea question.

1. **One or more answers are too broad.** Choice (A) goes well beyond the scope of the passage. While the passage mentions that the people of Crete developed the first commercial economy, it does not describe *the advantages and disadvantages of a commercial economy.*

2. **One or more answers are too narrow.** Choice (C) only applies to the second paragraph, while (E) is limited to the third paragraph.

3. **One or more answers will be inaccurate.** Inaccurate answers sound enticing, but don't be fooled. They are not supported by the passage. Choice (D), *prove that the Cretan kings were unpopular,* is inaccurate. The author provides details about daily life in the king's palace-city at Knossos which suggest that the Cretan kings were popular rulers.

4. **One answer will be correct.** Only choice (B), *describe an early culture,* summarizes the main idea of the entire passage.

Critical Reading Exercises 1-3 provide you with practice answering main idea questions. Critical Reading Exercises 4-5 give you an opportunity to write main idea questions.

CRITICAL READING PRACTICE EXERCISE ❶ "Main Idea"

DIRECTIONS: The following passage includes the first paragraph, the first two sentences of the middle paragraphs, and the last paragraph. Read the passage and then answer the main idea question. Next to each wrong answer choice, write the letter **B** for too broad, **N** for too narrow, or **I** for inaccurate. Mark the correct answer.

By 1916 the women of the NACW [National Association of Colored Women's Clubs] could point to a long list of achievements. . . . The NACW had grown to fifty thousand members and it
Line continued to sustain itself, without White largesse, as the first
(5) national Black organization (predating the NAACP and the Urban League) to deal with the needs of the race. The accomplishments of its members were formidable.

School founders like Charlotte Hawkins Brown, Lucy C. Laney, and Mary McLeod Bethune left inspiring legacies for generations to
(10) come. Scholarship loans for women to attend college had been provided. . . .

In the field of health, clubwoman Lugenia Burns Hope organized the Atlanta Neighborhood Union in 1908. Hope, whose parents had been free Blacks in Mississippi, had grown up in Chicago and,
(15) forced to leave school when her father died, had worked there for eight years as a dressmaker and bookkeeper. . . .

Such achievements were duplicated on a smaller scale throughout the country, and several NACW projects became models for the NAACP, the National Urban League, and in the case of the NACW's
(20) kindergarten program, the entire public school system of Washington, D.C.

from *When and Where I Enter* by Paula Giddings

1. The primary purpose of the passage is to
    (A) discuss the life and work of Lugenia Burns Hope
    (B) compare and contrast the NACW and the NAACP
    (C) outline the organization and structure of the NACW
    (D) criticize the contributions of Charlotte Hawkins Brown, Lucy C. Laney, and Mary McLeod Bethune
    (●) describe the accomplishments of the NACW

CRITICAL READING PRACTICE EXERCISE ② "Main Idea"

DIRECTIONS: The following passage includes the first paragraph, first two sentences of the middle paragraphs, and the last paragraph. Read the passage and then answer the main idea question. Next to each wrong answer choice, write the letter **B** for too broad, **N** for too narrow, or **I** for inaccurate. Mark the correct answer.

The cockroach, as it happens, is a popular test subject for laboratory research. It adapts well to captivity, lives relatively long, reproduces quickly, and will subsist in full vigor on Purina Dog
Line Chow. The largest American species, up to two inches in length and
(5) known as *Periplaneta americana*, is even big enough for easy dissection. One eminent physiologist has written fondly: "The laboratory investigator who keeps up a battle to rid his rat colony of cockroaches may well consider giving up the rats and working with the cockroaches instead. From many points of view the roach is
(10) practically made to order as a laboratory subject. Here is an animal of frugal habits, tenacious of life, eager to live in the laboratory and very modest in its space requirements." Tenacious of life indeed. . . .

The cockroach is roughly 250 million years old, which makes it the oldest of living insects, possibly even the oldest known air-
(15) breathing animal. . . . Those primitive early cockroaches possessed a simple and very practical anatomical design that remains almost unchanged in the cockroaches of today. . . .

Unlike most insects, they have mouthparts that enable them to take hard foods, soft foods, and liquids. They will feed on virtually
(20) any organic substance. . . . They are flattened enough to squeeze into the narrowest hiding place, either in human habitations or in the wild. They are quick on their feet, and can fly when they need to. . . .

Now one further quote from the experts, in summary, and
(25) because it has for our purposes here a particular odd resonance. "Cockroaches," say two researchers who worked under sponsorship of the United States Army, "are tough, resilient insects with amazing endurance and the ability to recover rapidly from almost complete extermination."

from *Natural Acts* by David Quammen

2. The primary purpose of the passage is to
   (A) explain why the cockroach is widely used in laboratory experiments
   (B) suggest a plan for exterminating cockroaches
   (C) describe a typical cockroach diet
   (D) discuss reasons for the longevity of cockroaches
   (E) explain why the cockroach received the name *Periplaneta americana*

CRITICAL READING PRACTICE EXERCISE ❸ "Main Idea"

DIRECTIONS: The following passage includes the first paragraph, first two sentences of the middle paragraphs, and the last paragraph. Read the passage and then answer the main idea question. Next to each wrong answer choice, write the letter **B** for too broad, **N** for too narrow, or **I** for inaccurate. Mark the correct answer.

Tanzania is a modern country located in eastern Africa. Although Tanzania is a very young nation, its ancient geological sites contain some of the world's oldest human and humanlike fossils. A flat
Line expanse known as Laetoli is one such place. Located in a remote
(5) corner of northern Tanzania, Laetoli's rich fossil beds yielded no human or humanlike remains until 1974. In that year, Mary Leakey led a scientific expedition hoping to find new clues about human origins.

As a veteran of many expeditions, Leakey knew that finding the
(10) remains of human ancestors requires great patience, expert knowledge, and luck. After a hard day of painstaking work, one scientist suddenly noticed strange footprints left by extinct animals in an exposed layer of volcanic ash. . . .

The footprints had been created by an extraordinary set of
(15) circumstances. First, a nearby volcano erupted, covering the surrounding landscape with a fresh layer of soft ash. . . .

Even more dramatic revelations soon followed the discovery of the animal footprints. In 1977, two of Leakey's assistants uncovered footprints remarkably similar to those of modern human beings. . . .
(20) After careful analysis, scientists concluded that the trail had been made by three creatures now called australopithecines. Human beings and other creatures that walk upright, such as australopithecines, are called hominids. . . .

The footprints are more than just scientific evidence. They are also
(25) reminders from our long-buried past about the human condition. Mary Leakey wrote that studying the footprints produced "a kind of poignant time wrench. At one point, and you need not be an expert tracker to discern this, she stops, pauses, turns to the left to glance at some possible threat or irregularity, and then continues to the north.
(30) This motion, so intensely human, transcends time."

3. The primary purpose of the passage is to
   (A) compare and contrast modern and ancient Tanzania
   (B) explain how the footprints were made
   (C) prove that hominids were incapable of walking erect
   (D) discuss a significant archaeological discovery
   (E) speculate about why hominids were present at Laetoli

CRITICAL READING PRACTICE EXERCISE ④ "Main Idea"

DIRECTIONS: Read the following topic sentences from a critical reading passage. Then write answer choices for the main idea question below. Label your wrong answer choices with **B** for too broad, **N** for too narrow, or **I** for inaccurate. Mark your correct answer.

The physical, chemical, and biological systems of lakes are complex and interrelated. Any one influences and is influenced by the others. . . .

Line   Limnologists [scientists who study freshwater ecosystems] have
(5) defined distinct zones in lakes, based upon the extent of light penetration in the water. The *littoral zone* is the shallow-water area where light reaches the bottom. . . .

The *limnetic zone* is the open-water area of a lake that extends from the surface to the depth where light intensity is reduced to
(10) about one percent of the surface light. In theory, the lower boundary of this zone is the *compensation level*, which is the depth at which oxygen uptake by bacteria, plant, and animal respiration equals photosynthetic oxygen release by green plants. . . .

The *profundal zone* is the deepwater area where only respiration
(15) and decomposition occur. Light intensity is too low in the profundal zone for photosynthesis to occur. . . .

The *benthic zone* is the lake bottom, where falling material accumulates and decomposes. It is inhabited by numerous types of burrowing animals. . . .
(20) The thermal properties of a lake are controlled by the length of exposure and intensity of the sun on the lake, by materials in the water which scatter and absorb light, and by wind mixing.

from *Geology in the Urban Environment* by Utgard, McKenzie, and Foley; originally extracted from USGS Circular 601-K, 1975.

4. The primary purpose of the passage is to

(A) Responses will vary. _____

(B) _____

(C) _____

(D) _____

(E) _____

CRITICAL READING PRACTICE EXERCISE ⑤ "Main Idea"

DIRECTIONS: Read the following topic sentences from a critical reading passage. Then write answer choices for the main idea question below. Label your wrong answer choices with **B** for too broad, **N** for too narrow, or **I** for inaccurate. Mark your correct answer.

Although lacking political unity, the Hellenistic world produced a number of impressive scientific and cultural achievements. Alexandria in Egypt became the foremost center of Hellenistic
Line civilization.
(5)   Alexandria occupied a strategic site on the western edge of the Nile delta. Ships from all around the Mediterranean docked in its spacious harbor. . . .
     Alexandria's thriving commerce enabled it to grow and prosper. By the third century B.C., it boasted a diverse population that
(10) exceeded half a million people. . . .
     Both residents and visitors admired Alexandria's great beauty. Broad avenues lined with statues of Greek gods divided the city blocks. . . .
     Alexandria's greatest attractions were its famous museum and
(15) library. The museum was a temple dedicated to the Muses, the Greek goddesses of arts and sciences. It contained art galleries, a zoo, botanical gardens, and even a dining hall. Teachers and students were only a short distance from the nearby library. Its collection of half a million papyrus scrolls included all the
(20) masterpieces of ancient literature. As the first true research library in the world, it helped promote the work of a gifted group of scholars.

5. Which of the following would be the most appropriate title for the passage?

(A) Responses will vary. _____

(B) _____

(C) _____

(D) _____

(E) _____

Vocabulary-in-Context

Many words in the English language have multiple meanings. For example, *Webster's New World Dictionary* lists 11 different definitions or uses of the word *common*. Possible definitions of *common* include: shared (common interests), widespread (a common saying), ordinary (a common person), coarse (common manners), familiar (a common sight), plain (a common face), and frequent (a common occurrence).

When a word has many different meanings, how do you know which one the author is using? The intended meaning clearly depends upon the *context* in which the word is being used. For example, what does the word *common* mean within the context of this sentence: "She didn't see herself as a hero but simply a common citizen." Since the author tells us that the woman didn't see herself as a hero, we are looking for a definition of *common* that means the opposite of hero. Within the context of this sentence, *common* means ordinary.

Identifying Vocabulary-In-Context Questions

Vocabulary-in-context questions are designed to test your ability to use contextual clues to determine the meaning of a word or phrase with multiple definitions. Your SAT will contain 4 to 7 vocabulary-in-context questions. Fortunately, they are very easy to spot. Here are three typical examples.

- In line 8, "domestic" most nearly means—
- In line 34, the phrase "sensitive to" is used to mean—
- The word "camp" (line 12) most nearly means—

A Case Example

Read the following paragraph and then answer the accompanying vocabulary-in-context question.

> In 1492, two complex but totally different cultures collided. Europeans believed that land could be bought, sold, and divided. In contrast, Native Americans viewed land as a common resource that, like water and air, could be used by everyone.

In line 3, "common" most nearly means

(A) coarse
(B) plain
(C) frequent
(D) familiar
(●) shared

All vocabulary-in-context questions provide a line reference. Your first step is to use this reference to go back to the passage and locate the appropriate sentence. It is wise to read both the sentence you are referred to and the one that precedes it. This will provide you with a more complete context.

Vocabulary-in-context questions are very similar to sentence completion questions. As you have learned, each sentence completion question contains a key word or phrase that will lead you to the correct answer. The same principle applies to vocabulary-in-context questions. In the example above, Native Americans are described as viewing land as a "common resource" that "could be used by everyone." In contrast, the Europeans' view "believed that land could be bought, sold, and divided." Native Americans viewed land as a resource that should be *shared* by everyone. Although choices (A), (B), (C), and (D) are all possible meanings of *common*, none of them fits within the context of this passage. Choice (E) is therefore the correct answer.

In this example, all of the answer choices were different definitions of the word *common*. It is important to remember that vocabulary-in-context answer choices can also include unrelated words. For example, in one recent question, SAT writers asked for a word that most nearly means "deliberate." Answer choices included *intentional, cautious, slow, compelling*, and *cunning*. While *intentional, cautious*, and *slow* are definitions of "deliberate," *compelling* and *cunning* are not. Don't let unrelated words fool you. They are distracters and should be *ZAPPED*.

Guided
PRACTICE

DIRECTIONS: Here are three more vocabulary-in-context questions. As you read each partial passage, use the context to help you determine the correct answer.

> The British barons who signed the Magna Carta irrevocably committed themselves to supporting the idea of limited monarchy.

1. In line 2, "committed" most nearly means
    (A) confined
    (B) withheld
    (●) pledged
    (D) released from
    (E) performed

> Impressionist paintings are now among the most popular works of art in the world. However, when they first appeared, art critics denounced the paintings, showing no appreciation for the Impressionists' bold new techniques.

2. In line 3, "appreciation" most nearly means
    (A) increase in value
    (●) understanding
    (C) scientific interest
    (D) anxiety about
    (E) gratitude for

> I am supposing, or perhaps only hoping, that our future may be found in the past's fugitive moments of compassion rather than in its solid centuries of warfare.

from *A People's History of the United States* by Howard Zinn

3. In line 3, "solid" most nearly means
    (●) unbroken
    (B) rugged
    (C) firm
    (D) reliable
    (E) unanimous

Discussion

1. *Committed* can mean "performed" (as that person committed a crime), "pledged" (as the senator was committed to a healthy environment), and "placed in custody or confined" (as the court committed the criminal to prison). Since *irrevocable* means "that which cannot be called back or reversed," the barons made a firm and lasting commitment, or pledge, to support the idea of limited monarchy. Choices (B) and (D) mean the opposite of committed and can be *ZAPPED* right away. Choice (C) is by far the best answer.

2. The most common use of the word *appreciate* is to express gratitude. However, *appreciate* can also mean "to increase in value" (as the land appreciated in value) and "understand" (as to appreciate how much work it takes to paint a house). In this example, "art critics denounced," or sharply criticized, Impressionist paintings. Since they denounced the paintings, we can *ZAP* choices (A) and (E). Choice (D) can be *ZAPPED* since the critics showed great, rather than "no," anxiety about the new style of art. Choice (C) can be *ZAPPED* since art critics would not show scientific interest in the paintings. Choice (B) is therefore the best answer. The art critics denounced the Impressionist paintings since they did not appreciate or understand them.

3. *Fugitive* is the key contextual word that will lead you to the correct answer. The author contrasts "the past's *fugitive* moments of compassion" with the "solid centuries of warfare." One meaning of *fugitive* is brief, short-lived. The author is saying that compassion is an all too brief occurrence, while warfare is continuous. Choice (A) best conveys this meaning. Choices (B), (C), (D), and (E) do not fit the context since they do not offer a contrast with *fugitive*.

Developing an Extra Edge

1. Vocabulary-in-context questions are not intended to test your knowledge of difficult words that have one meaning. As you have seen, vocabulary-in-context questions are designed to test your ability to use context clues to determine the correct use of a word or phrase with multiple meanings. Studying the context within which the word is placed is your best strategy. However, if you have trouble understanding the context, don't give up. A second strategy is to read the sentence substituting each answer for the stem word. Look for an answer that makes sense with the rest of the sentence. Answer choices that don't make sense or sound wrong can be *ZAPPED*.

2. Vocabulary-in-context questions can usually be answered very quickly since they are short and require you to read only one sentence. A test-wise student should never skip a vocabulary-in-context question. If you are running out of time and can't finish a passage, always do the vocabulary-in-context questions.

Independent PRACTICE

Critical Reading Practice Exercise 6 provides you with an opportunity to practice the skill of answering vocabulary-in-context questions.

CRITICAL READING PRACTICE EXERCISE 6 *"Vocabulary-in-Context"*

DIRECTIONS: Read each sentence or paragraph. Then use the context to determine the best answer for each question. Circle the correct answer.

Although the British victory in the French and Indian War gave them control over Canada, French-speaking settlers still remained the clear, and dominant, majority in Quebec.

1. In line 3, "clear" most nearly means

   (A) transparent   (D) untroubled
   (B) unmistakable   (E) logical
   (C) innocent

Disgruntled investors predicted that the company's final report would probably blame middle-managers and not top executives for failing to follow standard financial practices.

2. As used in line 3, the word "practices" most nearly means

   (A) procedures
   (B) exercises
   (C) rehearsals
   (D) preparations
   (E) rituals

Most professional athletes have short careers. As a result, it is very important for professional athletes to plan ahead so that when their playing days are over they will have other interests to sustain them.

3. The word "sustain" (line 3) most nearly means

   (A) endure
   (B) support
   (C) prolong
   (D) endorse
   (E) validate

After the Constitutional Convention adjourned, a local citizen approached Benjamin Franklin and asked: "Well, Doctor, what have we got, a republic or a monarchy?" Franklin responded with his usual eminent good sense, "A republic, if you can keep it."

4. As used in line 4, the word "eminent" means
   (A) ordinary
   (B) unremarkable
   (C) protruding
   (●) renowned
   (E) elevated

As she passed through the hospital wards in her plain dress, so quiet, so unassuming, she struck the casual observer simply as the pattern of a perfect lady.

5. As used in line 3, the word "pattern" means
   (A) configuration
   (B) duplicate
   (C) decoration
   (D) flawed version
   (●) model

When we want something to eat, we don't have to cultivate our food; we simply hop in the car and drive to the nearest fast-food restaurant. Even if we're feeling more domestic and want to cook at home, the food comes not from our own fields and labor, but from the supermarket.

6. In line 3, the word "domestic" most nearly means
   (A) wild
   (●) devoted to home life
   (C) imported from abroad
   (D) tame
   (E) native-grown

Recognizing a Paraphrase

Carefully examine each of the following pairs of phrases.

Column A	Column B
perceived the trek	viewed the journey
benefits and burdens	gifts and penalties
appeals to many people	widespread attraction
anonymous author	unknown source

What relationship does each pair of phrases have in common?

Each phrase in Column B is a paraphrase or rewording of the phrase in Column A. We frequently use paraphrasing in our everyday conversations. For example, if your best friend misses a class, you would help him or her catch up by paraphrasing key points from the lesson. Can you think of a recent example when you used paraphrasing to restate something that you read or heard?

SAT writers also use paraphrasing when they are writing answer choices. Many critical reading questions ask you to understand information presented in the passage. The correct answer is often a paraphrase or restatement of words found directly in the text.

A Case Example

Read the following paragraphs and then answer the accompanying questions.

> I had not realized that Shakespeare's plays could be so exciting. His treatment of topics as diverse as war, comedy, and romance struck me, as it still does, as a miracle of language and construction.

> To the author, Shakespeare's plays were
>
> (A) a miracle of language and construction
> (B) based upon obscure events and people
> (C) useless and boring
> (D) filled with biting satire
> (E) intended for professional scholars

Did you have any trouble answering this question? Probably not. Choice (A) provides the correct answer by giving you a direct quote from the passage. Now reread the passage and answer the following question.

> To the author, Shakespeare's plays were
>
> (A) wondrous and well crafted
> (B) based upon obscure events and people
> (C) useless and boring
> (D) filled with biting satire
> (E) intended for professional scholars

What is the difference between this test item and the previous version? As you can see, the two questions are identical with the exception of Choice (A). Although the two choice (A) answers do not have a single word in common, both are correct. The phrase *wondrous and well-crafted* is a paraphrase of the author's statement that Shakespeare's plays are "a miracle of language and construction." In this paraphrase *wondrous* is another way of saying "a miracle of language" and *well-crafted* is another way of saying "construction."

Guided PRACTICE

DIRECTIONS: Knowing how to identify a paraphrase is an important skill for answering critical reading questions. Carefully study each of the following passages. Look for answers that paraphrase words found directly in the text. Circle the correct answer.

> After each major event in his life, Washington always returned to Mount Vernon. His stately plantation overlooking the Potomac's serene waters provided a much needed place of calm from the turbulent events transforming America.

1. According to the passage, Mount Vernon served as a place where Washington could

    (A) avoid making decisions
    (B) make additional sacrifices for his country
    (C) enjoy being with his family
    (D) seek refuge from the swirl of daily news
    (E) find excitement and new challenges

> I could barely conceive of a world beyond our hometown in the Colorado Rockies. But my brother Gary had much wider horizons. He talked about the Vietnam War, the peace movement on college campuses, the civil rights movement in the South—and talked with the enthusiasm and zeal of the dedicated activist he would become.

2. The author's description stresses which of the following about Gary?

    (A) His limited understanding of life in Colorado
    (B) His philosophical differences with the author
    (C) His cosmopolitan world view and passion for politics
    (D) His problems with local authorities
    (E) His desire to become a reporter

Guided PRACTICE

Limnologists [scientists who study fresh water ecosystems] have defined distinct zones in lakes, based upon the extent of light penetration in the water. The *littoral zone* is the shallow water area where light reaches the bottom. At times, wave action may cause shoreline erosion and bring materials into suspension in the water.

from *Geology in the Urban Environment* by Utgard, McKenzie, and Foley

3. According to the passage, which of the following is true of the littoral zone?

   (A) It is a very fragile ecosystem.
   (B) It contains little plant and animal life.
   (C) It is very difficult for scientists to study.
   (D) It is the best zone for swimming.
   (E) It has little depth and is easily penetrated by light.

Discussion

1. The passage tells you that Mount Vernon provided Washington with "a much needed place of calm from the turbulent events transforming America." Choice (D) is clearly the best answer since *refuge* is a paraphrase for "place of calm," and *swirl of daily news* is another way of saying "turbulent events."

2. According to the author, what topics did Gary talk about? We are told that Gary's conversation ranged from "the Vietnam War" to "the peace movement on college campuses" and "the civil rights movement in the South." How did Gary discuss these topics? We are told that he talked about them "with the enthusiasm and zeal of the dedicated activist he would become." Which of the answers best paraphrases Gary's passionate views about national and world events? Choice (C) is the best answer since *cosmopolitan world view* summarizes Gary's global interests and *passion for politics* is another way of saying "the enthusiasm and zeal of the dedicated activist."

3. The passage tells you that the littoral zone "is the shallow water area where light reaches the bottom." Choice (E) is clearly the best answer since *has little depth* is a paraphrase for "shallow water area" and *easily penetrated by light* is a paraphrase for "where light reaches the bottom."

Critical Reading Exercise 7 provides you with an opportunity to recognize paraphrases and answer questions that use them.

CRITICAL READING PRACTICE EXERCISE 7 "Paraphrases"

DIRECTIONS: Carefully study each of the following passages. Look for answers that paraphrase words found directly in the text. Circle the correct answer.

Speculative risks hold forth the promise of gain or the chance of loss. Of major significance to businessmen is the speculative risk that arises from a changing price level. An increase in price level may bring a gain to one who holds a large inventory of goods; a decrease in price level may bring a loss.

from *Risk and Insurance* by Denenberg, Eilers, Hoffman, Kline, Melone, and Snider

1. According to the passage, which of the following is true of speculative risks?
   (A) They originate in individual events.
   (B) They are impersonal in origin and localized in consequences.
   (C) They are illegal in some states.
   (D) They involve the prospect for rewards and the risk of damages.
   (E) They apply only to merchants who own large stores.

Second, the laser beam is very uniform. Ordinary light is made up of photons of a variety of frequencies, while the laser beam is made up of nearly identical photons. It consists, therefore, of one tiny range of shades of one particular color. It is light that is essentially monochromatic (a term that comes from the Greek word meaning one color).

2. According to the passage, which of the following is true of laser beams?
   (A) They are unvarying and undisciplined.
   (B) They are consistent and have limited shades of one color.
   (C) They are dissimilar and have a variety of colors.
   (D) They are erratic and colorless.
   (E) They are uneven in quality and irregular in behavior.

The result of such commitment in Douglass's autobiography is a dual focus: one, public and social, setting forth to correct the moral and political ills arising from the fact of slavery; the other, personal and private, expressing Douglass's own thoughts, feelings, reactions, and emotions.

3. The author views Douglass's autobiography as being predominantly characterized by

    (A) an optimistic world view
    (B) a perplexing refusal to adjust to the realities of his era
    (C) a revealing discussion of the difficulties of writing an autobiography
    (D) a sense of personal entitlement
    (●) a mixture of social analysis and introspection

The ancient Sumerians worshipped over 3,000 gods. Archaeologists speculate that the Sumerians created clay dolls of their gods to help their children learn how to identify the various deities. The dolls thus functioned as learning tools and not as sacred objects to be venerated.

4. According to the passage, archaeologists speculate that the Sumerians used clay dolls of their gods as

    (●) tools for instruction
    (B) toys for amusement
    (C) idols to be revered
    (D) objects to be destroyed
    (E) instruments to be played

During the Reformation, leading theologians often displayed a penchant for endlessly disputing fine points of ceremony instead of concentrating upon the larger issue of rectifying corrupt practices.

5. According to the passage, leading theologians were often concerned with

    (A) reforming abuses in the Church
    (B) declaring high standards of spiritual conduct
    (●) arguing about trivial aspects of rituals
    (D) satirizing pompous priests
    (E) persecuting each other

As Temperate Zone people, we have long been ill-disposed toward deserts and expanses of tundra and ice. They have been wastelands for us; historically we have not cared at all what happened in them or to them. I am inclined to think, however, that their value will one day prove to be inestimable to us.

from *Arctic Dreams* by Barry Lopez

6. The author states that the Temperate Zone people view the uses made of "expanses of tundra and ice" with

(A) total apathy
(B) refined fascination
(C) confidence and satisfaction
(D) a view to the future
(E) a sense of awe

Putting It All TOGETHER

1 Your SAT will contain 4 reading passages and 40 critical reading questions.

2 The reading passages are drawn from the social sciences, natural sciences, humanities, and a variety of narrative sources.

3 Critical reading questions are not arranged in order of difficulty. However, they are usually presented in the order of their appearance in the passage.

4 *Active reading* means staying focused, asking mental questions, locating the main idea, and gaining a sense of the passage's overall structure.

5 Each SAT critical reading passage has a main idea. The main idea tells you what the passage is about or why the author wrote it.

6 The main idea of a passage is usually expressed in a topic sentence. Topic sentences can be located anywhere in a passage. The main idea of a hard passage is often found in the last paragraph. When looking for the main idea, carefully read the first paragraph, the first two sentences of each additional paragraph, and the final paragraph.

7 When answering main idea questions, immediately *ZAP* answers that are too broad, too narrow, or inaccurate. You need to think hard about the remaining choices.

8 Vocabulary-in-context questions are designed to test your ability to use contextual clues to determine the meaning of a word or phrase with multiple definitions. Your SAT will contain 4 to 7 vocabulary-in-context questions.

9 A paraphrase is a rewording or restatement of something that has been said or written. SAT writers often paraphrase the passage when they compose correct answers.

Answering Main Idea, Vocabulary-In-Context, and Paraphrase Questions

DIRECTIONS: Questions 1-8 are based on the following passage. The questions test your ability to find main ideas, answer vocabulary-in-context questions, and recognize paraphrased answers.

The following passage is based on information from a book written by two female historians about professional women who began their careers in science in the late nineteenth and early twentieth centuries.

The strong efforts to gain equality for women in the scientific workplace began to show results in the last quarter of the twentieth century; women have secured positions as research scientists and
Line won recognition and promotion within their fields. Though the
(5) modern struggle for equality in scientific fields is the same in many ways as it was in the early part of the century, it is also different. The women who first began undertaking careers in science had little support from any part of the society in which they lived. This vanguard had to struggle alone against the social conditioning they
(10) had received as women members of that society and against the male-dominated scientific community.

Women scientific researchers made a seemingly auspicious beginning. In the first quarter of the twentieth century, some women scientists who engaged in research worked at the most prestigious
(15) institutes of the period and enjoyed more career mobility than women researchers would experience again for several decades. Florence Sabin, an anatomist at the Rockefeller Institute of Medical Research noted for her research on the lymphatic system, is one important example. This encouraging beginning, however, was not
(20) to be followed by other successes for many decades. To have maintained an active role in research institutions, women would have had to share some of the decision-making power: they needed to be part of hiring, promotion, and funding decisions. Unfortunately, these early women scientists were excluded from the
(25) power structure of scientific research. As a result, they found it almost impossible to provide opportunities for a younger set of female colleagues seeking employment in a research setting, to foster their productivity and facilitate their career mobility, and eventually to allow them access to the top ranks.

(30) Even those with very high professional aspirations accepted subordinate status as assistants if doing so seemed necessary to gain access to research positions—and too often these were the only positions offered them in their chosen careers. Time and again they pulled back from offering any real resistance or challenge to the
(35) organizational structure that barred their advancement. But we must remember that these women scientists were few in number, their participation in decision-making positions was virtually nil,

and their political clout was minimal. Thus they could easily become highly visible targets for elimination from the staff,
(40) especially if their behavior was judged in the least imprudent.

Women's awareness that they were unequal colleagues, included in professional settings only on the sufferance of male colleagues, who held the positions of power, conflicted with their belief in meritocracy. They wanted to believe that achieving persons would
(45) be welcomed for their abilities and contributions. Yet they were surrounded by evidence to the contrary. An assistant professor of zoology observed that the men who were heads of departments were insistent on having other men in the department; they told her that women ought to be satisfied teaching high school. She relates
(50) that, during her ten years in the department, men were given at least six positions that she was qualified for and wanted desperately, but for which she was not even considered because she was a woman.

1. The passage is primarily concerned with

   (A) honoring the pioneering work of Florence Sabin
   (B) predicting the discoveries that leading women scientific researchers will make
   (C) explaining why leading women researchers opposed supporting a meritocracy
   (D) criticizing a zoology department for discriminating against women
   (E) describing the successes and problems of women who pursued scientific careers in the early twentieth century

2. In line 1, the word "strong" most nearly means

   (A) muscular
   (B) vigorous
   (C) courageous
   (D) forceful
   (E) highly flavored

3. In line 3, the word "secured" most nearly means

   (A) defended
   (B) freed from harm
   (C) guaranteed
   (D) gained possession of
   (E) tied down

4. In line 8, the word "support" most nearly means

   (A) promotion
   (B) help
   (C) boosting
   (D) bracing
   (E) financial aid

5. According to the passage, why were early women scientists unable to help younger female colleagues?

   (A) They were jealous of the younger women.
   (B) They were focused on their own career mobility.
   (●) They were barred from leadership positions.
   (D) They were unable to overcome the social conditioning from their youth.
   (E) They were unwilling to betray their belief in meritocracy.

6. Which of the following was NOT a reason why women refrained from challenging the organizational structure blocking their career advancement?

   (A) They lacked numerical strength.
   (B) They were denied fair access to legal remedies.
   (●) They were bound by a strict code of professional conduct.
   (D) They had little political influence.
   (E) They occupied almost no key administrative positions.

7. In line 47, the word "heads" most nearly means

   (A) geniuses
   (●) directors
   (C) fronts
   (D) sources
   (E) guides

8. The function of the final paragraph (lines 41-53) is to

   (●) illustrate the discrepancy between the ideal of meritocracy and the reality of male bias against women in scientific fields
   (B) point out the need to collect more evidence before drawing general conclusions
   (C) offer two different interpretations of how a meritocracy should function
   (D) compare and contrast the demands of teaching zoology in college and in high school
   (E) support the author's contention that women today face even more job discrimination than they did at the beginning of the twentieth century

Ascending the Staircase

CHAPTER 5
Vocabulary for Ascending the Staircase

CHAPTER 6
**Sentence Completions
for Ascending the Staircase**

CHAPTER 7
**Analogies for
Ascending the Staircase**

CHAPTER 8
Critical Reading for Ascending the Staircase

2

Vocabulary for Ascending the Staircase

After completing this chapter, you will be able to

1. give examples of words that begin with the prefixes IN-, IM-, UN-, and AB-.

2. define the roots LUC, LUMEN, ACRI, ACER, and FLU and give examples of words containing them.

3. recall what is meant by a synonym cluster.

4. give synonyms for *relieve, commonplace, introductory, temporary,* and *hasty.*

The Mighty Prefix, Part II

Every student should continually review the vocabulary presented in Chapter 1. Stress the idea that students must begin using their expanded vocabulary in their writing and daily conversations. They will not fully understand these new words until they are able to use them in context.

In Chapter 1 you learned that a prefix is a word part placed before a root in order to direct or change the root's meaning. As you saw, prefixes are valuable tools that can help you unlock the meaning of many words. So far, you have learned the meaning of the following prefixes.

1. E-/EX- = OUT, as in *exit, extinguish, extrovert, elusive, exorbitant, eminent,* and *expound.*

2. A-/AN- = NOT, as in *atypical, atheist, amorphous, atrophy, anonymous,* and *anomaly.*

3. RE- = BACK, AGAIN, as in *revoke, revitalize, renovate, resurge, redundant,* and *remuneration.*

In this lesson you'll learn three more key prefixes and 15 more key SAT words.

IN and IM ····▶ The Latin Way to Say NOT!

IN- is a Latin prefix meaning "not." IN- is one of the most often used prefixes on the SAT. It is important to note that IN- changes to IM- when it is attached to words and roots beginning with an M or P, as in *immature, immortal, impossible, impersonal,* and *imprecise.*

While IN- usually means "not," it is important to keep in mind that IN- can sometimes mean "with." For example, *insight* doesn't mean "not in sight." In this word, IN- means "with," so *insight* literally means "with great sight" and thus very perceptive. Most of the words in which IN- means "with" are very easy to recognize. The context in which the word is used will help you determine if IN- means "not" or "with." Here are six key SAT words in which the prefixes IN- and IM- mean "not."

1. *Interminable* – Do you remember the Terminator? He was a powerful android who put an end to all his enemies. *Terminate* means "to end." By attaching the prefix IN-, we create the word *interminable,* meaning "not having an end," or "endless."

   EXAMPLE: The trial was supposed to be short, but the prosecutor's *interminable* questions dragged out the proceedings for days.

2. *Incorrigible* – A person who is *corrigible* can be corrected or reformed. But someone who is *incorrigible* cannot be corrected or reformed.

   EXAMPLE: The *incorrigible* youth was finally expelled from school.

3. *Impious* – *Pious* is a word meaning "exhibiting reverence and earnest compliance with the observation of religious practices." *Impious* thus means "lacking reverence, disrespectful."

   EXAMPLE: His loud talking and other *impious* behavior offended many worshippers.

4. *Incorporeal* – Can you guess what the words *corpse* and *incorporeal* have in common? Both contain the Latin word *corpus*, meaning "body." A *corpse* thus refers to a dead body. *Incorporeal* means "having no body or substance."

   EXAMPLE: Many people believe that *incorporeal* beings exist and can influence human behavior.

5. *Intrepid* – *Trepidation* means "to tremble with fear." *Intrepid* thus means "having no fear." An *intrepid* person is therefore brave and courageous.

   EXAMPLE: The general praised the *intrepid* men and women who volunteered to take part in the dangerous mission.

6. *Inviolable* – When people *violate* a regulation or law, they break it. However, when something is *inviolable*, it is secure and cannot be violated.

   EXAMPLE: The United Nations Security Council guaranteed that the new countries' boundaries would be protected and therefore remain *inviolable*.

UN ····► The Old English Way to Say NOT!

UN- is an Old English prefix meaning "not." UN- is one of the most widely used prefixes in the English language. Here are five key SAT words that begin with UN-.

1. *Unfettered* – A *fetter* is a chain or shackle used to restrain prisoners. *Unfettered* means "not chained" and therefore free or liberated.

   EXAMPLE: Following the Civil War, many of the now *unfettered* former slaves tried to locate family members who had been sold to plantations in other states.

2. *Unfounded* – *Unfounded* means "lacking a sound basis." Something that is *unfounded* is groundless and thus untrue. *Unfounded* is part of an important synonym cluster that includes *unsubstantiated* and *unwarranted*.

   EXAMPLE: Stock prices rose as rumors of a crash proved to be *unfounded*.

3. *Unflappable* – *Flap* means "a state of excitement." *Unflappable* means "being calm, not showing excitement." A person with an *unflappable* appearance is controlled and unruffled.

   EXAMPLE: The defendant remained *unflappable* throughout the long and arduous trial.

4. *Unscathed* – *Scathe* means "to harm or injure." *Unscathed* thus means "unharmed, uninjured."

   EXAMPLE: Everyone was amazed that the passengers escaped *unscathed* from the terrible accident.

5. *Unorthodox* – *Orthodox* means "conforming to established doctrine." *Unorthodox* means the opposite, "not following established or traditional practices." Because they deviate from accepted norms, *unorthodox* people are often described as independent, radical, heretical, or even eccentric.

   EXAMPLE: While it may offend some people, *unorthodox* thinking can sometimes lead to important new insights.

AB ⸱⸱⸱▶ The Latin Way to Say Away From, Off.

1. *Abhor* – *Abhor* means "to intensely dislike someone or something." If you *abhor* someone, you want them as far away from you as possible.

   EXAMPLE: A pacifist *abhors* violence in any form.

2. *Abdicate* – *Abdicate* means "to surrender, to give away." History is filled with examples of rulers who *abdicated* their thrones.

   EXAMPLE: Edward VII of England *abdicated* his throne to marry a commoner.

3. *Abstain* – Have you ever turned down a dessert because you were trying to lose a little weight? If so, you *abstained* from eating the food. *Abstain* means "to voluntarily avoid, or stay away from, doing something."

   EXAMPLE: Vegetarians *abstain* from eating meat.

4. *Aberrant* – *Aberrant* means "not following" and thus being away from standard behavior. *Aberrant* can be used to describe an individual, group, or thing.

   EXAMPLE: The *aberrant* data forced the sociologist to conclude that the study was improperly conducted.

ODD WORD OUT

DIRECTIONS: Each question below consists of four words. Three of them are related in meaning. Circle the word that does not fit.

1. reverent   (impious)   devout   holy

2. intrepid   valiant   daring   (timid)

3. (substantiated) unfounded   baseless   unwarranted

4. calm   (agitated)   unfazed   unflappable

5. unorthodox   heretical   (conventional)   eccentric

6. loathe   disdain   abhor   (adore)

7. tractable   manageable   correctable   (incorrigible)

8. (unfettered)   restrained   confined   shackled

9. brief   ephemeral   temporary   (interminable)

10. (tangible)   incorporeal   immaterial   spiritual

MATCHING

DIRECTIONS: Match each word in the first column with its appropriate definition in the second column.

E	1. interminable		A.	groundless, untrue
H	2. abhor		B.	unreformable, past help
A	3. unfounded		C.	brave, bold, audacious
F	4. unscathed		D.	lacking material form or substance
B	5. incorrigible		E.	endless
I	6. abdicate		F.	safe, unharmed
J	7. unorthodox		G.	protected, secure, indestructible
C	8. intrepid		H.	dislike intensely, loathe
D	9. incorporeal		I.	surrender, give up
G	10. inviolable		J.	unconventional

APPLYING YOUR KNOWLEDGE

DIRECTIONS: In each of the items below, use your knowledge of the defined word to write a definition for the word in italics.

1. If PALATABLE means "acceptable to the palate or taste," what does *unpalatable* mean?

   not acceptable to the palate or taste

2. If MUTABLE means "changeable," what does *immutable* mean?

   not changeable or unable to change

3. If PARALLEL means "something equal or similar," what does *unparalleled* mean?

   something that has no equal

4. If NORMAL means "following a standard," what does *abnormal* mean?

not following a standard or deviating from the norm

5. If FAZED means "to disturb the composure of," what does *unfazed* mean?

to not be disturbed by something

Roots and Branches

If any of these words are unfamiliar, students should review pages 57–61.

In Chapter 1 you learned that a root is a word or word element from which other words are formed. As you saw, learning root families can be a very effective way of expanding your vocabulary. So far, you have learned five root families.

1. CORD = HEART, as in *cordial, accord,* and *discord.*

2. AMICUS = FRIEND, as in *amicable, amity,* and *amiable.*

3. GREG = GROUP, as in *gregarious, congregate, segregate, aggregate,* and *egregious.*

4. PATHOS = FEELINGS, as in *apathy, antipathy, sympathy,* and *empathy.*

5. FID = FAITH, as in *fidelity, confidant, diffident,* and *perfidious.*

In this lesson you will learn three more key roots and 14 more key SAT words.

Meet the LUC and LUMEN Families

They Will Light Up Your Life!

Students should cut pictures from magazines or newspapers and use them as stimulus materials to write descriptions of the events shown or to write interviews with the people shown. In their writing, they should use words from this lesson. Encourage them also to incorporate the vocabulary presented in Chapter 1.

LUC and LUMEN are Latin roots meaning "light." Here are four key members of this family.

1. *Lucid* – Since LUC means "light," *lucid* means "filled with light." Something that is lucid is clear.

   EXAMPLE: The witness persuaded the jury with her *lucid* account of what happened at the crime scene.

2. *Pellucid* – PEL- is derived from the prefix PER-, meaning "through." Something that is *pellucid* allows a maximum amount of light to pass through it. *Pellucid* thus means "crystal clear" and hence very easy to understand.

   EXAMPLE: After reading the convoluted writings of these amateur philosophers, I found your *pellucid* style very enjoyable.

3. *Elucidate* – The prefix E- means "out." *Elucidate* literally means "to bring out into the light" and thus make clear, or explain.

   EXAMPLE: The law professor is popular with students because of her ability to *elucidate* complex legal issues.

4. *Luminous* – The root LUMEN tells you that this word is bathed in light. *Luminous* means "giving off light, glowing."

   EXAMPLE: The sun is the most *luminous* body in the solar system.

Meet the ACRI and ACER Families

These Words Are Very Sharp

ACRI and ACER are Latin words meaning "sharp, very bitter." Here are five members of this family.

1. *Acute* – Quick, what is an *acute* angle? As you may recall from geometry, angles of less than 90 degrees are called *acute* angles. They are easily recognizable because they are sharply pointed. *Acute* is a prominent member of the ACER family. It can mean "sharp," as in an *acute* angle or an *acute* headache. It can also mean sharp in the sense of "keen or very perceptive."

   EXAMPLE: The writer was famous for his *acute* observations about human nature.

2. *Acumen* – *Acumen* refers to mental sharpness, keenness.

   EXAMPLE: Her business *acumen* should be a great asset to the company.

3. *Acid* – *Sharp* doesn't always have positive connotations. It can also mean "having a sharp, bitter taste." For example, would something that has an *acid* taste be palatable or unpalatable? Since *acid* means "sharp" in the sense of being bitter, it would definitely be unpalatable. While *acid* usually refers to a substance, it can also refer to a person's manner.

    EXAMPLE: His *acid* criticisms of my plan were unnecessary and hurt my feelings.

4. *Exacerbate* – *Exacerbate* combines the prefix EX-, meaning "out," and the root ACER, meaning "sharp, bitter." *Exacerbate* means "to make something out to be even more bitter."

    EXAMPLE: His insulting comments *exacerbated* relations between the two already hostile groups.

5. *Acrimonious* – The root ACRI tells you that this word will be filled with bitterness. *Acrimonious* means "full of spite, bitter, nasty."

    EXAMPLE: Relations between the rival candidates for class president became so *acrimonious* that each refused to speak to the other.

Meet the FLU Family

These Words Are Always in FLUX

FLU comes from the Latin word *fluvio*, meaning "river." FLU means "to flow." Here are five members of the FLU family.

1. *Fluent* – If a person is *fluent* in Spanish, does this mean that he or she knows or doesn't know how to speak Spanish? The root FLU, meaning "flow," tells you that the words flow naturally. *Fluent* means "flowing easily."

    EXAMPLE: After living in Mexico for three years, Paul spoke *fluent* Spanish.

2. *Confluence* – The prefix CON- means "with, together." *Confluence* means "to flow together."

    EXAMPLE: St. Louis is located at the *confluence* of the Missouri and Mississippi Rivers.

3. *Mellifluous* – *Melli* is a Latin word meaning "honey." *Mellifluous* literally means "to flow like honey." Today, *mellifluous* is used almost exclusively to describe voices, music, or sounds that flow sweetly.

    EXAMPLE: Megan's clarinet playing was *mellifluous*; the notes flowed smoothly and beautifully.

4. *Affluent* – *Affluent* means "to flow in abundance." Someone who is affluent is wealthy because he or she has an overflowing abundance of material goods.

   EXAMPLE: The pope called upon the world's *affluent* nations to increase their aid to countries with low standards of living.

5. *Superfluous* – The prefix SUPER- means "above." *Superfluous* means "to flow above" in the sense of exceeding what is necessary.

   EXAMPLE: The teacher cautioned his students to avoid *superfluous* details and instead concentrate on explaining the main ideas.

Using Your VOCABULARY

ODD WORD OUT

DIRECTIONS: Each question consists of four words. Three of them are related in meaning. Circle the word that does not fit.

1. (lucid)	ambiguous	muddled	convoluted
2. keen	penetrating	acute	(dull)
3. amiable	friendly	(acrimonious)	cordial
4. poor	(affluent)	destitute	impoverished
5. redundant	superfluous	excessive	(essential)
6. explain	elucidate	illustrate	(confuse)
7. comfort	(exacerbate)	relieve	soothe
8. (diverge)	confluence	link	juncture
9. hesitant	halting	(fluent)	stammering
10. harsh	(mellifluous)	discordant	raucous

RELATIONSHIPS

DIRECTIONS: For each question, decide whether the pair of words are synonyms (S), antonyms (A), or unrelated (U) to each other.

A	1. exacerbate	soothe
A	2. mellifluous	raucous
S	3. affluent	rich
S	4. elucidate	explain
U	5. luminous	perfidious
A	6. lucid	confused
A	7. acumen	stupidity
A	8. acute	obtuse
U	9. acrimonious	intrepid
S	10. confluence	convergence

COMPLETE THE HEADLINE

DIRECTIONS: The following headlines are taken from newspaper and magazine articles. Use one of the following five words to complete each headline: acrimony, lucid, acute, superfluous, affluent.

1. _____Lucid_____ Speech on Welfare Reform Wins Praise for Clarity

2. President Calls Crisis _____Acute_____, Urges Speedy Action

3. Renewed _____Acrimony_____ Between Owners and Players Stalls Contract Talks

4. Study Recommends That _____Affluent_____ Should Pay Higher Taxes

5. Governor Vetoes Bill Calling it Unnecessary and _____Superfluous_____

Synonym Clusters

To review these clusters (from pages 62–66), students should find and highlight these words in a magazine or newspaper article. Establish a bulletin board to post the articles.

In Chapter 1 you learned that a synonym cluster is a group of words that have similar meanings. So far, you have learned the following four synonym clusters.

1. The Thrill-of-Victory Cluster – exuberant, ebullient, exultant, elated, exhilarated, and ecstatic

2. The Agony-of-Defeat Cluster – despondent, dejected, dispirited, and disconsolate

3. The Stubborn Cluster – obstinate, obdurate, intransigent, recalcitrant, and dogged

4. The Secret Cluster – clandestine, surreptitious, stealthy, covert, and furtive

In this lesson you'll learn five more synonym clusters containing 23 key SAT words.

The Relieve Cluster

These Words Spell RELIEF

Have you ever taken an aspirin to relieve a headache or tried to soothe someone's anxieties? The English language provides us with several words to describe relief. Here are five members of the Relieve Cluster.

1. Alleviate – to relieve or lessen, as to *alleviate* pain

2. Allay – to relieve or lessen, as to *allay* someone's fears

3. Assuage – to relieve or lessen, as to *assuage* a person's grief

4. Mitigate – to relieve or lessen, as to *mitigate* a punishment

5. Mollify – to relieve or lessen, as to *mollify* someone's anger

The Commonplace Cluster

The Words Describe Clichés

Have you ever heard the sayings, "No pain, no gain," "When the going gets tough, the tough get going," and "Plan your work and work your plan"? These and other sayings have been repeated so many times that they become clichés. A *cliché* is something that is used so often that it

Use writing assignments to reinforce the use of SAT words in context. For example, given any set of ten vocabulary cards, write two paragraphs using as many of the words as possible.

becomes very familiar. The English language provides several words to describe commonplace sayings, things, and events. Here are four members of the Commonplace Cluster.

1. Trite – commonplace, as a *trite* plot

2. Banal – commonplace, as a *banal* lecture

3. Hackneyed – commonplace, as a *hackneyed* saying

4. Pedestrian – commonplace, as a *pedestrian* idea

The Introduction Cluster

These Words Get Things Started

What do the Preamble to the Constitution and an overture to a musical have in common? Both are formal *introductions*. Authors and composers frequently write introductions to their books, plays, laws, and musicals. Here are five members of the Introduction Cluster.

1. Preamble – an introduction to a constitution or law

2. Preface – an introductory statement to a book, article, or speech

3. Prologue – an introduction to a poem or play

4. Overture – an introduction to a musical

5. Prelude – an introduction to an opera or musical recital

The Temporary Cluster

These Words Are Short-Lived

Have you ever seen a beautiful rainbow or watched a colorful sunset? Although your memories of these events may last forever, the events themselves were short-lived. The English language provides us with several words to describe temporary events. Here are five members of the Temporary Cluster.

1. Momentary – temporary, short-lived

2. Ephemeral – temporary, short-lived

3. Evanescent – temporary, short-lived

4. Transient – temporary, short-lived

5. Fleeting – temporary, short-lived

The Hasty Cluster

These Words Do Things on the Spur of the Moment

Have you ever rushed into something without thinking it over? The English language provides us with several words to describe hasty actions that lack caution. Here are four key members of the Hasty Cluster.

1. Impetuous – hasty, lacking caution

2. Rash – hasty, lacking caution

3. Impulsive – hasty, lacking caution

4. Precipitate – hasty, lacking caution

Using Your VOCABULARY

ODD WORD OUT

DIRECTIONS: Each question below consists of four words. Three of them are related in meaning. Circle the word that does not fit.

1. (aggravate)   assuage   alleviate   mitigate

2. trite   (original)   banal   hackneyed

3. preface   preamble   (epilogue)   prologue

4. perpetual   (ephemeral)   permanent   enduring

5. (impetuous)   wary   deliberate   cautious

6. addendum   postscript   appendix   (overture)

7. (pedestrian)   imaginative   creative   original

8. exacerbate   (alleviate)   irritate   inflame

9. evanescent   fleeting   transient   (lasting)

10. impulsive   rash   (diligent)   precipitate

MATCHING

DIRECTIONS: Match each word in the first column with its appropriate definition in the second column.

C	1. trite	A. introduction to a constitution
D	2. assuage	B. rash, impetuous
B	3. impulsive	C. banal, commonplace
A	4. preamble	D. mollify, alleviate
E	5. ephemeral	E. fleeting, short-lived

RELATIONSHIPS

DIRECTIONS: For each question below, decide whether the pair of words are synonyms (S), antonyms (A), or unrelated (U) to each other.

U	1. hackneyed	inviolable
U	2. prologue	codicil
U	3. impetuous	lucid
S	4. evanescent	ephemeral
A	5. mollify	irritate
U	6. trite	acute
U	7. prologue	fluent
A	8. rash	wary
A	9. transient	sedentary
S	10. allay	alleviate

Sentence Completions for Ascending the Staircase

After completing this chapter, you will be able to

1. explain what is meant by a cause-and-effect word.

2. identify and answer cause-and-effect sentence completion questions.

3. explain what is meant by a support word.

4. use the synonym sentence strategy to solve sentence completion questions.

5. use the positive word/negative word strategy to answer sentence completion questions.

Cause-and-Effect Sentences

Every student should complete Chapter 2 prior to attacking these more advanced sentence completion questions. The strategies in this chapter build on the foundation established earlier.

In Chapter 2 you learned that your SAT will contain 19 sentence completion questions. As you read each sentence, your first step is to identify its key word or group of words. In some sentences the key word or group of words will be a definition. In others it will be a reversal word, such as *although*, *but*, or *however*, that signals a change in the flow of the sentence. Take a close look at the following three sentence completion questions. What signal word is used in all three sentences? How does this signal word affect each sentence?

1. The Food and Drug Administration rejected the experimental medicine because the patients who used it experienced ---- results.
   (A) nontoxic
   (B) refreshing
   (●) harmful
   (D) healthy
   (E) invigorating

2. Because he ---- many young artists, Renaissance scholars often describe Lorenzo de Medici as a patron of the arts.
   (●) supported
   (B) stifled
   (C) humiliated
   (D) rejected
   (E) regulated

3. Supporters of the new zoning law were ---- because there was no organized opposition to it within the community.
   (A) aggravated
   (B) interrupted
   (C) repudiated
   (D) weakened
   (●) relieved

Each sentence contains the signal word *because*. The word *because* signals the presence of a cause-and-effect relationship. For example, you are studying this book *because* you want to do well on the SAT. In Sentence 1, the *because* signals that there is a reason why the Food and Drug Administration rejected the experimental medicine. In Sentence 2, *because* signals that there is a reason why Renaissance scholars describe Lorenzo de Medici as a patron of the arts. And in Sentence 3, *because* signals that the lack of organized opposition had a positive impact upon supporters of the new zoning law.

The word *because* is by far the most frequently used cause-and-effect signal word. The list below gives the most commonly used signal words found in SAT sentence completion questions.

Key Cause-and-Effect Words

- BECAUSE
- IN ORDER TO
- AS A RESULT
- HENCE
- THEREFORE

- CONSEQUENTLY
- THUS
- WAS CAUSED BY
- DUE TO
- SINCE

As you might expect, sentences containing cause-and-effect words are called *cause-and-effect sentences*. In this type of sentence, the answer will be a word or words that provide a logical connection between a cause and an effect. For example, in the three previous sentences, the Food and Drug Administration would reject the experimental medicine *because* patients experienced *harmful* results; Renaissance scholars would describe Lorenzo de Medici as a patron *because* he *supported* young artists; and supporters of the new zoning law would be *relieved because* there was no organized opposition.

A Case Example

After completing this lesson, students should find sentences in published articles that fit the cause-and-effect format. By inserting appropriate blanks, students can construct sentence completion questions for their classmates.

As you read the following sentence completion question, first identify the cause-and-effect signal word. Then select the answer that fits the logic of the sentence.

> Because they had expected the spacecraft *Voyager 2* to be able to gather data only about the planets Jupiter and Saturn, scientists were ---- the wealth of information it sent back from Neptune 12 years after leaving Earth.
>
> (A) disappointed in
> (B) concerned about
> (C) confident in
> (D) elated by
> (E) anxious for

The signal word *because* alerts you to expect a cause-and-effect relationship. What impact did the information *Voyager 2* sent back about Neptune have upon the scientists? The first phrase in the sentence tells you that the scientists had expected to receive information only about Jupiter and Saturn. Because of this limited expectation, you could logically anticipate that they would be excited and happy about getting the additional information. With this understanding, you can *ZAP* (A), (B), and (E). Now you need to think hard about (C) and (D). The best choice is clearly (D).

DIRECTIONS: Here are three more cause-and-effect sentences. First locate and underline the cause-and-effect signal word or words. Then mark the answer that best fits the logic of the sentence.

1. The commission criticized the legislature for making college attendance dependent on the ability to pay, charging that, <u>as a result</u>, hundreds of qualified young people would be ---- further education.

   (A) entitled to
   (B) striving for
   (●) deprived of
   (D) uninterested in
   (E) participating in

2. <u>Because</u> their experimental findings are ----, the researchers have been praised for announcing a major breakthrough on the causes of cancer.

   (A) incomplete
   (●) indisputable
   (C) peculiar
   (D) contradictory
   (E) tentative

3. <u>Because</u> of the presence of so many ----, it was reasonable to expect immediate ---- the plan.

   (A) adversaries . . . embracing of
   (B) adherents . . . opposition to
   (C) supporters . . . resistance to
   (D) antagonists . . . agreement with
   (●) backers . . . support for

Guided PRACTICE

Discussion

1. The group of words *as a result* signals you to look for a cause-and-effect relationship. The first part of the sentence tells you that the legislature made *college attendance dependent on the ability to pay*. What impact do you think this will have on the ability of *qualified young people* to attend college? Would this action help or prevent young people from going to college? Since it would logically make it more difficult to go to college, you are looking for a word related somehow to restriction, obstruction, or loss of educational opportunity. The correct choice is (C).

2. The word *because* signals you to look for a cause-and-effect relationship. What quality of the experimental findings would result in researchers being praised *for announcing a major breakthrough on the causes of cancer*? Choices (A), (C), (D), and (E) would not result in praise for the researchers. On the other hand, *indisputable* experimental findings would be a cause for praise. The answer is (B).

3. When a cause-and-effect sentence contains two blanks, the missing words must combine to form a logical connection. Let's take a look at each answer choice.

    *   In this case, depending on what word goes in the first blank, any of the choices would fit the second blank. We need to look at both of the words together. Would you expect to find *adversaries* engaged in the *embracing of* the plan? No. *Adversaries* are opponents who would probably disagree with the plan. *ZAP* (A).

    *   Would it be reasonable to expect *adherents* to show immediate *opposition to* the plan? Of course not. *Adherents* would support the plan. *ZAP* (B).

    *   Would it be reasonable to expect *supporters* to show *resistance to* the plan? No. *Supporters* would defend the plan. *ZAP* (C).

    *   Would it be reasonable to expect *antagonists* to show *agreement with* the plan? No. *Antagonists* would more likely show hostility. *ZAP* (D).

    *   Would it be reasonable to expect *backers* to show *support for* the plan? Yes, it would. *Backers* would join together to *offer support* for the plan. Choice (E) is clearly the best answer.

Sentence Completion Practice Exercise 1 provides you with an opportunity to practice your skill of answering cause-and-effect sentences.

SENTENCE COMPLETION PRACTICE EXERCISE ① "Cause and Effect"

DIRECTIONS: First locate and underline the cause-and-effect signal word in each sentence. Then mark the answer that best completes the logic of the sentence.

1. Because no comprehensive ---- exist, we cannot positively identify the most prolific writer in human history.

    (A) cures
    (B) aptitudes
    (●) records
    (D) resolutions
    (E) advertisements

2. We gained confidence in Susan's leadership abilities because she always ---- the campaign promises she made.

    (A) forgot about
    (B) wearied of
    (C) withdrew from
    (D) reneged on
    (●) delivered on

3. As late as 1891, a speaker assured his audience that since profitable farming was the result of natural ability rather than learning, an education in agriculture was ----.

    (A) crucial
    (B) arduous
    (C) tedious
    (●) pointless
    (E) indispensable

4. The President's advisors are experiencing great difficulty in developing a consensus on welfare reform because their opinions are derived from such ---- sources.

    (A) similar
    (●) divergent
    (C) inconsequential
    (D) precise
    (E) candid

5. The paintings of contemporary abstract artists are often ---- the general public because the artists use abstract symbols that are deliberately ----.

    (●) incomprehensible to . . . obscure
    (B) insensitive to . . . obstinate
    (C) objectionable to . . . obsolete
    (D) supported by . . . obscene
    (E) denounced by . . . obvious

6. Unhappy customers complained that <u>because</u> of the ---- of the popular new automobile, dealers were charging ---- prices.

   (A) dearth . . . reasonable
   (B) surplus . . . excessive
   (C) popularity . . . equitable
   (D) obscurity . . . extravagant
   (●) scarcity . . . exorbitant

7. <u>Because</u> Marty Zweig's careful analysis of leading economic indicators made him almost ---- in his ability to predict changes in major stock averages, many investors ---- his financial advice.

   (A) perfect . . . ignored
   (B) foolproof . . . shunned
   (●) infallible . . . followed
   (D) undependable . . . accepted
   (E) unreliable . . . imitated

8. The historian's essay raised new questions on how Native Americans first reached North America <u>because</u> she ---- important parts of the archaeological record that other scholars have ----.

   (A) explores . . . noticed
   (B) ignores . . . considered
   (●) examines . . . neglected
   (D) mocks . . . ridiculed
   (E) tolerates . . . supported

9. Although supernovas are among the most ---- of cosmic events, these stellar explosions are often hard to ----, either <u>because</u> they are enormously far away or <u>because</u> they are dimmed by intervening dust and gas clouds.

   (A) remote . . . observe
   (●) luminous . . . detect
   (C) predictable . . . foresee
   (D) ancient . . . determine
   (E) violent . . . disregard

10. Ernest Hemingway's prose is noted for its ---- <u>because</u> he rarely uses a ---- word or group of words.

    (A) eloquence . . . comprehensible
    (B) ingenuity . . . clever
    (C) ambiguity . . . vague
    (●) economy . . . superfluous
    (E) arrogance . . . vain

Synonym Sentences

In Chapter 2 you learned that words such as *but, although,* and *however* are reversal words that signal a contrast or change of direction in a sentence. In Lesson 4 in this chapter, you learned that words such as *because, consequently,* and *therefore* signal a cause-and-effect relationship in a sentence. Now take a look at the following three sentence completion questions. What signal word is used in all three sentences? How does this signal word affect each sentence?

1. Churchill urged an uncompromising and ---- attitude with Hitler, rather than the policy of appeasement advocated by Neville Chamberlain.
    (A) flexible
    (B) resolute
    (C) desperate
    (D) docile
    (E) obedient

2. The long drought left the once fertile fields barren and ----.
    (A) luxuriant
    (B) productive
    (C) soggy
    (D) arid
    (E) lush

3. Outgoing and ---- by nature, Ursula became even more gregarious at the company party.
    (A) affable
    (B) reclusive
    (C) solitary
    (D) belligerent
    (E) deceptive

Each sentence contains the signal word *and.* The word *and* signals that you are looking for an answer that supports or continues a thought. The answer is often a synonym or closely related word. For example, in Sentence 1 *resolute* is synonymous with *uncompromising*; in Sentence 2 *arid* is synonymous with *barren*; and in Sentence 3 *affable* is synonymous with *outgoing*.

And is by far the most frequently used support signal word. The list below gives the most commonly used support signal words used on the SAT. Sentence completion questions in which these words play a key role are called *synonym sentences*.

Key Support Signal Words

- AND
- ALSO
- ADDITIONALLY
- SINCE
- MOREOVER
- AS WELL AS
- FURTHERMORE
- INDEED

A Case Example

After completing this lesson, students should find and highlight supporting signal words in newspaper and magazine articles. By inserting appropriate blanks, they can construct their own sentence completion questions.

As you read the following sentence completion question, first identify the support signal word. Next identify the key word that is linked with the support word. Then select an answer that is synonymous with or closely related to the key word.

> Though few and ----, the provisions were sufficient to sustain the stranded travelers until the search party located them.
>
> (A) abundant
> (B) intrepid
> (C) inept
> (D) toxic
> (E) meager

The signal word *and* alerts you to look for a word that is closely related to *few*. If you know the meanings of *abundant* (plentiful), *intrepid* (courageous), *inept* (unskilled), and *toxic* (poisonous), you can ZAP (A), (B), (C), and (D). Choice (E) is the correct answer because *meager* (having a limited supply) is the only choice that supports *few*.

Guided
PRACTICE

DIRECTIONS: Here are three more synonym sentences. First locate and underline the support signal word. Next identify and circle the key word that is linked with the support word. Then mark an answer that is synonymous or closely related to the key word.

1. Theatergoers across America fell in love with the play's (charming) and ---- heroine.
   - (A) bland
   - (B) vivacious
   - (C) lethargic
   - (D) merciless
   - (E) erratic

2. Since the king believed his prime minister to be both ---- and (trustworthy,) he refused to consider the possibility that his advisor could be a traitor.
   - (A) perfidious
   - (B) deceitful
   - (C) seditious
   - (D) steadfast
   - (E) elusive

3. In temperament they were radically different: the older man was (quiet) and ----; the younger was ---- and (uninhibited.)
   - (A) reserved . . . raucous
   - (B) aloof . . . restrained
   - (C) harsh . . . restless
   - (D) taciturn . . . laconic
   - (E) agitated . . . noisy

Guided PRACTICE

Discussion

1. The signal word *and* alerts you to look for a word that is closely related to *charming*. Choices (A), (C), (D), and (E) can all be ZAPPED since *bland* means "unoriginal," *lethargic* means "lazy," *merciless* means "ruthless," and *erratic* means "unstable." Only choice (B), *vivacious* (full of life), complements *charming* and fits the logic of the sentence.

2. Before looking at the choices, you should get an indication from the sentence that you're looking for a positive character trait. (If you don't get this idea, you're not reading the sentence carefully.) With this idea in mind, you can ZAP (A), (B), (C), and (E).

   Unfortunately, for many students the words in this problem are very difficult. If you don't know that *perfidious* means "treacherous," *deceitful* means "dishonest," *seditious* means "rebellious," and *elusive* means "hard to catch," all you can do is ZAP the words you do know and then select from the leftovers. Since *steadfast* fits the general meaning of the sentence, you should choose (D) even if you're not sure of some of the other words.

3. The signal word *and* is used twice in this sentence. In the first instance, it signals you to look for a word that is closely related to *quiet*. Choices (C) and (E) can be ZAPPED since the words *harsh* and *agitated* are not related to *quiet*. The second use of *and* signals you to look for a word that is closely related to *uninhibited*. Choices (B) and (D) can be ZAPPED since *restrained* and *laconic* do not support or complement *uninhibited*. After ZAPPING, your only choice is (A). Since *reserved* means "aloof and shy," it complements *quiet*. And since *raucous* means "loud and noisy," it complements *uninhibited*.

Sentence Completion Practice Exercise 2 provides an opportunity to practice your skill of answering synonym sentences.

SENTENCE COMPLETION PRACTICE EXERCISE ② "Synonyms"

DIRECTIONS: First locate and underline the support signal word. Next identify the key word that is linked with the support word. Then mark the answer that is synonymous with or closely related to the key word.

1. Japan is famous for its violent typhoons, which are perhaps the most dramatic examples of the ---- and tempestuous weather conditions in the area.

   (A) decorous
   (B) fragile
   (C) placid
   (D) turbulent
   (E) ephemeral

2. Though her demeanor with most people is carefree, those who know her insist she is actually serious and ---- in private.

   (A) frivolous
   (B) flippant
   (C) unfettered
   (D) subdued
   (E) boisterous

3. Copernicus' revolutionary heliocentric theory removed the earth from the center of the solar system, thus stirring up disagreement and even ---- among his contemporaries.

   (A) antagonism
   (B) harmony
   (C) amity
   (D) banter
   (E) empathy

4. As part of their struggle for national and religious unity, Ferdinand and Isabella established the Inquisition, a powerful tribunal charged with suppressing heresy and ----.

   (A) conformity
   (B) unorthodoxy
   (C) modesty
   (D) diffidence
   (E) decorum

5. Because of their carnivorous and ---- nature, sharks are perhaps the most feared creatures in the ocean.

   (A) erratic
   (B) exuberant
   (C) pragmatic
   (D) apprehensive
   (E) predatory

6. Maya Angelou has always been generous in her praise and ---- of young writers.

   (A) ridicule
   (B) derision
   (C) encouragement
   (D) sarcasm
   (E) caricature

7. T. S. Eliot was often a subtle writer who made telling points through indirection and ----.

   (A) elaboration
   (B) audacity
   (C) adulation
   (D) intransigence
   (E) allusion

8. Having chosen the rigors of an ascetic life, he dedicated himself to the twin goals of sanctity and ----.

   (A) hedonism
   (B) self-denial
   (C) extravagance
   (D) revenge
   (E) dominance

9. Despite the priority the manager placed on consensus, his assistants continued to argue and ---- over petty details.

   (A) concur
   (B) harmonize
   (C) exult
   (D) unwind
   (E) quibble

10. Scientists rejected the radical new theory saying it rested on incomplete and ---- data that had not been fully tested.

    (A) reliable
    (B) substantial
    (C) definitive
    (D) authoritarian
    (E) misleading

Using Positive and Negative Words

SAT sentence completion questions frequently use challenging vocabulary words and complex sentence structures. As a result, even the best students will not always be sure of the answer to each question.

If you are having trouble answering a sentence completion question, don't give up. There are effective strategies you can use to *ZAP* distracters and zero in on the correct answer.

A Strategy for Using Positive and Negative Words

Stress the idea that this strategy requires concentration and practice. Although it will take considerable time in the beginning, the strategy will later tend to speed up the problem-solving process.

Suppose a friend said to you, "I don't recommend the movie, it was long and ——." What word would you put in the missing blank? Words like *boring*, *dull*, and *monotonous* quickly come to mind. Why is that? Why didn't words like *exciting*, *interesting*, and *entertaining* come to mind?

The answer, of course, is that your friend specifically said, "I don't recommend the movie." As a result, you expect to hear negative words that explain this statement. If your friend said, "I strongly recommend the movie," you would expect to hear positive words to explain this statement.

Like your everyday conversations, SAT sentence completion questions often use positive and negative words. Knowing this can help you master some of the toughest sentence completion questions on the SAT. Here's a three-step strategy for using positive and negative words.

1. First, use contextual clues to determine if the missing word (or words) is most likely a *positive* word or a *negative* word. A positive word is one with good connotations, while a negative word is one with bad connotations. As you determine the meaning of the sentence, write a positive sign (+) in the blank if it requires a positive word or a negative sign (–) if it requires a negative word.

2. Second, write a positive or negative sign next to each of the answer choices.

3. Third, match the symbols you placed in the sentence blanks with the symbols you placed beside the choices.

A Case Example

Let's apply this three-step procedure to the following example.

> The critic liked nothing about the movie; she called the plot ---- and the acting ----.
>
> (A) dreary . . . inspiring
> (B) trite . . . dazzling
> (C) exhilarating . . . enthralling
> (D) stirring . . . unprofessional
> (E) tedious . . . amateurish

STEP 1   **Use** contextual clues to determine if the missing word or words are positive or negative. This sentence clearly tells you that *the critic liked nothing about the movie. Liked nothing* is the key group of words. It tells you that both blanks will require negative words. Write negative symbols (–) in each blank.

STEP 2   **Write** positive or negative symbols beside each answer choice.

(A) *Dreary* means "gloomy and depressing" and is a negative word. *Inspiring* means "stimulated, filled with motivation" and is a positive word.

(B) *Trite* means "commonplace" and is a negative word. *Dazzling* means "electrifying" and is a positive word.

(C) *Exhilarating* means "filled with enthusiasm" and is a positive word. *Enthralling* means "fascinating" and is a positive word.

(D) *Stirring* means "deeply moving" and is a positive word. *Unprofessional* means "lacking the standards of a profession or job" and is a negative word.

(E) *Tedious* means "very boring" and is a negative word. *Amateurish* means "lacking in experience or expertise" and is a negative word.

STEP 3   **Find** answer symbols that match the sentence symbols. Since we are looking for a negative-negative combination, you can ZAP any of the answers that include positive words. You should ZAP (A), (B), (C), and (D). Even if you don't know what *enthralling* means, you can still ZAP (C) because *exhilarating* is a positive word. The best answer is (E).

Guided
PRACTICE

DIRECTIONS: Here are three more practice examples. Let's use the three-step procedure to answer each question.

1. No one is neutral about Davis; he inspires either uncritical ---- from his supporters or profound ---- from his opponents.
    - (A) adulation . . . antipathy
    - (B) enthusiasm . . . exuberance
    - (C) apathy . . . revulsion
    - (D) condemnation . . . veneration
    - (E) disgust . . . aversion

STEP 1

Use contextual clues to determine if the missing word or words are positive or negative. The sentence tells you that people have two very different views of Davis. The group of words *from his supporters* tells you that the first blank will require a positive word. The group of words *from his opponents* tells you that the second blank will require a negative word.

STEP 2

Write positive and negative symbols beside each answer choice.
- (A) *Adulation* means "to greatly admire" and is a positive word. *Antipathy* means "great dislike" and is a very negative word.
- (B) *Enthusiasm* and *exuberance* both mean "great excitement" and are positive words.
- (C) *Apathy* means "indifferent" and is a negative word. *Revulsion* means "intense dislike" and is a negative word.
- (D) *Condemnation* means "to express strong disapproval" and is a negative word. *Veneration* means "to show great respect" and is a positive word.
- (E) Both *disgust* and *aversion* mean "intense dislike" and are negative words.

STEP 3

Find answer symbols that match the sentence symbols. Since you are looking for a positive-negative combination, you can *ZAP* choices (B), (C), (D), and (E). Note that since *condemnation* is a negative word, choice (D) can be *ZAPPED* even if you don't know what *veneration* means. Only choice (A) provides the correct combination of a positive word followed by a negative word.

2. As a result of her long career and many controversial positions, the Senator's popularity has swung between overwhelming ---- and wide-spread rejection.

(A) disapproval
(B) criticism
(C) approbation
(D) dismissal
(E) disfavor

STEP 1

Use contextual clues to determine if the missing word or words are positive or negative. The sentence tells us that the Senator's popularity has *swung* because of her *many controversial positions*. Since we are told she has experienced widespread rejection, we can assume that the blank requires a positive word.

STEP 2

Write positive and negative symbols beside each answer choice.

(A) *Disapproval* is clearly a negative word.
(B) *Criticism* is clearly a negative word.
(C) *Approbation* means "strong approval" and is thus a positive word.
(D) *Dismissal* is clearly a negative word.
(E) *Disfavor* is clearly a negative word.

STEP 3

Find the answer symbol that matches the sentence symbol. Since choices (A), (B), (D), and (E) are all negative words, they can be ZAPPED. The only choice left is (C). Note that you can correctly answer this question even if you don't know what *approbation* means.

Guided
PRACTICE

3. Although the novel was bold and ----, the movie version disappointed many viewers who thought it was ---- and bland.

   (A) obsolete . . . captivating
   (B) distinctive . . . unique
   (C) routine . . . commonplace
   (D) innovative . . . conventional
   (E) exciting . . . appealing

STEP 1

Use contextual clues to determine if the missing word or words are positive or negative. The sentence contrasts the characteristics of a novel with its movie version. The support word *and* tells you to look for a positive word that complements *bold*. Since the movie version *disappointed many viewers*, you can assume that the second blank calls for a negative word to complement *bland*.

STEP 2

Write positive or negative symbols beside each answer choice.
   (A) *Obsolete* means "out-of-date" and is a negative word. *Captivating* means "fascinating" and is a positive word.
   (B) *Distinctive* and *unique* are both positive words meaning "one of a kind."
   (C) *Routine* and *commonplace* are both negative words meaning "ordinary."
   (D) *Innovative* means "new, creative," and is a positive word. *Conventional* means "ordinary" and is a negative word.
   (E) *Exciting* and *appealing* are both positive words.

STEP 3

Find the answer symbols that match the sentence symbols. You can ZAP choices (A), (B), (C), and (E) because they do not fit the required positive-negative pattern. The best answer is (D).

Developing an Extra Edge

Remind students that **ZAPPING** doesn't always give them the correct answer; it simply narrows the choices.

1. The positive word/negative word strategy can be a very effective way to ZAP many wrong choices. While you may not always be able to ZAP four choices, you can frequently ZAP two or three. As long as you can ZAP at least one choice, you should guess from the remaining choices.

2. The positive word/negative word strategy is a very powerful technique. However, it is important to remember that it cannot be applied to every sentence completion question.

Sentence Completion Practice Exercise 3 provides you with an opportunity to practice your skill of using the positive word/negative word strategy to answer sentence completion questions.

SENTENCE COMPLETION PRACTICE EXERCISE 3 *"Positive/Negative"*

DIRECTIONS: Use the three-step procedure to answer each of the following sentence completion questions.

1. Since it was first published in 1848, reaction to the *Communist Manifesto* has oscillated between complete -±- and outright hostility.

   (A) antagonism
   (B) devotion
   (C) disregard
   (D) repudiation
   (E) condescension

2. Although the feeding activities of whales and walruses give the seafloor of the Bering Shelf a devastated appearance, these activities seem to be actually -±- to the area, -±- its productivity.

   (A) destructive . . . counterbalancing
   (B) rehabilitative . . . diminishing
   (C) beneficial . . . enhancing
   (D) detrimental . . . redirecting
   (E) superfluous . . . encumbering

3. Far from being a ---- area as the first settlers feared, the Great Plains turned out instead to contain an abundance of -±- land.

   (A) barren . . . fertile
   (B) desolate . . . arid
   (C) productive . . . fruitful
   (D) sterile . . . dry
   (E) luxuriant . . . poor

4. Although the passage of time has softened the overwhelmingly hostile reaction to his paintings, even now only a few independent observers -±- his works.

   (A) denounce
   (B) applaud
   (C) reprove
   (D) disapprove
   (E) avoid

5. Upton Sinclair's book *The Jungle*, which graphically exposed the -=- and unsanitary practices in meat-packing plants, is widely credited with having -±- the muckraking movement of the early 1900's.

   (A) nutritious . . . retarded
   (B) unhealthy . . . promoted
   (C) hygienic . . . stymied
   (D) hazardous . . . hindered
   (E) beneficial . . . launched

6. Monica was acutely aware of how easily the -±- she currently enjoyed as a celebrity could vanish and become indifference or even -=-.

   (A) affection . . . warmth
   (B) rewards . . . reverence
   (C) reprimands . . . loathing
   (D) disdain . . . esteem
   (E) attention . . . boredom

7. Eric was neither loyal nor devoted but was as -=- and -=- a man as I have ever met.

   (A) perfidious . . . treacherous
   (B) reliable . . . dutiful
   (C) traitorous . . . allegiant
   (D) dependable . . . faithless
   (E) rebellious . . . scrupulous

8. Seeking to settle the strike, the mediator proposed several compromises which -=- leaders on both sides refused to consider much less accept.

   (A) conciliatory   (D) obdurate
   (B) reasonable   (E) skillful
   (C) concerned

9. Although Henry VIII began his reign as -±- leader who hoped to accomplish great deeds, he ended as a -=- ruler who ruthlessly imposed his will upon the English people.

   (A) a hedonistic . . . vicious
   (B) a lethargic . . . philanthropic
   (C) an enlightened . . . humane
   (D) a benevolent . . . tyrannical
   (E) a cruel . . . compassionate

10. Though she modestly refused to accept any credit, Sonal was actually -±- who knew every detail about the project.

    (A) a demagogue   (D) a tyrant
    (B) a master   (E) a novice
    (C) an apprentice

Putting It All
TOGETHER

1) There will be 19 sentence completion questions on your SAT. Each question consists of a sentence in which one or two words have been deliberately omitted. Your job is to select the one or two words that best complete the sentence.

2) Each sentence completion question has a key word or phrase that will help guide you to the correct answer.

3) Signal words such as *because, in order to,* and *as a result of* indicate that the sentence will involve a cause-and-effect relationship.

4) Signal words such as *and, also,* and *furthermore* indicate that you are looking for an answer that supports or continues a thought. The answer is often a synonym or closely related thought.

5) Many SAT sentence completion questions use positive and negative words. Use contextual clues to determine if the missing word (or words) is a positive word or a negative word. Place a positive sign (+) in the blank that requires a positive word and a negative sign ( ) in the blank requiring a negative word. Next place a positive or negative symbol beside each of the answer choices. Then match the +/− symbols you placed in the sentence blanks with the +/− symbols you placed beside the answers.

Answering Definition, Contrast, Cause-and-Effect, and Synonym Sentences

DIRECTIONS: The 10 sentence completion questions in this exercise illustrate all four types of sentences you have studied so far. First underline all signal words. Then circle the key word or phrase in each sentence. Draw a line from the key word or phrase to the correct answer.

1. Animals that have tasted unpalatable plants tend to ---- them afterward on the basis of their most conspicuous features, such as their flowers.

   (A) recognize
   (B) hoard
   (C) trample
   (D) retrieve
   (E) approach

2. During his adventures as the captain of the Golden Hind, Francis Drake proved to be a resourceful and ---- leader who overcame many obstacles and ----.

   (A) intrepid . . . benefits
   (B) accomplished . . . advantages
   (C) timid . . . difficulties
   (D) inept . . . imitations
   (E) resilient . . . hardships

3. The defense attorney passionately argued that the charges against her client were fabricated and therefore ----.

   (A) lucid
   (B) fastidious
   (C) unfounded
   (D) corroborated
   (E) ancient

4. Since she believed him to be both candid and trustworthy, she refused to consider the possibility that his statements had been ----.

   (A) critical
   (B) satirical
   (C) honorable
   (D) insincere
   (E) genuine

5. As a result of Damon's ---- assertions the discussion quickly deteriorated into a (an) ---- name-calling contest.

    (A) antagonistic . . . amiable
    (B) belligerent . . . acrimonious
    (C) jovial . . . antagonistic
    (D) idealistic . . . affable
    (E) perceptive . . . cordial

6. Since her philosophy draws liberally on several traditions and methodologies, it can justifiably be termed ----.

    (A) paradoxical
    (B) patriotic
    (C) conventional
    (D) heretical
    (E) eclectic

7. The professor's lecture covered all the salient points so effectively that any additional commentary would be ----.

    (A) redundant
    (B) impulsive
    (C) warranted
    (D) essential
    (E) persuasive

8. Always ----, she never acted in a spontaneous or ---- manner.

    (A) deliberate . . . cautious
    (B) wary . . . prudent
    (C) impetuous . . . careful
    (D) prudent . . . impulsive
    (E) unpredictable . . . planned

9. Although the report had initially seemed to be legitimate, further investigation revealed that it was based upon ---- data that had been improperly collected.

    (A) spurious
    (B) notable
    (C) sound
    (D) verified
    (E) impressive

10. Like most ---- writing, this pamphlet presented a one-sided and ---- view of the issue.

    (A) passionate . . . fair
    (B) balanced . . . partial
    (C) polemic . . . biased
    (D) vernacular . . . objective
    (E) anecdotal . . . hurried

7

Analogies for Ascending the Staircase

After completing this chapter, you will be able to

1. recall the three-step procedure for solving an analogy.

2. identify and solve *Relative Size* analogies.

3. identify and solve *Is Characteristic Of* analogies.

4. identify and solve *Antonym* analogies.

5. identify and solve *Definitional* analogies.

"Relative Size" Analogies

Reviewing Analogies

Every student should complete Chapter 3 prior to attacking these more advanced analogy questions. The strategies in this chapter build on the foundation established earlier.

In Chapter 3 you learned that each SAT contains 19 analogies. Begin each analogy question by first establishing a clear relationship between the two stem words. Then form a short specific sentence connecting the stem words. After you apply your sentence to each of the choices, select the answer that best matches your sentence. By using this three-step strategy to attack analogies, you avoid the added effort of determining a relationship between the words in every choice.

Most SAT analogies can be grouped into nine basic types of relationships. If you've mastered the material in Unit 1, you have already learned to identify and solve the following four types of analogies.

- IS A TYPE OF   e.g. ELBOW : JOINT
- IS A PART OF   e.g. WORD : LANGUAGE
- IS A PLACE WHERE   e.g. COURTROOM : LAWYER
- IS USED TO   e.g. SPONGE : ABSORB

Identifying *RELATIVE SIZE* Analogies

Analogy Relationship 5

Take a close look at the following six analogies.

- hill : mountain
- puddle : pond
- river : creek
- ripple : tidal wave
- flood : trickle
- breeze : hurricane

What type of relationship do these six analogies have in common? All six illustrate a type of analogy called *Relative Size*. This type of analogy is easy to spot. The SAT writers provide you with two objects or things, one of which is smaller (or larger) than the other.

Is Smaller (or Larger) Than is the connection that solves each of these six analogies.

- a hill *is smaller than* a mountain
- a puddle *is smaller than* a pond
- a river *is larger than* a creek
- a ripple *is smaller than* a tidal wave
- a flood *is larger than* a trickle
- a breeze *is smaller than* a hurricane

A Case Example

Let's apply our three-step procedure to the following analogy.

POND : LAKE ::

(A) shirt : fabric
(B) hill : mountain
(C) clay : potter
(D) mile : distance
(E) valley : river

STEP 1 **Relate** the stem words and form a sentence connecting them. POND : LAKE is a good example of a *Relative Size* analogy. We can form a sentence connecting POND and LAKE by saying, "A POND is smaller than a LAKE." Note that we could also read the analogy from right to left by saying, "A LAKE is larger than a POND."

STEP 2 **Apply** this sentence to each of the answer choices.

(A) shirt : fabric	Is a shirt smaller than a fabric? No. There is a relationship between shirt and fabric, but you don't need to waste time thinking about it. What is clear is that your original connecting sentence doesn't make any sense. *ZAP* (A).
(B) hill : mountain	Is a hill smaller than a mountain? Yes. As always, let's check the other choices.
(C) clay : potter	Is clay smaller than a potter? Again, there is a relationship, but the connecting sentence doesn't make any sense. *ZAP* (C).
(D) mile : distance	Is a mile smaller than a distance? No. *ZAP* (D).
(E) valley : river	Is a valley smaller than a river? No. *ZAP* (E).

STEP 3 **Select** the answer that best matches your original sentence. In this example, (B) is the only choice that makes sense. It is the correct answer.

Guided PRACTICE

DIRECTIONS: Here are three more *Relative Size* analogies. Use our three-step process to find the correct answers.

1. BREEZE : GALE ::

   (A) surf : shore
   (B) decibel : sound
   (C) flower : plant
   (D) cloudburst : rainfall
   (●) trickle : flood

2. METROPOLIS : CITY ::

   (A) precaution : danger
   (●) highway : street
   (C) heart : muscle
   (D) crown : tree
   (E) nightmare : sleep

3. HOLE : CAVE ::

   (A) pencil : eraser
   (B) tunnel : mountain
   (C) fence : gate
   (●) ripple : tidal wave
   (E) fault : earthquake

Analogy 1

Relate the stem words and then form a sentence connecting them. BREEZE : GALE is an example of a *Relative Size* analogy. We can form a sentence connecting BREEZE and GALE by saying, "A BREEZE is smaller than a GALE."

Apply this sentence to each of the answer choices.

Discussion

(A)	surf : shore	Is a surf smaller than a shore? No. *ZAP* it.
(B)	decibel : sound	Is a decibel smaller than a sound? If you know that a decibel is a measure of sound, you can *ZAP* this choice. Otherwise, leave it for now.
(C)	flower : plant	Is a flower smaller than a plant? No. *ZAP* it.
(D)	cloudburst : rainfall	Is a cloudburst smaller than a rainfall? This is sort of connected but not too clear. Leave it for now.
(E)	trickle : flood	Is a trickle smaller than a flood? Yes. This looks very attractive.

Select the answer that best matches your original sentence. In this example, the answer is (E) because "A BREEZE is smaller than a GALE in the same way as a TRICKLE is smaller than a FLOOD."

Analogy 2

Relate the stem words and then form a sentence connecting them. METROPOLIS : CITY is another example of a *Relative Size* analogy. We can form a sentence connecting METROPOLIS and CITY by saying, "A METROPOLIS is larger than a CITY."

Apply this sentence to each of the answer choices.

(A)	precaution : danger	Is a precaution larger than a danger? No. *ZAP* it.
(B)	highway : street	Is a highway larger than a street? Yes. But let's look at the other choices.
(C)	heart : muscle	Is a heart larger than a muscle? No. *ZAP* it.
(D)	crown : tree	Is a crown larger than a tree? This will trick many students who are thinking about the skyline of a big city because the crown is the top of the tree. It's an attractive SAT trap.
(E)	nightmare : sleep	Is a nightmare larger than a sleep? No. *ZAP* it.

Select the answer that best matches your original sentence. In this example, the answer is (B) since "A METROPOLIS is larger than a CITY in the same way as a HIGHWAY is larger than a STREET."

Analogy 3

Relate the stem words and then form a sentence connecting them. HOLE : CAVE is another example of a *Relative Size* analogy. We can form a sentence connecting HOLE and CAVE by saying, "A HOLE is smaller than a CAVE."

Apply this sentence to each of the answer choices.

(A)	pencil : eraser	Is a pencil smaller than an eraser? No. *ZAP* it.
(B)	tunnel : mountain	Is a tunnel smaller than a mountain? There is a relationship, but not one based on size. *ZAP* it.

(C) fence : gate — Is a fence smaller than a gate? This could be trouble because you might remember seeing low fences with towering gate posts. Leave it for now.

(D) ripple : tidal wave — Is a ripple smaller than a tidal wave? Yes. As always, let's compare it to the other choices.

(E) fault : earthquake — Is a fault smaller than an earthquake? No. *ZAP* it.

Select the answer that best matches your original sentence. In this example, you'll need to think hard about (C) and (D). The answer is (D) because "A HOLE is smaller than a CAVE in the same way as a RIPPLE is smaller than a TIDAL WAVE."

Developing an Extra Edge

1. *Relative Size* analogies often use concrete geographic terms. As a result, it is often possible to make a visual image of the stem words and the answer choices. For example, take a look at the pictures below showing a POND and a LAKE and a HILL and a MOUNTAIN. They graphically illustrate the analogy that "A POND is smaller than a LAKE in the same way as a HILL is smaller than a MOUNTAIN." Try using your mind's eye to visualize the analogy that "A HOLE is smaller than a CAVE in the same way as a RIPPLE is smaller than a TIDAL WAVE."

2. *Relative Size* analogies typically occur in the early part of the middle third of a set of analogies. They are typically the second or third question in a set of six analogies and the third to fifth questions in a set of 13 analogies.

Independent
PRACTICE

Analogy Practice Exercise 5 provides you with 10 more *Relative Size* analogies. Use the three-step process to answer each one. Remember, practice is the first step in building confidence.

ANALOGY PRACTICE EXERCISE ⑤ "Relative Size"

DIRECTIONS: For each question, first write a sentence linking the stem words. Then mark the correct answer.

1. DITCH : CANYON ::

   (A) sun : cloud
   (B) eye : hurricane
   (C) gulf : coast
   (D) puddle : lake
   (E) tunnel : mine

   A ditch is smaller than a canyon.
   _____
   _____
   _____
   _____

2. SQUALL : BREEZE ::

   (A) cloudburst : drizzle
   (B) forest : trail
   (C) bridge : river
   (D) swamp : water
   (E) prairie : grass

   A squall is larger than a breeze.
   _____
   _____
   _____
   _____

3. HILL : MOUNTAIN ::

   (A) crest : wave
   (B) breeze : hurricane
   (C) highway : road
   (D) harbor : port
   (E) hail : ice

   A hill is smaller than a mountain.
   _____
   _____
   _____
   _____

4. GULLY : RAVINE ::

   (A) peak : mountain
   (B) director : cast
   (C) cloud : rain
   (D) portal : arch
   (E) pebble : boulder

   A gully is smaller than a ravine.
   _____
   _____
   _____
   _____

5. DRIZZLE : DELUGE ::

   (A) breeze : typhoon
   (B) tree : root
   (C) sunshine : warmth
   (D) gusher : oil
   (E) forest : fire

   A drizzle is smaller than a deluge.
   _____
   _____
   _____
   _____

6. SQUABBLE : FIGHT ::

   (A) song : repertoire
   (B) lecture : assignment
   (●) tiff : quarrel
   (D) exclamation : state
   (E) puncture : tire

A squabble is smaller than a fight.

_____

_____

_____

7. FLURRY : BLIZZARD ::

   (A) lightening : thunder
   (B) forest : tree
   (C) gust : breeze
   (D) beach : sand
   (●) drizzle : downpour

A flurry is smaller than a blizzard.

_____

_____

_____

8. SPECK : STAIN ::

   (A) desert : oasis
   (B) beach : wave
   (C) drench : damp
   (D) breath : inhale
   (●) trickle : torrent

A speck is smaller than a stain.

_____

_____

_____

9. CONFLAGRATION : CAMPFIRE ::

   (A) misdemeanor : crime
   (●) city : village
   (C) injunction : court
   (D) dearth : surplus
   (E) fruit : jam

A conflagration is larger than a campfire.

_____

_____

10. ABYSS : DITCH ::

   (A) alley : street
   (B) peak : roof
   (●) mountain : knoll
   (D) spray : foam
   (E) plateau : land

An abyss is larger than a ditch.

_____

_____

_____

"Is Characteristic Of" Analogies

Identifying *IS CHARACTERISTIC OF* Analogies

Analogy Relationship 6

Take a close look at the following six analogies.

- braggart : boastful
- daredevil : reckless
- coward : fearful
- egoist : selfish
- bigot : biased
- optimist : hopeful

Remind students that these strategies require study and practice before they can be applied in an actual testing situation.

What type of relationship do these six analogies have in common? All six illustrate a type of relationship called *Is Characteristic Of*. An *Is Characteristic Of* analogy presents you with a person and his or her most characteristic or defining attribute.

Is Characteristic Of is the connecting phrase that solves each of the six analogies listed above.

- being BOASTFUL is the defining *characteristic of* a BRAGGART
- being RECKLESS is the defining *characteristic of* a DAREDEVIL
- being FEARFUL is the defining *characteristic of* a COWARD
- being SELFISH is the defining *characteristic of* an EGOIST
- being BIASED is the defining *characteristic of* a BIGOT
- being HOPEFUL is the defining *characteristic of* an OPTIMIST

ZAP SOMETIMES and *COULD BE* Distracters

Take a close look at the following three possible answers.

- pirate : merciless
- salesclerk : courteous
- warrior : reckless

Do you think these are examples of *Is Characteristic Of* analogies? Remember, the test of an *Is Characteristic Of* analogy is that it must provide the person's defining characteristic. In the first example, although pirates are *sometimes* merciless, being merciless is not a *defining characteristic of* a pirate. Therefore, it is possible for a pirate to sometimes be merciful. Similarly, in the second example, salesclerks are often courteous. But is being courteous a *defining characteristic* of a salesclerk? No, because it is possible for a salesclerk to *sometimes* be rude. And finally, warriors are *sometimes* reckless. But is being reckless a *defining characteristic* of a warrior? No, because successful warriors usually tend to be cautious.

A Case Example

Let's apply our three-step procedure to the following analogy.

MISER : STINGY ::

(A) laborer : idle
(B) amateur : expert
(C) coward : brave
(D) liar : compulsive
(E) dunce : ignorant

STEP **1**   **Relate** the stem words and then form a sentence connecting them. A MISER is by definition a greedy, stingy person who hoards money. Thus, "Being STINGY is characteristic of a MISER."

STEP **2**   **Apply** this sentence to each of the answer choices.

(A) laborer : idle	Is being idle characteristic of a laborer? *ZAP* (A).
(B) amateur : expert	Is being an expert characteristic of an amateur? No. If someone's an expert, they won't be called an amateur. *ZAP* (B).
(C) coward : brave	Is being brave characteristic of a coward? Quite the opposite. *ZAP* it.
(D) liar : compulsive	Is being compulsive characteristic of a liar? This choice will trick many students because they will think of the idea of a *compulsive liar*. It's a bad choice, but leave it for now.
(E) dunce : ignorant	Is being ignorant characteristic of a dunce? Yes. A dunce is by definition someone who is ignorant. Excellent choice.

STEP **3**   **Select** the answer that best matches your original sentence. In this example, you need to consider (D) and (E). The answer is (E) because "Being STINGY is characteristic of a MISER in the same way that being IGNORANT is characteristic of a DUNCE."

Guided PRACTICE

DIRECTIONS: Here are three more *Is Characteristic Of* analogies. Use our three-step process to find the correct answers.

1. OPTIMIST : HOPEFUL ::

   (A) braggart : boastful
   (B) oaf : graceful
   (C) liar : truthful
   (D) soldier : peaceful
   (E) athlete : cheerful

2. RASH : HOTHEAD ::

   (A) prompt : procrastinator
   (B) kind : tyrant
   (C) cautious : daredevil
   (D) foolish : simpleton
   (E) abusive : critic

3. EXPLORER : CURIOSITY ::

   (A) acrobat : agility
   (B) student : knowledge
   (C) scientist : integrity
   (D) artist : fame
   (E) rebel : obedience

Analogy 1

Relate the stem words and then form a sentence connecting them. OPTIMIST : HOPEFUL is an example of an *Is Characteristic Of* analogy. Using this phrase, we can form a sentence connecting OPTIMIST and HOPEFUL by saying, "Being HOPEFUL is characteristic of an OPTIMIST."

Apply this sentence to each of the answer choices.

Discussion

(A)	braggart : boastful	Is being boastful characteristic of a braggart? Yes. But, as always, let's check the remaining answers.
(B)	oaf : graceful	Is being graceful characteristic of an oaf? If you're not sure what an *oaf* is, leave this for now. Otherwise, you could *ZAP* (B) because an oaf is rarely graceful.
(C)	liar : truthful	Is being truthful characteristic of a liar? Of course not. *ZAP* it.

(D) soldier : peaceful   Is being peaceful characteristic of a soldier? A soldier's profession is to fight. *ZAP* it.

(E) athlete : cheerful   Is being cheerful characteristic of an athlete? An athlete could be cheerful, but that's not the quality that defines an athlete. *ZAP* (E).

Select the answer that best matches your original sentence. In this example, you need to think about (A) and (B) if you don't know the meaning of *oaf*. Since (A) fits quite well, you should select it; "Being HOPEFUL is characteristic of an OPTIMIST in the same way as being BOASTFUL is characteristic of a BRAGGART."

Analogy 2

Relate the stem words and then form a sentence connecting them. RASH : HOTHEAD is an example of an *Is Characteristic Of* analogy. Using this phrase, we can form a sentence connecting RASH and HOTHEAD by saying, "Being RASH is characteristic of a HOTHEAD."

Apply this sentence to each of the answer choices.

(A) prompt : procrastinator   Is being prompt characteristic of a procrastinator? If you know both of these words, you can *ZAP* (A). Otherwise, leave it for now.

(B) kind : tyrant   Is being kind characteristic of a tyrant? Absolutely not. *ZAP* (B).

(C) cautious : daredevil   Is being cautious characteristic of a daredevil? No. *ZAP* (C).

(D) foolish : simpleton   Is being foolish characteristic of a simpleton? Yes. Let's check the remaining choice.

(E) abusive : critic   Is being abusive characteristic of a critic? Sometimes, but not always. You can *ZAP* (E).

Select the answer that best matches your original sentence. In this example, the answer is (D) because "Being RASH is characteristic of a HOTHEAD in the same way as being FOOLISH is characteristic of a SIMPLETON."

Analogy 3

Relate the stem words and then form a sentence connecting them. EXPLORER : CURIOSITY is another example of an *Is Characteristic Of* analogy. Using this phrase, we can form a sentence connecting EXPLORER and CURIOSITY by saying, "CURIOSITY is characteristic of an EXPLORER."

Apply this sentence to each of the answer choices.

   (A) acrobat : agility   Is agility characteristic of an acrobat? Yes, but let's keep checking.

   (B) student : knowledge Is knowledge characteristic of a student? This will attract many test takers because they relate being a student with getting more knowledge. Sometimes students have knowledge, but not always. You can leave this for now, but it's not as good as choice (A).

   (C) scientist : integrity   Is integrity characteristic of a scientist? Only sometimes. *ZAP* (C).

   (D) artist : fame   Is fame characteristic of an artist. Again, only sometimes. *ZAP* (D).

   (E) rebel : obedience   Is obedience characteristic of a rebel? No. *ZAP* it.

Select the answer that best matches your original sentence. In this example, the answer is (A) since "CURIOSITY is characteristic of an EXPLORER in the same way as AGILITY is characteristic of an ACROBAT."

Developing an Extra Edge

1. *Is Characteristic Of* analogies are rarely found in the easy third of a set of analogies. However, they are a popular choice in the middle third.

2. *Is Characteristic Of* analogies are very easy to spot. The stem and each of the answers contain a person. This list of people tells you that you are being asked to solve an *Is Characteristic Of* analogy.

3. Don't be tricked into choosing an answer in which you can use the words *sometimes* and *could be*. These words are a signal that the answer is a distracter that should be *ZAPPED*.

Analogy Practice Exercise 6 provides you with 10 more *Is Characteristic Of* analogies. Use the three-step process to answer each one. Remember, practice is the first step in building confidence.

ANALOGY PRACTICE EXERCISE 6 "Is Characteristic Of"

DIRECTIONS: For each question, first write a sentence linking the stem words. Then mark the correct answer.

1. VETERAN : EXPERIENCE ::   Experience is characteristic of a veteran.

   (A) soldier : bravery
   (B) child : curiosity
   (C) physician : practice
   (D) expert : skill
   (E) actor : fame

2. MISER : GREED ::   Greed is characteristic of a miser.

   (A) traitor : loyalty
   (B) cynic : trust
   (C) judge : partiality
   (D) rebel : defiance
   (E) coward : courage

3. ZEALOT : ENTHUSIASM ::   Enthusiasm is characteristic of a zealot.

   (A) sage : wisdom
   (B) mentor : enmity
   (C) guest : rudeness
   (D) prophet : frigidity
   (E) egoist : humility

4. CYNIC : DISTRUSTFUL ::   Being distrustful is characteristic of a cynic.

   (A) hypocrite : insincere
   (B) author : prolific
   (C) optimist : uncertain
   (D) extrovert : bashful
   (E) loafer : energetic

5. DEXTERITY : JUGGLER ::   Dexterity is characteristic of a juggler.

   (A) modesty : braggart
   (B) honesty : politician
   (C) flexibility : accountant
   (D) sincerity : merchant
   (E) agility : acrobat

6. PHILANTHROPIST : GENEROUS ::

    (A) loafer : industrious
    (B) miser : thrifty
    (C) idealist : pragmatic
    (D) enthusiast : idle
    (E) adolescent : likable

Being generous is characteristic of a philanthropist.

_____

_____

7. PAUPER : DESTITUTE ::

    (A) defendant : honest
    (B) exhibitionist : embarrassed
    (C) adherent : loyal
    (D) cynic : generous
    (E) nomad : stationary

Being destitute is characteristic of a pauper.

_____

_____

8. TARDY : LAGGARD ::

    (A) eloquent : minister
    (B) thankful : ingrate
    (C) tolerant : bigot
    (D) evil : benefactor
    (E) energetic : dynamo

Being tardy is characteristic of a laggard.

_____

_____

_____

9. HEDONIST : PLEASURE ::

    (A) exhibitionist : attention
    (B) pacifist : belligerence
    (C) pessimist : adventure
    (D) seditionist : obedience
    (E) abolitionist : dominance

Seeking pleasure is characteristic of a hedonist.

_____

_____

10. PERFIDIOUS : TRAITOR ::

    (A) gregarious : recluse
    (B) diffident : genius
    (C) amiable : coach
    (D) impetuous : hothead
    (E) despondent : gambler

Being perfidious is characteristic of a traitor.

_____

_____

_____

"Antonym" Analogies

Identifying *ANTONYM* Analogies

Analogy Relationship 7

Take a look at the following six analogies.

- purify : contaminate
- eternity : end
- doubt : conviction
- arid : fertile
- inane : significance
- peerless : equal

Point out that the SAT once included an entire section on "opposites" which has been eliminated on the new SAT. On the new test, the opposites, or antonyms, tend to appear frequently in the analogy section.

What type of relationship do you think these six analogies have in common? All six illustrate a type of relationship called *Antonym* or opposites. An *Antonym* analogy provides you with a pair of words that are nearly opposite in meaning. Once you have determined that the stem words are antonyms, examine the answer choices and select another pair of antonyms.

The simplest way to phrase the relationship between two antonyms is to say, "Word 1 *is the opposite of* Word 2." For example, "PURIFY is the opposite of CONTAMINATE."

Many *Antonym* analogies can also be connected by using the phrases *is without*, *lack of*, or *won't*. In the examples listed above, ETERNITY won't END, DOUBT is the lack of CONVICTION, ARID is without FERTILE soil, INANE is without SIGNIFICANCE, and PEERLESS is without EQUAL.

A Case Example

Let's apply our three-step procedure to the following analogy.

VETERAN : ROOKIE ::
- (A) epic : story
- (B) comedian : amusement
- (C) bread : crumb
- (D) principal : school
- (E) old-timer : newcomer

 STEP **1**

Relate the stem words and then form a sentence connecting them. Since a VETERAN has experience and a ROOKIE lacks experience, "VETERAN is the opposite of ROOKIE."

STEP **2** **Apply** this sentence to each of the answer choices.

(A) epic : story	Is an epic the opposite of a story? No, it's just a special type of lengthy story or poem. *ZAP* (A).
(B) comedian : amusement	Is a comedian the opposite of an amusement? No. *ZAP* it.
(C) bread : crumb	Is bread the opposite of crumb? No. *ZAP* it.
(D) principal : school	Is principal the opposite of school? No. *ZAP* it.
(E) old-timer : newcomer	Is an old-timer the opposite of a newcomer? Sort of. An old-timer has experience and a newcomer doesn't.

STEP **3** **Select** the answer that best matches your original sentence. In this example, the answer is (E) since "A VETERAN is the opposite of a ROOKIE in the same way as an OLD-TIMER is the opposite of a NEWCOMER."

Guided PRACTICE

DIRECTIONS: Here are three more *Antonym* analogies. Let's use our three-step process to find the correct answers.

1. ANONYMOUS . NAME ..

   (A) informal : style
   (B) vast : area
   (C) analogous : parallel
   (D) aimless : goal
   (E) fleeting : fame

2. PERPETUAL : STOP ::

   (A) brittle : break
   (B) immobile : move
   (C) perishable : spoil
   (D) incredible : grow
   (E) elastic : stretch

3. RASH : PATIENCE ::

   (A) adroit : skill
   (B) authentic : validity
   (C) ridiculous : laughter
   (D) merciful : forgiveness
   (E) ambivalent : conviction

Analogy 1

Relate the stem words and then form a sentence connecting them. Since *anonymous* means "to be without a known name," ANONYMOUS : NAME is an *Antonym* analogy.

Apply this sentence to each of the answer choices.

Discussion

(A)	informal : style	Is informal without style? Not really. Informal is more of a casual style. Depending on your certainty, you could leave this or *ZAP* it.
(B)	vast : area	Is vast without area? No. *ZAP* (B).
(C)	analogous : parallel	Is analogous without parallel? If you know both words, you can *ZAP* this choice. Otherwise, leave it for now.
(D)	aimless : goal	Is aimless without a goal? Yes. By definition aimless is without a goal. As always, let's check the final choice.
(E)	fleeting : fame	Is fleeting without fame? No. This choice will attract many students only because these two words are often associated with each other. *ZAP* it.

Select the answer that best matches your original sentence. In this example, the answer is (D) since "ANONYMOUS is without a NAME in the same way as AIMLESS is without a GOAL."

Analogy 2

Relate the stem words and then form a sentence connecting them. Since *perpetual* means "to last or endure forever," PERPETUAL : STOP is an *Antonym* analogy that can be expressed as "PERPETUAL won't STOP."

Apply this sentence to each of the answer choices.

(A)	brittle : break	Are brittle and break antonyms? No. *ZAP*.
(B)	immobile : move	Are immobile and move antonyms? Yes. Something immobile won't move. As always, let's check the remaining choices.
(C)	perishable : spoil	Are perishable and spoil antonyms? No. *ZAP* (C).
(D)	incredible : grow	Are incredible and grow antonyms? No. *ZAP* (D).
(E)	elastic : stretch	Are elastic and stretch antonyms? Something elastic will stretch. They are not opposites. *ZAP* (E).

Select the answer that best matches your original sentence. In this example, the answer is (B) since "PERPETUAL won't STOP in the same way as IMMOBILE won't MOVE."

Analogy 3

Relate the stem words and then form a sentence connecting them. Since *rash* means "to act in a hasty, impulsive manner," RASH : PATIENCE is an *Antonym* analogy that can be expressed as "RASH lacks PATIENCE."

Apply this sentence to each of the answer choices.

(A) adroit : skill	Does adroit lack skill? No. *ZAP* (A).
(B) authentic : validity	Does authentic lack validity? No. *ZAP*!
(C) ridiculous : laughter	Does ridiculous lack laughter? No. Something ridiculous might cause laughter. It doesn't lack laughter.
(D) merciful : forgiveness	Does merciful lack forgiveness? No. *ZAP* (D).
(E) ambivalent : conviction	Does ambivalent lack conviction? Yes. Ambivalent means to have conflicting feelings toward a person or thing.

Select the answer that best matches your original sentence. In this example, the answer is (E) since "RASH lacks PATIENCE in the same way as AMBIVALENT lacks CONVICTION."

Developing an Extra Edge

1. *Antonym* analogies can be found at all levels of difficulty. However, they are an especially popular choice for the middle level analogies. Overall, about 10 percent of all SAT analogies fall into this category.

2. Most *Antonym* analogies can be connected by the words *lack*, *without*, and *won't*. However, it is often enough to simply recognize that the stem words are opposite in meaning. Then look for an answer choice that is also opposite in meaning.

Analogy Practice Exercise 7 provides you with 10 more *Antonym* analogies. Use the three-step process to answer each one. Remember, practice is the first step in building confidence.

ANALOGY PRACTICE EXERCISE 7 "Antonyms"

DIRECTIONS: For each question, first write a sentence linking the stem words. Then mark the correct answer.

1. BEGINNING : END ::

   (A) chapter : book
   (B) birth : life
   (C) dawn : day
   (D) greeting : farewell
   (E) proposal : suggestion

   The beginning is the opposite of the end.

2. REQUEST : INJUNCTION ::

   (A) ask : reply
   (B) suggest : order
   (C) praise : honor
   (D) leave : departure
   (E) chat : discussion

   An injunction is an order, which is the opposite of a request.

3. BARREN : FERTILITY ::

   (A) juvenile : maturity
   (B) cautious : timidity
   (C) inhuman : cruelty
   (D) spontaneous : originality
   (E) ambitious : inferiority

   To be barren is to lack fertility.

4. EXTRAVAGANT : RESTRAINT ::

   (A) trivial : importance
   (B) obvious : apparition
   (C) resilient : maturity
   (D) stoic : patience
   (E) enormous : size

   An extravagant person is without restraint.

5. APATHETIC : EMOTION ::

   (A) unconcerned : indifference
   (B) ambitious : promotion
   (C) doubtful : conviction
   (D) brilliant : talent
   (E) artistic : success

   An apathetic person is without emotion.

6. EXORBITANT : MODERATION ::   Something exorbitant lacks

    (A) stagnant : stillness   moderation.
    (B) brief : significance
    (C) momentary : fame
    (D) mobile : movement
    (E) arid : fertility

7. PERFIDIOUS : LOYALTY ::   A perfidious person is without loyalty.

    (A) culpable : guilt
    (B) amorphous : shape
    (C) heterogeneous : variety
    (D) despondent : dejection
    (E) ingenious : design

8. INTRACTABLE : COMPROMISE ::   An intractable person won't

    (A) durable : last   compromise.
    (B) clever : think
    (C) arbitrary : decide
    (D) modest : boast
    (E) guilty : repent

9. LETHARGIC : ENERGY ::   Being lethargic is the opposite of

    (A) exotic : interest   having energy.
    (B) gigantic : size
    (C) ebullient : enthusiasm
    (D) premeditative : intent
    (E) despondent : hope

10. DESULTORY : DIRECTION ::   A desultory person lacks direction.

    (A) ambitious : promotion
    (B) wise : intelligence
    (C) nefarious : virtue
    (D) zealous : passion
    (E) generous : taste

"Definitional" Analogies

Identifying *DEFINITIONAL* Analogies

Analogy Relationship 8

Take a close look at the following six analogies.

- birth : life
- captain : ship
- linguistics : speech

- amiable : company
- embezzle : money
- obstinate : persuade

What type of relationship do you think these six analogies have in common? All four illustrate a type of analogy called *Definitional*. In this type of analogy, SAT writers provide you with a word and a part of its definition. Your job is to fill in the blanks to make a complete definition. In the above examples, BIRTH is the beginning of LIFE, a CAPTAIN is in charge of a SHIP, LINGUISTICS is the study of SPEECH, an AMIABLE person loves COMPANY, EMBEZZLE is to steal MONEY, and OBSTINATE is hard to PERSUADE.

A Case Example

Let's apply our three-step procedure to the following analogy.

CREST : WAVE ::
(A) frame : picture
(B) summit : mountain
(C) step : ladder
(D) floor : wall
(E) delta : river

STEP 1

Relate the stem words and then form a sentence connecting them. By definition, "A CREST is the top of a WAVE."

STEP 2

Apply this sentence to each of the answer choices.

(A) frame : picture	Is a frame the top of a picture? No. *ZAP!*
(B) summit : mountain	Is a summit the top of a mountain? Yes. But, as always, let's check the remaining answers.
(C) step : ladder	Is a step the top of a ladder? No. *ZAP* (C).

(D) floor : wall   Is a floor the top of a wall? No.
                          ZAP (D).

(E) delta : river   Is a delta the top of a river? If you're
                          not sure, leave this for now.

STEP **Select** the answer that best matches your original sentence. In this example, the answer is (B) since "A CREST is the top of a WAVE in the same way as a SUMMIT is the top of a MOUNTAIN."

DIRECTIONS: Here are three more *Definitional* analogies. Let's use our three-step process to find the correct answers.

1. CURATOR : MUSEUM ::
    (A) critic : theater
    (B) nurse : hospital
    (C) guest : hotel
    (D) lawyer : courtroom
    (E) captain : ship

2. EMBARK : JOURNEY ::
    (A) conclude : activity
    (B) interrupt : performance
    (C) launch : mission
    (D) receive : gift
    (E) reject : membership

3. PSYCHOLOGY : BEHAVIOR ::
    (A) aesthetics : health
    (B) meteorology : rocks
    (C) plagiarism : ideas
    (D) etymology : insects
    (E) dynamics : motion

Analogy 1

Relate the stem words and then form a sentence connecting them. CURATOR : MUSEUM is a good example of a *Definitional* analogy since "A CURATOR is in charge of a MUSEUM."

Apply this sentence to each of the answer choices.

(A)	critic : theater	Is a critic in charge of a theater? No. *ZAP* (A).
(B)	nurse : hospital	Is a nurse in charge of a hospital? No. *ZAP* (B).
(C)	guest : hotel	Is a guest in charge of a hotel? No. *ZAP* (C).
(D)	lawyer : courtroom	Is a lawyer in charge of a courtroom? No. *ZAP* (D).
(E)	captain : ship	Is a captain in charge of a ship? Yes. By definition, a captain is in charge of a ship.

Discussion

Select the answer that best matches your original sentence. In this example, the answer is (E) since "A CURATOR is in charge of a MUSEUM in the same way as a CAPTAIN is in charge of a SHIP."

Analogy 2

Relate the stem words and then form a sentence connecting them. EMBARK : JOURNEY is a good example of a *Definitional* analogy, since "To EMBARK is to begin a JOURNEY."

Apply this sentence to each of the answer choices.

(A)	conclude : activity	Does conclude mean to begin an activity. No. *ZAP!*
(B)	interrupt : performance	Does interrupt mean to begin a performance? No. *ZAP!*
(C)	launch : mission	Does launch mean to begin a mission? Yes. But, as always, let's check the remaining choices.
(D)	receive : gift	Does receive mean to begin a gift? No. *ZAP* this choice.
(E)	reject : membership	Does reject mean to begin a membership? No. *ZAP* (E).

Select the answer that best matches your original sentence. In this example, the answer is (C) since "To EMBARK is to begin a JOURNEY in the same way as to LAUNCH is to begin a MISSION."

Analogy 3

Relate the stem words and then form a sentence connecting them. PSYCHOLOGY : BEHAVIOR is a good example of a *Definitional* analogy since "PSYCHOLOGY is the study of BEHAVIOR."

Apply this sentence to each of the answer choices.

(A) aesthetics : health — Is aesthetics the study of health? No. *ZAP* it.

(B) meteorology : rocks — Is meteorology the study of rocks? No. *ZAP* (B).

(C) plagiarism : ideas — Is plagiarism the study of ideas? If you know these words, you can *ZAP* (C), otherwise leave it for now.

(D) etymology : insects — Is etymology the study of insects? Tricky, but you can easily *ZAP* (D) if you're a proficient etymologist.

(E) dynamics : motion — Is dynamics the study of motion? Yes.

Select the answer that best matches your original sentence. In this example, the answer is (E) since "PSYCHOLOGY is the study of BEHAVIOR in the same way as DYNAMICS is the study of MOTION."

Developing an Extra Edge

1. *Definitional* analogies can be found at all levels of difficulty. However, they are an especially popular choice for the middle and difficult thirds.

2. *Definitional* analogies are the most popular type of analogy. Approximately 40 percent of all analogies fit into this category.

Analogy Practice Exercise 8 provides you with 10 more *Definitional* analogies. Use the three-step process to answer each one. Remember, practice is the first step in building confidence.

ANALOGY PRACTICE EXERCISE 8 "Definitional"

DIRECTIONS: For each question, first write a sentence linking the stem words. Then mark the correct answer.

1. ALLURING : RESIST ::

   (A) elusive : catch
   (B) fragile : break
   (C) vivid : imagine
   (D) perishable : waste
   (E) valuable : steal

   Something alluring is hard to resist.

2. PROLOGUE : PLAY ::

   (A) suffix : word
   (B) climax : story
   (C) chapter : book
   (D) location : address
   (E) preamble : document

   A prologue is an introduction to a play.

3. SAVORY : TASTE ::

   (A) offensive : odor
   (B) vanilla : flavor
   (C) inaudible : sound
   (D) fragrant : smell
   (E) discordant : voice

   Something savory has a pleasant taste.

4. SYLLABUS : COURSE ::

   (A) codicil : will
   (B) rule : game
   (C) journal : trip
   (D) agenda : meeting
   (E) overture : opera

   A syllabus is an outline of a course.

5. ELEGY : SORROW ::

   (A) diatribe : approval
   (B) eulogy : praise
   (C) parody : esteem
   (D) epic : shame
   (E) fable : awe

   An elegy expresses sorrow.

6. ALLEVIATE : PAIN ::

   (A) allay : anxiety
   (B) deviate : norm
   (C) terminate : discussion
   (D) inflame : hatred
   (E) evade : issue

   To alleviate is to lessen pain.

   _____

   _____

   _____

   _____

7. PROTAGONIST : STORY ::

   (A) moral : fable
   (B) paragraph : essay
   (C) subject : painting
   (D) demagogue : prejudice
   (E) flashback : novel

   A protagonist is the main character in a

   story.

   _____

   _____

8. FASTIDIOUS : PLEASE ::

   (A) docile : manage
   (B) obstinate : persuade
   (C) practical : utilize
   (D) young : rejuvenate
   (E) lucid : understand

   Someone who is fastidious is hard to please.

   _____

   _____

   _____

9. TIRADE : BITTER ::

   (A) cliché : creative
   (B) skit : lengthy
   (C) quibble : trivial
   (D) quotation : tedious
   (E) harangue : complimentary

   A tirade is speech that has a bitter quality.

   _____

   _____

   _____

10. EXPLICATE : ELABORATION ::

    (A) substantiate : evidence
    (B) confiscate : wealth
    (C) debilitate : strength
    (D) fabricate : information
    (E) alleviate : fear

    To explicate is to provide elaboration.

    _____

    _____

    _____

Putting It All
TOGETHER

1 There will be 19 analogies on your SAT. One 30-minute section will have a set of 13 analogies and one 30-minute section will have a set of 6 analogies.

2 Each analogy consists of a pair of stem words and five pairs of answers.

3 Begin each analogy by establishing a clear relationship between the two stem words. Then form a short, specific sentence connecting the stem words. Next apply your sentence to each of the answer choices. Select the answer that best matches your sentence.

4 In *Relative Size* analogies, the SAT writers provide you with two objects or things, one of which is smaller (or larger) than the other.

5 In *Is Characteristic Of* analogies, the SAT writers provide you with a person and his or her most characteristic or defining attribute.

6 In *Antonym* analogies, the SAT writers provide you with a pair of words that are opposite in meaning.

7 In *Definitional* analogies, the SAT writers provide you with a word and a part of its definition.

Answering Relative Size, Is Characteristic Of, Antonym, and Definitional Analogies

DIRECTIONS: The following 10 analogies illustrate six of the eight types of analogies you have studied thus far. First fill-in the blank with a short specific sentence connecting the stem words. Then circle the answer that best matches your sentence.

1. MOCCASIN : FOOTWEAR ::   A moccasin is a type of footwear.

   (A) pattern : dress
   (B) frame : picture
   (C) beret : cap
   (D) bone : skeleton
   (E) belt : waist

2. DOWNPOUR : RAIN ::   A downpour is a heavy rain.

   (A) thunder : clap
   (B) flurry : blizzard
   (C) summit : mountain
   (D) gust : wind
   (E) beach : sand

3. IMAGE : COLLAGE ::   An image is part of a collage.

   (A) pedestal : statue
   (B) shore : ocean
   (C) catalog : shopper
   (D) tile : mosaic
   (E) sketch : artist

4. RACONTEUR : WIT ::   Wit is a characteristic of a raconteur.

   (A) sage : wisdom
   (B) infant : maturity
   (C) diplomat : insensitivity
   (D) miser : generosity
   (E) genius : witless

5. OVERTURE : OPERA ::   An overture is an introduction to an opera.

   (A) agenda : book
   (B) draft : essay
   (C) joke : satire
   (D) act : play
   (E) preface : book

6. MELLIFLUOUS : HEAR ::

(A) raucous : touch
(B) coarse : feel
(C) savory : taste
(D) stench : smell
(E) distressing : see

Something mellifluous is pleasant to hear.

_____

_____

_____

_____

7. FABLE : INSTRUCT ::

(A) parody : amuse
(B) elegy : joy
(C) epic : shame
(D) parable : mislead
(E) polemic : calm

A fable is used to instruct.

_____

_____

_____

_____

8. LUCID : UNDERSTAND ::

(A) lethargic : arouse
(B) resilient : defeat
(C) unstable : topple
(D) heavy : lift
(E) fleeting : preserve

Something lucid is easy to understand.

_____

_____

_____

_____

9. EPHEMERAL : PERMANENCE ::

(A) intrepid : adventure
(B) jovial : merry
(C) rational : logic
(D) brilliant : insight
(E) insensitive : feeling

Something ephemeral lacks

permanence.

_____

_____

10. REPROBATE : INCORRIGIBLE ::

(A) traitor : reliable
(B) radical : unorthodox
(C) ingrate : gracious
(D) bigot : tolerant
(E) pilgrim : impious

Being incorrigible is characteristic of

a reprobate.

_____

_____

Critical Reading for Ascending the Staircase

After completing this chapter, you will be able to

1. explain what is meant by a fact.

2. explain what is meant by an inference.

3. identify and answer inferential questions.

4. explain what is meant by attitude and mood.

5. identify and answer attitude, mood, and tone questions.

6. describe the characteristics of a paired passage.

7. explain the five-step strategy for attacking paired passages.

Making Inferences

Every student should complete Chapter 4 prior to attacking these more advanced critical reading questions. The strategies in this chapter build on the foundation established earlier.

In Chapter 4 you learned strategies for answering main idea and vocabulary questions. In this chapter you will start by learning how to make sound inferences based on facts.

Suppose your best friend avoided you at a party. What would you conclude from this behavior? You would probably conclude that your friend was mad at you.

In this situation, you reached a conclusion by using inferential thinking. First, you began with the facts. A *fact* is a statement that may be checked and proven true or false. For example, your friend's failure to talk with you at a party is a statement of fact. Based upon this fact, you inferred that your friend was angry at you. An *inference* is a conclusion arrived at by reasoning from facts. It is important to note that an inference may or may not be true. For example, your friend may have been in a bad mood and didn't want to ruin your evening.

Learning how to make inferences is an important part of being a skilled critical reader. Since authors do not always explicitly state their opinions or conclusions, it is often necessary to make inferences "by reading between the lines." As in everyday life, you begin by first identifying the relevant facts. You then use these facts to help you make a reasonable inference or conclusion.

Identifying Inferential Questions

Inferential questions are very easy to identify. Here are examples of recent inferential questions.

- It can be inferred from the passage that...
- Which of the following can be inferred?
- The author implies that...
- The passage as a whole suggests that...

The words *infer*, *imply*, and *suggest* are signal words that should alert you to expect an inferential question.

A Case Example

Read this excerpt from a passage on ancient Sparta and answer the inference question that follows. Mark the letter of the best response and then make a note of the supporting evidence that led you to that answer.

> Sparta, which had also grown from an organization of conquerors, was by its location less exposed to the influence of trade. . . . Sparta developed into a civilization more like that of
> *Line* modern Junker Prussia, that is, feudal landlords bound together by
> (5) holding down their serfs or *helots*. The organization of Sparta always reflected internal tension by the necessity for remaining perpetually armed, as much against internal revolution from the serfs or *helots*, who were the conquered older inhabitants, as against external attack.

from *Western Political Heritage* by William Y. Elliott and Neil A. McDonald

The author implies that the helots were

(A) privileged
(B) cruel
(C) greedy
(D) confused
(E) rebellious

Supporting Evidence:

Responses will vary.

_____

_____

_____

The author never explicitly tells us how the helots acted toward the Spartans. However, the author does provide a number of useful facts. First, we are told that the landowning Spartans were unified by "holding down" the helots. Second, the Spartans remained "perpetually armed" to guard against the possibility of "internal revolution." Finally, the helots were "conquered older inhabitants" of the area. Taken together, these facts support the inference that the Spartans must have faced a possible helot revolt. The best answer is therefore (E).

Guided PRACTICE

DIRECTIONS: Read each passage. Then answer the inferential questions that follow. Mark the letter of the best response and then make a note of the supporting facts that led you to that answer.

> To be chosen to compete in the drama competition was itself a great honor, and the cream of Athens' leadership vied for the right. For example, Aeschylus, one of the most revered and successful
> *Line* playwrights, was also one of Athens' most honored generals; for
> (5) Aeschylus to win first prize for tragedy, a feat he accomplished repeatedly, was roughly comparable to having General Dwight Eisenhower win the Pulitzer Prize for drama.
>
> from *Theatre: The Dynamics of Art* by Brian Hansen

1. It can be inferred from the passage that
    (A) Aeschylus successfully based his tragedies on his own military experiences
    (B) Dwight Eisenhower equaled Aeschylus as a general and playwright
    (C) the drama competition's prestige attracted Athens' most distinguished citizens
    (D) Aeschylus was a better general than playwright
    (E) few Athenians entered the drama competition

Supporting Evidence:

Responses will vary.

If curiosity, cunning, adaptability, inurement to repetition were—along with sociability—the prime virtues of early man, the later Paleolithic hunter needed still other traits: courage,
Line imagination, adroitness, readiness to face the unexpected. At a
(5) critical moment in the hunt, when an enraged buffalo, already wounded, turned upon the hunters closing in upon him, the ability to act in concert at the command of the most experienced and daring hunter was the price of avoiding injury and sudden death. There was no parallel to this situation in food gathering, nor
(10) yet in the later modes of Neolithic agriculture.

from *The Myth of the Machine* by Lewis Mumford

2. The author infers that late Paleolithic groups developed highly disciplined practices from the knowledge that

(A) hunting brought more prestige than food gathering
(B) the supply of big game animals had begun to dwindle
(C) they lived during a period of adverse weather conditions
(D) the animals they hunted were dangerous
(E) they competed with early farmers for good land

Supporting Evidence:

Responses will vary.

Guided PRACTICE

Many of the members of the Constitutional Convention were cynics who distrusted the abilities of the average person. It thus comes as no surprise that the Framers of the Constitution
Line envisioned the Senate as a small deliberative body that would be
(5) insulated from public opinion. As a result, Senators were given six-year terms, in contrast to the two-year terms served by members of the House of Representatives. Although many political scientists now contend that six years is too long, there were Framers who argued for even longer terms. For example, Alexander Hamilton
(10) suggested that Senators be given life tenure.

3. It can be inferred from the passage that Alexander Hamilton

   (A) wanted to be elected to the Senate
   (B) would not support the Constitution
   (C) trusted the people and believed that they should have a significant role in the new government
   (D) was a very popular member of the Constitutional Convention
   (E) wanted to make it difficult for the public to influence the Senate

Supporting Evidence:

Responses will vary.

_____

_____

Guided PRACTICE

Discussion

1. The passage tells us that it was "a great honor" to compete in the drama competition. As a result, the competition attracted "the cream," or top, of the city's leadership. These two facts support choice (C).

2. The author does not specifically tell us why late Paleolithic groups developed highly disciplined hunting practices. However, we are told that the hunters had to act together ("in concert") to avoid "injury and sudden death." We can therefore infer that the animals they hunted must have been very dangerous. Choice (D) is thus the best answer.

3. Although the passage tells us that Alexander Hamilton suggested that the Senators be given life tenure, it doesn't tell us why. However, we do know that the framers of the Constitution wanted "to insulate senators from public opinion." Clearly, Hamilton's life tenure proposal would have made it all but impossible for the public to influence the Senate. We can infer that choice (E) is the best answer.

Developing an Extra Edge

When answering inferential questions, it is helpful to keep these two key points in mind.

1. SAT inferences are almost always straightforward and consistent with the main idea of the passage. Always stay within the scope of the passage and its main idea.

2. Eliminate choices that go beyond the facts. Avoid jumping to extreme conclusions that are not supported by facts in the passage.

Independent PRACTICE

Critical Reading Practice Exercises 10 and 11 provide you with an opportunity to practice the skill of answering inference questions.

CRITICAL READING PRACTICE EXERCISE 10 *"Inference Questions"*

Remind students that they should be active readers. They need to underline key points, circle words, or make notes directly on the reading passage. Writing on the passage as they read will help them stay focused, and it will speed the process of referring back to the reading selection.

DIRECTIONS: Read each passage. Then answer the questions that follow. Mark the letter of the best response and then write, in the space provided, the supporting facts that led you to that answer.

Hot on the trail of finding the truth about sky-stones was a young lawyer-turned-physicist, Ernst Chladni, at the University of Berlin. Ignoring popular superstition and scientific scorn alike, Chladni
Line started his investigation from scratch by plucking his way through
(5) musty libraries and archives . . . centuries-old accounts of "fallen masses." . . . He analyzed numerous specimens of curiously heavy rocks gathered from diverse parts of the globe. . . . Chladni was coming to the unorthodox but inevitable conclusion that meteorites are extraterrestrial objects.

from *Stones from the Stars* by T.R. LeMaire

1. The author implies which of the following?
   (A) Recorded reports of "falling rocks" conclusively proved the extraterrestrial origin of meteorites.
   (B) Historical accounts of meteorite falls had been previously neglected by most scientists.
   (C) Meteorite showers occurred less frequently in Chladni's time than in previous centuries.
   (D) Chladni recognized the link between superstition and scientific inquiry.
   (E) Chladni placed more emphasis on eyewitness accounts than on chemical analysis.

Supporting Evidence:

Responses will vary.

_____

_____

In 1974 archaeologist Mary Leakey led a scientific expedition to Tanzania hoping to find clues about the origins of human life. Although Leakey's team found numerous animal fossils, two years
Line of careful searching only produced a few jaw fragments and teeth
(5) from human-like creatures. But lucky breaks often come in unexpected ways. Letting off steam after a hard day of painstaking

work, several scientists began throwing chunks of dried elephant dung at one another. As one scientist searched the ground for more ammunition, he noticed strange marks in a recently exposed layer of
(10) volcanic ash. A closer investigation revealed that the marks were footprints left by extinct species of early hominids.

2. It can be inferred from the passage that the discovery of the fossilized footprints was a result of

   (A) long hours of careful research
   (B) a lucky excavation in an unlikely place
   (●) an accidental discovery of an exposed surface
   (D) a meticulous study of modern animal tracks in the area
   (E) a tip provided by an amateur archaeologist

Supporting Evidence:

Responses will vary.

It is April 1959, I'm standing at the railing of the *Batory's* upper deck, and I feel that my life is ending. I'm looking out at the crowd that has gathered on the shore to see the ship's departure from
Line Gdynia—a crowd that, all of a sudden, is irrevocably on the other
(5) side—and I want to break out, run back, run toward the familiar excitement, the waving hands, the exclamations. We can't be leaving all of this behind—but we are. I am thirteen years old, and we are emigrating. It's a notion of such crushing, definitive finality that to me it might as well mean the end of the world.

from *Lost in Translation* by Eva Hoffman

3. The author's description of the crowd on the shore suggests that

   (A) her family does not expect to find a warm welcome
   (B) her relatives will not be able to visit her
   (C) her family's friends have now turned against them
   (D) she will find it difficult to communicate with her friends
   (●) the step she is taking is irreversible

Supporting Evidence:

Responses will vary.

CRITICAL READING PRACTICE EXERCISE **11** "Inference Questions"

DIRECTIONS: Read each passage. Then answer the questions that follow. Mark the letter of the best response and then write, in the space provided, the supporting facts that led you to that answer.

> It is frequently assumed that the mechanization of work has a revolutionary effect on the lives of the people who operate the new machines and on the society into which the machines have been
> *Line* introduced. For example, it has been suggested that the employment
> (5) of women in industry took them out of the household, their traditional sphere, and fundamentally altered their position in society.

1. It can be inferred from the passage that, before the Industrial Revolution, the majority of women's work was done in which of the following settings?

   (A) textile mills
   (●) private households
   (C) offices
   (D) factories
   (E) small shops

Supporting Evidence:

Responses will vary.

_____

> The absence of recorded sunspot activity in the notes kept by European observers in the late seventeenth and early eighteenth centuries has led some scholars to postulate a brief cessation of
> *Line* sunspot activity at that time (a period called the Maunder
> (5) minimum). The Maunder minimum has been linked to a span of unusual cold in Europe extending from the sixteenth to the early nineteenth centuries. The reality of the Maunder minimum has yet to be established, however, especially since the records that Chinese naked-eye observers of solar activity made at that time appear to
> (10) contradict it.

2. It can be inferred from the passage that Chinese observations of the Sun during the late seventeenth and early eighteenth centuries

   (A) are ambiguous because most sunspots cannot be seen
   (B) probably were made under the same weather conditions as those made in Europe
   (C) are more reliable than European observations
   (●) recorded some sunspot activity during this period
   (E) have been employed by scientists seeking to argue that a change in solar activity occurred during this period

Supporting Evidence:

Responses will vary.

_____

_____

Scholars often fail to see that music played an important role in the preservation of African culture in the United States. They correctly note that slavery stripped some cultural elements from
Line Black people—their political and economic systems—but they
(5) underestimate the significance of music in sustaining other African cultural values. African music, unlike the music of some other cultures, was based on a total vision of life in which music was not an isolated social domain. In African culture music was pervasive, serving not only religion, but all phases of life, including birth,
(10) death, work, and play. The methods that a community devises to perpetuate itself come into being to preserve aspects of the cultural legacy that that community perceives as essential. Music, like art in general, was so inextricably a part of African culture that it became a crucial means of preserving the culture during and after the dislocations of slavery.

3. Which of the following statements concerning the function of African music can be inferred from the passage?

(A) It preserved cultural values because it was thoroughly integrated into the lives of the people.
(B) It was more important in the development of African religious life than in other areas of culture.
(C) It was developed in response to the loss of political and economic systems.
(D) Its pervasiveness in African culture hindered effectiveness in minimizing the impact of slavery.
(E) Its isolation from the economic domains of life enabled it to survive the destructive impact of slavery.

Supporting Evidence:

Responses will vary.

_____

_____

LESSON
12

Recognizing Attitude, Mood, and Tone

Take a close look at the following list of words. What do they all have in common?

- anger
- joy
- frustration
- sadness
- fear

Each of these words describes a different mood. A *mood* is a predominant emotion. If you are with a friend, how can you determine if he or she is angry or happy? In our everyday conversations, we pay close attention to a person's tone of voice and body language. For example, a person who is angry will often raise his or her voice and frown. In contrast, a person who is happy will probably speak normally and smile.

Interpreting a person's mood requires good human relations skills. Interpreting a writer's mood requires good critical thinking skills. Each author has an *attitude,* or state of mind, toward the subject he or she is writing about. While authors cannot literally frown or smile at the reader, they can reveal their attitudes by the descriptive phrases and examples they use.

Identifying Attitude, Mood, and Tone Questions

The SAT writers often ask you to determine an author's attitude, mood, or tone. These questions are easy to spot. Here are examples of the formats used on recent PSATs and SATs.

- The author's attitude toward _____ is best described as
- The author's tone in the passage is best described as
- The author uses the word "_____" to express
- The author's perspective on _____ is that of

Key Words in Questions on Attitude, Mood, and Tone

Students should identify celebrities or historical figures and describe them using these words.

The SAT writers often draw upon a small but important group of words to describe different attitudes. For purposes of easy reference, here is a list of 12 key words.

1. *Cynical* – having or showing a distrustful attitude toward human nature

2. *Skeptical* – having or showing doubts about a person, idea, or belief

3. *Optimism* – an inclination to put the most favorable construction upon an action or to anticipate the best possible outcome

4. *Pessimism* – an inclination to emphasize adverse aspects, conditions, and possibilities or to expect the worst possible outcome

5. *Nostalgia* – a sentimental yearning to return to the past or to an irrevocable condition

6. *Scorn* – to show disdain, contempt

7. *Indifference* – a lack of interest, concern, or enthusiasm

8. *Sarcasm* – a sharp and often satirical utterance designed to cut or give pain

9. *Ambivalence* – simultaneous and contradictory attitudes or feelings, as to be both attracted and repelled by a person

10. *Condescension* – to assume an air of superiority, to patronize

11. *Esteem* – to hold in high regard

12. *Flippant* – lacking seriousness or proper respect

Two Keys for *ZAPPING* Attitude, Mood, and Tone Questions

1. **Identify positive and negative words.** In Chapter 6, Lesson 6, you learned how to use positive and negative words to help you answer sentence completion questions. The same skill can help you master attitude, mood, and tone questions. Since most attitude questions direct you to a sentence or paragraph, always carefully examine these lines for positive and negative words and phrases. Positive words and phrases indicate that the author approves of a person, place, or idea. Negative words and phrases indicate that the author disapproves of a person, place, or idea. Once you have gained a sense of whether the author is positive or negative about a subject, *ZAP* choices that do not reflect this view.

2. *ZAP* **negative choices regarding ethnic groups.** One of your passages will reflect the concerns or accomplishments of an ethnic group. You can be sure that answer choices making negative statements about these groups will be incorrect. Often, after you *ZAP* every negative statement, you will be left with only two or three choices from which to pick.

A Case Example

Read the following passage and then answer the accompanying question.

> As soon as the Army set Michael free he went to Harvard, mostly because that was where his father had urged him to apply, and at first he was determined not to be taken in by any of the myths or legends of Harvard, either: he didn't even care to acknowledge, let
> *Line* alone to admire, the physical beauty of the place. It was "school," a
> (5) school like any other, and as grimly eager as any other to collect its share of his GI Bill of Rights money.
>
> But after a year or two he began to relent a little. Most of the courses *were* stimulating; most of the books *were* the kind he had always wanted to read; the other students, some of them, anyway,
> (10) were turning out to be the kind of men he had always craved as companions.

from *Young Hearts Crying* by Richard Yates

Michael's attitude toward Harvard changed from

(A) disconnection to ingratitude
(B) admiration to indifference
(C) esteem to understanding
(D) anxiety to skepticism
(E) detachment to appreciation

Phrases such as "he was determined not to be taken in by any of the myths or legends of Harvard," and "he didn't even care to acknowledge, let alone to admire, the physical beauty of the place" clearly establish Michael's negative attitude when he first entered Harvard. However, this attitude soon changed. The reversal word *but*, which opens the second paragraph, signals a change in Michael's mood. The author now describes Michael's positive reaction to the courses, books, and other students. The best answer will be one describing a change from a negative to a positive attitude. Choices (B) and (C) can be *ZAPPED* since "admiration" and "esteem" are positive words. Choices (A) and (D) can be *ZAPPED* since "ingratitude" and "skepticism" do not describe Michael's new positive attitude. Only choice (E) correctly describes Michael's shift from a negative to a positive attitude.

Guided PRACTICE

DIRECTIONS: Knowing how to identify an author's attitude, mood, and tone is an important skill for answering critical reading questions. Carefully study each of the following examples. Examine the author's choice of words and describe if he or she has a positive or a negative attitude toward the subject. Then mark the answer that best describes this attitude.

> The Federalist Party completely discounted the ability and intelligence of the ordinary citizen. Indeed, scorn and disdain for the so-called "middling sort" were cornerstones of Federalist
>
> *Line* ideology. For Jefferson and his followers, the essential political
> (5) question was thus, "How can we respond to these misconceptions?"

1. The author uses the question, "How can we respond to these misconceptions?" to express Jefferson's

    (A) objections to the views of the Federalists
    (B) ambivalence toward the views of the Federalists
    (C) detachment from the views of the Federalists
    (D) optimistic appraisal of the views of the Federalists
    (E) tentative support for the views of the Federalists

> It is April 1959, I'm standing at the railing of the *Batory's* upper deck, and I feel that my life is ending. I'm looking out at the crowd that has gathered on the shore to see the ship's departure from
>
> *Line* Gdynia—a crowd that, all of a sudden, is irrevocably on the other
> (5) side—and I want to break out, run back, run toward the familiar excitement, the waving hands, the exclamations. We can't be leaving all of this behind—but we are. I am thirteen years old, and we are emigrating. It's a notion of such crushing, definitive finality that to me it might as well mean the end of the world.

from *Lost in Translation* by Eva Hoffman

2. Within the context of this paragraph, the author's statement, "We can't be leaving all of this behind—but we are," expresses her growing mood of

    (A) skepticism
    (B) indifference
    (C) despair
    (D) exuberance
    (E) optimism

Certainly the blue crab is superbly designed for speed in the water. Its body is shallow, compressed, and fusiform, or tapering at both ends. Although strong, its skeletal frame is very light, as
Line anyone who picks up a cast-off shell readily appreciates. At the
(5) lateral extremities are wickedly tapered spines, the Pitot tubes, one might say, of the crab's supersonic air frame. (These spines grow very sharp in large crabs; and good-sized specimens falling to a wooden deck occasionally impale themselves on them, quivering like the target knives of a sideshow artist.) This lateral adaptation
(10) is as it should be, of course, for an animal given to sideways travel.

from *Beautiful Swimmers* by William Warner

3. In this paragraph, the author adopts the tone of a
   (A) tentative novice
   (B) knowledgeable authority
   (C) concerned citizen
   (D) cynical critic
   (E) provocative commentator

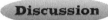

1. The first two sentences in this passage summarize the Federalist's view of the average person. Jefferson could approve, disapprove, or be neutral about these views. By calling Federalist views "misconceptions," Jefferson clearly expresses a negative attitude. Since choices (B), (C), (D), and (E) all express neutral or positive attitudes, they can be ZAPPED. Only choice (A) expresses the author's negative attitude toward the views of the Federalists.

2. How does the author describe how she feels about leaving Gdynia and becoming an emigrant? The first part of her statement, "We can't be leaving all of this behind," expresses her shock and disbelief at what is happening. The second part, "but we are," expresses the "definitive finality" of what is happening. The author then describes this feeling as "crushing" and says "it might as well mean the end of the world." This statement clearly expresses a negative attitude. Choices (D) and (E) can be ZAPPED since they are both positive words. Choice (A) can be ZAPPED since *skepticism* means "to have doubts" and the author stresses the "definitive finality" of what is happening to her. Choice (B) can be ZAPPED since *indifference* means "a lack of concern" and the author tells us that she feels as if her world is ending. Only choice (C), *despair*, conveys the author's growing sense of hopelessness and discouragement.

3. The author provides a precise and detailed explanation of how the blue crab's anatomy is "superbly designed for speed in the water." As we have often stressed, your answer must be supported by statements in the passage. Since none of the statements in this passage present the author as *concerned* or *cynical*, choices (C) and (D) can be ZAPPED. Since the author never makes a *provocative* statement and his mastery of the subject clearly shows that he is not a *novice*, choices (E) and (A) can be ZAPPED. Instead, the author's mastery of the subject establishes him as a *knowledgeable authority*. Choice (B) is thus the best answer.

Critical Reading Practice Exercises 12 and 13 provide you with an opportunity to answer attitude, mood, and tone questions.

CRITICAL READING PRACTICE EXERCISE 12 "Attitude, Mood, & Tone"

DIRECTIONS: Carefully read each of the following passages and questions. Examine the author's choice of words and decide if he or she has a positive or negative attitude. Then mark the answer that best describes this attitude.

> Harlem in the 1930's might well have struck a sensitive boy as a valley of bones. The Depression had fallen savagely on a not very wealthy economic community to begin with. . . . Jacob Lawrence was
> *Line* what might pass as a statistically average kid in that world. His
> (5) parents had long been separated and his mother was on welfare a good part of the time. He was a high school dropout. . . .
> A bleak enough picture, but for an imaginative, healthy, very quiet but very determined boy, it was enormously exciting. Those overcrowded streets in the West 130s and 140s were full of vivid,
> (10) racy life. People were living somehow.

from *Jacob Lawrence* by Robert Wernick

1. The author's perspective on Harlem in the 1930's is that of
   (A) an unsympathetic outsider
   (B) an outraged reformer
   (C) a hopeful commentator
   (D) a sad observer
   (E) a cynical scholar

Music expresses, at different moments, serenity or exuberance, regret or triumph, fury or delight. It expresses each of these moods, and many others. . . . It may even express a state of meaning for
Line which there exists no adequate word. . . . In that case, musicians
(5) often like to say that it has only a purely musical meaning. . . . What they really mean is that no appropriate word can be found to express the music's meaning and that . . . they do not feel the need of finding it.

from *What to Listen for in Music* by Aaron Copland

2. The author's attitude toward music is best described as

(A) delight and wonder
(B) concern and anxiety
(C) nostalgia and regret
(D) mockery and sarcasm
(E) anger and indignation

Our current views of both the terrestrial and the mechanical New Worlds have been falsely colored by the opaque religious prejudices of the leaders of the eighteenth-century Enlightenment. Thinkers
Line like Voltaire and Diderot, judging medieval institutions by the
(5) decayed survivals of their own day, took for granted that the Middle Ages were a period of besotted ignorance and superstition; and in their desire to throw off the influence of the Established Church, they converted the High Middle Ages, one of the great moments in European culture, into a neo-Gothic horror story, assuming that no
(10) serious progress had been made in any department until their own period.

from *The Pentagon of Power* by Lewis Mumford

3. The author's attitude towards the leaders of the eighteenth-century Enlightenment is best described as one of

(A) awe for their achievements
(B) sympathy for their dilemma
(C) respect for their scholarship
(D) criticism for their misconceptions
(E) gratitude for their insights

CRITICAL READING PRACTICE EXERCISE 13   "Attitude, Mood, & Tone"

DIRECTIONS: Carefully read each of the following passages and questions. Examine the author's choice of words and decide if he or she has a positive or negative attitude. Then mark the answer that best describes this attitude.

Once in winter I was far out on the sea ice north of Melville Island in the high Arctic with a drilling crew. I saw a seal surface at some hourless moment in the day in a moon pool, the open water
Line directly underneath the drilling platform that lets the drill string
(5) pass through the ice on its way to the ocean floor. The seal and I regarded each other in absolute stillness, I in my parka, arrested in the middle of an errand, the seal in the motionless water, its dark brown eyes glistening in its gray, catlike head. Curiosity held it. What held me was: how far out on the edge of the world I am. A
(10) movement of my head shifted the hood of my parka slightly, and the seal was gone in an explosion of water. Its eyes had been enormous. I walked to the edge of the moon pool and stared into the dark ocean. I could not have been more surprised by the seal's appearance if it had fallen out of the winter sky overhead, into the
(15) spheres of light that embraced the drill rig and our isolated camp. To contemplate what people are doing out here and ignore the universe of the seal, to consider human quest and plight and not know the land, I thought, to not listen to it, seemed fatal. Not perhaps for tomorrow, or next year, but fatal if you looked down the
(20) long road of our determined evolution and wondered at the considerations that had got us this far.

from *Arctic Dreams* by Barry Lopez

1. The author's overall attitude toward the future of the Arctic is best described as

   (A) avaricious
   (B) nostalgic
   (C) pessimistic
   (D) inquisitive
   (E) meditative

My mother and her friends were, after all, the female counterpart of Ralph Ellison's invisible man. Indeed, you might say they suffered a triple invisibility, being black, female, and foreigners.
Line They really didn't count in American society except as a source of
(5) cheap labor. But given the kind of women they were, they could not tolerate the fact of their invisibility, their powerlessness. And they fought back, using the only weapon at their command: the spoken word.

from *Reena and Other Stories* by Paule Marshall

2. The author's attitude toward her mother and the other women is best described as one of

(A) admiration
(B) amusement
(C) apathy
(D) confusion
(E) scorn

Vindication came in 1803, when even the vaunted French Academy of Science caved in—no doubt prompted by a thundering load of . . . meteorites that landed in Normandy, practically in the
Line academy's lap. As Dr. H.H. Nininger jests in *Our Stone-Pelted Planet,*
(5) "It became possible for a meteorite to land in France without fear of embarrassment."

from *Stones from the Stars* by T.R. LeMaire

3. The author's tone in describing how the French Academy of Sciences responded to the meteorites that landed in Normandy is best described as

(A) shock
(B) scorn
(C) confidence
(D) compassion
(E) reverence

Introducing Paired Passages

Have you ever asked your friends what they thought of a new television program? Did everyone have the same opinion? Probably not. Some of your friends may have liked the actors, while others may have thought the plot was boring. People often have different opinions about the same television program, event, or problem because they look at these things from different points of view.

A person's point of view is the way he or she interprets topics or events. Learning how to identify and compare different points of view is an important critical thinking skill. As citizens of a democracy, you are often asked to evaluate different viewpoints on an issue. Because of the importance of this skill, each SAT includes a pair of passages written by two authors who have different points of view on a topic.

Known as "paired passages," the two readings are each about one column in length. On most SATs, the paired passages will be located in a separate 15-minute section. However, it is important to know that the paired passages do not have to be in a separate section. On some recent SATs, the paired passages have appeared within one of the standard 30-minute verbal sections. If this occurs, be sure to reserve at least 15 minutes to read the paired passages and answer their questions.

Kinds of Passages

Like other critical reading passages, paired passages deal with topics drawn from the social sciences, natural sciences, and humanities. So far, about half of the paired passages have dealt with topics drawn from the social sciences. For example, in one paired passage the author of Passage 1 argued that the Enlightenment ideals of political leaders, such as Jefferson and Madison, were most responsible for America's constitutional guarantee of religious freedom. In contrast, the author of Passage 2 argued that religious freedom grew out of political necessity since no one Protestant group was strong enough to impose its will on the entire country.

Kinds of Questions

Each paired passage will be followed by between 11 and 13 questions. The first three to five questions will concern the first passage alone. The next three to five questions will concern the second passage alone. The final three to four questions will ask you to compare and contrast the two passages.

The questions relating to an individual passage will be the same as the questions you have dealt with on single passages. The questions relating to both passages will be different. Lesson 10 in Chapter 12 will show you how to answer these questions.

A Basic Strategy: Divide and Conquer

On first glance a paired passage may look twice as hard as a single reading selection. Fortunately, appearances are deceiving. There is no reason for you to be worried. The best way to approach a paired passage is to cut it down to size by using the following five-step "divide and conquer" strategy.

STEP **1** **Read** the first passage. As always, look for the main idea by focusing on the topic sentence.

STEP **2** **Answer** the questions that relate to the first passage. Paired passage questions are ordered so that the first few apply to Passage 1 and the next apply to Passage 2. In addition, paired passage questions contain specific lines and passage references that will enable you to determine which passage they relate to.

STEP **3** **Read** the second passage. Once again, look for the main idea by focusing on the topic sentence. The main idea will oppose, support, or in some way complement the main idea presented in the first passage.

STEP **4** **Answer** the questions that relate to the second passage.

STEP **5** **Answer** the questions that ask about the relationship between the two passages.

Critical Reading Practice Exercise 14 provides you with an opportunity to answer questions about paired passages.

CRITICAL READING PRACTICE EXERCISE **14** "Paired Passages"

DIRECTIONS: Use the first four steps of our five-step approach to read the following paired passages. The questions do not include items that relate to both passages. Chapter 12, Lesson 10, will provide a detailed explanation of how to answer these type of questions.

Passage 1

A well-organized, well-financed group with a focused agenda was able to use the media to scare the wits out of an uninformed public who, until they sat down that night to watch *60 Minutes*, had never
Line heard of Alar.
(5)   The panic produced by the *60 Minutes* report was almost like yelling "fire!" in a theater, except that in the case of Alar there certainly was time for reasonable people to ask if CBS and Meryl Streep were the best authorities on this subject, and if their opinions ought to be substituted for all the health regulators in the FDA, the
(10) EPA and the rest of the federal government.

More and more, public policy is decided this way. The scare and reaction method has become a primary prod for decision making at policy levels in this country.

A focused, highly motivated minority, often a very small minority,
(15) is able to overwhelm and capture the decision making process because the majority is unfocused, or focused on other matters. Too often, the style of our debate is turned into a shouting match, where lies and half-truths are acceptable tools, and where reason and evidence counts for little.

(20)   Let me make another related point before I go on: government is only one of the institutions making the rules we live by. Schools, the media, special interest groups and others, as in the case of Alar, are able to create and enforce actions which bypass our representative legislative bodies or administrative offices.

(25)   A good example of this relates once again to the Alar incident.

Within a few hours of the *60 Minutes* broadcast, the New York City Public Schools took all apples out of their lunch program.

We spoke to the school officials to tell them how mistaken this decision was.

(30)   We were told frankly that science had nothing to do with it. The administrators in New York simply were not willing to face alarmed parents. This decision was later reversed, but only after several weeks passed and many wholesome apples were destroyed and others went unpurchased.

from "Economic Properties and the Environmentalist" by Richard McGuire

Passage 2

(35)   Listening to a well regarded environmental program on the radio last winter, I heard the commentator take on the nuclear industry for the "deceit" behind its new PR[†] campaign: *"The ads boast that nuclear energy doesn't pollute the air. Now that may be technically correct, but it completely avoids the huge problem . . . of what happens when*

(40) *accidents occur. You know, the ones they assured us could never happen. But when they do, the cancer rates in the vicinity soar, and the entire region's landscape is blighted for who knows how long. Accidents like Chernobyl*."*

     The commentator's reporting might be, uh, "technically correct"

(45) regarding Chernobyl. But her piece was focusing on the nuclear industry in the *United States.* In fact, there is no documented evidence of increased cancer rates resulting from this nation's worst accident, at Three Mile Island in 1979. There has never been an accident at a U.S. nuclear reactor which has blighted the landscape.

(50)   The facts: People living within 50 miles of TMI were exposed to about 1.5 millirems of radiation. (The average annual dose for a U.S. resident is 360 millirems, from background radiation.) Of quite a different magnitude is the widely accepted estimate that, over the next 50 years, 17,000 people will die from cancers induced by

(55) Chernobyl's runaway nuclear reaction.

     Evidently, then, Chernobyl does *not* equal Three Mile Island.

     It's not that I think the "Living on Earth" radio commentator had no legitimate quarrel with the PR campaign. Certainly, she had reason to critique the nuclear industry's worker-safety record, as

(60) well as their avoidance of the unresolved issue of radwaste disposal. But why hype the commentary with blighted landscapes and soaring cancer rates? "Living on Earth" is generally an excellent environmental program, yet even the best resort to hyperbole when nukes come up.

(65)   Reporting that diverts us from rational, informed debate about energy options fuels the public's nuclear phobia. And it belongs in the dumpster.

* Chernobyl: an explosion in a Soviet nuclear power plant in the city of Chernobyl released large amounts of radioactive materials into the environment

[†] PR: public relations

from "Media Meltdown" by Scott Menchin

1. In line 1, the phrase "well-organized, well-financed group" refers to

   (A) the producers of *60 Minutes*
   (B) the manufacturers of the chemical Alar
   (C) opponents of the use of Alar
   (D) journalists and media decision makers
   (E) the industry which grows and markets apples

2. In comparing the *60 Minutes* report to yelling "fire!" in a theater (lines 5-10), the author of Passage 1 suggests that

   (A) the report was worse because it used a celebrity for credibility
   (B) the report was worse because it was based only on opinions
   (C) the report was worse because it appeared on television
   (D) yelling "fire!" would be worse because it leaves reasonable people no choice other than to react in fear
   (E) yelling "fire!" would be worse because it represented an attempt to do physical harm to people

3. The author of Passage 1 mentions the "health regulators in the FDA" (line 9) in order to suggest that they

   (A) had already considered the issues raised by the use of Alar
   (B) are frequently misled by powerful industry groups
   (C) need more funding to adequately protect the public
   (D) are always ignored by lawmakers and other federal agencies
   (E) made serious mistakes in the way they regulated the use of Alar

4. The author of Passage 1, in lines 25-34, holds that the New York City Public Schools decision was wrong because

   (A) it was later reversed
   (B) it was made in response to concerned parents
   (C) it ignored scientific considerations
   (D) it had economic consequences
   (E) Alar has been proven harmless by scientific studies

5. In line 38, the statement that nuclear industry ads "may be technically correct" is intended to emphasize the point that the ads

   (A) may also be technically incorrect
   (B) never use accepted statistical methods
   (C) have been proven wrong by later research
   (D) assume that major accidents will not happen
   (E) have been denounced by many scientists

6. The author of Passage 2 claims that radiation levels experienced by people after the Three Mile Island accident were

   (A) so insignificant that they could not be measured by existing equipment
   (B) a serious threat to the environment and public health in the future
   (C) of no significance as an environmental and public health problem
   (D) larger than authorities reported at the time of the accident
   (E) small compared to current standards for acceptable radiation levels

7. The author of Passage 2 acknowledges that the nuclear power industry could be fairly criticized for

   (A) denying the possibility of a nuclear accident in the United States
   (B) covering up reports on the Chernobyl accident
   (C) increasing cancer rates in the United States
   (D) failing to adequately protect nuclear industry workers
   (E) using a public relations campaign to influence public policy decisions

8. In line 63, what is the meaning of the word "hyperbole"?

   (A) dishonesty
   (B) exaggeration
   (C) self-importance
   (D) defensiveness
   (E) cautiousness

9. In line 66, the word "phobia" most nearly means

   (A) legitimate concern
   (B) utter confusion
   (C) wishful thinking
   (D) unreasonable fear
   (E) bored indifference

Putting It All
TOGETHER

1 A *fact* is a statement that may be checked and proven true or false.

2 An *inference* is a conclusion arrived at by reasoning from facts. An inference may or may not be true.

3 When you answer inference questions, first identify the relevant facts. Then use these facts to help you make a reasonable inference or conclusion.

4 A *mood* is a predominant emotion.

5 Each author has an *attitude,* or state of mind, toward the subject he or she is writing about.

6 When you answer attitude and mood questions, first look for positive and negative words in the passage. Once you have gained a sense of whether the author is positive or negative about a subject, *ZAP* choices that do not reflect this view.

7 *ZAP* all negative choices about ethnic groups.

8 Each SAT includes a pair of passages written by two authors who have different points of view on a topic.

9 When you work on paired passages, begin by reading the first passage and answering the questions that apply to it. Then read the second passage and answer the questions that apply to it. Finally, answer the questions that ask about the relationship between the two passages.

Answering Main Idea, Vocabulary-In-Context, Paraphrase, Inference, and Attitude Questions

DIRECTIONS: Carefully read the passage. Then answer the questions that follow. Mark the letter of the best response.

Practically speaking, the artistic maturing of the cinema was the single-handed achievement of David W. Griffith (1875-1948). Before Griffith, photography in dramatic films consisted of little more than
Line placing the actors before a stationary camera and showing them in
(5) full length as they would have appeared on stage. From the beginning of his career as a director, however, Griffith, because of his love of Victorian painting, employed composition. He conceived of the camera image as having a foreground and a rear ground, as well as the middle distance preferred by most directors. By 1910, he
(10) was using close-ups to reveal significant details of the scene or of the acting and extreme long shots to achieve a sense of spectacle and distance. His appreciation of the camera's possibilities produced novel dramatic effects. By splitting an event into fragments and recording each from the most suitable camera position, he could
(15) significantly vary the emphasis from camera shot to camera shot.
Griffith also achieved dramatic effects by means of creative editing. By juxtaposing images and varying the speed and rhythm of their presentation, he could control the dramatic intensity of the events as the story progressed. Despite the reluctance of his
(20) producers, who feared that the public would not be able to follow a plot that was made up of such juxtaposed images, Griffith persisted, and experimented as well with other elements of cinematic syntax that have become standard ever since. These included the flashback, permitting broad psychological and emotional exploration as well as
(25) narrative that was not chronological, and the crosscut between two parallel actions to heighten suspense and excitement. In thus exploiting fully the possibilities of editing, Griffith transposed devices of the Victorian novel to film and gave film mastery of time as well as space.
(30) Besides developing the cinema's language, Griffith immensely broadened its range and treatment of subjects. His early output was remarkably eclectic: it included not only the standard comedies, melodramas, westerns, and thrillers, but also such novelties as adaptations from Browning and Tennyson, and treatments of social
(35) issues. As his successes mounted, his ambitions grew, and with them the whole of American cinema. When he remade *Enoch Arden* in 1911, he insisted that a subject of such importance could not be treated in the then conventional length of one reel. Griffith's introduction of the American-made multireel picture began an
(40) immense revolution. Two years later, *Judith of Bethulia*, an elaborate historicophilosophical spectacle, reached the unprecedented length of four reels, or one hour's running time. From our contemporary

viewpoint, the pretensions of this film may seem a trifle ludicrous, but at the time it provoked endless debate and discussion and gave
(45) a new intellectual respectability to the cinema.

1. The primary purpose of the passage is to
   (A) discuss the importance of Griffith to the development of the cinema
   (B) describe the impact on cinema of the flashback and other editing innovations
   (C) deplore the state of American cinema before the advent of Griffith
   (D) analyze the changes in the cinema wrought by the introduction of the multireel film
   (E) document Griffith's impact on the choice of subject matter in American films

2. In line 7, the word "employed" most nearly means
   (A) hired
   (B) retained
   (C) utilized
   (D) discharged
   (E) worked

3. The author's attitude toward D.W. Griffith's work is best described as
   (A) scornful
   (B) ambivalent
   (C) skeptical
   (D) laudatory
   (E) flippant

4. In line 23, the word "standard" most nearly means
   (A) banner
   (B) foundation
   (C) required
   (D) irregular
   (E) accepted

5. It can be inferred from the passage that before 1910 the normal running time of a film was
   (A) 15 minutes or less
   (B) between 15 and 30 minutes
   (C) between 30 and 45 minutes
   (D) between 45 minutes and 1 hour
   (E) 1 hour or more

6. In the final paragraph (lines 30-45) the author presents evidence to show that

    (A) Griffith achieved artistic acclaim but limited financial rewards
    (B) Griffith vastly expanded the scope and manner of dealing with cinematic topics
    (C) Griffith outraged audiences with his ludicrous plots
    (D) Griffith recognized the artistic limitations inherent in filmmaking
    (E) Griffith preferred to use American authors and to draw upon American themes

7. It can be inferred from the passage that Griffith would be most likely to agree with which of the following statements?

    (A) The good director will attempt to explore new ideas as quickly as possible.
    (B) The most important element contributing to a film's success is the ability of the actors.
    (C) The camera must be considered an integral and active element in the creation of a film.
    (D) The cinema should emphasize serious and sober examinations of fundamental human problems.
    (E) The proper composition of scenes in a film is more important than the details of their editing.

8. The author's attitude toward photography in the cinema before Griffith can best be described as

    (A) sympathetic
    (B) nostalgic
    (C) amused
    (D) condescending
    (E) hostile

Rising to the Top of the Tower

3

CHAPTER 9

**Vocabulary for
Rising to the Top of the Tower**

CHAPTER 10

**Sentence Completions for
Rising to the Top of the Tower**

CHAPTER 11

**Analogies for
Rising to the Top of the Tower**

CHAPTER 12

**Critical Reading for
Rising to the Top of the Tower**

Vocabulary for Rising to the Top of the Tower

After completing this chapter, you will be able to

1. give examples of words that begin with the prefixes BENE-, MAL-, SUPER-, and MIS-.

2. define the roots PLAC, CHRON, SPEC, and PUG and give examples of words containing them.

3. give synonyms for *talkative, brief and to the point, freed from blame, disgusting,* and *uneasy about the future.*

The Mighty Prefix, Part III

Prior to attacking this unit, students should review the vocabulary presented in Chapters 1 and 5. Remind students that they need to strive to apply their new vocabulary in the context of their writing and conversation.

In Chapters 1 and 5, you learned that a prefix is a word part placed before a root in order to direct or change the root's meaning. As you saw, prefixes are valuable tools that can help you unlock the meaning of many words. So far, you have learned the meaning of the following prefixes.

1. E-/EX- = OUT, as in *exit, extinguish, extrovert, elusive, exorbitant, eminent,* and *expound.*

2. A-/AN- = NOT, as in *atypical, atheist, amorphous, atrophy, anonymous,* and *anomaly.*

3. RE- = BACK, AGAIN, as in *revoke, revitalize, renovate, resurge, redundant,* and *remuneration.*

4. IN-/IM- = NOT, as in *interminable, incorrigible, impious, incorporeal, intrepid,* and *inviolable.*

5. UN- = NOT, as in *unfettered, unfounded, unflappable, unscathed,* and *unorthodox.*

6. AB- = AWAY FROM, OFF, as in *abhor, abdicate, abstain,* and *aberrant.*

In this lesson you'll learn four more key prefixes and 17 more key SAT words.

BENE or BEN ·····► When BENE- or BEN- is part of a word, things go WELL.

BENE- is a Latin prefix meaning "well." Here are five words that begin with BENE- or BEN-.

1. *Benefit* – One thing people look for when they apply for a job is the *benefit* package. A *benefit* is anything that promotes or enhances well-being.

   EXAMPLE: The *benefits* of the job include two weeks of paid vacation, free use of the company fitness center, and inexpensive health insurance.

2. *Benevolent* – Does a *benevolent* person want to help or hurt you? The prefix BENE- tells you that *benevolent* means "kindly, full of good will."

   EXAMPLE: Contributing presents to needy children is a *benevolent* act.

3. *Benefactor* – A *benefactor* is one who does good by giving financial or other aid.

   EXAMPLE: The school's new computer lab was the gift of a generous *benefactor*.

4. *Benediction* – The root DIC means "to say." A *benediction* is the act of saying a blessing.

   EXAMPLE: The minister gave a *benediction* at the end of the funeral service.

5. *Benign* – If your doctor told you that the tumor she removed was *benign*, would that be good news or bad news? The prefix BEN- tells you that it would be good news. A *benign* tumor is harmless. *Benign* means "kind, gentle."

   EXAMPLE: The *benign* grandparents gave everything they could to their grandchildren.

MAL ····➤ When MAL- is part of a word, things go BADLY.

MAL- is a Latin prefix meaning "bad or badly." Here are six key SAT words that begin with MAL-.

1. *Malign* – If someone *maligns* your reputation, is that good or bad? The prefix MAL- tells you that it is bad. *Malign* means "to speak badly of, to slander, defame."

   EXAMPLE: Many people complained that the politicians were more interested in *maligning* each other than in debating the issues.

2. *Malicious* – *Malicious* means "filled with malice or ill will." A *malicious* person is driven by hatred and wants to harm others.

   EXAMPLE: He was the unfortunate victim of a *malicious* rumor spread by a jealous rival.

3. *Malevolent* – Does a *malevolent* person want to help or harm you? The prefix MAL- tells you that a *malevolent* person is not benevolent. *Malevolent* means "wishing harm to others."

   EXAMPLE: Her *malevolent* remark hurt his feelings.

4. *Malediction* – Since the root DIC means "to say," what do you think *malediction* means? As you undoubtedly deduced, a *malediction* is the act of saying evil or a curse.

  EXAMPLE: The malevolent wizard uttered a *malediction* against his enemies.

5. *Malignant* – If your doctor told you that the tumor she removed was *malignant*, would that be good news or bad news? The prefix MAL-tells you that it would be bad news. *Malignant* means "deadly, very harmful."

  EXAMPLE: The *malignant* rumors severely damaged his reputation.

6. *Malingerer* – Would you expect a *malingerer* to be a model employee? Probably not. The prefix MAL- warns you to expect the worst. A *malingerer* is someone who procrastinates or avoids work.

  EXAMPLE: Danielle turned out to be a *malingerer* who rarely did her chores.

SUPER ····► The SUPERhero of Prefixes.

What qualities made Superman so super? SUPER- is a Latin prefix meaning "above or beyond." Superman is appropriately named since his powers are "far beyond those of mortal humans." Here are three key SAT words that begin with SUPER-.

1. *Supercilious* – Since *super* means "above" and *cilium* means "eyelid," *supercilious* literally means "above one's eyebrows." A *supercilious* look thus expresses pride, disdain, and even haughtiness.

  EXAMPLE: After winning the lottery, the once humble employee became *supercilious* and obnoxious.

2. *Superficial* – *Superficial* literally means "just above the surface." *Superficial* has thus come to mean "a lack of depth, shallow."

  EXAMPLE: Jeff would be the first to admit that he only has a *superficial* knowledge of physics.

3. *Supersede* – *Supersede* is composed of the prefix SUPER- and the Latin root SEDERE, which means "to sit." *Supersede* thus means "to sit above" in the sense of replacing or taking the place of.

  EXAMPLE: The high school's new attendance policy will *supersede* all previous regulations.

MIS ⋯➤ The Anglo-Saxon way to say WRONGLY and BAD.

MIS- is an Anglo-Saxon prefix meaning WRONGLY and BAD. Here are three key SAT words that begin with MIS-.

1. *Misnomer* – NOMEN is a Latin root meaning "name." A *misnomer* is thus a name that is wrongly or unsuitably applied to a person or object.

    EXAMPLE: In the army, "gun" is considered a *misnomer* for "rifle."

2. *Misconception* – A *misconception* is a wrong interpretation or misunderstanding of an idea, person, or event.

    EXAMPLE: Many students have *misconceptions* about how to apply to colleges and universities.

3. *Miscreant* – Would you predict that a *miscreant* is a good person or an evil person? The prefix MIS- tells you that a *miscreant* is an evildoer or scoundrel.

    EXAMPLE: The *miscreant* proudly boasted about his evil plans.

Using Your
VOCABULARY

MATCHING

DIRECTIONS: Match each word in the first column with its appropriate definition in the second column.

_D_	1. benevolent	A.	lacking depth
_J_	2. supercilious	B.	an unsuitable name
_B_	3. misnomer	C.	evildoer, scoundrel
_H_	4. benefactor	D.	full of good will
_I_	5. malign	E.	a curse
_F_	6. supersede	F.	take the place of
_C_	7. miscreant	G.	someone who avoids work
_A_	8. superficial	H.	someone who does good
_E_	9. malediction	I.	speak badly of
_G_	10. malingerer	J.	haughty, disdainful

ODD WORD OUT

DIRECTIONS: Each question below consists of four words. Three of them are related in meaning. Circle the word that does not fit.

1. disdainful   supercilious   haughty   (modest)

2. cruel   selfish   (benevolent)   unkind

3. amiable   (malicious)   affable   benign

4. (profound)   superficial   incomplete   shallow

5. (benevolent)   spiteful   resentful   malevolent

6. praise   compliment   eulogize   (malign)

7. malicious   defamatory   (commendable)   slanderous

8. acrimonious   (benign)   malevolent   vicious

9. (hero)   scoundrel   miscreant   evildoer

10. patron   benefactor   (miser)   donor

APPLYING YOUR KNOWLEDGE

DIRECTIONS: In each of the items below, use your knowledge of the defined word to write a definition for the word in italics.

1. If ADROIT means "skillful," what does *maladroit* mean?

   to have "bad" skill; to be clumsy or awkward

2. If NATURAL means "normal or usual," what does *supernatural* mean?

   above or beyond what is normal or natural

3. If CONSTRUE means "to give an explanation or interpretation," what does *misconstrue* mean?

   to give a wrong explanation or interpretation

4. If FEASANCE means "the performance of an act or obligation," what does *malfeasance* mean?

   the performance of an act that is wrong or unlawful

5. If ANTHROPE means "human," how does a *misanthrope* view human beings?

   A misanthrope views humans as "bad" or unlikable.

Roots and Branches

In Chapters 1 and 5, you learned that a root is a word or word element from which other words are formed. As you saw, learning root families can be a very effective way of expanding your vocabulary. So far, you have learned eight root families.

1. CORD = HEART, as in *cordial, accord,* and *discord.*

2. AMICUS = FRIEND, as in *amicable, amity,* and *amiable.*

3. GREG = GROUP, as in *gregarious, congregate, segregate, aggregate,* and *egregious.*

4. PATHOS = FEELINGS, as in *apathy, antipathy, sympathy,* and *empathy.*

5. FID = FAITH, as in *fidelity, confidant, diffident, and perfidious.*

6. LUC/LUMEN = LIGHT, as in *lucid, pellucid, elucidate,* and *luminous.*

7. ACRI/ACER = SHARP or BITTER, as in *acute, acumen, acid, exacerbate,* and *acrimonious.*

8. FLU = FLOW, as in *fluent, confluence, mellifluous, affluent,* and *superfluous.*

In this lesson you will learn four more key roots and 17 more key SAT words.

Meet the PLAC Family

They Will Help Make You CALM

PLAC is a Latin root meaning "to make calm." Here are four key members of the PLAC family.

1. *Placid* – *Placid* means "to be outwardly calm and composed."

   EXAMPLE: The coach's *placid* disposition enabled her to remain calm and focused despite the raucous crowd.

2. *Placate* – *Placate* means "to calm the anger of," especially by appeasing or yielding concessions.

   EXAMPLE: The baby sitter *placated* the crying child by allowing him to eat his favorite candy.

3. *Complacent* – *Complacent* means "to be so calm as to be self-satisfied or smug."

   EXAMPLE: After signing for a huge bonus, the rookie became *complacent* and soon lost his starting position.

4. *Implacable* – Do you think an *implacable* opponent can be pleased? The prefix IM-, meaning "not," tells you that an *implacable* opponent cannot be either pleased or appeased. *Implacable* means "incapable of appeasement and therefore relentless."

   EXAMPLE: The presence of two such *implacable* foes made it impossible to negotiate a peace treaty.

Meet the CHRON Family

They Are Always on TIME

Chronos is a Greek word meaning "time." Here are five key members of this timely family.

1. *Chronological* – Suppose someone asked you to place the following dates in *chronological* order: 1776, 1066, 476, and 1492. Since *chronological* means "arranged in order of occurrence," the correct order would be: 476, 1066, 1492, and 1776.

   EXAMPLE: After completing her first draft, the novelist decided to tell her story in *chronological* order, rather than shifting from present to past.

2. *Synchronize* – The Greek prefix SYN- means "same or together." *Synchronize* thus means "to occur together at the same time, simultaneous."

   EXAMPLE: We *synchronized* our clocks so we could arrive at the prom at precisely the same time.

3. *Chronicle* – Many newspapers around the country have the word *chronicle* in their name. The explanation is that a *chronicle* is a record of events in order of time.

> EXAMPLE: His *chronicle* of the Civil War began with the firing on Fort Sumter and ended with Lee's surrender at Appomatox.

4. *Chronic* – *Chronic* refers to a habit, condition, or disease that continues over a long period of time.

> EXAMPLE: Diane was a *chronic* complainer who annoyed everyone in the department.

5. *Anachronism* – Since the prefix AN- means "not," *anachronism* refers to something that is not happening in its proper time.

> EXAMPLE: The clock that strikes twelve in Shakespeare's *Julius Caesar* is an *anachronism* since there were no striking clocks in ancient Rome.

Meet the SPEC/SPIC Family

They Are Happy to SEE You

SPEC and SPIC are Latin roots meaning "to see or observe." For example, a *spectator* is someone who sees an event. Here are four key members of this family.

1. *Conspicuous* – *Conspicuous* means "easy to see" and thus impossible to miss.

> EXAMPLE: The tour group leader wore a *conspicuous* red, white, and blue hat that made her impossible to miss.

2. *Perspective* – Have you ever disagreed with a friend on an issue? Perhaps it is because you and your friend viewed the problem from different *perspectives*. A *perspective* is a point of view.

> EXAMPLE: Environmentalists and lumber companies often have different *perspectives* on how to best use the forests in the Pacific Northwest.

3. *Circumspect* – The prefix CIRCUM- means "around." *Circumspect* thus means "to look around" in the sense of being cautious and careful.

> EXAMPLE: A political leader cannot afford to accept advice from just anyone; he or she must learn to be as *circumspect* as possible in choosing advisors.

4. *Specious* – Rumors often appear at first to be true, but later turn out to be false. When this happens, the original reports were probably *specious*. *Specious* means "seemingly fair, attractive or true, but actually not so; deceptive."

   EXAMPLE: Henderson's argument for the plan impressed the new council members but struck the more experienced leaders as *specious*.

5. *Perspicacity* – The prefix PER- means "through." *Perspicacity* thus means "to see through" in the sense of being very perceptive or astute.

   EXAMPLE: The *perspicacity* of Leonardo da Vinci impressed his contemporaries; his farsighted ideas and novel inventions demonstrated a brilliant mind blessed with great insight.

Meet the PUG Family

They Are Spoiling for a FIGHT

Pugnus is a Latin word meaning "fist." For example, a *pugilist* is a professional boxer. Here are three key members of the PUG family.

1. *Pugnacious* – *Pugnacious* literally means "eager to use one's fists." A *pugnacious* person is combative and quick to fight.

   EXAMPLE: Shawn's quick temper and *pugnacious* personality made a fight inevitable.

2. *Repugnant* – The prefix RE- means "back, again." *Repugnant* thus literally means "to be hit by a fist again and again." Since something that hits you again and again is repulsive, *repugnant* means "offensive, very distasteful."

   EXAMPLE: Pat's willingness to steal confidential files and then lie about it is *repugnant* to any reasonable way of thinking.

3. *Impugn* – *Impugn* means "to fight against" in the sense of questioning, criticizing, or challenging the accuracy or honesty of something.

   EXAMPLE: Stephen's critics *impugned* his motives as being based upon pure self-interest.

Using Your VOCABULARY

DIRECTIONS: For each question, decide whether the pair of words are synonyms (S), antonyms (A), or unrelated (U) to each other.

A	1. circumspect	reckless
S	2. repugnant	disgusting
S	3. complacent	smug
S	4. perspicacity	astuteness
U	5. chronic	flippant
U	6. implacable	pious
A	7. placate	irritate
S	8. pugnacious	belligerent
S	9. specious	spurious
U	10. anachronism	hedonist

ODD WORD OUT

DIRECTIONS: Each question consists of four words. Three of them are related in meaning. Circle the word that does not fit.

1. defend	support	advocate	(impugn)
2. rash	impetuous	impulsive	(circumspect)
3. discontent	restless	(complacent)	troubled
4. (chronic)	temporary	infrequent	fleeting
5. specious	(valid)	deceptive	spurious
6. (conciliatory)	contentious	belligerent	pugnacious
7. (ordinary)	notable	outstanding	conspicuous
8. repugnant	(pleasant)	unsavory	unpalatable
9. turbulent	agitated	(placid)	perturbed
10. placate	(antagonize)	mollify	appease

COMPLETE THE HEADLINE

DIRECTIONS: The following headlines are taken from newspaper and magazine articles. Use one of the following five words to complete each headline: Implacable, Specious, Placate, Chronicle, Chronic.

1. Once _____Implacable_____ Foes Negotiate Bosnian Settlement

2. Doctors Urge Long-term Care for _____Chronic_____ Problems

3. New Biography to _____Chronicle_____ the Life of Richard Nixon

4. President Tries to _____Placate_____ Critics by Offering Changes in Welfare Reform Bill

5. Reviews Blast Movie Saying It Is a _____Specious_____ Adaptation of a Classic Novel

LESSON 3

Synonym Clusters

Students should establish a daily routine of reviewing the flash cards and using the new words in their personal conversation and writing.

In Chapters 1 and 5, you learned that a synonym cluster is a group of words that have similar meanings. So far, you have learned the following nine synonym clusters.

1. The Thrill-of-Victory Cluster – exuberant, ebullient, exultant, elated, exhilarated, and ecstatic

2. The Agony-of-Defeat Cluster – despondent, dejected, dispirited, and disconsolate

3. The Stubborn Cluster – obstinate, obdurate, intransigent, recalcitrant, and dogged

4. The Secret Cluster – clandestine, surreptitious, stealthy, covert, and furtive

5. The Relieve Cluster – alleviate, allay, assuage, mitigate, and mollify

6. The Commonplace Cluster – trite, banal, hackneyed, and pedestrian

7. The Introduction Cluster – preamble, preface, prologue, overture, and prelude

8. The Temporary Cluster – momentary, ephemeral, evanescent, transient, and fleeting

9. The Hasty Cluster – impetuous, rash, impulsive, and precipitate

In this lesson, you'll learn five more synonym clusters containing 22 key SAT words.

The Talkative Cluster

These Words Have a Lot to Say

Have you ever had a friend who just didn't know when to stop talking? Someone who would keep you on the phone long after the conversation was over? The English language provides us with several words to describe this person. Here are five key members of the Talkative Cluster.

1. Loquacious – talkative

2. Verbose – talkative, wordy

3. Garrulous – talkative, noisy

4. Prattle – talkative, babbling

5. Bombastic – talkative, in the sense of being pompous

The Brief-and-to-the-Point Cluster

A Very Uncommunicative Group

President Coolidge was famous for being a man of few words. Once a lady told him that she had bet she could get him to say three words to her. Coolidge *laconically* replied, "You lose." The word *laconic* is an important member of a cluster of synonyms that describe people whose conversation is brief and to the point. Here are four members of the Brief-and-to-the-Point Cluster.

1. Succinct – brief and to the point

2. Laconic – brief and to the point

3. Terse – brief and to the point

4. Taciturn – brief and to the point

The Freed-from-Blame Cluster

These Words Mean You Are Free to Go!

One of the greatest feelings is to be proven right after being blamed for something you didn't do. Has this ever happened to you? The English language provides us with several words to describe this condition. Here are five members of the Freed-from-Blame cluster.

1. Exculpate – free from blame

2. Exonerate – free from blame

3. Vindicate – free from blame

4. Absolve – free from blame

5. Acquit – free from blame

The Disgusting Cluster

These Words Describe Things That Are Horrible

The news media today loves to report on crimes that everyone agrees are horrible and disgusting. When possible, they gather these stories from every corner of the world and report them as if they're happening in your own backyard. Reporters use a large number of words to describe things we find horrible and disgusting. Here are five key members of the Disgusting Cluster.

1. Abhorrent – disgusting, revolting, horrible

2. Appalling – disgusting, revolting, horrible

3. Despicable – disgusting, revolting, horrible

4. Repulsive – disgusting, revolting, horrible

5. Heinous – disgusting, revolting, horrible

The Uneasy-about-the-Future Cluster

These Words Are Worried Something Bad Will Happen

It's not unusual for a person to get an uneasy feeling that something bad is about to happen. The English language provides several words to express this feeling. Here are three key members of the Uneasy-about-the-Future Cluster.

1. Apprehension – a fearful or uneasy feeling about the future

2. Foreboding – a fearful or uneasy feeling about the future

3. Premonition – a fearful or uneasy feeling about the future

Using Your VOCABULARY

ODD WORD OUT

DIRECTIONS: Each question below consists of four words. Three of them are related in meaning. Circle the word that does not fit.

1. verbose   (taciturn)   garrulous   loquacious
2. (bombastic)   quiet   simple   unaffected
3. exculpate   acquit   vindicate   (convict)
4. beneficial   laudable   (heinous)   admirable
5. repugnant   (pleasant)   appalling   abhorrent
6. (confidence) apprehension foreboding   premonition
7. taciturn   (loquacious) laconic   terse
8. blame   censure   condemn   (exculpate)
9. despicable   appalling   repulsive   (admirable)
10. optimistic   favorable   (foreboding)   encouraging

MATCHING

DIRECTIONS: Match each word in the first column with its appropriate definition in the second column.

C	1. foreboding	A. free from blame
E	2. loquacious	B. saying little, terse
D	3. abhorrent	C. uneasy about the future
A	4. exculpate	D. appalling, horrible
B	5. taciturn	E. talkative, garrulous

RELATIONSHIPS

DIRECTIONS: For each question below, decide whether the pair of words are synonyms (S), antonyms (A), or unrelated (U) to each other.

A	1. bombastic	quiet
S	2. garrulous	verbose
S	3. heinous	loathsome
U	4. exculpate	extravagant
S	5. succinct	terse
S	6. acquit	vindicate
S	7. premonition	foreboding
U	8. taciturn	malignant
U	9. loquacious	surreptitious
S	10. repugnant	repulsive

Sentence Completions for Rising to the Top of the Tower

After completing this chapter, you will be able to

1. explain what is meant by a Level 5 question.

2. describe two characteristics of a Level 5 question.

3. correctly answer Level 5 sentence completion questions.

4. complete a set of 10 sentence completion questions in 7 minutes and a set of 9 sentence completion questions in 6 minutes.

Answering the Toughest Sentence Completion Questions

Prior to attempting the strategies in this chapter, students should review Chapters 2 and 6. These advanced strategies are for excellent readers who have already mastered the previous material.

Without marking an answer at this time, review the following two sentence completion questions.

1. An apparently gratuitous gesture, whether it is spiteful or solicitous, arouses our suspicion, while a gesture recognized to be ---- gives no reason for surprise.

   (A) warranted
   (B) dubious
   (C) affected
   (D) benevolent
   (E) rancorous

2. The novelist brings out the ---- of human beings time and time again by ---- their lives to the permanence of the vast landscape.

   (A) absurdity . . . relating
   (B) transience . . . likening
   (C) evanescence . . . contrasting
   (D) complexity . . . comparing
   (E) uniqueness . . . opposing

Would you rate these two questions easy, medium, or hard? Most students taking the SAT would describe these questions as hard. The SAT writers would agree with this rating. The SAT has an evaluation system in which they rate each question on a scale of 1 to 5, with 1 being very easy and 5 being very hard. They assigned a 5 to both of the above questions. Normally, 80 percent or more of the students who answer a Level 5 question will select the wrong answer.

Characteristics of Level 5 Sentence Completion Questions

Level 5 sentence completion questions are easy to find. They always appear ninth or tenth in a set of ten questions and eighth or ninth in a set of nine questions. But what characteristics make these questions so difficult? Their degree of difficulty is based upon two key factors.

1. **Challenging vocabulary** Level 5 sentence completion questions contain a number of challenging vocabulary words. Difficult words are used in both the answer choices and the sentence. For example, Sentence 1 above contains such high-level words as *gratuitous*, *spiteful*, and *solicitous*. The answer choices include such difficult words as

warranted, dubious, affected, benevolent, and *rancorous.* In order to successfully answer Level 5 sentence completion questions, you must have a strong vocabulary. The Appendix offers several powerful tools for improving your SAT vocabulary.

2. **Complex sentence structure** In Chapters 2 and 6, you studied sentence completion questions that use easy vocabulary and relatively simple sentence structure. In contrast, the most challenging sentence completion questions contain combinations of definitions, reversal words, cause-and-effect words, and support words. As a result, it is imperative that you have a full command of the sentence completion skills presented earlier. For easy reference, here is a brief review of the key points of Chapters 2 and 6.

- Each sentence completion question has **a key word or group of words** that will help guide you to the correct answer. There are no exceptions to this rule. It applies to both the easiest sentence completion questions and the hardest.

- The key word or group of words is sometimes **a definition or explanation**. The answer is thus a word that is defined or explained in the sentence.

- **Contrast sentences** contain reversal words such as *but, although,* and *however.* In this type of sentence, the answer will be a word that contrasts with the key word or phrase.

- **Cause-and-effect sentences** contain signal words such as *because, in order to,* and *a result of.* In this type of sentence, the answer will be a word that completes a cause-and-effect relationship.

- **Synonym sentences** contain signal words such as *and, also,* and *furthermore.* In this type of sentence, the answer will somehow form a synonym or closely related thought.

- Many SAT sentence completion questions use **positive and negative words**. It is often helpful to use contextual clues to determine if the answer is a positive or negative word.

Let's apply these skills to the two Level 5 sentence completion questions that we used to introduce this lesson.

Case Example 1

An apparently gratuitous gesture, whether it is spiteful or solicitous, arouses our suspicion, while a gesture recognized to be ---- gives no reason for surprise.

(**A**) warranted
(B) dubious
(C) affected
(D) benevolent
(E) rancorous

This sentence asks you to compare two gestures—a *gratuitous* (uncalled for) *gesture* that *arouses our suspicion* and an unnamed gesture that *gives no reason for surprise*. The correct answer will thus be a word that fulfills two conditions. First, it must contrast with *gratuitous*. And second, it must be compatible with the key group of words *gives no reason for surprise*. Let's apply these two conditions to each of the five answer choices.

(A) **warranted** *Warranted* means "justified" in the sense of having reasonable grounds for an act or statement. *Warranted* thus contrasts with *gratuitous* and is compatible with our key group of words since a gesture that is *warranted* would give no reason for surprise. Let's hold this answer. As always, we'll check the remaining choices.

(B) **dubious** *Dubious* means "doubtful, uncertain." It doesn't offer a contrast with *gratuitous* and is not compatible with our key group of words since a *dubious* gesture would give reason for surprise. Since this answer fails to pass our two tests, it should be ZAPPED.

(C) **affected** *Affected* means "behaving in an artificial way to impress people." It doesn't offer a contrast with *gratuitous* and is not compatible with our key group of words since an *affected* gesture would probably give reason for surprise. Since this answer fails to pass our two tests, it should be ZAPPED.

(D) **benevolent** *Benevolent* means "kind, compassionate." *Benevolent* doesn't offer a sharp contrast with *gratuitous*. However, it could be compatible with our key group of words since a *benevolent* gesture would probably give no reason for surprise. Let's hold this answer for now. Although it is not a perfect fit, it is a possible answer.

(E) **rancorous** *Rancorous* means "causing resentment and feelings of bitterness." It doesn't offer a contrast with *gratuitous* and is not compatible with our key group of words since a *rancorous* gesture would give reason for surprise.

Conclusion: Choices (B), (C), and (E) can all be ZAPPED since they clearly fail to match our two conditions. Although choice (D) is close, *benevolent* doesn't offer a really sharp contrast with *gratuitous*. In contrast, *warranted* is a direct antonym of *gratuitous*. Since the action is "justified," it would give no reason for surprise. Choice (A) is therefore the correct answer.

Case Example 2

The novelist brings out the ---- of human beings time and time again by ---- their lives to the permanence of the vast landscape.
(A) absurdity . . . relating
(B) transience . . . likening
(●) evanescence . . . contrasting
(D) complexity . . . comparing
(E) uniqueness . . . opposing

The first blank in this sentence asks you to select a word describing a human trait that the novelist brings out *time and time again*. Unfortunately, the first word in all five of the answer choices meets this test. The second blank asks you to select a word that logically relates to the key word *permanence*. However, once again all five answer choices could fit. The challenge in this sentence is to select an answer that establishes a logical relationship among three words — the key word, *permanence*, and the two missing words. Let's apply this test to each answer choice.

(A) **absurdity . . . relating . . . permanence** Is it logical to bring out the *absurdity* of human beings by *relating* their lives *to the permanence of the vast landscape*? No. *Absurd* means "unreasonable, illogical." You can ZAP (A) because there isn't any sensible connection between the first and second part of this statement.

(B) **transience . . . likening . . . permanence** Is it logical to bring out the *transience* of human beings by *likening* their lives *to the permanence of the vast landscape*? No. *Transience* means "brief, short-lived." You could underscore the *transience* of human life by contrasting it to something more permanent, but not by *likening* it to something more permanent. ZAP (B).

(C) **evanescence . . . contrasting . . . permanence** Is it logical to bring out the *evanescence* of human beings by *contrasting* their lives with something permanent? An author could underscore the *evanescence* of human life by contrasting it with *the permanence of the vast landscape*. Let's keep this one. As always, let's examine the remaining choices.

(D) **complexity . . . comparing . . . permanence** Is it logical to bring out the *complexity* of human beings by *comparing* their lives to something permanent? No. *Complexity* means "intricate, complicated." An author who is trying to underscore the *complexity* of human life would probably compare it to the qualities of simplicity or straightforwardness, rather than to *permanence*.

(E) **uniqueness . . . opposing . . . permanence** Is it logical to bring out the *uniqueness* of human beings by *opposing* their lives *to the permanence of the vast landscape*? No. *Uniqueness* means "distinctive, one of a kind." Why would an author try to underscore the *uniqueness* of human life by *opposing* it to *the permanence of a vast landscape*?

Conclusion: Choices (A), (B), (D), and (E) can all be *ZAPPED* since they fail to meet our test of logically relating to the key word *permanence*. Only choice (C) meets this test.

Guided
PRACTICE

DIRECTIONS: Here are two more Level 5 sentence completion questions. Use the skills you have learned so far to answer each question. Explain your answer in the space provided. Then compare your reasoning with the answers that follow.

1. Like a true iconoclast, Ann was ---- who ---- conventional styles of management.

   (A) a nonconformist . . . spurned
   (B) a miscreant . . . embraced
   (C) an aesthete . . . encouraged
   (D) a loafer . . . enforced
   (E) a dissenter . . . advocated

   Responses will vary.

   _____

2. The history of science is replete with examples of bold new theories that were ---- when they first appeared but were subsequently ---- by future researchers.

   (A) corroborated . . . verified
   (B) assailed . . . derided
   (C) boycotted . . . repudiated
   (D) vilified . . . substantiated
   (E) lauded . . . revered

   Responses will vary.

   _____

Discussion

1. This sentence contains two key words, *iconoclast* and *conventional*. An *iconoclast* is a person who attacks, ridicules, or criticizes *conventional* (traditional, established) institutions and ideas. The sentence asks you to select an answer choice in which the first word is synonymous with an *iconoclast* and the second word describes how an *iconoclast* would react to *conventional styles of management*. Since an *iconoclast* would oppose *conventional styles of management*, the second word must have a negative connotation.

   (A) **nonconformist . . . spurned** A *nonconformist* is similar to an *iconoclast* in that both oppose conventional ways of doing things. *Spurn* is a negative word meaning "to reject" and thus describes how an *iconoclast* would react to *conventional styles of management*. Let's keep (A) for now.

   (B) **miscreant . . . embraced** A *miscreant*, or evildoer, is unrelated to an *iconoclast*. *Embraced* is a positive word that does not describe how an *iconoclast* would react to *conventional styles of management*. Choice (B) fails to meet both our tests and can be ZAPPED.

   (C) **aesthete . . . encouraged** An *aesthete*, or lover of beauty, is unrelated to an *iconoclast*. *Encouraged* is a positive word that does not describe how an *iconoclast* would react to *conventional styles of management*. Choice (C) fails to meet both our tests and can be ZAPPED.

   (D) **loafer . . . enforced** A *loafer*, or idler, is someone who avoids work and is unrelated to an *iconoclast*. *Enforced* is a positive word that does not describe how an *iconoclast* would react to *conventional styles of management*. Choice (D) fails to meet both our tests. ZAP it.

   (E) **dissenter . . . advocated** A *dissenter* is similar to an *iconoclast* in that both express opposition to conventional ways of doing things. *Advocated*, however, is a positive word that does not express how an *iconoclast* would react to *conventional styles of management*. Choice (E) thus fails our second test and can be ZAPPED.

   Conclusion: Only choice (A) meets both our tests by providing a synonym of *iconoclast* and a negative word describing how an *iconoclast* would react to *conventional styles of management*.

2. The reversal word *but* signals that you are looking for a contrast between how new theories were received when they *first appeared* and how they were received by *future researchers*. The contrast could be between a positive first word and a negative second word (+/-) or between a negative first word and a positive second word (-/+). Let's take a look at each answer choice.

(A) **corroborated . . . verified** *Corroborate* (supported, proved) and *verified* are both positive words. Since there is no contrast, this choice can be ZAPPED.

(B) **assailed . . . derided** *Assailed* (attacked, sharply criticized) and *derided* (ridiculed, scorned) are both negative words. Since there is no contrast, ZAP (B).

(C) **boycotted . . . repudiated** *Boycotted* (refused to buy, rejected) and *repudiated* (rejected, disavowed) are both negative words, again we have no contrast. ZAP (C).

(D) **vilified . . . substantiated** *Vilified* (to have used abusive or slanderous language) and *substantiated* (verified) do form a contrast that fits the logic of this sentence, making (D) an attractive choice. Let's check (E) before we mark it as the correct answer.

(E) **lauded . . . revered** *Lauded* (strongly praised) and *revered* (treated with honor, esteem) are both positive words. We can ZAP (E) because there is no contrast.

Conclusion: Only choice (D) provides contrasting words that fit the logic of the sentence.

Developing an Extra Edge

1. Level 5 sentence completion questions are evenly divided between double-blank and single-blank questions. Most of the single blank questions are definitional while most of the double-blank questions require contrasting answers.

2. In the Introduction (pages 1–20), you learned that easy questions have easy answers and hard questions have hard answers. This principle applies to Level 5 sentence completion questions. Always *ZAP* relatively easy answers. If you are having trouble choosing between two answers, it is generally wise to select the answer with the toughest words.

   Be careful with this tip. In the previous question, for example, if you recognized that (D) was a good, logical answer, but you were not sure of the meaning of *corroborated* or *repudiated*, don't move away from your sensible choice just because the other choices have words you don't know.

Independent PRACTICE

Sentence Completion Practice Exercise 1 provides you with an opportunity to practice your skill of answering Level 5 sentence completion questions.

SENTENCE COMPLETION PRACTICE EXERCISE 1 "Level 5"

DIRECTIONS: This exercise contains ten Level 5 sentence completion questions. Use all of your skills to attack each question. After marking your answer, explain your logic in the space provided.

1. The belief that people belonging to the Clovis tradition were the first inhabitants of the Americas is ---- by new data that have severely shaken a long-standing ---- among archaeologists.

   (A) assailed . . . consensus
   (B) strengthened . . . debate
   (C) supported . . . dilemma
   (D) stymied . . . vacillation
   (E) refuted . . . dissension

   Responses will vary.

2. Like most absolute rulers, Louis XIV was a ruthless despot who gave orders in such ---- way that it was obvious he expected to be obeyed without question.

   (A) a loquacious
   (B) a surreptitious
   (C) a superfluous
   (D) a circuitous
   (E) an imperious

   Responses will vary.

3. It is a ---- confession because William seems anything but ---- : he makes it clear that although he has acted wrongly, he has done so through no fault of his own.

   (A) boring . . . concerned
   (B) typical . . . relieved
   (C) singular . . . penitent
   (D) prejudiced . . . involved
   (E) permissible . . . sorry

   Responses will vary.

4. They sought to oust their party chair because her proposal seemed
----; it contradicted their fundamental economic policies.

   (A) garrulous
   (B) remedial
   (C) formulaic
   (D) heretical
   (E) cursory

   Responses will vary.

5. She was a woman of contrasts: periods of ---- alternated with
periods of frenetic activity.

   (A) animation
   (B) torpor
   (C) invincibility
   (D) profundity
   (E) ebullience

   Responses will vary.

6. Though difficult, it is ---- to study shearwaters in their land-based
breeding colonies; studying these birds at sea, however, poses an
almost ---- problem.

   (A) enterprising . . . inventive
   (B) helpful . . . salutary
   (C) necessary . . . facile
   (D) feasible . . . insuperable
   (E) possible . . . implausible

   Responses will vary.

7. Supporters of the woman suffrage movement hailed Elizabeth Cady
Stanton's "Declaration of Sentiments" as a convincing ---- that
powerfully ---- the prevailing notion that women should not
participate in political activities.

   (A) diagnosis . . . confirmed
   (B) ultimatum . . . espoused
   (C) polemic . . . refuted
   (D) supplication . . . bolstered
   (E) solicitation . . . advocated

   Responses will vary.

8. During the early stages of his film career, D. W. Griffith's output was remarkably ----: it included not only the standard comedies, melodramas, westerns, and thrillers, but also such novelties as adaptations from Browning and Tennyson, and treatments of social issues.

   (A) eclectic
   (B) acrimonious
   (C) impromptu
   (D) theoretical
   (E) pragmatic

   Responses will vary.

   _____

9. Because Alexander the Great was an omnipotent ruler, his death was a ----, marking the end of the old order and the beginning of chaos.

   (A) tribute
   (B) watershed
   (C) verdict
   (D) reparation
   (E) connotation

   Responses will vary.

   _____

10. Well-publicized disagreements in the scientific community have so ---- many lay persons that they now ---- new warnings about the health effects of popular foods.

    (A) inundated . . . regulate
    (B) exasperated . . . discount
    (C) bedazzled . . . ridicule
    (D) vindicated . . . exaggerate
    (E) disqualified . . . minimize

    Responses will vary.

    _____

Pacing Your Work on Sentence Completion Questions

Pacing is most important for students who have an honest chance at carefully completing the entire test. On the SAT, a careful pace is always better than rushing forward with the risk of making unnecessary errors.

Try to recall a situation where you were performing under the pressure of a moving clock. Athletes, entertainers, and writers often have to "beat the clock," "keep a schedule," and "make a deadline." **The pressure builds whenever you feel like you don't have enough time to do what you are capable of doing.** Learning how to handle time pressure requires practice, patience, and confidence.

The SAT will require you to perform well while working at a brisk pace. Students aspiring to reach for the top of the SAT verbal tower should strive to answer all of the sentence completion questions. The strategies and practice exercises you have completed so far are designed to enable you to master even the most challenging sentence completion questions.

As you know, your SAT will include one set of 10 sentence completion questions and one set of 9 sentence completion questions. You should spend an average of about 40 seconds on each question. This means devoting about 7 minutes to the set of 10 sentence completion questions and 6 minutes to the set of 9 sentence completion questions. This pace is designed to leave you with ample time to complete the critical reading passages.

Sentence Completion Practice Exercises 2 and 3 give you an opportunity to time yourself on a set of 10 sentence completion questions and a set of 9 sentence completion questions.

SENTENCE COMPLETION PRACTICE EXERCISE 2 *"Timed Test"*

DIRECTIONS: Mark the answer for each of the following 10 sentence completion questions. **Try to complete the entire set in 7 minutes.** When you have finished, use the space provided to record how long it took you to complete the set.

1. Like other ---- animals, owls are rarely seen during the day.

   (A) migratory
   (B) herbivorous
   (C) equatorial
   (D) nocturnal
   (E) hybrid

2. Because the island is only ---- by boat, it appeals to tourists looking for ---- vacation away from large crowds and busy shopping centers.

   (A) reachable . . . an agitated
   (B) trampled . . . a confused
   (C) accessible . . . a tranquil
   (D) relocated . . . a disordered
   (E) executed . . . a cordial

3. Marine biologists are concerned that ---- substances in San Francisco Bay are ---- the population of harbor seals.

   (A) savory . . . diminishing
   (B) fragrant . . . highlighting
   (C) toxic . . . endangering
   (D) invigorating . . . squandering
   (E) harmless . . . weakening

4. As the pace of suburban development increases, the amount of rural land has begun to ---- thus ---- the habitat of many animals.

   (A) diminish . . . protecting
   (B) dwindle . . . threatening
   (C) expand . . . exposing
   (D) shrink . . . shielding
   (E) flourish . . . endangering

5. The name of the neighborhood is a ----; although it is called "The Bottom," it is located on a hill overlooking the rest of the town.

   (A) misfortune
   (B) miscalculation
   (C) misinterpretation
   (D) misstep
   (●) misnomer

6. Only Carter's ---- personality could have turned such a tedious party into a lively event that everyone enjoyed.

   (●) effervescent
   (B) belligerent
   (C) subdued
   (D) efficient
   (E) intolerant

7. Far from being --- who avoided publicity, the author is actually a very ---- person who enjoys meeting people and talking about her new books.

   (A) a loner . . . introverted
   (B) an exhibitionist . . . lethargic
   (C) a regal . . . withdrawn
   (D) a philanthropist . . . insecure
   (●) a recluse . . . gregarious

8. As scientists have learned more about the universe, phenomena that were once ---- and mysterious are now ----.

   (A) enigmatic . . . misunderstood
   (B) manifest . . . irrevocable
   (●) baffling . . . comprehensible
   (D) puzzling . . . ambiguous
   (E) apparent . . . insignificant

9. Although usually regarded as a pragmatic politician, Senator Halpern initiated what many skeptics called ---- plan to run for president as the leader of a new party.

   (A) an eminent
   (●) a quixotic
   (C) an authentic
   (D) an unsentimental
   (E) a venal

10. Ken exhibited unexpected patience and guile when he ---- plotted a series of ---- that helped him gain control over the business.

    (A) ineptly . . . disavowals
    (B) benevolently . . . stratagems
    (C) diffidently . . . intrigues
    (●) cleverly . . . machinations
    (E) superficially . . . schemes

Time: _____

SENTENCE COMPLETION PRACTICE EXERCISE **3** "Timed Test"

DIRECTIONS: Mark the answer in each of the following 9 sentence completion questions. **Try to complete the entire set in 6 minutes.** When you have finished, use the space provided to record how long it took you to complete the set.

1. On December 3, 1967, a five-surgeon team headed by Dr. Christiaan N. Barnard ---- the first successful heart transplant thus ---- a new medical procedure that would save thousands of lives.

   (A) executed . . . terminating
   (B) neglected . . . commencing
   (C) proposed . . . restricting
   (D) resisted . . . launching
   (E) performed . . . initiating

2. The Soviet Union's successful launch of Sputnik, the world's first man-made satellite, acted as a catalyst ---- the rapid expansion of America's space program.

   (A) igniting
   (B) checking
   (C) suffocating
   (D) exposing
   (E) restraining

3. Although the early impressionists were all ----, with disparate ideas and attitudes, they were united in their desire to achieve a greater naturalism in art.

   (A) individualistic
   (B) indistinguishable
   (C) fused
   (D) consolidated
   (E) inconspicuous

4. Danielle Martinez's ---- personality and ability to work with temperamental actors and actresses established her as one of the most promising young directors in Hollywood.

   (A) contentious
   (B) biased
   (C) timorous
   (D) amiable
   (E) caustic

5. Although usually ----, the district attorney was ---- the dramatic and unexpected increase in the city's crime rate.

   (A) obstinate . . . appeased by
   (B) unflappable . . . alarmed by
   (C) unapproachable . . . comforted by
   (D) impulsive . . . agitated by
   (E) submissive . . . elated by

6. Since the highway commissioner's program to alleviate traffic congestion produced few improvements, critics called his efforts ----.

   (A) fruitful
   (B) notable
   (C) futile
   (D) climatic
   (E) farsighted

7. Leaders of the environmental movement angrily charged that the accusations against their organization were ---- and meant to ---- their position on how to best protect endangered animals.

   (A) fraudulent . . . bolster
   (B) authentic . . . distort
   (C) slanderous . . . enhance
   (D) spurious . . . misrepresent
   (E) sensible . . . champion

8. At the peak of his popularity, Mahatma Gandhi had a ---- of devoted followers who ---- his strategy of non-violent civil disobedience.

   (A) throng . . . mocked
   (B) host . . . derided
   (C) legion . . . supported
   (D) smattering . . . tolerated
   (E) horde . . . undermined

9. When he matter-of-factly stated, "I seen my opportunities and I took 'em," George Washington Plunket succinctly summarized the ---- behavior of corrupt nineteenth-century politicians who gladly accepted bribes and appointed cronies to public jobs.

   (A) anachronistic
   (B) venal
   (C) trivial
   (D) negligible
   (E) altruistic

Time: _____

Putting It All
TOGETHER

1. There will be 19 sentence completion questions on your SAT. Each question consists of a sentence in which one or two words have been deliberately omitted. Your job is to select the one or two words that best complete the sentence.

2. Each sentence completion question has a key word or phrase that will help guide you to the correct answer.

3. The SAT rates all questions on a scale of 1 to 5, with 5 being very hard. Normally, 80 percent or more of the students answering a Level 5 question will miss it.

4. Level 5 sentence completion questions have a challenging vocabulary and a complex sentence structure. Level 5 sentences often contain combinations of definitions, reversal words, cause-and-effect words, and support words.

5. Strive to answer a set of 10 sentence completion questions in 7 minutes and a set of 9 sentence completions in 6 minutes.

Sentence Completions

DIRECTIONS: Mark the answer for each of the following sentence completion questions. **Try to complete the entire set in 7 minutes.**

1. Because they take up space at feeders and consume a disproportionate amount of food, grackles are usually regarded as the most ---- of the blackbird visitors.

    (A) annoying
    (B) tranquil
    (C) valuable
    (D) friendly
    (E) subdued

2. Renowned as ---- worker, Thomas Edison spent days and nights on his experiments, often not even taking time to eat and sleep.

    (A) an indifferent
    (B) an indefatigable
    (C) a clumsy
    (D) an inexperienced
    (E) a sluggish

3. Marc Chagall was a highly ---- artist whose paintings stand alone, defying categorization and ----.

    (A) predictable . . . evaluation
    (B) conservative . . . duplication
    (C) careless . . . interpretation
    (D) original . . . imitation
    (E) commonplace . . . reproduction

4. A rainbow is ---- thing; it quickly disappears, leaving only a beautiful memory.

    (A) a chaotic
    (B) a heinous
    (C) a resilient
    (D) an ephemeral
    (E) a perpetual

5. Although she had once been a world traveler, Tasha now leads ---- life, spending most of her time reading books and working in her garden.

    (A) a provocative
    (B) a clandestine
    (C) a sedentary
    (D) an animated
    (E) a nomadic

6. Becky was ---- about her new art course; that is, her feelings about learning how to paint were contradictory.

   (A) unwavering
   (B) focused
   (C) passionate
   (D) ambivalent
   (E) euphoric

7. As the growing population of the Southwestern states continues to ----, it will inevitably ---- the region's limited supply of water.

   (A) mushroom . . . replenish
   (B) diminish . . . exhaust
   (C) shrivel . . . augment
   (D) dwindle . . . demolish
   (E) burgeon . . . deplete

8. Cheryl prided herself on being a ---- administrator who ignored theoretical and ---- proposals in favor of a down-to-earth search for practical solutions.

   (A) profound . . . challenging
   (B) pragmatic . . . idealistic
   (C) pessimistic . . . discouraging
   (D) stoical . . . substantive
   (E) superficial . . . shallow

9. Like a true ----, Peter demonstrated unswerving ---- his country's controversial and expensive program of military expansion.

   (A) pacifist . . . support for
   (B) jingoist . . . devotion to
   (C) loiterer . . . criticism of
   (D) skinflint . . . commitment to
   (E) nonpartisan . . . dedication to

10. Although the governor's public career was a model of ----, his biographer uncovered some private ---- that raised inevitable doubts about his character.

    (A) rectitude . . . wrongdoings
    (B) dishonor . . . immorality
    (C) decorum . . . righteousness
    (D) probity . . . humility
    (E) ignominy . . . piety

11

Analogies for Rising to the Top of the Tower

After completing this chapter, you will be able to

1. recall the three-step procedure for solving analogies.

2. identify and solve *Degree* analogies.

3. solve analogies using the strategies for recognizing unrelated pairs.

4. solve analogies using the three-step procedure for Working in Reverse.

5. complete a set of 13 analogies in 9 minutes and a set of 6 analogies in 4 minutes.

"Degree" Analogies

Reviewing Analogies

Prior to attempting the strategies in this chapter, students should review Chapters 3 and 7. These advanced strategies are for excellent readers who have already mastered the previous material.

In Chapter 3 you learned that each SAT contains 19 analogies and that you should attack each analogy by using the three-step strategy. Your first step, as always, is to establish a clear relationship between the two stem words. Your next step is to form a short specific sentence connecting the stem words. Finally, after you apply your sentence to each of the answer choices, you should select the answer that best matches your sentence.

Most SAT analogies can be grouped into nine basic types of relationships. In Chapters 3 and 7, you learned to identify and solve the following types of analogies.

- IS A TYPE OF   e.g. GOLD : METAL
- IS A PART OF   e.g. TREE : FOREST
- IS A PLACE WHERE   e.g. CLASSROOM : TEACHER
- IS USED TO   e.g. SCALE : WEIGHT
- RELATIVE SIZE   e.g. HILL : MOUNTAIN
- IS CHARACTERISTIC OF e.g. WISDOM : SAGE
- ANTONYM   e.g. INTREPID : FEAR
- DEFINITIONAL   e.g. CREST : WAVE

Identifying *DEGREE* Analogies

Analogy Relationship 9

Study the following six analogies.

Base Word	Greater Degree of Base Word
angry	infuriated
distasteful	repugnant
happy	elated
tired	exhausted
frightened	terrified
talkative	loquacious

What type of relationship do these six analogies have in common? All six illustrate a type of analogy called *Degree*. This type of analogy is easy to spot. The SAT writers provide you with two words, one of which is an intensified version of the other.

Very is the connecting phrase that solves each of the six analogies.

- infuriated is *very* angry
- repugnant is *very* distasteful
- elated is *very* happy
- exhausted is *very* tired
- terrified is *very* frightened
- loquacious is *very* talkative

A Case Example

Let's apply our three-step procedure to the following analogy.

ENRAGED : ANGRY ::

(A) ambitious : idle
(B) cunning : vague
(C) elated : happy
(D) concerned : indifferent
(E) generous : polite

STEP **1**   **Relate** the stem words and then form a sentence connecting them. ENRAGED : ANGRY is a good example of a *Degree* analogy. We can form a sentence relating ENRAGED and ANGRY by saying, "To be ENRAGED is to be very ANGRY."

STEP **2**   **Apply** this sentence to each of the answer choices and *ZAP* the choices that clearly don't fit.

(A) ambitious : idle	Is to be ambitious to be very idle? No. These words are related, but as opposites. *ZAP* it.
(B) cunning : vague	Is to be cunning to be very vague? No. *ZAP* it.
(C) elated : happy	Is to be elated to be very happy? Yes. As always, let's check the other choices.
(D) concerned : indifferent	Is to be concerned to be indifferent? No. *ZAP* it.
(E) generous : polite	Is to be generous to be polite? These words are somewhat related, but the relationship is not strong and clear. *ZAP* it.

STEP **3**   **Select** the answer that best matches your original sentence. The answer is (C) since "To be ENRAGED is to be very ANGRY in the same way as to be ELATED is to be very HAPPY."

DIRECTIONS: Here are three more *Degree* analogies. Use our three-step process to find the correct answers.

1. MINUSCULE : SMALL ::
   - (A) erratic : stable
   - (B) complex : simple
   - (C) difficult : impossible
   - (D) mammoth : big
   - (E) rugged : smooth

2. METICULOUS : EXACT ::
   - (A) impious : holy
   - (B) vicious : deceptive
   - (C) humorous : grave
   - (D) ambitious : failure
   - (E) cautious : careful

3. SUPERFICIAL : SHALLOW ::
   - (A) forlorn : cheerful
   - (B) arduous : difficult
   - (C) heinous : jealous
   - (D) frequent : irregular
   - (E) hilarious : sad

Analogy 1

Relate the stem words and then form a sentence connecting them. MINUSCULE : SMALL is an example of a *Degree* analogy. We can form a sentence connecting MINUSCULE and SMALL by saying, "MINUSCULE is very SMALL."

Apply this sentence to each of the answer choices.

Discussion

(A)	erratic : stable	Is erratic very stable? No. *ZAP* it.
(B)	complex : simple	Is complex very simple? No. *ZAP* it.
(C)	difficult : impossible	Is difficult very impossible? This will trick students who lose track of the order of the two words. Something that is difficult is not a greater degree of something that is impossible. *ZAP* it.
(D)	mammoth : big	Is mammoth very big? Yes. But as always, let's look at the other choices.
(E)	rugged : smooth	Is rugged very smooth? No. *ZAP* it.

Select the answer that best matches your original sentence. In this example, the answer is (D) since "MINUSCULE is very small in the same way as MAMMOTH is very BIG."

Analogy 2

Relate the stem words and then form a sentence connecting them. We can form a sentence connecting METICULOUS and EXACT by saying, "METICULOUS is very EXACT."

Apply this sentence to each of the answer choices.

(A)	impious : holy	Is impious very holy? No. *ZAP* it.
(B)	vicious : deceptive	Is vicious very deceptive? This choice will trip up many good students. Don't let yourself get off the track of your initial sentence. If you're not sure, save this one for now.
(C)	humorous : grave	Is humorous very grave? No. *ZAP* it.
(D)	ambitious : failure	Is ambitious very failure? No. *ZAP* it.
(E)	cautious : careful	Is cautious very careful? Yes.

Select the answer that best matches your original sentence. In this example, you may need to give final consideration to (B) and (E). The answer is (E) since "METICULOUS is very EXACT in the same way as CAUTIOUS is very CAREFUL."

Analogy 3

Relate the stem words and then form a sentence connecting them. We can form a sentence connecting SUPERFICIAL and SHALLOW by saying, "SUPERFICIAL is very SHALLOW."

Apply this sentence to each of the answer choices.

(A)	forlorn : cheerful	Is forlorn very cheerful? No. *ZAP* it.
(B)	arduous : difficult	Is arduous very difficult? Yes. But as always, let's look at the other choices.
(C)	heinous : jealous	Is heinous very jealous? No. *ZAP* it.
(D)	frequent : irregular	Is frequent very irregular? No. *ZAP* it.
(E)	hilarious : sad	Is hilarious very sad? No. *ZAP* it.

Select the answer that best matches your original sentence. In this example, the answer is (B) since "SUPERFICIAL is very SHALLOW in the same way as ARDUOUS is very DIFFICULT."

Developing an Extra Edge

1. *Degree* analogies are an especially popular choice for the hard third analogies.

2. *Degree* analogies often combine a very difficult vocabulary word with a relatively easy word. For example, EXCRUCIATING : PAINFUL combines a tough word, EXCRUCIATING, and a very easy word, PAINFUL.

   When you spot this type of pattern, it is often helpful to place a double ++ beside the stronger word (EXCRUCIATING ++) and a single + beside the less intense word (PAINFUL +). Then use the double plus/single plus pattern to find a parallel relationship in the answer choices.

Independent PRACTICE

nalogy Practice Exercise 4 provides you with 10 more *Degree* analogies. Use the three-step process to answer each one. Remember, practice is the first step in building confidence.

ANALOGY PRACTICE EXERCISE **4** "Degree"

DIRECTIONS: For each question, first write a sentence linking the stem words. Then mark the correct answer.

1. ARID : DRY ::

   (A) hot : scalding
   (B) puny : huge
   (C) wild : tame
   (D) volatile : bright
   (E) frigid : cold

   Arid is very dry.
   _____
   _____
   _____

2. CONFUSED : BEWILDERED ::

   (A) pleased : exasperated
   (B) angered : embarrassed
   (C) frightened : terrified
   (D) open-minded : bigoted
   (E) frenzied : dignified

   Bewildered is very confused.
   _____
   _____
   _____

3. LIVID : ANGRY ::

   (A) envious : proud
   (B) hilarious : funny
   (C) benevolent : flammable
   (D) anxious : curious
   (E) prevalent : scarce

   Livid is very angry.
   _____
   _____
   _____

4. FASTIDIOUS : NEAT ::

   (A) fragrant : foul
   (B) courageous : foolish
   (C) gorgeous : tempting
   (D) punctual : active
   (E) appalling : shocking

   Fastidious is very neat.
   _____
   _____
   _____

5. OMINOUS : ALARMING ::

   (A) hideous : unattractive
   (B) homogeneous : varied
   (C) industrious : important
   (D) ridiculous : amusing
   (E) hilarious : somber

   Ominous is very alarming.
   _____
   _____
   _____

6. IRONCLAD : FIRM ::

(A) stiff : malleable
(●) feeble : weak
(C) cracked : bruised
(D) smooth : polished
(E) lazy : lethargic

Ironclad is very firm.

_____

_____

_____

7. PELLUCID : CLEAR ::

(A) anonymous : popular
(B) suspicious : talkative
(C) vicious : noble
(●) excruciating : painful
(E) virtuous : obsessive

Pellucid is very clear.

_____

_____

_____

8. EMBRYONIC : EARLY ::

(A) malicious : sincere
(B) extravagant : essential
(●) vigilant : alert
(D) exalted : common
(E) trite : memorable

Embryonic is very early.

_____

_____

_____

9. EGREGIOUS : BAD ::

(A) remarkable : normal
(B) interminable : concise
(C) amiable : resourceful
(D) impressionable : intense
(●) precarious : unstable

Egregious is very bad.

_____

_____

_____

10. GARRULOUS : TALKATIVE ::

(A) pious : profound
(B) malicious : incomplete
(C) supercilious : successful
(●) zealous : enthusiastic
(E) luminous : kindly

Garrulous is very talkative.

_____

_____

_____

Eliminating Unrelated Pairs

SAT analogy questions use a wide variety of challenging words. As a result, even the best students will not know every word in each analogy question.

If you don't know what a stem word means, should you give up and move on to the next question? Not necessarily. There are powerful strategies you can use to answer analogies containing words you don't know. In fact, you can almost always *ZAP* one or two choices, even when you don't know either of the stem words.

Recognizing Related Pairs

Always remember that a true SAT analogy consists of a clear and logical relationship between two words. So far, you have already studied nine types of analogy relationships.

- IS A TYPE OF   e.g. EAGLE : BIRD
- IS A PART OF   e.g. ACTOR : CAST
- IS A PLACE WHERE   e.g. GREENHOUSE : PLANT
- IS USED TO   e.g. THERMOMETER : TEMPERATURE
- RELATIVE SIZE   e.g. HILL : MOUNTAIN
- IS CHARACTERISTIC OF   e.g. PAUPER : DESTITUTE
- ANTONYM   e.g. IRRATIONAL : LOGIC
- DEFINITIONAL   e.g. ELUSIVE : CATCH
- DEGREE   e.g. ASTONISHED : SURPRISED

Recognizing Unrelated Pairs

Study the following four analogies. Which of the nine relationships does each one illustrate?

- CONFIDENT : WIN   • SOLDIERS : BRAVE
- PALACE : INTRIGUE   • CURIOUS : FACTS

If you had trouble determining which relationships are illustrated by these analogies, don't worry. In fact, all four are unrelated pairs of words that do not form an SAT analogy. For example, is there a clear and logical relationship between CONFIDENT and WIN? Don't CONFIDENT players usually WIN? Maybe, but CONFIDENT players also lose sometimes. Although these two words are associated with each other, there is no clear and logical relationship between CONFIDENT and WIN. Similarly, a PALACE is a place where INTRIGUE *sometimes* occurs. *Some* SOLDIERS are BRAVE while some are not, and *some* FACTS are CURIOUS, but many are not.

Any answer choice containing words that are NOT related to each other in a clear and logical way does not form an SAT analogy and should be eliminated. *At least one-fifth of all SAT analogy answer choices are unrelated.* If you *ZAP* unrelated pairs, you will reduce your mental work load and dramatically improve your odds of finding the correct answer.

Developing an Extra Edge

The following four tips will help you recognize unrelated word pairs.

1. True SAT analogies must have a clear and logical relationship. If you need the words *sometimes* or *maybe* to connect a word pair, the answer choice is not a true SAT analogy.

2. Beware of answer choices that sound good simply because there is a familiar association between them. For example, BIRTHDAY : CELEBRATE, MEAT : POTATOES, and EXPLORER : FAME all are frequently associated pairs of words. But does *everyone* celebrate his or her birthday? Do meat and potatoes *always* go together? And does *every* explorer win fame? No, no, and no.

3. The nine types of relationships you have studied account for more than 95% of all SAT analogies. You should be immediately suspicious of any answer choice that doesn't fit into one of these nine categories.

4. The few types of analogies that we haven't examined are fairly easy to recognize and appear only once in a great while. Here are three relationships that appear infrequently in analogy sections.

RELATIONSHIP	EXAMPLE	SENTENCE
Is Used By	DRILL : DENTIST	A DRILL is used by a DENTIST.
Is a Measure Of	DECIBEL : SOUND	A DECIBEL is a measure of SOUND.
Is an Expression Of	KISS : AFFECTION	A KISS is an expression of AFFECTION.

Independent
PRACTICE

Analogy Practice Exercises 5-7 give you an opportunity to practice the skill of identifying unrelated pairs.

ANALOGY PRACTICE EXERCISE 5 "Unrelated Pairs"

DIRECTIONS: Read each pair of words and note what type of analogy is being tested. Use the codes below to classify each word pair. Place a Z (for *ZAPS*) beside any pair of unrelated words.

Is a Type Of . . . . T		Antonym . . . . A	
Relative Size . . . . RS		Is Used To . . . . U	
Is a Part Of . . . . P		Definitional . . . . DEF	
Is Characteristic Of C		Degree . . . . DEG	
		Is a Place Where . . . . . PW	

Z	1.	KNIGHT : BEAUTY
DFF	2.	ELEGY : SORROW
DEF	3.	JURISPRUDENCE : LAW
Z	4.	INTERPRETATION : READER
DEF	5.	GOVERNMENT : POLICY
Z	6.	HILL : TREES
C	7.	EVIL : MALEFACTOR
Z	8.	EULOGY : CANDID
U	9.	ADHESIVE : BOND
DEG	10.	RAGE : ANGER
Z	11.	GEOLOGY : RUINS
T	12.	CUMULUS : CLOUD
A	13.	NEFARIOUS : VIRTUE
U	14.	ANALGESIC : PAIN
Z	15.	BACON : EGGS
Z	16.	RODENTS : MAZE
P	17.	STAR : CONSTELLATION
A	18.	FLIPPANT : DEFERENTIAL
PW	19.	LITIGATION : COURT
RS	20.	DITCH : RAVINE
DEF	21.	ASSUAGE : SORROW
Z	22.	STRENUOUS : EXERCISE
DEG	23.	PARAMOUNT : IMPORTANT
Z	24.	PAINT : CREATIVITY
Z	25.	CLAUSE : CONTRACT

ANALOGY PRACTICE EXERCISE ⑥ "Unrelated Pairs"

DIRECTIONS: Read each pair of words and note what type of analogy is being tested. Use the codes below to classify each word pair. Place a Z (for *ZAPS*) beside any pair of unrelated words.

Is a Type Of	. . . . T	Antonym	. . . . A
Relative Size	. . . . RS	Is Used To	. . . . U
Is a Part Of	. . . . P	Definitional	. . . . DEF
Is Characteristic Of	 C	Degree	. . . . DEG
		Is a Place Where	. . . . . PW

Z	1.	ENVY : SUCCESS
Z	2.	PLEASURABLE : INDULGED
DEF	3.	PROLOGUE : PLAY
Z	4.	ADVENTURE : DANGER
P	5.	CAT : FELINE
DEF	6.	BUOYANT : FLOAT
U	7.	SCALE : WEIGHT
Z	8.	PLAGIARIST : IMAGINATION
A	9.	IMPIOUS : REVERENT
Z	10.	LARCENY : PERJURY
Z	11.	WISE : DETACHED
DEG	12.	EXCRUCIATING : PAINFUL
C	13.	MISCREANT : WICKED
DEF	14.	INSIGHT : INTUITION
Z	15.	JEALOUS : BLESSED
PW	16.	AQUARIUM : FISH
RS	17.	CREEK : RIVER
DEF	18.	CODICIL : WILL
Z	19.	MOODY : JEALOUS
DEG	20.	SUPERCILIOUS : ARROGANT
DEF	21.	EPIC : LENGTHY
Z	22.	REPULSIVE : DISTANCE
Z	23.	SERMON : DUTY
DEG	24.	ACRIMONIOUS : BITTER
DEF	25.	ALLAY : ANXIETY

ANALOGY PRACTICE EXERCISE ❼ "Unrelated Pairs"

DIRECTIONS: Read each pair of words and note what type of analogy is being tested. Use the codes below to classify each word pair. Place a Z (for *ZAPS*) beside any pair of unrelated words.

Is a Type Of . . . . T		Antonym . . . . A	
Relative Size . . . . RS		Is Used To . . . . U	
Is a Part Of . . . . P		Definitional . . . . DEF	
Is Characteristic Of C		Degree . . . . DEG	
		Is a Place Where . . . . PW	

A	1.	MERCILESS : SYMPATHETIC
A	2.	IMPLACABLE : RELENTING
Z	3.	GOSSIP : TRUTHFUL
Z	4.	COACH : WINNER
Z	5.	COFFEE : SUGAR
DEG	6.	AUSPICIOUS : FAVORABLE
Z	7.	DEPRECIATE : DISCARDED
DEF	8.	DELIBERATE : ACTION
Z	9.	QUOTATION : MEMORABLE
C	10.	LOITERER : IDLE
Z	11.	SCIENTIST : CATALYST
U	12.	ODOMETER : DISTANCE
P	13.	MUSICIAN : ORCHESTRA
Z	14.	OPTIMISTIC : LUCKY
DEF	15.	AMIABLE : COMPANY
DEG	16.	EUPHORIA : HAPPINESS
A	17.	QUIXOTIC : PRAGMATIC
Z	18.	ICING : CAKE
DEF	19.	FOREBODING : DISASTER
Z	20.	BROOD : INSULT
Z	21.	MERCIFUL : JUSTICE
DEF	22.	EXONERATE : BLAME
U	23.	PIPELINE : OIL
A	24.	MITIGATE : SEVERITY
T	25.	RUBY : GEMSTONE

Working in Reverse

Carefully examine the following four analogies.

- MARTYR : SELF-ABNEGATING
- JINGOIST : NATION
- SANCTIMONIOUS : HYPOCRISY
- CORROBORATE : TESTIMONY

Do you know the meaning of the words in these four analogies? Don't worry if you don't. SELF-ABNEGATING (lack of consideration for oneself), JINGOIST (a super patriot, chauvinist), SANCTIMONIOUS (pretending to be very holy, pious), and CORROBORATE (to strengthen) are examples of the most difficult words used on the SAT.

Normally you begin working on an analogy by establishing a relationship between the stem words and then forming a sentence connecting them. But what if you don't know what the stem words mean and are therefore unable to construct a sentence?

Fortunately, there is a very powerful strategy for dealing with this type of problem. It's called *Working in Reverse*. Working in Reverse is based upon a simple but important principle. Each SAT analogy question contains at least two analogous pairs: the stem words and one of the answer choices. Working in Reverse utilizes the fact that one of the answer choices must be an analogy. Your job is to use the skills you have developed so far to find the correct answer. Here is a three-step procedure for accomplishing this task.

1. ***ZAP* all unrelated pairs.** A true SAT analogy consists of a clear and logical relationship between two words. As you learned in Lesson 7, unrelated pairs lack a clear and logical relationship. Your first step is to carefully examine all five answer choices and *ZAP* any unrelated pairs.

2. ***ZAP* answer choices that have the same relationship.** Closely examine the following analogy.

   <u>XXXX</u> : <u>XXXX</u> ::
   (A) inflexible : bend
   (B) perpetual : stop
   (C) slippery : grasp
   (D) dense : penetrate
   (E) brittle : break

The stem words are blocked out to illustrate an analogy where you don't know the meaning of the words. Take a look at the five answer choices.

(A) inflexible : bend	Is there a clear and logical relationship between inflexible and bend? Yes. Something that is inflexible won't bend. We can't *ZAP* this choice at this time.
(B) perpetual : stop	Is there a clear and logical relationship between perpetual and stop? Yes. Something that is perpetual won't stop. We can't *ZAP* this choice at this time.
(C) slippery : grasp	Is there a clear and logical relationship between slippery and grasp? Yes. Something that is slippery is hard to grasp. We can't *ZAP* this choice at this time.
(D) dense : penetrate	Is there a clear and logical relationship between dense and penetrate? Yes. Something that is dense is hard to penetrate. We can't *ZAP* this choice at this time.
(E) brittle : break	Is there a clear and logical relationship between brittle and break? Yes. Something that is brittle will break. We can't *ZAP* this choice at this time.

At first glance we seem to have solved nothing since we were unable to *ZAP* any unrelated pairs. But looks are deceiving. Based on our first pass, answers (A) and (B) have the same relationship. Whenever two answer choices have the same relationship, neither one can be the correct response. You can therefore *ZAP* (A) and (B), even though you don't know the main pair of words. Using this same procedure you can also *ZAP* answers (C) and (D). *ZAPPING* leaves (E) as the only remaining choice.

3. **After *ZAPPING*, guess from the remaining choices.** Working in Reverse should help you *ZAP* two or more answer choices. Guess from the remaining answer choices. As you learned in the Introduction, never leave a blank if you can *ZAP* even one choice.

Guided PRACTICE

DIRECTIONS: Let's use our three-step procedure to solve the following analogy by Working in Reverse. We've blocked the stem words to illustrate how powerful a strategy Working in Reverse can be.

XXXX : XXXX ::

(A) scientist : inventive
(B) liar : compulsive
(C) hothead : impulsive
(D) politician : eloquent
(E) amateur : skillful

(A) scientist : inventive	Is there a clear and logical relationship between scientist and inventive? No. Scientists are *sometimes* inventive, but not always. *ZAP* it.
(B) liar : compulsive	Is there a clear and logical relationship between liar and compulsive? No. *Some* liars are compulsive, but others are not. This is an unrelated pair. *ZAP.*
(C) hothead : impulsive	Is there a clear and logical relationship between hothead and impulsive? Yes. Being impulsive is characteristic of a hothead. Let's keep this one.
(D) politician : eloquent	Is there a clear and logical relationship between politician and eloquent? No. *Some* politicians are eloquent, but some of them are quite poor at public speaking.
(E) amateur : skillful	Is there a clear and logical relationship between amateur and skillful? No. *Some* amateurs are skillful, but others are not. *ZAP* it.

Conclusion: Working in Reverse leaves you with choice (C) as the only possible answer.

Guided PRACTICE

DIRECTIONS: Here are three more analogies. Solve them by Working in Reverse.

1. <u>XXXX</u> : <u>XXXX</u> ::
    (A) heroic : conflict   (D) elated : happy
    (B) worried : apathetic   (E) request : command
    (C) ambition : success

2. <u>XXXX</u> : <u>XXXX</u> ::
    (A) hurricane : land   (D) earthquake : valley
    (B) avalanche : snow   (E) fire : forest
    (C) tornado : air

3. <u>XXXX</u> : <u>XXXX</u> ::
    (A) vain : flattery   (D) staid : levity
    (B) adroit : skill   (E) amiable : company
    (C) profound : depth

Analogy 1

Discussion

(A) heroic : conflict — Is there a clear and logical relationship between heroic and conflict? No. Some conflicts are heroic, but others are not. *ZAP* this unrelated pair.

(B) worried : apathetic — Is there a clear and logical relationship between worried and apathetic? Yes. Worried and apathetic are antonyms. Hold this one for now.

(C) ambition : success — Is there a clear and logical relationship between ambition and success? No. Ambition sometimes leads to success and sometimes it does not. *ZAP* it.

(D) elated : happy — Is there a clear and logical relationship between elated and happy? Yes. Elated means to be very happy. Hold this one for now.

(E) request : command — Is there a clear and logical relationship between request and command? Yes. Request and command are antonyms. Hold onto this one for now.

Conclusion: Choices (A) and (C) can be *ZAPPED* because they are unrelated pairs. Choices (B) and (E) are both antonym analogies. The stem words therefore cannot be an antonym analogy since there would then be two possible answers. Therefore *ZAP* both (B) and (E). After *ZAPPING*, choice (D) is the only possible answer.

Analogy 2

(A) hurricane : land	Is there a clear and logical relationship between hurricane and land? No. Some hurricanes strike land, but others do not. *ZAP* this unrelated pair.
(B) avalanche : snow	Is there a clear and logical relationship between avalanche and snow? Yes. By definition, an avalanche is a large mass of moving snow. Hold onto this one.
(C) tornado : air	Is there a clear and logical relationship between tornado and air. Yes. By definition, a tornado is a whirlpool of moving air. Hold onto this one.
(D) earthquake : valley	Is there a clear and logical relationship between earthquake and valley? No. Some earthquakes occur in a valley, but others occur in mountains or in the ocean. This is an unrelated pair. *ZAP* it.
(E) fire : forest	Is there a clear and logical relationship between fire and forest? No. Some fires occur in forests, but many do not. This is an unrelated pair. *ZAP* it.

Conclusion: Choices (A), (D), and (E) are unrelated pairs and can be *ZAPPED*. Choices (B) and (C) both form analogous relationships so both could be the answer. At this point, you should simply guess between (B) or (C). The correct answer may not be known to you, but on problems like this, you will tend to be right half the time.

Analogy 3

(A) vain : flattery   Is there a clear and logical relationship between vain and flattery? Yes. A vain person likes flattery. Hold onto this one.

(B) adroit : skill   Is there a clear and logical relationship between adroit and skill? Yes. By definition, an adroit person has great skill. Hold onto this one.

(C) profound : depth   Is there a clear and logical relationship between profound and depth? Yes. By definition, something profound has great depth. Hold onto this one.

(D) staid : levity   Is there a clear and logical relationship between staid and levity? Let's assume that you don't know what the words staid and levity mean. Now what do you do? Stay calm. Remember your indomitable will! Let's put this answer on hold and move on to the next choice.

(E) amiable : company   Is there a clear and logical relationship between amiable and company? Yes. By definition, an amiable person enjoys company. Hold onto this one.

Conclusion: Choices (A) and (E) have the same relationship and can therefore be *ZAPPED*. Similarly, choices (B) and (C) have the same relationship and can be *ZAPPED*. After *ZAPPING*, you are left with choice (D). Even though you don't know what the words mean, you can make a logical assumption that they form an SAT analogy.

Developing an Extra Edge

1. It is important to remember that the technique of Working in Reverse may not enable you to *ZAP* every answer choice. However, you should always guess if you can *ZAP* even one of the choices.

2. The technique of Working in Reverse works especially well on *Is Characteristic Of* analogies. This type of analogy always provides you with five choices involving a person and a characteristic. Since an analogy cannot have two or more answers with the same relationship, you should always be able to *ZAP* four answers in *Is Characteristic Of* analogies.

Independent PRACTICE

Analogy Practice Exercise 8 gives you an opportunity to practice the skill of Working in Reverse.

ANALOGY PRACTICE EXERCISE 8 "Working in Reverse"

The most likely answers have been marked.

DIRECTIONS: Use the Working in Reverse strategies to eliminate unlikely choices. After you have *ZAPPED* three or four choices, mark one or two possible answers.

1. XXXX : XXXX ::
   - (A) hand : fingers
   - (B) alphabet : letters
   - (C) foot : toes
   - (●) bird : feathers
   - (E) scale : notes

2. XXXX : XXXX ::
   - (●) etymologist : words
   - (B) potter : clay
   - (C) exterminator : pests
   - (D) barber : razor
   - (E) dramatist : costumes

3. XXXX : XXXX ::
   - (A) gambler : poverty
   - (B) scholar : plagiarism
   - (C) braggart : modesty
   - (●) philanthropist : generosity
   - (E) detective : maturity

4. XXXX : XXXX ::
   - (A) fragrant : smell
   - (B) savory : taste
   - (C) melodious : sound
   - (D) successful : tune
   - (●) dim : light

5. XXXX : XXXX ::
   - (A) sermon : duty
   - (B) benefit : burden
   - (C) discharge : intern
   - (D) burglary : perjury
   - (●) speck : stain

6. XXXX : XXXX ::

   (A) dejected : hopeless
   (B) wise : detached
   (●) enraged : angry
   (D) shy : lazy
   (E) shapeless : formless

7. XXXX : XXXX ::

   (A) event : random
   (●) watershed : significant
   (C) conclusion : vague
   (D) decision : crushing
   (E) memory : forgivable

8. XXXX : XXXX ::

   (A) polemic : soothe
   (B) parody : praise
   (C) cliché : imagination
   (●) skit : lengthy
   (E) elegy : lament

9. XXXX : XXXX ::

   (A) hostage : lawless
   (B) hypocrite : devout
   (C) jingoist : tolerant
   (D) zealot : indifferent
   (●) optimist : hopeful

10. XXXX : XXXX ::

    (A) elusive : catch
    (●) wan : vitality
    (C) impetuous : temporary
    (D) benevolent : perfection
    (E) obstinate : persuade

Pacing Your Work on Analogies

Remind students that it is more important to be careful than to rush and risk making careless errors. These pacing guidelines are for students who are capable of completing the entire test in a careful, thoughtful manner.

Students aspiring to reach for the top of the SAT verbal tower should strive to answer all of the analogy questions. The strategies and practice exercises you have completed so far are designed to enable you to master even the most challenging analogy questions.

As you know, your SAT will include one set of 13 analogies and one set of 6 analogies. You should spend an *average* of about 40 seconds on each analogy question. This means devoting about 9 minutes to the set of 13 analogies and 4 minutes to the set of 6 analogies. This pace is designed to leave you with ample time to complete the critical reading passages.

Independent PRACTICE

Analogy Practice Exercises 9 and 10 give you an opportunity to time yourself on a set of 13 analogies and a set of 6 analogies.

ANALOGY PRACTICE EXERCISE 9 "Timed Test"

DIRECTIONS: Mark the best answer in each of the following 13 analogies. Try to complete the entire set in 9 minutes. When you have finished, use the space provided to record how long it took you to complete the set.

1. CAPTAIN : SHIP ::

   (A) guard : fort
   (B) principal : school
   (C) writer : editor
   (D) teacher : faculty
   (E) guest : party

2. DISTANCE : ODOMETER ::

   (A) exposure : camera
   (B) temperature : thermometer
   (C) reflection : telescope
   (D) mold : plastic
   (E) plow : tractor

3. APEX : PYRAMID ::

   (A) summit : mountain
   (B) edge : knife
   (C) outline : report
   (D) recess : school
   (E) shore : lake

4. ARBORETUM : TREES ::

   (A) hospital : patients
   (B) supermarket : shoppers
   (C) bank : depositors
   (D) aquarium : fish
   (E) dormitory : students

5. ADJOURNMENT : TRIAL ::

   (A) bone : skeleton
   (B) preface : book
   (C) annex : building
   (D) strike : factory
   (E) intermission : play

6. COMBUSTIBLE : IGNITE ::

   (A) parallel : meet
   (B) extinct : live
   (C) soluble : dissolve
   (D) dense : penetrate
   (E) buoyant : spirit

7. ANTIDOTE : POISONING ::

   (A) tranquilizer : anxiety
   (B) sedative : drowsiness
   (C) sandpaper : friction
   (D) analgesic : sleep
   (E) fertilizer : growth

8. PRELUDE : PERFORMANCE ::

   (A) itinerary : trip
   (B) signature : document
   (C) preamble : statute
   (D) addendum : book
   (E) movement : symphony

9. MALADROIT : SKILL ::

   (A) juvenile : youth
   (B) surprise : shock
   (C) sociable : company
   (D) ardent : passion
   (E) aimless : purpose

10. REPROBATE : DEPRAVED ::

   (A) coward : brave
   (B) pauper : destitute
   (C) cynic : hopeful
   (D) rebel : loyal
   (E) patron : miserly

11. QUELL : DISTURBANCE ::

   (A) articulate : theory
   (B) multiply : anxiety
   (C) mute : sound
   (D) dismantle : fortress
   (E) shift : blame

12. OBDURATE : COMPROMISE ::

   (A) bargain : purchase
   (B) summons : invite
   (C) brittle : bend
   (D) momentary : change
   (E) revolt : mutiny

13. FLAMBOYANT : GAUDY ::

   (A) intriguing : boring
   (B) difficult : arduous
   (C) innocence : patience
   (D) effervescent : animated
   (E) discordant : harmonious

TIME: _____

ANALOGY PRACTICE EXERCISE ⑩ "Timed Test"

DIRECTIONS: Mark the best answer in each of the following six analogies. Try to complete the entire set in 4 minutes. When you have finished, use the space provided to record how long it took you to complete the set.

1. THESAURUS : SYNONYM ::

   (A) atlas : map
   (B) footnote : definition
   (C) prescription : drug
   (D) blueprint : building
   (E) flour : wheat

2. OYSTER : PEARL ::

   (A) petroleum : refinery
   (B) apple : core
   (C) crab : claw
   (D) bear : cub
   (E) sheep : wool

3. DELUGE : SHOWER ::

   (A) rumble : thunder
   (B) freeze : thaw
   (C) blizzard : flurry
   (D) breathe : inhale
   (E) desert : oasis

4. SYLLABUS : COURSE ::

   (A) index : book
   (B) document : portfolio
   (C) recess : school
   (D) title : play
   (E) resume : career

5. ITEM : COMPENDIUM ::

   (A) census : population
   (B) poem : anthology
   (C) conductor : orchestra
   (D) oration : speech
   (E) itinerary : voyage

6. INCORPOREAL : FORM ::

   (A) fleeting : fame
   (B) amendable : plan
   (C) anonymous : name
   (D) tempting : offer
   (E) alterable : position

TIME: _____

Putting It All

TOGETHER

1 There will be 19 analogies on your SAT. One 30-minute section will have a set of 13 analogies and one 30-minute section will have a set of 6 analogies.

2 Each analogy consists of a pair of stem words and five pairs of choices.

3 Begin each analogy by establishing a clear relationship between the two stem words. Then form a short, specific sentence connecting the stem words. Next apply your sentence to each of the answer choices. Select the answer that best matches your sentence.

4 In *Degree* analogies, the SAT writers provide you with two words, one of which is an intensified version of the other.

5 Any answer choice containing words that are NOT related to each other in a clear and logical way is not an SAT analogy and should be eliminated.

6 Working in Reverse is a powerful strategy when you don't know the meaning of the stem words. First, *ZAP* all unrelated pairs in the answer choices. Second, *ZAP* all answer choices that have the same relationship. Finally, guess from the remaining answer choices.

7 Strive to answer the set of 13 analogies in 9 minutes and the set of 6 analogies in 4 minutes.

Answering Analogies: Timed Test

DIRECTIONS: Mark the best answer for each of the following analogy questions. Try to complete the entire set in nine minutes.

1. BELT : WAIST ::

   (A) sole : shoe
   (B) pocket : pants
   (C) link : locket
   (D) ring : finger
   (E) beret : cap

2. COPPER : METAL ::

   (A) wave : fuel
   (B) thunder : lightning
   (C) pup : seal
   (D) oil : fuel
   (E) passenger : bus

3. RESERVOIR : WATER ::

   (A) clinic : treatment
   (B) highway : traffic
   (C) tank : fuel
   (D) mine : gold
   (E) mountain : tunnel

4. DECIBEL : SOUND ::

   (A) letter : alphabet
   (B) minute : time
   (C) weight : mineral
   (D) verse : poem
   (E) diameter : circle

5. ASTOUNDED : SURPRISED ::

   (A) dejected : sad
   (B) repulsed : interested
   (C) bored : curious
   (D) frustrated : patient
   (E) encouraged : hindered

6. SAGE : WISDOM ::

   (A) extrovert : reserve
   (B) explorer : curiosity
   (C) traitor : loyalty
   (D) acrobat : popularity
   (E) daredevil : caution

7. CODICIL : WILL ::

(A) climax : story
(B) sketch : drawing
(C) agenda : meeting
(D) annex : building
(E) excerpt : book

8. MARINE : SEA ::

(A) glacial : valley
(B) conflagrant : fire
(C) confluent : river
(D) carnivorous : animal
(E) terrestrial : land

9. ALLEVIATE : CONCERN ::

(A) appease : demand
(B) demean : reputation
(C) rearrange : plan
(D) resolve : dilemma
(E) inflame : passion

10. APHORISM : ENLIGHTEN ::

(A) satire : ridicule
(B) eulogy : condemn
(C) elegy : arouse
(D) fable : obscure
(E) epic : shame

11. MEANDERING : ROUTE ::

(A) renovated : building
(B) digressive : statement
(C) devastated : plan
(D) depreciating : asset
(E) revitalized: program

12. ABSTRUSE : UNDERSTAND ::

(A) fragile : break
(B) savory : enjoy
(C) naughty : disobedient
(D) elusive : catch
(E) tangled : confine

13. CHAUVINIST : NATION ::

(A) plagiarist : thought
(B) idealist : compromise
(C) exhibitionist : embarrassment
(D) egoist : self
(E) nonconformist : norm

Critical Reading for Rising to the Top of the Tower

After completing this chapter, you will be able to

1. describe the skill of making comparisons.

2. identify five types of comparison questions used in paired passages.

3. define and give examples of an assumption.

4. complete a single reading passage and answer its questions in 20 minutes.

5. complete two reading passages and answer their questions in 15 minutes.

6. complete a paired passage and answer its questions in 15 minutes.

Prior to attempting the strategies in this chapter, students should review Chapters 4 and 8. These advanced strategies are for excellent readers who have already mastered the previous material.

Have you ever had one of those days when you disagreed with every comment you heard from the minute you got out of bed? Some days it seems that the whole universe is devoid of facts—nothing but one opinion after another. Our classrooms, newspapers, television programs, electronic bulletin boards, and family discussions are crammed full of opinions of every kind. Although variety has been called the "spice of life," it is also one of the challenges of living with other people. As citizens of a democracy, we are often asked to identify, evaluate, and choose from a number of differing points of view.

The SAT writers recognize the importance of comparing different points of view. That's why each SAT includes a "paired passage" consisting of two passages on the same or related topics. Chapter 8 provided you with basic information about the passages and questions used in paired passages. As you learned, the paired passages and the first 7–8 questions are identical to the other SAT reading passages and questions. However, the final 3–4 questions are different. These "comparison questions" ask you to recognize similarities and differences between the two passages. This lesson will focus on the skills you need to answer comparison questions. Answering these questions is essential for students striving to climb to the top of the SAT tower.

Five Types of Comparison Questions

Making comparisons is an important part of our everyday lives. For example, as high school students you compare teachers, colleges, cars, singers, computers, movies, ideas, and many other things. But what does it mean to "make comparisons"? Making a comparison means examining two or more ideas, objects, people, or events to discover ways they are alike and ways they are different. For example, two cars can be compared on the basis of their cost, gas mileage, engine size, and a host of other features. Similarly, two reading passages can be compared in a number of different ways. The SAT writers have focused upon the following five distinct types of comparison questions.

1. **Comparing Main Ideas** In Chapter 4 you learned that each SAT passage contains a main idea and supporting details. About half of the comparison questions ask you to identify the similarities between main ideas and key supporting points presented in the paired passages.

2. **Comparing Tone** In Chapter 8 you learned that each author has a tone or attitude toward the subject he or she is writing about. Many paired passages include a question asking you to evaluate the differences in tone between the two passages.

3. **Comparing Assumptions** An assumption is a belief that underlies a statement or action. Although assumptions may be stated, they are often unstated. For example, Alexander Hamilton's statement that the government should be entrusted to the "rich, well-born, and able" was based upon the assumption that the mass of people were incapable of self-government. Many paired passage questions ask you to evaluate the assumptions upon which the authors base their arguments.

4. **Determining a Point of Agreement** The authors of the two paired passages often disagree on key issues and ideas. However, this does not mean that they disagree on everything. One often asked comparison question asks you to recognize a statement the two authors would agree with.

5. **Determining How One Author Would React to the Other Author** The most challenging comparison questions ask you to use your knowledge of one author's viewpoint to determine how he/she would react to a point made by the other author. For example, a comparison question on a recent PSAT asked, "What would be the likely response of the author of Passage 2 to the discussion on cars in lines 10–18 of Passage 1?"

Although comparison questions are challenging, they are not impossible. Like Level 5 Sentence Completion and Analogy questions, they require good skill and a lot of practice. When answering comparison questions, it is often helpful to visualize the passages as overlapping circles. For example, in the diagram below, the circle on the left represents Passage 1 and the circle on the right represents Passage 2. The area where the two passages overlap represents the similarities between the passages.

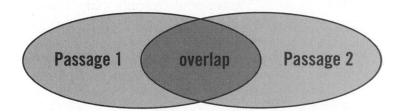

A Case Example

In Chapter 8, you read a paired passage and then answered the passage specific questions. The passages are reprinted below. Read the two passages and then answer the five comparison questions that follow. The questions are designed to illustrate the five major types of comparison questions.

Passage 1

A well-organized, well-financed group with a focused agenda was able to use the media to scare the wits out of an uninformed public who, until they sat down that night to watch *60 Minutes*, had
Line never heard of Alar.
(5)   The panic produced by the *60 Minutes* report was almost like yelling "fire!" in a theater, except that in the case of Alar there certainly was time for reasonable people to ask if CBS and Meryl Streep were the best authorities on this subject, and if their opinions ought to be substituted for all the health regulators in the FDA, the
(10) EPA and the rest of the federal government.

More and more, public policy is decided this way. The scare and reaction method has become a primary prod for decision making at policy levels in this country.

A focused, highly motivated minority, often a very small minority,
(15) is able to overwhelm and capture the decision making process because the majority is unfocused, or focused on other matters. Too often, the style of our debate is turned into a shouting match, where lies and half-truths are acceptable tools, and where reason and evidence counts for little.

(20)   Let me make another related point before I go on: government is only one of the institutions making the rules we live by. Schools, the media, special interest groups and others, as in the case of Alar, are able to create and enforce actions which bypass our representative legislative bodies or administrative offices.

(25)   A good example of this relates once again to the Alar incident.

Within a few hours of the *60 Minutes* broadcast, the New York City Public Schools took all apples out of their lunch program.

We spoke to the school officials to tell them how mistaken this decision was.

(30)   We were told frankly that science had nothing to do with it. The administrators in New York simply were not willing to face alarmed parents. This decision was later reversed, but only after several weeks passed and many wholesome apples were destroyed and others went unpurchased.

from "Economic Priorities and the Environmentalist" by Richard McGuire

Passage 2

(35)   Listening to a well regarded environmental program on the radio last winter, I heard the commentator take on the nuclear industry for the "deceit" behind its new PR[†] campaign: *"The ads boast that nuclear energy doesn't pollute the air. Now that may be technically correct, but it completely avoids the huge problem … of what happens when*

(40) *accidents occur. You know, the ones they assured us could never happen. But when they do, the cancer rates in the vicinity soar, and the entire region's landscape is blighted for who knows how long. Accidents like Chernobyl *."*

    The commentator's reporting might be, uh, "technically correct"

(45) regarding Chernobyl. But her piece was focussing on the nuclear industry in the *United States*. In fact, there is no documented evidence of increased cancer rates resulting from this nation's worst accident, at Three Mile Island in 1979. There has never been an accident at a U.S. nuclear reactor which has blighted the landscape.

(50)   The facts: People living within 50 miles of TMI were exposed to about 1.5 millirems of radiation. (The average annual dose for a U.S. resident is 360 millirems, from background radiation.) Of quite a different magnitude is the widely accepted estimate that, over the next 50 years, 17,000 people will die from cancers induced by

(55) Chernobyl's runaway nuclear reaction.

    Evidently, then, Chernobyl does *not* equal Three Mile Island.

    It's not that I think the "Living on Earth" radio commentator had no legitimate quarrel with the PR campaign. Certainly, she had reason to critique the nuclear industry's worker-safety record, as

(60) well as their avoidance of the unresolved issue of radwaste disposal. But why hype the commentary with blighted landscapes and soaring cancer rates? "Living on Earth" is generally an excellent environmental program, yet even the best resort to hyperbole when nukes come up.

(65)   Reporting that diverts us from rational, informed debate about energy options fuels the public's nuclear phobia. And it belongs in the dumpster.

[†] PR: public relations

* Chernobyl: an explosion in a Soviet nuclear power plant in the city of Chernobyl released large amounts of radioactive materials into the environment

from "Media Meltdown" by Scott Menchin

1. **Comparing Main Ideas**

   Both authors see serious problems in the way that

   (A) environmental pollutants are regulated
   (B) environmental research is conducted
   (C) elected officials investigate scientific stories
   (D) small groups always dominate public policy debates
   (●) media coverage often influences scientific debates

Since both passages emphasize problems in the way *media coverage often influences scientific debates*, choice (E) is the best answer. For example, Passage 1 points out that a *60 Minutes* segment on the pesticide Alar "scared the wits out of an uninformed public." The author of Passage 2 reinforces this concern with media coverage saying that "Reporting that diverts us from rational, informed debate about energy options ... belongs in the dumpster." Choices (A), (B), (C), and (D) can be eliminated since they are not mentioned in both passages and are not the focus of either passage.

2. **Comparing Tone**

   In both passages, the author's attitude toward ill-considered reporting is best described as

   (A) offended
   (B) delighted
   (C) indifferent
   (D) ambivalent
   (E) amused

Both authors are critical of ill-considered reporting. You can therefore delete choices (B), (C), (D), and (E) as being either too positive or neutral. Only choice (A), *offended*, conveys the negative reaction the two authors have toward ill-considered reporting.

3. **Comparing Assumptions**

   What best describes an assumption about the public held by the authors of Passages 1 and 2?

   (A) Most people are well-informed and highly focused on public issues.
   (B) The public places too much trust in school officials and government bureaucrats.
   (C) The public usually ignores media reports.
   (D) The public has given too much authority to the nuclear power industry.
   (E) The public can be easily misled by emotional charges and undocumented assertions.

Choice (A) can be ZAPPED since Passage 1 states (lines 14-16) that the majority of the public is "unfocused." Choice (B) can be ZAPPED since Passage 1 criticizes school administrators for ignoring scientific facts and giving in to emotional parents. Choice (C) can be ZAPPED since both authors agree that the public pays attention to media reports. Choice (D) can be ZAPPED since it is not discussed in Passage 1 and is not supported by Passage 2. Choice (E) is the best response since both passages portray the public as "unfocused" and thus easily "diverted" by emotional charges about pesticides and undocumented assertions about the nuclear power industry.

4. **Determining a Point of Agreement**
   The authors of both passages would most probably agree that
   (A) all reporting on environmental matters is harmful to the public interest
   (B) fear of sickness from environmental causes in the United States is irrational
   (C) scientists are best qualified to make decisions about public environmental policy
   (D) industry groups can be trusted to regulate themselves to protect the general public
   (E) a realistic environmental policy requires the acceptance of some degree of potential risks

Since neither author suggests that *all reporting on environmental matters is harmful* or that *industry groups can be trusted to regulate themselves*, choices (A) and (D) can be ZAPPED. Choice (B) is not correct because only author 1 says that an uninformed public needs to direct questions to authorities before panicking; justified fear would not be irrational. Choice (C) is tempting because author 1 expresses this belief in lines 9-11, but author 2 doesn't actually state this. In fact, scientists are never mentioned at all as being the most qualified in Passage 2, only "the facts" are mentioned in lines 50-55. This does not indicate that the author clearly believes scientists are the best qualified to make decisions on public policy. Both authors realize that a realistic environmental policy does have to accept a certain level of potential risks, which makes (E) the best answer.

5. **Determining How One Author Would React to the Other Author**
   What would be the likely response of the author of Passage 1 to the report by the "Living on Earth" radio commentator in lines 37-43?
   (A) cautious approval
   (B) indignant criticism
   (C) enthusiastic endorsement
   (D) detached neutrality
   (E) anxious anticipation

The author of Passage 1 strongly criticizes the media for what he calls a "scare and react method" of reporting. The author of Passage 1 would thus be very critical of the broadcast by the "Living on Earth" commentator. Since choices (A), (C), (D), and (E) describe positive or neutral responses, they can be ZAPPED. Only choice (B) describes the negative reaction we would expect from the author of Passage 1.

Guided PRACTICE

DIRECTIONS: First read the following paired passages. Then answer the five comparison questions that follow.

Both of the following excerpts discuss how two teenagers felt about immigrating to North America. The author of Passage 1 emigrated from Russia to America in 1894. The author of Passage 2 emigrated from Poland to Canada in 1959.

Passage 1

Passover was celebrated in tears that year. In the story of the Exodus we would have read a chapter of current history, only for us there was no deliverer and no promised land. But what said
Line some of us at the end of the long service? Not "May we be next
(5) year in Jerusalem," but "Next year—in America!" So there was our promised land, and many faces were turned towards the West. . . .

My father was carried away by the westward movement, glad of his own deliverance, but sore at heart for us whom he left behind. It was the last chance for all of us. We were so far reduced
(10) in circumstances that he had to travel with borrowed money to a German port, whence he was forwarded to Boston, with a host of others, at the expense of an emigrant aid society. . . .

I am sure I made as serious efforts as anybody to prepare myself for life in America on the lines indicated in my father's letters. In
(15) America, he wrote, it was no disgrace to work at a trade. Workmen and capitalists were equal. The employer addressed the employee as *you*, not, familiarly, as *thou*. The cobbler and the teacher had the same title, "Mister." And all the children, boys and girls, Jews and Gentiles, went to school! Education would be ours for the asking,
(20) and economic independence also, as soon as we were prepared. He wanted Fetchke and me to be taught some trade; so my sister was apprenticed to a dressmaker and I to a milliner. . . .

This was during our last year in Russia, when I was between twelve and thirteen years of age: My father's letters soon warned
(25) us to prepare for the summons, and we lived in a quiver of expectation.

Not that my father had grown suddenly rich. He was so far from rich that he was going to borrow every cent of the money for our third-class passage; but he had a business in view which he
(30) could carry on all the better for having the family with him; and, besides, we were borrowing right and left anyway, and to no definite purpose. With the children, he argued, every year in Russia was a year lost. They should be spending the precious years in school, in learning English, in becoming Americans.
(35) United in America, there were ten chances of our getting to our feet again to one chance in our scattered, aimless state.

So at last I was going to America! Really, really going, at last! The boundaries burst. The arch of heaven soared. A million suns shone out for every star. The winds rushed in from outer space,
(40) roaring in my ears, "America! America!"

from *The Promised Land* by Mary Antin

Passage 2

It is April 1959, I'm standing at the railing of the *Batory's* upper deck, and I feel that my life is ending. I'm looking out at the crowd that has gathered on the shore to see the ship's departure from Gdynia—a crowd that, all of a sudden, is irrevocably on the other
(45) side—and I want to break out, run back, run toward the familiar excitement, the waving hands, the exclamations. We can't be leaving all this behind—but we are. I am thirteen years old, and we are emigrating. It's a notion of such crushing, definitive finality that to me it might as well mean the end of the world. . . .
(50) When the brass band on the shore strikes up the jaunty mazurka rhythms of the Polish anthem, I am pierced by a youthful sorrow so powerful that I suddenly stop crying and try to hold still against the pain. I desperately want time to stop, to hold the ship still with the force of my will. I am suffering my first, severe attack
(55) of nostalgia, or *tesknota*—a word that adds to nostalgia the tonalities of sadness and longing. It is a feeling whose shades and degrees I'm destined to know intimately, but at this hovering moment, it comes upon me like a visitation from a whole new geography of emotions, an annunciation of how much an absence
(60) can hurt. Or a premonition of absence, because at this divide, I'm filled to the brim with what I'm about to lose—images of Cracow, which I loved as one loves a person, of the sun-baked villages where we had taken summer vacations, of the hours I spent poring over passages of music with my piano teacher, of conversations
(65) and escapades with friends.

Looking ahead, I come across an enormous, cold blankness—a darkening, an erasure, of the imagination, as if a camera eye has snapped shut, or as if a heavy curtain has been pulled over the future. Of the place where we're going—Canada—I know nothing.
(70) There are vague outlines of half a continent, a sense of vast spaces and little habitation. When my parents were hiding in a branch-covered forest bunker during the war, my father had a book with him called *Canada Fragrant with Resin* which, in his horrible confinement, spoke to him of majestic wilderness, of animals
(75) roaming without being pursued, of freedom. That is partly why we are going there, rather than to Israel, where most of our Jewish friends have gone. But to me, the word "Canada" has ominous echoes of the "Sahara." No, my mind rejects the idea of being taken there, I don't want to be pried out of my childhood, my
(80) pleasures, my safety, my hopes for becoming a pianist. The *Batory* pulls away, the foghorn emits its lowing, shofar sound, but my being is engaged in a stubborn refusal to move. My parents put their hands on my shoulders consolingly; for a moment, they allow themselves to acknowledge that there's pain in this
(85) departure, much as they wanted it.

from *Lost in Translation* by Eva Hoffman

1. Both authors are primarily concerned with

   (●) adjusting to an irreversible change in their lives
   (B) dealing with an irrational fear that they will be separated from their families
   (C) coping with a severe state of depression
   (D) facing an unsettling fear that they will not survive the voyage across the Atlantic
   (E) explaining why their fathers chose to emigrate

2. The two authors differ in their attitudes toward emigrating to a new country in that Author 1 is

   (A) alarmed, whereas Author 2 is skeptical
   (B) exultant, whereas Author 2 is encouraged
   (●) exhilarated, whereas Author 2 is despondent
   (D) cautious, whereas Author 2 is somber
   (E) annoyed, whereas Author 2 is exuberant

3. Which best describes an assumption about emigrating held by the fathers of both authors?

   (A) America is a better country than Canada.
   (B) Going to a new country will force their daughters to become more responsible.
   (C) Urban life is better than rural life.
   (●) Life in the new countries will be better than life in the old countries.
   (E) If their families don't like the new countries they can always return to their old homes.

4. The authors of both passages would most probably agree that at the time they were emigrating

   (A) it was impossible to imagine what their future lives would be like
   (B) they were leaving lives of hardship for something much better
   (C) their fathers showed a callous disregard of how their children felt about emigrating
   (D) they were too young to understand what was happening to them
   (●) they knew they would be deeply affected by the experience of emigrating

5. What would be the likely response of the author of Passage 1 to the author of Passage 2's discussion of *tesknota* in lines 54-56?

(A) She would probably empathize with the author of Passage 2 saying that she feels the same emotion.

(B) She would probably criticize the author of Passage 2 for being overly sentimental and weak.

(C) She would probably urge the author of Passage 2 to refuse to emigrate.

(D) She would probably explain why America is a much better country than Canada.

(●) She would probably urge the author of Passage 2 to think more about the benefits of living in Canada.

Discussion

1. Both authors describe how they feel about leaving their homelands and emigrating to new countries. Although their feelings are quite different, both authors are trying to come to terms with the problem of *adjusting to an irreversible change in their lives*. Choices (B) and (D) can be ZAPPED since neither author expresses fear of being separated from her family or not surviving the voyage across the Atlantic. Choice (C) can be ZAPPED since the author of Passage 1 is clearly not depressed about emigrating to America. Choice (E) is tempting since both authors provide explanations of why their fathers chose to emigrate. However, this information is of secondary importance. This is particularly true in Passage 2, where the author only hints at why her father wanted to leave Poland. Since both authors are *adjusting to an irreversible change in their lives*, choice (A) is the best answer.

2. The two authors have very different views about emigrating. Since the author of Passage 1 is eagerly looking forward to emigrating while the author of Passage 2 dreads it, you are looking for an answer with a positive word and negative word combination. Choice (C) *exhilarated, despondent* is the only answer that clearly meets this criteria. Choices (A), (B), (D), and (E) all fail to meet this positive/negative criteria and can therefore be ZAPPED.

Discussion

3. Both fathers are willing to uproot their families because they believe their families will enjoy much better lives in America and Canada. Only choice (D) expresses this shared assumption. Choices (A), (B), (C), and (E) can all be *ZAPPED* since they are unsupported by the passages.

4. Although the two authors have very different views about leaving their homelands, both clearly understand that they would be *deeply affected by the experience of emigrating.* Choice (E) is thus the best answer. Choice (A) can be *ZAPPED* since the author of Passage 1 clearly envisions a bright future where "there were ten chances of our getting to our feet again to one chance in our scattered, aimless state." Choice (B) can be *ZAPPED* since the author of Passage 2 enjoyed her life in Poland and doesn't want "to be pried out of my childhood, my pleasures, my safety, my hopes of becoming a pianist." Choice (C) can be *ZAPPED* since the author of Passage 1 and her father share a common vision of America as a land of opportunity. In addition, the author of Passage 2 reveals that her parents do understand how she feels when they acknowledge her pain by putting their hands on her shoulders. And finally, choice (D) can be *ZAPPED* since both authors are fully aware of what is happening to them.

5. The author of Passage 2 is overwhelmed by a simultaneous feeling of nostalgia and sadness called *tesknota.* In contrast, the author of Passage 1 is overwhelmed by feelings of excitement and anticipation. Choice (A) can be *ZAPPED* since the author of Passage 1 has a very different feeling about emigrating and thus could not empathize with the author of Passage 2. Choice (B) is tempting. However, as an emigrant herself, the author of Passage 1 would probably not criticize a fellow teenager for feeling sad about leaving her friends and home. Choice (C) can be *ZAPPED* since the author of Passage 1 strongly supports emigrating. Choice (D) can be *ZAPPED* since there is no evidence that the author of Passage 1 has any knowledge about Canada. Given the author of Passage 1's positive views toward emigration, she would probably try to encourage the author of Passage 2 to think about the advantages of emigrating to Canada. Choice (E) is therefore the best answer.

Critical Reading Practice Exercise 11 provides you with an opportunity to answer comparison questions.

CRITICAL READING PRACTICE EXERCISE ⑪ "Comparison"

DIRECTIONS: First read the following paired passages. Then answer the five comparison questions that follow.

During the latter part of the fifth century B.C., most of the Greek world was divided into two powerful alliances led by the Athenians and the Lacedæmonians [commonly known to us as Spartans]. As tensions rose, the Spartans summoned a meeting to debate the issue of war or peace. The following passages are taken from an account of the meeting by a Greek historian. The first passage presents the views of the Corinthians, the second the views of the Spartan king.

Passage 1 (Corinthians)

Lacedæmonians! The confidence which you feel in your constitution and social order inclines you to receive any reflections
Line of ours or other powers with a certain skepticism. Hence springs
(5) your moderation, but hence also the rather limited knowledge which you betray in dealing with foreign politics. Time after time was our voice raised to warn you of the blows about to be dealt us by Athens, and time after time, instead of taking the trouble to ascertain the worth of our communications, you contented yourself
(10) with suspecting the speakers of being inspired by private interest. And so, instead of calling these allies together before the blow fell, you have delayed to do so till we are smarting under it. . . .

You, Lacedæmonians, of all the Hellenes are alone inactive, and defend yourselves not by doing anything but by looking as if you
(15) would do something; you alone wait till the power of an enemy is becoming twice its original size instead of crushing it in its infancy. . . .

We hope that none of you will consider these words of remonstrance to be rather words of hostility; men remonstrate with
(20) friends who are in error, accusations they reserve for enemies who have wronged them. Besides, we consider that we have as good a right as anyone to point out a neighbor's fault, particularly when we contemplate the great contrast between the two national characters; a contrast of which, as far as we can see, you have little
(25) perception, having never yet considered what sort of antagonists you will encounter in the Athenians, how widely, how absolutely different from yourselves.

The Athenians are addicted to innovation, and their designs are characterized by swiftness alike in conception and execution; you

(30) have a genius for keeping what you have got, accompanied by a total want of invention, and when forced to act you never go far enough. Again, they are adventurous beyond their power, and daring beyond their judgment, and in danger they are sanguine; your wont is to attempt less than is justified by your power, to

(35) mistrust even what is sanctioned by your judgment, and to fancy that from danger there is no release. Further, there is promptitude on their side against procrastination on yours; they are never at home, you are never from it: for they hope by their absence to extend their acquisitions, you fear by your advance to endanger

(40) what you have left behind. They are swift to follow up a success, and slow to recoil from a reverse. . . .

Such is Athens, your antagonist. And yet, Lacedæmonians, you still delay. . . . Let your procrastination end. For the present, assist your allies and Potidæ in particular, as you promised by a speedy

(45) invasion of Attica, and do not sacrifice friends and kindred to their bitterest enemies, and drive the rest of us in despair to some other alliance.

Passage 2 (Spartan king)

I do bid you not to take up arms at once, but to send and remonstrate with them in a tone not too suggestive of war, nor again

(50) too suggestive of submission, and to employ the interval in perfecting our own preparations. . . . If they listen to our embassy, so much the better; but if not, after the lapse of two or three years our position will have become materially strengthened, and we can then attack them if we think proper. . . .

(55) The slowness and procrastination, the parts of our character that are most assailed by their criticism, need not make you blush. If we undertake the war without preparation, we should by hastening its commencement only delay its conclusion: further, a free and famous city has through all time been ours. The quality which they

(60) condemn is really nothing but a wise moderation; thanks to its possession, we alone do not become insolent in success and give way less than others in misfortune; we are not carried away by the pleasure of hearing ourselves cheered on to risks which our judgment condemns; nor, if annoyed, are we any the more

(65) convinced by attempts to exasperate us by accusation. We are both warlike and wise, and it is our sense of order that makes us so. . . .

These practices, then, which our ancestors have delivered to us, and by whose maintenance we have always profited, must not be given up. And we must not be hurried into deciding in a day's brief

(70) space a question which concerns many lives and fortunes and many cities, and in which honour is deeply involved,—but we must decide calmly. This our strength peculiarly enables us to do.

from *The Complete Writings of Thucydides, The Peloponnesian War*, Crawley translation

1. Both speeches discuss the

    (A) strengths and weaknesses of Athens
    (B) reasons for declaring war on Athens
    (C) Spartan's policy of deliberate action
    (D) differences between Sparta and Athens
    (E) terms of a peace treaty with Athens

2. In comparison to the tone of Passage 1, the tone of Passage 2 is more

    (A) conciliatory
    (B) condemnatory
    (C) belligerent
    (D) arrogant
    (E) pessimistic

3. Which best describes an assumption about the future held by the speakers in Passages 1 and 2?

    (A) War can be avoided if the Spartans become more innovative and assertive.
    (B) War is certain if Athens continues its aggressive policies.
    (C) Athens and Sparta will become more alike.
    (D) The Corinthians will become the leading power in Greece.
    (E) The Persians will conquer both the Athenians and the Spartans.

4. The Corinthian ambassador and the Spartan king would most probably agree that

    (A) sea power is preferable to land power
    (B) it is better to be warlike than wise
    (C) caution is always a virtue
    (D) the Spartans do not fully understand their own character
    (E) foreign policy is closely related to national character

5. The view expressed in Passage 1 that war must be declared on Athens is challenged by the implication in Passage 2 that

    (A) the Athenians might listen to firm but reasonable arguments
    (B) Sparta is too preoccupied with its own internal affairs to fight Athens
    (C) Sparta is irrevocably committed to a policy of peace with its neighbors
    (D) Sparta distrusts the Corinthians
    (E) the Athenians are about to give up their aggressive policies

Pacing Your Work on Critical Reading

Students aspiring to reach for the top of the SAT verbal tower should strive to answer all of the critical reading questions. The strategies and practice exercises you have completed so far are designed to enable you to master even the most challenging critical reading passages and questions.

One of your verbal sections will contain 10 sentence completions, 13 analogies, and either a single reading passage or a paired passage. Regardless of whether it is a single passage or a paired passage, the reading will be between 85 and 100 lines long and contain 12 or 13 questions. If you spend an average of 40 seconds on each sentence completion and analogy, you will have 15 minutes to complete the critical reading passage.

Independent PRACTICE

Critical Reading Practice Exercise 12 provides you with an opportunity to answer a complete set of reading questions.

CRITICAL READING PRACTICE EXERCISE 12 "Timed Passage"

DIRECTIONS: Time yourself on the following critical reading passage and the 11 questions that accompany it. Try to read the passage and answer the questions in 15 minutes.

Questions 1-11 are based on the following passage.

The following passage is taken from a history of women artists.

In Italy during the Renaissance a revolutionary change occurred in artists' images of themselves in relation to society. They struggled to give the status and rewards of an intellectual profession to what
Line had hitherto been classified and rewarded as a craft. This change
(5) should have made it more difficult for women to become artists. A seven-year apprenticeship in a master's shop no longer sufficed. Artists were expected to have a liberal arts education with special emphasis on mathematics and the laws of perspective and to have considerable knowledge of ancient art, both from literary texts and
(10) from the objects themselves, which were best seen in Rome. . . . It became accepted that the training of every ambitious, serious artist would include the study of the human body, at first from corpses and clothed models but increasingly from the nude male model, and travel to the major art centers to study the achievements of
(15) one's rivals and of the best artists of the previous generation or two. Such a level of education and freedom of movement were hardly possible for women in the fifteenth and sixteenth centuries. . . .

Strangely enough, it was easier for a woman to conform to this new conception of the artist as a divinely inspired genius than it
(20) had been for her to emerge from the conservative, traditional medieval workshop. While artists were winning new status in Renaissance society, there was an important shift in the attitudes toward the education of women that had prevailed in the fourteenth and fifteenth centuries. Early in the sixteenth century at the court of
(25) Federigo da Montefeltro in Urbino, Baldassare Castiglione wrote his *Il Cortegiano*, which was first published in 1528. Before the century was out, over thirty editions had been printed in Italy, France, England, and Spain. Castiglione devoted an entire chapter to the ideal female member of an aristocratic household. . . . Almost all the
(30) attributes and accomplishments necessary to the male courtier were also declared appropriate to the female, including a high level of educational attainment and the ability to paint, play musical

instruments and sing, write poetry, and make witty, stimulating conversation.

(35)   These ideas were not in themselves new. They can be found much earlier in medieval treatises on courtly behavior, but the invention of printing in the meantime meant that a far wider audience had access to Castiglione's ideas of ideal courtly behavior than could ever have learned about these customs in the Middle Ages. *Il*
(40) *Cortegiano* was enormously popular; its influence on social behavior and educational theory extended far beyond the Renaissance courts, where it originated, to all lesser noble families and to all successful merchants wealthy enough to emulate that way of life. Thus Castiglione helped to emancipate women from the bondage of
(45) illiteracy and minimal education, extending the privileges and opportunities of a few women to those of a much wider social stratum. He made it proper, even praiseworthy, for women to engage in a wide range of artistic, musical, and literary pursuits, and if most women only dabbled as amateurs and formal education
(50) for women remained poor, there is still no shortage after the mid-sixteenth century of references to women who were regarded by their contemporaries as exceptionally fine artists, musicians, and writers. . . .

        Sofonisba Anguissola, the eldest daughter of a provincial
(55) nobleman, fits neatly into the category of daughters of minor aristocrats whose educational horizons were expanded by Castiglione. She and her sisters were all taught to play musical instruments and to read Latin as well as to paint. . . . Thus she is a good example of the new female courtier. . . .

(60)   Sofonisba's fame was made first as a portrait painter and the demand for examples of her phenomenal skill in this specialty made it difficult . . . for her to extend her range to more prestigious categories of painting. By producing one large, full-length portrait of her father with one of her sisters and her brother . . . shortly before
(65) she left for Spain, she evidently wished to declare her ability to manage multi-figure compositions and thus perhaps to try history painting at a later date. . . .

        The adulation of Sofonisba by patrons . . . and the publicity given to these outward signs of success were of great historical importance
(70) for later women artists. The fabulous wealth her talents gained for her must have inspired other fathers with talented daughters to think of training them in hopes of similar success.

from *Women Artists: 1550-1950* by Ann Sutherland Harris

1. The passage is best described as

   (A) a refutation of a common misconception
   (B) a discussion of a trend
   (C) a definition of a concept
   (D) an unraveling of a paradox
   (E) a profile of a controversial artist

2. Which of the following is NOT suggested in the first paragraph?

   (A) Prior to the Renaissance women faced many obstacles that excluded them from artistic careers.
   (B) Renaissance artists admired and studied ancient art.
   (C) Pre-Renaissance art included few if any nudes.
   (D) Prior to the Renaissance artists were amateurs who devoted little if any time to their trade.
   (E) The status and prestige of artists improved during the Renaissance.

3. Castiglione's book probably appealed to certain merchants because of their

   (A) belief in the inherent value of education
   (B) desire to assume courtly ways
   (C) fascination with antiquity
   (D) wish to increase the size of their markets
   (E) urge to maintain the status quo

4. The third paragraph (lines 35-53) suggests that one reason for the great influence of Castiglione's book was the

   (A) higher levels of education of its audience compared to medieval audiences
   (B) high political rank and power of the duke of Urbino
   (C) accessibility of its language
   (D) increased availability of books
   (E) greater prevalence of women at royal courts than in earlier times

5. In line 50, "poor" most nearly means

   (A) impoverished
   (B) barren
   (C) unproductive
   (D) sterile
   (E) inferior

6. The author most likely includes the example of Sofonisba Anguissola (lines 54-72) in order to

   (A) show the effect of Castiglione's ideas on one woman's career
   (B) show the typical educational attainments of women during the Renaissance
   (C) demonstrate the difficulty of a woman's becoming as artist
   (D) show that conditions for women had not changed since the medieval period
   (E) refute the belief that women were hindered in their efforts to pursue artistic careers

7. The passage implies

   (A) women were better portrait painters than men
   (B) Anguissola was a better musician than artist
   (C) paintings of historic events were more lucrative then portraits
   (D) there was a strong link between Anguissola's noble origins and the high fees she commanded
   (E) Anguissola was more popular in Spain than in Italy

8. The author would most likely agree with which of the following statements about women artists living during the Renaissance?

   (A) They failed to produce works of high quality.
   (B) They enjoyed greater opportunities than the women who preceded them.
   (C) They ultimately could not reconcile their traditional family roles with having an artistic career.
   (D) They experienced a promising beginning but were thwarted by jealous male rivals.
   (E) They created the distinctive characteristics of what is now called the Renaissance style.

9. Which of the following Renaissance influences does the passage see as counterbalancing the forces that kept women subordinate?

   (A) The rising popularity of the idea of artistic "genius."
   (B) Greater public roles for artists.
   (C) The dissipation of class distinctions.
   (D) The spread of Castiglione's ideas.
   (E) A change in artistic styles.

10. The primary function of the final paragraph (lines 68–72) is to
    (●) indicate that Anguissola influenced future generations of women artists
    (B) illustrate the discrepancy between Castiglione's ideals of courtly behavior and the way male artists treated successful female artists
    (C) point out the need for more research on the changing role of women artists during the Renaissance
    (D) rebuke wealthy patrons for being too stingy
    (E) criticize the avarice of ambitious Italian fathers

11. The author's attitude toward Anguissola's work is one of
    (A) stunned incredulity
    (B) gleeful satire
    (●) emphatic approval
    (D) quiet reflection
    (E) intense exasperation

One of your verbal sections will contain 9 sentence completions, 6 analogies, and 2 reading passages. The passages will vary in length from as short as one column (50 lines) to as long as 1 1/2 columns (75 lines). Each passage will contain as few as 5 questions and as many as 11 questions. There will be a total of either 15 or 16 questions. If you spend an average of 40 seconds on each sentence completion and analogy, you will have 20 minutes to complete both critical reading passages. Time yourself on the following two critical reading passages and the 15 questions that accompany them.

Independent
PRACTICE

Critical Reading Practice Exercise 13 provides you with an opportunity to answer two complete sets of reading questions.

CRITICAL READING PRACTICE EXERCISE 13 "Timed Passages"

DIRECTIONS: Carefully read each of the following passages and questions. Then mark the correct answers.

The following passage is taken from a book on the blue crab and the Chesapeake Bay. Callinectes sapidus *(meaning "beautiful swimmer") is the blue crab's zoological name.*

A female crab born in May or June will produce eggs and hatchlings at the same time of year two years later. This statement has a definitive and tidy ring. In fairness to the reader, however, it
Line must be said that sponge crabs bearing eggs ready to hatch are not
(5) unknown as late as November. Or that crabs may mate in the first part of the summer instead of the last, giving rise to autumn larvae that may not survive the winter. To think properly about the blue crab, therefore, it is first necessary to assume that the species can and will perform anything in its life cycle at any time, dead of
(10) winter excepted. Bearing this in mind, we must then recognize that there are definite *peak periods* during which *most crabs* go through a given stage in the cycle. . . . The trouble is that a great many crabs do not observe them. The timetable of the great migrations between salty and fresher water, believed to be unique to *Callinectes*, can
(15) often go way off schedule. . . . Worse, the peak period timetable simply falls apart as one travels south from the Chesapeake. Blue crabs on the Gulf Coast typically have one or two spawns in the spring, but some may do it in December, even though cooler waters in the latter month may make them rather sluggish. Even the range
(20) of the blue crab constantly shifts, either naturally or by man's intervention. . . .
Dr. Willard Van Engel of the Virginia Institute of Marine Sciences, a leading authority whose annual crab forecast is widely respected by Chesapeake watermen, well sums up the dilemmas of blue crab
(25) research. "It is so difficult," he says. "We don't even have any real age standards, like the otoliths of a fish's skull. Moulting means there are no permanent hard parts. It's a wonderfully tolerant animal, but also so variable, so enigmatic."
To the very end. As the summer of their spawns nears its close,
(30) old females go out to sea in great numbers to die. Inexplicably, lesser numbers of these ocean-journeying crabs may return the next year to eke out a purposeless existence for yet a few more summer days. Those that return can be easily recognized. Barnacles stud their shells and sea moss dulls their once bright colors. They are known

(35) as "sea runs" and appear just inside Cape Henry in late July or early
August. Often they travel up into the James River, passing through
the waters in which most of them were born. It is almost as if these
crabs cannot decide. Like other crabs, *Callinectes sapidus* probably
evolved from the oceans. But it is now an estuarine organism,

(40) having found its best place in life where river and ocean waters
blend. What primal drive, then, impels females to die in their
evolutionary cradle? Why are they not accompanied by males, who
are believed to seek out the deepest Bay channels when their
moment comes? And what can we say of the sea runs who return,

(45) befouled and spent, to sample briefly once more the estuarine
gardens of their youth?

Discussing these questions, a retired Smith Island waterman once
looked hard at me and raised his arms in supplication. "Oh, my
blessed," he said very slowly. "That old crab is hard to figure out."

So it is, all along the way.

from *Beautiful Swimmers* by William W. Warner

1. The passage is primarily concerned with
   (A) providing a definitive guide to the mating habits of blue crabs
   (B) forecasting the timetable of the great migrations between salty
       and fresh water
   (C) explaining the differences between Chesapeake crabs and Gulf
       Coast crabs
   (D) describing the varied and often perplexing behavior of blue
       crabs
   (E) explaining why sea runs return to their home waters to die

2. In line 13, "observe" most nearly means
   (A) celebrate   (D) make out
   (B) adhere to   (E) comment upon
   (C) watch

3. It can be inferred that "the otoliths of a fish's skull" (line 26) can be
   used to
   (A) determine the age of a fish
   (B) predict when blue crabs will mate
   (C) pinpoint the blue crabs' migrations between salty and fresh
       water
   (D) explain why sea runs and males die in different places
   (E) help Dr. Engel make his annual forecasts

4. The author uses the phrase "evolutionary cradle" (line 42) to refer to
   (A) deep Bay channels
   (B) the cool waters on the Gulf Coast
   (C) the waters just beyond Cape Henry
   (D) the months of May and June when most female crabs are born
   (E) the place where sea runs are born

5. Dr. Van Engel and the retired Smith Island waterman agree that

   (A) blue crabs probably originated in the ocean
   (B) sea runs live longer than males
   (C) blue crabs follow precise patterns of behavior
   (D) otoliths provide useful tools for studying blue crabs
   (E) blue crabs often exhibit puzzling behavior

6. In line 45, "spent" most nearly means

   (A) paid out   (D) wasteful
   (B) occupied   (E) robust
   (C) exhausted

7. The author's attitude toward blue crabs is best described as

   (A) pleasure in its amusing antics
   (B) awe of its great longevity
   (C) irritation at its eccentricity
   (D) fascination with its great diversity
   (E) respect for its strength and cunning

8. The author uses the concluding sentence, "So it is, all along the way," to

   (A) express his exasperation with the retired Smith Island waterman for failing to answer his questions
   (B) signal his intent to conduct further research on the migratory habits of blue crabs
   (C) refine his original statement that female crabs follow "definite and tidy" patterns of behavior
   (D) invite the Smith Island waterman to accompany him on a visit to the Virginia Institute of Marine Sciences
   (E) emphasize his contention that the blue crab is difficult to predict

Questions 9-15 are based on the following passage.

In the following passage, a famous psychologist discusses his views on creativity.

I first had to change my ideas about creativity as soon as I began studying people who were positively healthy, highly evolved and matured, self-actualizing. I had first to give up my stereotyped
Line notion that health, genius, talent and productivity were
(5) synonymous. A fair proportion of my subjects, though healthy and creative in a special sense that I am going to describe, were *not* productive in the ordinary sense, nor did they have great talent or genius, nor were they poets, composers, inventors, artists, or creative intellectuals. It was also obvious that some of the greatest
(10) talents of mankind were certainly not psychologically healthy people, Wagner, for example, or Van Gogh or Byron. Some were and

some weren't, it was clear. I very soon had to come to the conclusion that great talent was not only more or less independent of goodness or health of character but also that we know little about it. For
(15) instance, there is some evidence that great musical talent and mathematical talent are more inherited than acquired. It seemed clear then that health and special talent were separate variables, maybe only slightly correlated, maybe not. We may as well admit at the beginning that psychology knows very little about special talent
(20) of the genius type. I shall say nothing more about it, confining myself instead to that more widespread kind of creativeness which is the universal heritage of every human being that is born, and which seems to co-vary with psychological health.

   Furthermore, I soon discovered that I had, like most other people,
(25) been thinking of creativeness in terms of products, and secondly, I had unconsciously confined creativeness to certain conventional areas only of human endeavor, unconsciously assuming that *any* painter, *any* poet, *any* composer was leading a creative life. Theorists, artists, scientists, inventors, writers could be creative.
(30) Nobody else could be. Unconsciously I had assumed that creativeness was the prerogative solely of certain professionals.

   But these expectations were broken up by various of my subjects. For instance, one woman, uneducated, poor, a full-time housewife and mother, did none of these conventionally creative things and
(35) yet was a marvelous cook, mother, wife and homemaker. With little money, her home was somehow always beautiful. She was the perfect hostess. Her meals were banquets. Her taste in linens, silver, glass, crockery and furniture was impeccable. She was in all these areas original, novel, ingenious, unexpected, inventive. I just *had* to
(40) call her creative. I learned from her and others like her that a first-rate soup is more creative than a second-rate painting, and that, generally, cooking or parenthood or making a home could be creative while poetry need not be; it could be uncreative.

   It dawned on me once that a competent cellist I had reflexly
(45) thought of as "creative" (because I associated her with creative music? with creative composers?) was actually playing well what someone else had written. She was a mouthpiece, as the average actor or "comedian" is a mouthpiece. A good cabinet maker or gardener or dressmaker *could* be more truly creative. I had to make
(50) an individual judgment in each instance, since almost any role or job could be either creative or uncreative. . . .

   In other words, I learned to apply the word "creative" (and also the word "esthetic") not only to products but also to people in a characterological way, and to activities, processes, and attitudes.
(55) And furthermore, I had come to apply the word "creative" to many products other than the standard and conventionally accepted poems, theories, novels, experiments or paintings.

from *Toward a Psychology of Being* by Abraham H. Maslow

9. The primary purpose of the passage is to

   (A) define and give examples of genius
   (B) discuss the origins of musical and mathematical talent
   (C) praise the housewife as a model homemaker
   (D) critique the work of the cellist
   (●) explore the meaning of creativity

10. As used in line 12, "clear" most nearly means

   (●) unmistakable   (D) vindicate
   (B) unimportant   (E) pass over
   (C) unclouded

11. The author believes that genius is

   (A) most often found in psychologically healthy people
   (B) more inherited than acquired
   (●) not yet fully understood by psychology
   (D) strongly correlated with a person's character
   (E) clearly linked with great productivity

12. The author's attitude toward the housewife is one of

   (A) disdain   (●) respect
   (B) envy   (E) bewilderment
   (C) skepticism

13. Which of the following would the author think the most creative?

   (A) An artist whose paintings are almost identical with Van Gogh's.
   (B) A coach who follows the same strategy each game.
   (●) A psychiatrist who deals with each patient in a personal and intuitive manner.
   (D) A singer whose style is similar to a well-known recording artist.
   (E) An architect with a carefully prepared blueprint that is meticulously followed in each house.

14. The author employs all of the following in the development of the passage EXCEPT

   (A) a personal point of view
   (B) a specific example of creativity
   (C) an illustration of a stereotyped attitude about creativity
   (●) a reference to another psychologist
   (E) an opinion about the nature of genius

15. The author uses the final paragraph (lines 52-57) to

   (A) admit that psychology knows very little about creativity
   (B) emphasize his conviction that all human beings are creative
   (C) redefine his earlier definition of genius
   (●) summarize his conclusions about creativity
   (E) invite the reader to become more creative

Putting It All
TOGETHER

1 Each SAT will include one paired passage. The paired passage will contain 3-4 comparison questions that ask you to recognize similarities and differences between the two passages.

2 There are five major types of comparison questions.
- comparing main ideas
- comparing tone
- comparing assumptions
- determining a point of agreement
- determining how one author would react to another author

3 About half of the comparison questions ask you to identify the similarities between main ideas and key supporting points presented in the paired passages.

4 Many paired passages include a question asking you to evaluate the differences in tone between two passages.

5 An assumption is a belief that underlies a statement or action. Many comparison questions ask you to evaluate the assumptions upon which the authors base their arguments.

6 The authors of the two paired passages sometimes agree on key issues and ideas. One often used comparison question asks you to recognize a statement the two authors would agree with.

7 The most challenging comparison questions ask you to use your knowledge of one author's viewpoint to determine how he/she would react to a point made by the other author.

8 One verbal section will contain 10 sentence completions, 13 analogies, and either a single passage or a paired passage. By spending an average of 40 seconds on each sentence completion and analogy, you will have 15 minutes to complete the critical reading passage.

9 One verbal section will contain 9 sentence completions, 6 analogies, and 2 reading passages. By spending an average of 40 seconds on each sentence completion and analogy, you will have 20 minutes to complete the two critical reading passages.

Answering Paired Passage Questions

DIRECTIONS: Use the information contained in the paired passage and the introductory material below to answer the questions that follow. Strive to finish this exercise in 15 minutes.

Questions 1-13 are based on the following pair of passages.

The following passages describe the pioneering work of two early biologists.

Passage 1

Vesalius' book *The Construction of the Human Body* (1543) was intended to reveal the inadequacy and even falsity of the current Galenic anatomy and to institute a reform of the subject, which at
Line that time was taught inadequately. Vesalius not only sought
(5) graphically and verbally to correct the errors of Galen but also argued that medical students and physicians should base their knowledge of the human body on direct dissection.

There were a number of new ideas in Vesalius' book, many of which contradicted Galen's statements. It was definitely unheard of
(10) to base anatomical knowledge on the direct experience of dissecting human bodies and those of animals for comparative purposes, and to exhort all medical students, anatomical scientists, and physicians to perform their own dissections of the human body. Not only did Vesalius show by examples that such actual dissections had
(15) produced new knowledge, he also gave explicit directions as to how the reader should proceed in making a dissection so as either to verify Vesalius' own presentation or to "arrive at an independent conclusion." This revolutionary aspect of his book was enhanced by beautiful and detailed artistic illustrations. There can be no doubt
(20) that Vesalius successfully inaugurated a reform of the subject of anatomy and the method of teaching it.

It is therefore surprising to observe that Vesalius did not assume a radical anti-Galenic stance. The non-revolutionary attitude of Vesalius may be seen most clearly in his discussions of the pores
(25) alleged by Galen to exist in the septum (wall) separating the right ventricle of the heart from the left. These pores, or passages, were an essential part of Galenic physiology, providing a necessary pathway for the blood to ooze a drop at a time from the so-called "arterial vein" (for us, the pulmonary artery) into the "venal vein" (or
(30) pulmonary vein). Galen taught that air was carried to the heart from the lungs by means of this "venal artery," where it combined with the trickle of blood through the pores in the septum to produce arterial blood.

That there are no such passages going from one side of the heart
(35) to the other was at once made evident to Vesalius by actual dissections of the human heart. A true revolutionary would, I believe, have simply concluded that the whole Galenic physiology, and perhaps even the Galenic medicine based on it, must be false and should be cast out at once. But not Vesalius! Instead, he
(40) confesses in the second edition of his book to a lack of that self-

confidence that would have enabled him to reform the Galenic teachings about the heart and blood. We are told that he consciously "accommodated" the doctrines of Galen to a great extent in his text. Vesalius failed to overturn the physiological doctrines of Galen not
(45) because he sincerely believed in their truth but because, scholars maintain, he did not feel equal to the task of sweeping reform.

Passage 2

Usually this designation ["father of modern biology"] is given to William Harvey. In the early 1600's, Harvey observed that the beating heart expelled the blood within it. He then reasoned: if the
(50) heart contains two ounces of blood and beats sixty-five times each minute, then it must eject into the body over ten pounds of blood per minute. It had previously been thought that blood was derived from the food that is eaten. But one cannot imagine ten pounds of blood being formed anew each minute from the amount of food a
(55) man consumes. Reflection on this observation and simple deduction led Harvey to postulate that blood expelled by the heart must circulate through the body whence it returns to the heart. He then performed experiments to investigate the hypothesis. He showed that obstruction of a vein causes pooling of blood on the side of the
(60) obstruction away from the heart. He showed that the bleeding arises from the nearest end to the heart of a severed artery and the farthest end of a severed vein. And he demonstrated with elegant simplicity the function of the venous valves, concerning which he wrote that "so provident a cause as nature had not plac'd many valves without
(65) design."

Harvey's discovery of the circulation of blood was a monumental and many-sided contribution to science. In the first place, it discredited the beliefs of fourteen centuries that the heart was not a muscular organ and that the blood passed through the septum
(70) between the right and left ventricles. In addition, Harvey knowingly or unknowingly used the scientific method in almost astoundingly modern fashion; and, finally, he bolstered his already incontrovertible claim to immortality by conceiving the heart as a pump, for in this notion Harvey heralded a new view concerning
(75) living organisms—though . . . he did not appreciate the meaning of his own work on this score. But to his successors his work gave proof to the concept that life, like the rest of the universe, could be viewed as a material machine. Descartes was quick to praise Harvey for "having broken the ice in this matter," and in his own discourses
(80) he relied heavily on the work of Harvey to illustrate the mechanical nature of living objects. Their only difference from man-made machines, he insisted, was in the degree of complexity. With these assertions, sudden new excitement entered the realm of biological thought. For it now seemed reasonable that if the living organism
(85) were a material mechanism then it, too, could be investigated by the new method of science.

from *Modern Science and the Nature of Life* by William S. Beck

1. Passage 1 is primarily concerned with

   (A) describing revolutionary ideas that changed the history of science
   (B) describing Vesalius' contributions to the study of human anatomy and his attitude toward Galen's physiological teachings
   (C) tracing the history of anatomical studies from Galen to Vesalius
   (D) praising the artistic illustrations in Vesalius' book
   (E) criticizing Galen's conception of how the heart functions

2. Which of the following would best fit the author of Passage 1's concept of "a true revolutionary?" (lines 36-39)

   (A) A scientist who strives to make discoveries that would benefit society.
   (B) A researcher who conducts studies independently of other experts.
   (C) A philosopher who refutes a fallacious system of thought.
   (D) A doctor who does not separate politics from the practice of medicine.
   (E) A painter who sacrifices personal happiness in the pursuit of perfection.

3. In line 39, "cast" most nearly means

   (A) to scatter
   (B) to throw
   (C) to pick
   (D) to mold
   (E) to look

4. According to the author of Passage 1, Vesalius did not openly reject Galenic physiology because of

   (A) a reluctance to antagonize religious authorities
   (B) a lingering suspicion that Galen was right
   (C) a refusal to accept new ideas
   (D) a lack of irrefutable evidence that Galen was wrong
   (E) a sense of diffidence about his abilities

5. The author of Passage 1's attitude toward Vesalius' work can best be described as a mixture of

   (A) awe and reverence
   (B) contempt and disdain
   (C) superciliousness and pride
   (D) respect and disappointment
   (E) condescension and reserve

6. It can be inferred that Harvey is considered the "father of modern biology" because he was the first to

   (A) accurately describe how the heart functions
   (B) publish accurate illustrations of the heart
   (C) dissect the human body
   (D) invent the scientific method
   (E) challenge the concept of mechanism

7. It can be inferred that Harvey's observation of pooling of blood on the side of a vein obstruction away from the heart led him to the conclusion that

   (A) the blood was returning to the heart
   (B) blood was manufactured as it circulated
   (C) blood was expelled from the heart with each beat
   (D) the heart had to pump harder when the blood was far away from it
   (E) previous calculations as to the amount of blood contained by the body were incorrect

8. In line 76, "score" most nearly means

   (A) test result
   (B) large number
   (C) keep a tally
   (D) amount owed
   (E) area of study

9. According to Passage 2, Descartes believed that

   (A) the new methods of science could not be applied to living objects
   (B) Harvey failed to appreciate the significance of his work
   (C) living organisms and man-made machines only differed in their level of intricacy
   (D) he should be called the "father of modern biology"
   (E) man-made machines were more complex than living objects

10. It can be inferred from Passage 2 that the concept of mechanism was important to the scientific method because it supported the idea that

   (A) living organisms were part of a universal design
   (B) scientists could work together, each one performing part of an experiment
   (C) hypotheses must be based on experimental evidence
   (D) the somewhat complicated method could lead to a simplistic theory of life
   (E) organisms could be expected to function in understandable and regular ways

11. The author of Passage 1 would most likely regard Harvey's work as which of the following?

(A) controversial
(B) speculative
(C) deceptive
(D) revolutionary
(E) premature

12. The authors of both passages would most probably agree that

(A) both Vesalius and Harvey failed to refute Galen's physiological doctrines
(B) both Vesalius and Harvey had non-revolutionary attitudes toward their work
(C) Galenic physiology supported Descartes' view that a living organism could be viewed as a material machine
(D) both Vesalius and Harvey made significant contributions to the study of human anatomy
(E) Vesalius is more deserving than Harvey of the title "father of modern biology"

13. Both Vesalius and Harvey assumed that

(A) dissections are the best way to gain knowledge about how the human body functions
(B) traditional knowledge from authorities such as Galen should be respected and accepted
(C) the heart was not a muscular organ
(D) blood was derived from the food that we eat
(E) the "venal artery" carried air to the heart

A

SAT Posttest

After completing this posttest, you will be able to estimate your verbal score on the SAT.

SECTION 1

Time–30 Minutes
30 Questions
For each question in this section, select the best answer from among the choices given.

Each sentence below has one or two blanks, each blank indicating that something has been omitted. Beneath the sentence are five words or sets of words labeled A through E. Choose the word or set of words that, when inserted in the sentence, <u>best</u> fits the meaning of the sentence as a whole.

Example:

Medieval kingdoms did not become constitutional republics overnight; on the contrary, the change was ----.

(A) unpopular
(B) unexpected
(C) advantageous
(D) sufficient
(●) gradual

1. As a result of a conservation program begun in the 1960's, the southern white rhinos of South Africa are no longer ----.

   (A) fragile
   (B) relevant
   (●) endangered
   (D) frantic
   (E) fugitive

2. When the Industrial Revolution began, the new textile equipment was regarded as so ---- that the British government ---- anyone from taking plans or machinery out of the country.

   (A) insignificant . . . forbade
   (B) trivial . . . banned
   (C) precious . . . encouraged
   (D) useless . . . blocked
   (●) valuable . . . prohibited

3. Like a true ----, Matt was ---- in all of the skills of his profession.

   (●) expert . . . proficient
   (B) dabbler . . . inexperienced
   (C) bungler . . . talented
   (D) master . . . inept
   (E) dolt . . . practiced

4. On paper, the new coach's game plan seemed interesting and ----, but the plays he called were usually routine and ----.

   (A) daring . . . novel
   (●) innovative . . . repetitive
   (C) unique . . . special
   (D) commonplace . . . unusual
   (E) mundane . . . predictable

5. Some people remain imperturbed under the most trying circumstances; in contrast, others react with great ---- to minor problems.

   (A) tranquillity
   (●) agitation
   (C) serenity
   (D) indifference
   (E) aloofness

6. Early astronomers such as Copernicus and Kepler were not unfamiliar with ---- since they had to endure more than their fair share of criticism and ridicule.

   (A) affluence
   (B) acclaim
   (C) incompetence
   (D) respect
   (●) adversity

7. In temperament they were diametrically opposite: Ryan was ----, while Sam was always looking to become involved in a new project.

   (●) lethargic
   (B) animated
   (C) audacious
   (D) perceptive
   (E) malicious

GO ON TO THE NEXT PAGE >

SECTION

1

8. Regan was neither argumentative nor supercilious but was as ---- and as ---- a person as I have ever met.

   (A) cordial . . . unassuming
   (B) congenial . . . arrogant
   (C) combative . . . conceited
   (D) contentious . . . modest
   (E) affable . . . disagreeable

9. ---- and ----, General Andrew Jackson Goodpaster was a man who gauged the impact of every word he spoke and always acted with complete self-control.

   (A) Shy . . . eccentric
   (B) Succinct . . . naive
   (C) Ruthless . . . reserved
   (D) Stodgy . . . colorless
   (E) Laconic . . . unflappable

Each question below consists of a related pair of words or phrases, followed by five pairs of words or phrases labeled A through E. Select the pair that best expresses a relationship similar to that expressed in the original pair.

Example:

CRUMB : BREAD ::

   (A) ounce : unit
   (B) splinter : wood
   (C) water : bucket
   (D) twine : rope
   (E) cream : butter

10. LAWYER : COURTROOM ::

    (A) artist : studio
    (B) patient : ward
    (C) commuter : car
    (D) spectator : auditorium
    (E) diner : restaurant

11. LIE : COT ::

    (A) face : wall
    (B) stand : screen
    (C) push : chair
    (D) open : cabinet
    (E) sit : bench

12. SCHEDULE : TIME ::

    (A) quench : thirst
    (B) satiate : appetite
    (C) budget : money
    (D) arouse : sleep
    (E) solve : problem

13. ANECDOTE : STORY ::

    (A) film : theater
    (B) chapter : novel
    (C) lyric : song
    (D) joke : parody
    (E) skit : play

14. VIRTUOSO : SKILL ::

    (A) miser : wealth
    (B) zealot : fervor
    (C) advocate : resistance
    (D) performer : artistry
    (E) rebel : idle

15. INSOLENT : RESPECT ::

    (A) lavish : extravagance
    (B) impulsive : restraint
    (C) cunning : duplicity
    (D) sluggish : fatigue
    (E) ardent : passion

GO ON TO THE NEXT PAGE

SECTION

1

Questions 16-23 are based on the following passage.

The following passage is from a discussion of women poets in world history.

Poetry begins in life and its necessities, but in order to flourish as a written art it requires leisure, the time to pursue and to perfect. The
Line Heian Period (794-1185 A.D.) in Japan provided an
(5) abundance of that leisure and the desire to perfect a tradition which is unique in the histories of world literature.

The word *Heian* itself means "peace," "tranquillity." Culture—visual arts, literature,
(10) philosophy, music—was concentrated in Kyoto, where an elegant court gathered around the Emperor and his family. Outside of the capital there was little of interest to these perhaps two thousand people; enormous energy was
(15) concentrated in just a few square miles, an energy which could be devoted entirely to clothing, poetry, food, incense and intrigue. There were no wars, no invasions from outside this insulated and insular country, no popular uprisings to
(20) distract attention from the refinement of the senses. . . .

Japanese was, during the entire Heian era, considered unsuited to the lofty thoughts of serious poetry, for which the Chinese language
(25) was reserved. Japanese would be used for occasional poems, love verses, the literature of seduction and lament. It was left to women to write in Japanese, in the vernacular, while men reserved the supposedly more difficult Chinese
(30) for themselves, unaware that what they were writing was imitation Chinese literature, inferior to the original, and, above all, inferior to what contemporary women were writing in their native tongue. . . . But in time it became apparent
(35) that all that once appeared trivial and marginal was in fact the outstanding achievement in Japanese literature, and one of the greatest achievements in all of world literature. Women produced the best, the greatest classics in
(40) Japanese: not simply *The Tale of Genji*, Murasaki's *Diary*, the *Pillow Book of Sei Shonagon*, but the

poetry of Ono no Komachi, Ise, Otomo no Sakanoe and others. So important were women to the native literature that when men set their
(45) hands to writing poetic diaries, as Ki no Tsurayuki did in the *Tosa Diary*, they often wrote under the persona of a woman.

It is clear then that women occupied a strong position in Japan during the first centuries
(50) following the development of literacy, so long as the vernacular remained outside the realm of power and prestige. During these first five hundred years they created the themes, forms and moods which shaped subsequent Japanese
(55) literary tradition: the *tanka*, with its elegiac tone and characteristic imagery; the diary; and the novel.

Deeply embedded in the poems of [Japanese women] are feelings of regret about the shortness
(60) of life, the fickleness of love, and the ravages of age, which imbue them with a brooding melancholy. They rapidly became conventionalized and traditional, a sorrowful lament, perhaps, for the passing of desire as
(65) much as for the torment of it. These elegiac feelings, and a dark mysteriousness, are an essential part of the tradition, with special literary terms and meanings; they are no longer confined to women.
(70) At the end of the Heian era, when political and military upheaval destroyed the leisurely culture in Kyoto, men, and martial virtues, took over the vernacular as well as official culture. Then poetry became something to occupy the rare moments of
(75) rest in a soldier's life, or in the lives of hermits, priests, or courtiers confined to the distant court far from important events.

The imitation of Chinese poetry became a secondary occupation even for men; women
(80) surrendered their pre-eminence in the vernacular literature, and finally, as in so many other cultures, nearly vanished from the anthologies. The tradition they had done so much to shape was carried on by men.

from Rob Swigart's "Introduction" to the section "Japan," from *Women Poets of the World* edited by Joanna Bankier and Deirdre Lashgari

GO ON TO THE NEXT PAGE

SECTION **1**

16. The primary purpose of the passage is to

   (A) describe the role and contributions of women writers during the Heian era
   (B) explain what factors led to the collapse of the Heian era
   (C) evaluate the influence of Chinese literature upon Japanese culture during the Heian era
   (D) discuss the linkage between leisure time and literary output during the Heian era
   (E) discuss the impact of military and political upheavals on Japanese culture during the Heian era

17. With which of the following statements about the writing of poetry would the author of the passage most likely agree?

   (A) Poetry derives its most penetrating insights from periods of great upheaval.
   (B) Poetry is most often written by people who speak out against life's injustices.
   (C) Poetry most often flourishes in monasteries and barracks far from the distractions of the royal court.
   (D) Poetry begins with insights from daily life and thrives when writers have free time.
   (E) Poetry is most often stimulated by the challenge of writing in a language that is not the poet's native tongue.

18. In line 48, "strong" most nearly means

   (A) mighty
   (B) advantageous
   (C) bright
   (D) devoted
   (E) concentrated

19. It can be inferred from the passage that all of the following were present in Heian literature EXCEPT

   (A) novels in Japanese by women
   (B) love verses in Chinese by men
   (C) tanka's in Japanese by women
   (D) diaries in Japanese by women under the persona of a man
   (E) poetry in Chinese by women

20. The passage implies that the most important element that female authors contributed to Japanese literature was

   (A) vivid observations of the customs and traditions of the imperial court
   (B) psychological insights into human behavior
   (C) the skillful use of the Chinese language
   (D) a reexamination of the role of women in Japanese society
   (E) the creation of traditional literary forms

21. According to the author, the poems of Japanese women have a "brooding melancholy" (lines 61-62) that expresses their

   (A) pleasure in finally receiving more recognition than male writers
   (B) alarm at the political and military upheavals threatening Japanese society
   (C) sadness at the transience of life
   (D) enjoyment of the abundance and leisure provided by the imperial court
   (E) concern for the poverty and suffering of the people living in Kyoto

22. What impact did the end of the Heian era have upon women poets?

   (A) Their focus shifted to exposing political corruption in the imperial court.
   (B) Their attention was diverted to creating a new antiwar literature.
   (C) They began to experiment with writing novels and poetic diaries in Chinese.
   (D) They lost their importance and their work disappeared from literary collections.
   (E) They concentrated upon writing romantic poems that helped people escape from the boredom of life.

23. The author's tone in the passage is best described as that of

   (A) a skeptic trying to raise doubts
   (B) a critic looking to find fault
   (C) a scholar describing an event
   (D) a polemicist presenting an argument
   (E) an iconoclast attacking a traditional belief

GO ON TO THE NEXT PAGE

SECTION 1

Questions 24-30 are based on the following passage.

The following passage is from a novel written by an African American woman. The novel takes place in an unspecified Northern city in the United States.

Children bloomed on Brewster Place during July and August with their colorful shorts and tops plastered against gold, ebony, and nut-
Line brown legs and arms; they decorated the street,
(5) rivaling the geraniums and ivy found on the manicured boulevard downtown. The summer heat seemed to draw the people from their cramped apartments onto the stoops, as it drew the tiny drops of perspiration from their
(10) foreheads and backs.

The apple-green car with the white vinyl roof and Florida plates turned into the street like a greased cobra. Since Etta had stopped at a Mobil station three blocks away to wash off the
(15) evidence of a hot, dusty 1,200-mile odyssey home, the chrome caught the rays of the high afternoon sun and flung them back into its face. She had chosen her time well.

The children, free from the conditioned
(20) restraints of their older counterparts, ran along the sidewalks flanking this curious, slow-moving addition to their world. Every eye on the block, either openly or covertly, was on the door of the car when it opened. They were rewarded by the
(25) appearance of a pair of white leather sandals attached to narrow ankles and slightly bowed, shapely legs. The willow-green sundress, only ten minutes old on the short chestnut woman, clung to a body that had finished a close second in its
(30) race with time. Large two-toned sunglasses hid the weariness that had defied the freshly applied mascara and burnt-ivory shadow. After taking twice the time needed to stretch herself, she reached into the back seat of the car and pulled
(35) out her plastic clothes bag and Billie Holiday* albums.

The children's curiosity reached the end of its short life span, and they drifted back to their various games. The adults sucked their teeth in
(40) disappointment, and the more envious felt self-righteousness twist the corners of their mouths. It was only Etta. Looked like she'd done all right by herself—this time around. . . .

Any who bothered to greet her never used her
(45) first name. No one called Etta Mae "Etta," except

in their minds; and when they spoke to each other about her, it was Etta Johnson; but when they addressed her directly, it was always Miss Johnson. This baffled her because she knew what
(50) they thought about her, and she'd always call them by their first names and invited them to do the same with her. But after a few awkward attempts, they'd fall back into the pattern they were somehow comfortable with. Etta didn't
(55) know if this was to keep the distance on her side or theirs, but it was there. . . .

Mattie sat in her frayed brocade armchair, pushed up to the front window, and watched her friend's brave approach through the dusty
(60) screen. Still toting around them oversized records, she thought. That woman is a puzzlement.

Mattie rose to open the door so Etta wouldn't have to struggle to knock with her arms full.
(65) "Lord, child, thank you," she gushed, out of breath. "The younger I get, the higher those steps seem to stretch."

She dumped her load on the sofa and swept off her sunglasses. She breathed deeply of the
(70) freedom she found in Mattie's presence. Here she had no choice but to be herself. The carefully erected decoys she was constantly shuffling and changing to fit the situation were of no use here. Etta and Mattie went way back, a singular term
(75) that claimed co-knowledge of all the important events in their lives and almost all of the unimportant ones. And by rights of this possession, it tolerated no secrets.

*Billie Holiday (1915-1959) was a famous African American jazz singer

from *The Women of Brewster Place* by Gloria Naylor

24. The author's description of Etta's car as a "greased cobra" (line 13) suggests that it is

(A) small and cramped
(B) a symbol of poverty
(C) worn but dependable
(●) fast and sleek
(E) restored and reliable

GO ON TO THE NEXT PAGE ▶

SECTION

1

25. The author's description of Etta as having a body "that had finished a close second in its race with time" suggests that she was

   (A) a young girl who would soon become a beautiful woman
   (B) ● an attractive woman who had aged gracefully
   (C) an older woman who was temperamental
   (D) a homely woman who had a pleasant personality
   (E) a plain woman who had a streak of independence

26. The children's initial reaction to Etta's arrival differed from that of the adults in that the children were

   (A) more affectionate toward a returning neighbor
   (B) more envious of the show of wealth
   (C) more accustomed to Etta's manners
   (D) less interested in strange travelers
   (E) ● less reserved in their display of curiosity

27. Why was Etta "baffled" (line 49) that residents of the neighborhood resisted calling her by her first name?

   (A) She always made a point of building close personal relationships with them.
   (B) She had lived in the neighborhood a long time and was well known.
   (C) She was usually surprised when people didn't do what she specifically told them to do.
   (D) ● She knew that they generally disapproved of her even though they spoke in terms of respect.
   (E) She thought that they would have been more anxious to please her since she had money.

28. The author uses Etta's sunglasses as a recurring detail that

   (A) suggests Etta's distorted view of the world
   (B) ● reveals Etta's need to shield herself in public
   (C) indicates Etta's contradictory responses to Mattie's neighbors
   (D) demonstrates Etta's sensible approach to driving in bright sunlight
   (E) emphasizes Etta's detachment from Mattie and the neighbors

29. The narrator primarily conveys which of the following regarding Etta Mae Johnson?

   (A) amused wonderment
   (B) reluctant gratitude
   (C) ● unresolved mystery
   (D) unrestrained jealousy
   (E) suppressed resentment

30. By describing Etta and Mattie's relationship as tolerating no secrets, the author suggests that it is

   (A) too fragile to survive sustained tensions
   (B) so intense that secrets would destroy it
   (C) ● of such long standing that neither can deceive the other
   (D) similar to most relationships in a close-knit community
   (E) like the friendship of children, open and naive

IF YOU FINISH BEFORE TIME IS CALLED, YOU MAY CHECK YOUR WORK ON THIS SECTION ONLY. DO NOT TURN TO ANY OTHER SECTION IN THE TEST.

STOP

SECTION 2

Time–30 Minutes
35 Questions
For each question in this section, select the best answer from among the choices given.

Each sentence below has one or two blanks, each blank indicating that something has been omitted. Beneath the sentence are five words or sets of words labeled A through E. Choose the word or set of words that, when inserted in the sentence, best fits the meaning of the sentence as a whole.

Example:

Medieval kingdoms did not become constitutional republics overnight; on the contrary, the change was ----.

(A) unpopular
(B) unexpected
(C) advantageous
(D) sufficient
(●) gradual

1. In her highly influential book, *Silent Spring*, Rachel Carson pointed out that DDT is a deadly insecticide that can persist in water and soil and thus ---- beneficial insects and wildlife.

(A) inspire
(B) repair
(C) enlarge
(●) contaminate
(E) gratify

2. Although the *Principia Mathematica* by Bertrand Russell and Alfred North Whitehead is one of the most respected intellectual achievements of the twentieth century, almost all of its conclusions were ---- within a decade of its publication, and few scholars agree with its ideas today.

(●) challenged
(B) acknowledged
(C) acclaimed
(D) endorsed
(E) authenticated

3. Despite Amanda's bold plan and well thought out presentation, most business leaders remained ----, and their ---- attitude prevented immediate action.

(A) restrained .. eager
(B) hesitant .. energetic
(C) enthusiastic .. evasive
(●) reluctant .. cautious
(E) pleasant .. positive

4. In *The Grapes of Wrath*, the Land and Cattle Company is a faceless beast of prey: there is no individual to blame or hate, only ---- Board of Directors.

(A) a generous
(B) a jovial
(C) an articulate
(D) a compassionate
(●) an anonymous

5. Some of the artifacts archaeologists have discovered at Mesa Verde remain ----, but others provide glimpses into a civilization that ---- for 700 years in the southwest corner of Colorado and then vanished.

(A) unknowable .. terminated
(●) baffling .. flourished
(C) understandable .. matured
(D) obvious .. perished
(E) sacred .. thrived

6. Although labor and management were far apart when contract talks began, Luisa proved to be a skillful mediator who helped the two sides ---- their differences and reach an equitable compromise.

(A) inflame
(●) reconcile
(C) magnify
(D) embellish
(E) exaggerate

7. College libraries are usually places of quiet study, but in the days before exams they become bustling centers of often ---- activity.

(A) unruffled
(B) impractical
(C) frivolous
(D) obsolete
(●) frenetic

8. Taylor was admired for being a ---- who gave generously to local charities and to people who needed help.

(A) hypocrite
(B) demagogue
(●) philanthropist
(D) loiterer
(E) miscreant

GO ON TO THE NEXT PAGE

SECTION 2

9. Critics ---- the candidate's twisted arguments and ---- reasoning saying that he contributed little if anything to clarifying the difficult issues facing his constituents.

(A) championed .. aimless
(B) assailed .. convoluted
(C) applauded .. lucid
(D) denounced .. persuasive
(E) imitated .. instantaneous

10. The successful testing of ENIAC, the first electronic digital machine, was a ---- event marking the beginning of a new information revolution that would ---- change the world.

(A) trivial .. irresponsibly
(B) riveting .. irrationally
(C) watershed .. irrevocably
(D) ephemeral .. irresistibly
(E) petty .. irrefutably

Each question below consists of a related pair of words or phrases, followed by five pairs of words or phrases labeled A through E. Select the pair that best expresses a relationship similar to that expressed in the original pair.

Example:

CRUMB : BREAD ::

(A) ounce : unit
(B) splinter : wood
(C) water : bucket
(D) twine : rope
(E) cream : butter

11. HYDROGEN : GAS ::

(A) leaf : plant
(B) lead : pencil
(C) wool : fabric
(D) ring : finger
(E) lock : door

12. WEB : SPIDER ::

(A) nest : bird
(B) canal : otter
(C) flower : bee
(D) acorn : squirrel
(E) bait : fish

13. CHOIR : SINGER ::

(A) election : voter
(B) anthology : poet
(C) cast : actor
(D) orchestra : composer
(E) convention : organizer

14. PINNACLE : CAREER ::

(A) crest : wave
(B) valley : hill
(C) shingle : roof
(D) spoke : wheel
(E) slope : angle

15. PAGE : KNIGHT ::

(A) princess : king
(B) essay : novelist
(C) defendant : judge
(D) apprentice : master
(E) clue : detective

16. CONDENSE : STORY ::

(A) avoid : controversy
(B) abbreviate : word
(C) duplicate : page
(D) introduce : speaker
(E) communicate : idea

17. SEDATIVE : PACIFY ::

(A) scalpel : cauterize
(B) analgesic : discomfit
(C) surgery : operate
(D) antiseptic : sterilize
(E) stimulant : induce

18. MISNOMER : NAME ::

(A) error : mishap
(B) variability : change
(C) exception : rule
(D) misconception : idea
(E) misdeed : apology

GO ON TO THE NEXT PAGE

SECTION 2

19. PARABLE : ILLUSTRATIVE ::

    (A) newspaper : daily
    (B) joke : amusing
    (C) cliché : creative
    (D) lecture : spoken
    (E) film : exposed

20. INVINCIBLE : CONQUERED ::

    (A) expensive : bought
    (B) invaluable : insured
    (C) incredible : disputed
    (D) suspicious : doubted
    (E) invulnerable : subdued

21. UNBALANCED : EQUILIBRIUM ::

    (A) imaginary : mind
    (B) adept : skill
    (C) indifferent : interest
    (D) substantial : significance
    (E) polished : refinement

22. EPICURE : FOOD ::

    (A) aesthete : art
    (B) gourmet : cook
    (C) hypochondriac : illness
    (D) carpenter : woodwork
    (E) child : candy

23. MUNIFICENT : GENEROSITY ::

    (A) candid : credibility
    (B) prosperous : poverty
    (C) influential : opinion
    (D) haughty : arrogance
    (E) obstinate : persuasion

GO ON TO THE NEXT PAGE

SECTION

2

Each passage below is followed by questions based on its content. Answer the questions following each passage on the basis of what is <u>stated</u> or <u>implied</u> in that passage and in any introductory material that may be provided

Questions 24-35 are based on the following passage.

The passage is from a book written by an American scientist who traveled in Africa for two years and met with scientists who were working on that continent. The following excerpt is from the author's description of the work of an ornithologist* named Jamie. Jamie had been working in Mali, planning a conservation reserve for water birds that was to be located in the Niger delta. The flood plain of the Niger River is an extremely dry region known as the Sahel.

"Birds get massacred in the slide to monoculture,**" is Jamie's succinct way of characterizing one problem with developing the
Line Niger flood plain. As precious as they are, these
(5) waters are bound to be developed. But developed for whom? A nomad looking over the delta sees a landscape in motion, an array of shifting opportunities overlaid by an ancient network of social relations. A Western engineer, on the other
(10) hand, sees a resource waiting to be exploited, a good place to build dams and other projects cast in concrete. . . .

Overlooked or ignored in these schemes is the fact that every technological fix attempted in the
(15) Sahelian wetlands over the past fifty years has failed. Either the technology was wrong for the culture, or the technology itself was faulty. Permanent waterworks require social hierarchies to run them: managers on top, workers below.
(20) But the network or relationships in the Sahel tends to stretch horizontally among peers rather than vertically between figures of authority. . . .

The land itself has also resisted the imposition of Western technology. The soils have proved too
(25) fragile to support the irrigation projects already built in the Sahel. Most of these have been plagued by waterlogging and salinization before finally being abandoned. A telling example comes from the agricultural schemes on the
(30) Senegal River, which, along with Lake Chad and the Niger, used to be the third great wetlands in the Sahel. Two new dams at the headwaters and mouth of the river will put an end to its existence as a seasonal flood plain. But they will do

(35) nothing to alter the fact that other irrigation projects already built along the Senegal have greatly impoverished the lives of its riverine citizens: every newly created acre of paddy field has resulted in four acres of flood plain reverting
(40) to desert.

The figures are not more encouraging for the Niger delta. Over the past fifteen years more than one hundred million dollars have been invested here in cattle-ranching and rice-growing schemes.
(45) During the drought of 1984, this Sahelian herd totaled a million well-watered cattle, but two thirds of them died for lack of pasture. Their plight was worsened by the conversion of twenty percent of the delta from grazing land to rice
(50) polders that produced no rice that year. Undaunted by its previous failures, the World Bank is investing another fifty million dollars in the delta for irrigated agriculture. A further threat to the area comes from twenty dams planned for
(55) the river all the way back to its headwaters in the Fouta Djallon in Guinea.

In the face of this onslaught, Jamie's original assignment was little more than a holding action. He was supposed to survey the delta and find a
(60) watery ark to be set aside as a national reserve for the ducks and water birds that winter here. Many of Africa's parks have been established under similar conditions. They represent an amelioration of doubtful policies, an itch in the
(65) conscience of northerners as they work their will on the south. Cynics might say that establishing a bird reserve in Mali is of particular interest to European duck hunters worried about their supply of fowl. Whatever the motive behind it,
(70) Jamie abandoned the project when he realized there was no way the delta could be turned into a park.

"You can't tell someone not to eat a pelican when they're hungry, " he says. "And pelican
(75) eating itself is less of a threat to the bird populations than other factors."

*ornithologist: a scientist who studies birds
**monoculture: the use of an area for a single economic purpose

GO ON TO THE NEXT PAGE

SECTION 2

In a locale that shifts from dusty plain to watery world in a matter of days, where mud, marsh, and flood make transportation impossible
(80) for six months of the year, it is impossible to establish and police a European-style park. "Most of what you do in conservation is untenable here. When the flood arrives you're surrounded by a sea of water. So forget about driving your car.
(85) Then when the flood recedes you're surrounded by mud. So you can't travel by boat either."

Late in 1984 Jamie sent a report to Switzerland explaining why he wanted to drop the idea of bird reserves in the delta. The birds are
(90) threatened locally by four trends: the extension and intensification of agriculture, the use of contact poisons on cropland, the destruction of *bourgou* pasture through overgrazing, and the hunting of ducks and other waterfowl by the
(95) Bozo. But in Jamie's opinion, none of these trends is alarming, and all are relatively benign compared to other threats lying upstream.

"In fact the desired reserve system exists already—it is the thousands of square kilometers
(100) of seasonally flooded pastures managed traditionally for fishing and grazing activities, neither of which excludes healthy bird populations," his report concluded. "While current land use practices continue, the role of
(105) the conservationist will be to fine-tune improvements at the local level of resource use, which will probably have few dramatic effects. The single most long-reaching contribution to be made is in ensuring the water supply, and let the
(110) vast surface area and tradition do the rest."

from *Camping with the Prince* by Thomas A. Bass

24. In line 1, "slide" most nearly means

  (A) soft glide
  (B) rapid movement
  (C) slip
  (D) slither
  (E) gradual slope

25. The author implies (lines 1-17) that the "slide to monoculture" in the Niger flood plain will be both

  (A) insignificant and arduous
  (B) infallible and fruitful
  (C) incomprehensible and beneficial
  (D) indisputable and effortless
  (E) inevitable and unsuccessful

26. The contrast between the way the nomads and Western engineers view the Niger delta (lines 5-12) emphasizes the differences between

  (A) opportunistic and cynical perspectives
  (B) skeptical and confident perspectives
  (C) fanciful and realistic perspectives
  (D) traditional and scientific perspectives
  (E) pessimistic and optimistic perspectives

27. According to the passage, technologically sound waterworks plans for the Niger flood plain, as discussed in lines 13-22, turned out to be a failure because

  (A) the technology was not explained to local residents before being turned over to them
  (B) the technology produced changes that didn't fit the region's social customs
  (C) the soils in the region turned out to be unsuitable for agricultural purposes
  (D) the waterworks plans were designed for the Senegal River, not the Niger
  (E) rainfall in the area drained by the Niger River was unusually low for several decades

28. The author's use of the phrase "resisted the imposition of" (lines 23-24) emphasizes the fact that

  (A) the waterworks introduced new factors whose effects could not be predicted
  (B) the planners didn't care about possible damage to the local environment
  (C) the people of the Sahel were strongly opposed to the waterworks
  (D) modern European technology is simply replacing earlier technologies introduced by outsiders
  (E) Europeans usually develop soil conservation plans before constructing waterworks

GO ON TO THE NEXT PAGE

SECTION 2

29. The passage suggests that cattle ranching and rice growing schemes described in lines 41-50 were harmful to the region because

    (A) they took water away from pasture land
    (B) their success created a demand for more dams
    (C) they convinced Europeans that few problems existed
    (D) they led to attempts by outsiders to make profits in the region
    (E) the irrigated land became unsuitable for waterfowl

30. The author's attitude toward the World Bank (lines 51-53) can best be described as

    (A) respectful
    (B) hopeful
    (C) critical
    (D) understanding
    (E) indifferent

31. The words "In the face of this onslaught" in line 57 suggest that the author sees the waterworks development plans as

    (A) an eventual source of political problems
    (B) insignificant compared to the forces of nature
    (C) a much needed economic stimulus
    (D) the victims of recurring bad luck
    (E) more harmful than beneficial to the delta

32. The author suggests that the original plan for a waterfowl refuge in the delta resulted from

    (A) a misunderstanding about the effects of dam construction on waterfowl populations
    (B) a plan to encourage hunting of waterfowl as a food source in the region
    (C) an awareness that more flood plain development would reduce waterfowl habitat
    (D) large losses of waterfowl during the drought of 1984
    (E) a view of waterfowl as a resource to be exploited for economic benefits

33. The passage suggests that, at the time the author is writing, Jamie has come to believe that

    (A) saving waterfowl is not an appropriate goal for scientists
    (B) the best thing for the region would be to allow regular flooding
    (C) Europeans are interested in waterfowl preservation mostly for selfish reasons
    (D) a highway system that allows year-round travel on the flood plain is badly needed
    (E) waterfowl preserves should be built further upstream on the Niger river

34. Jamie's eventual decision to abandon the waterfowl reserve resulted from

    (A) lack of support from European conservation groups
    (B) a recognition that no threats to waterfowl exist
    (C) opposition of the local population to the plan
    (D) the selection of a better site for a reserve
    (E) a realization that the idea wasn't practical

35. The author's attitude toward Jamie's views is primarily

    (A) dubious
    (B) neutral
    (C) disdainful
    (D) supportive
    (E) uncomprehending

IF YOU FINISH BEFORE TIME IS CALLED, YOU MAY CHECK YOUR WORK ON THIS SECTION ONLY. DO NOT TURN TO ANY OTHER SECTION IN THE TEST. STOP

SECTION

3

Time–15 Minutes
13 Questions

For each question in this section, select the best answer from among the choices given.

The two passages below are followed by questions based on their content and on the relationship between the two passages. Answer the questions on the basis of what is <u>stated</u> or <u>implied</u> in the passages and in any introductory material that may be provided.

Questions 1-13 refer to the following passages.

Gregor Mendel and Barbara McClintock were pioneering figures in genetic research, the science of inherited traits. The following two passages discuss the difficulties both had in communicating their new ideas to other scientists.

Passage 1

When Gregor Mendel presented his research to the Brunn Society for the Study of Natural Science in 1865, no one—including Mendel
Line himself—ever imagined that this unpretentious
(5) high school teacher would someday be venerated as the founder of modern genetics.

Mendel was an Augustinian monk who had been educated in science and mathematics at the University of Vienna. After completing his
(10) studies, he returned to the monastery and was assigned a position at a local high school, where he taught physics and biology.

During this time, Mendel became intrigued by scientific reports describing the results of cross-
(15) pollinating different species of plants to develop hybrids. Researchers had been vainly searching for evidence that would allow them to formulate a basic principle of inheritance, but experimental results were puzzling. When certain species of
(20) plants were crossed, they produced hybrids with identical traits; however, when hybrids were crossbred, they yielded a variety of inexplicable new combinations.

Mendel's varied academic background led him
(25) to hypothesize that the transmission of traits through generations of plants might be charted as simple mathematical relationships. He used the monastery garden to test his hypothesis, planting experimental plots of a variety of peas.
(30) In the course of his research, Mendel crossbred thousands of plants. With each successive generation, he meticulously counted, classified, and recorded seven observable traits in the offspring peas, including such factors as whether
(35) the peas were round or wrinkled and the plants short or tall.

Based on these longitudinal studies, Mendel developed a number of theories about the hereditary elements at work in plant traits. While
(40) his findings are today universally known as the Mendelian laws, the members of the Brunn Society greeted his report with little more than polite attention. His experiments were discussed briefly and perhaps a few questions were asked,
(45) but, for the most part, no one took Mendel seriously. To the skeptical Society members, Mendel was an undistinguished, modest monk lacking both advanced academic credentials and previously published research.
(50) Mendel postulated that parent plants each provide one gene for each pair of genes in their offspring, and that a plant inherits each trait independently. While some exceptions have been documented, later research has validated
(55) Mendel's findings and his two conclusions are today known as Mendel's *Law of Segregation* and his *Law of Independent Assortment*.

As primary evidence for his conclusions, Mendel presented the Society with his algebraic
(60) computations. At the time, the use of algebra to unravel botanical mysteries was in itself a mystery to the Society members. While Mendel's results were published in 1866, it wasn't until 1900 that the scientific community began to see
(65) that this humane scientist and monk had indeed revealed a nearly universal pattern of heredity.

GO ON TO THE NEXT PAGE

SECTION

Passage 2

In 1951 when Barbara McClintock presented to the scientific community her findings on the

(70) transposition of genes in maize, most scientists dismissed her research findings as unintelligible. Yet in 1984 she was awarded the Nobel Prize in Physiology for the same work. What factors can cause a scientific breakthrough to be initially

(75) underrated by virtually everyone?

As a rule, the more a scientific claim is at odds with accepted beliefs, the more resistance it encounters. Any divergent claim is by its nature hard to understand; in 1951 the results and

(80) implications of McClintock's research were totally at variance with the predominant view of how genes behaved. Not until after the helical structure of DNA was elucidated in 1953 did geneticists revise drastically their views on the

(85) behavior of genes.

Furthermore, the kinds of evidence McClintock presented in 1951, specifically the patterns her data revealed, were unusually difficult for her to explain in terms her colleagues could readily

(90) understand. Scientists and philosophers of science tend to speak as if the language of scientific discourse were intrinsically precise, as if those who use it understand one another's meaning automatically even when they differ

(95) substantially in the models they use. But, in fact, scientific language, like ordinary language, can give rise to ambiguities, misunderstandings, and confusion.

In everyday practice, the rules of scientific

(100) methodology are combined with a generous admixture of intuition, aesthetics, and philosophy. A special type of careful observation was central to McClintock's scientific experience; the analyses of her data and conclusions required

(105) a particularly well-trained eye as well as frame of mind receptive to unpredictable evidence. For McClintock, the reciprocity between cognition and visual perception was so intimate that, in effect, she knew by seeing and saw by knowing.

(110) Another factor contributing to the initial cool reception that McClintock received was a general lack of familiarity with her type of work, since so many geneticists at that time focused on experiments with the fruit fly.

(115) For McClintock the spots on the kernels of maize were codes in a text that, with her unusual skill at making logical connections by visual observation, she could read directly and thereby

infer a genetic message. Changes and variations

(120) in generations of plants revealed patterns of genetic behavior. However, she did not convey, in conventional scientific language, the full structure of the reading that had emerged with such clarity for her. Scientists who understood

(125) McClintock's work attributed their success to the experience of observing the patterns of actual kernels of maize, finding, in one biologist's words, "a single color photograph more illuminating than all her papers."

(130) McClintock's problem in communication resembled that of a visual artist—success depended on a like-minded vision in the viewer. For decades, her reading of the genetics of maize remained largely her own.

1. In line 27 of Passage 1, "simple" most nearly means

   (A) natural
   (B) innocent
   (C) credulous
   (D) plain-spoken
   (E) easily understood

2. Passage 1 indicates that members of the Brunn Society reacted to Mendel's presentation with

   (A) irrational fear
   (B) undisguised contempt
   (C) courteous indifference
   (D) unrestrained enthusiasm
   (E) cautious interest

3. In lines 46–50 of Passage 1, the authors imply that the members of the Brunn Society would have been more receptive to Mendel's presentation if

   (A) he used more complex algebraic formulas to prove his points
   (B) he used humorous anecdotes to illustrate key points
   (C) he compiled a more extensive bibliography to support his research
   (D) he had more impressive academic credentials
   (E) he could demonstrate that the peas grown in his monastery garden could also be raised in nearby villages

GO ON TO THE NEXT PAGE

SECTION 3

4. Which of the following best describes the author's attitude toward those who failed to appreciate the importance of Mendel's findings?

   (A) admiration for their willingness to stand by their beliefs
   (B) indignation toward their rude behavior
   (C) suspicion of their selfish motives
   (D) recognition of the obstacles they faced
   (E) ridicule of the positions they adopted

5. The phrase "revealed a nearly universal pattern" (line 66) conveys the author's opinion that

   (A) Mendel's research had been ingenious
   (B) Mendel's findings were actually easy to understand
   (C) Mendel's data was important but too subtle for most people to understand
   (D) Mendel's discoveries would be reversed by twentieth-century scientists
   (E) Mendel's experiments uncovered truths far beyond the facts explained by his data

6. Passage 2 is best described as

   (A) a definition of a concept
   (B) a refutation of a new theory
   (C) an answer to a question
   (D) a portrait of a famous scientist
   (E) a plea for a compromise between two opposing views

7. The author of Passage 2 implies that if the helical structure of DNA had been known before 1951, McClintock's findings would have been

   (A) welcomed because they were compatible with accepted views
   (B) condemned because they plagiarized someone else's work
   (C) rejected because they contradicted a new theory
   (D) ignored because they were uninteresting and unimportant
   (E) admired because they were clear and easily understood

8. In line 108, "intimate" most nearly means

   (A) personal
   (B) guarded
   (C) cherished
   (D) confidential
   (E) intertwined

9. The author suggests that which of the following tasks would be most similar to McClintock's analysis of genetic patterns in maize?

   (A) finding one object hidden in an enormous pile
   (B) using past events to predict future developments
   (C) decoding a brief communication as part of a contest
   (D) translating a text written in an unusual alphabet
   (E) building a model based on detailed instructions

10. According to the author of Passage 2, which of the following contributed the most to helping scientists understand McClintock's ideas?

    (A) their ability to study color photographs depicting patterns on actual kernels of maize
    (B) their ability to transfer ideas from experiments with fruit flies to McClintock's work with kernels of maize
    (C) their ability to speak a common scientific language that was universally understood
    (D) their ability to read and comprehend the difficult ideas presented in McClintock's scholarly papers
    (E) their ability to relate McClintock's new theories to commonly held assumptions about how genes behaved

GO ON TO THE NEXT PAGE

SECTION

3

11. The authors of both passages would agree with which statement about why scientists initially dismissed Mendel's and McClintock's ideas?

   (A) McClintock and Mendel were loners who were disliked by many prominent scientists.
   (B) McClintock and Mendel used unorthodox ways of communicating their new ideas.
   (C) McClintock and Mendel performed pioneering research in fields that were considered unimportant.
   (D) McClintock and Mendel refused to recognize their debt to earlier scientists.
   (E) McClintock and Mendel had long histories of repeated failures and thus lacked credibility.

12. What would be the likely response of the authors of Passage 1 to the author of Passage 2's statement (lines 76–78) that "the more a scientific claim is at odds with accepted beliefs, the more resistance it encounters"?

   (A) They would support the statement saying that it is corroborated by Mendel's experience.
   (B) They would dismiss the statement saying that it has no relevance to their discussion on Mendel.
   (C) They would reject the statement saying that it is contradicted by the response Mendel received from the Brunn Society.
   (D) They would disregard the statement saying that Mendel and McClintock's experiences have nothing in common.
   (E) They would suppress the statement saying that it posed a threat to any scientists who espouse it.

13. Which statement best expresses the primary differences between the experiences of McClintock and Mendel?

   (A) McClintock became an artist while Mendel returned to his monastery.
   (B) McClintock wrote a bestselling book describing her research while Mendel wrote algebraic equations that few scientists could understand.
   (C) McClintock was honored by her contemporaries while Mendel was vindicated by posterity.
   (D) McClintock became an impoverished scientist while Mendel became a famous humanitarian.
   (E) McClintock withdrew into a life of seclusion while Mendel became a world famous scientist.

IF YOU FINISH BEFORE TIME IS CALLED, YOU MAY CHECK YOUR WORK ON THIS SECTION ONLY. DO NOT TURN TO ANY OTHER SECTION IN THE TEST. **STOP**

Calculating Your Score on the Posttest

STEP **1**   **Count**

Total Number of Blanks: _____ + _____ + _____ = _____
　　　　　　　　　　　　　　Sec. 1　　Sec. 2　　Sec. 3

Total Number Correct: _____ + _____ + _____ = _____
　　　　　　　　　　　　　Sec. 1　　Sec. 2　　Sec. 3

Total Number Incorrect: _____ + _____ + _____ = _____
　　　　　　　　　　　　　　Sec. 1　　Sec. 2　　Sec. 3

ADD to CHECK YOUR COUNTING. The Sum should be 78: _____

STEP **2**   **Determine Your Score Adjustment**

The Score Adjustment is:

Total Number Incorrect x .25 = _____

STEP **3**   **Determine Your RAW SCORE**

Your RAW SCORE is the Total Number Correct minus the Adjustment:

Total Correct:　　　_____

Minus Adjustment:　– _____

RAW SCORE　　　= _____

STEP **Convert Your RAW SCORE to an SAT Score**

SCORE CONVERSION TABLE

Raw Score	Verbal Scaled Score	Raw Score	Verbal Scaled Score	Raw Score	Verbal Scaled Score
78	800	51	590	24	440
77	800	50	580	23	430
76	800	49	580	22	430
75	800	48	570	21	420
74	790	47	570	20	410
73	780	46	560	19	410
72	760	45	560	18	400
71	750	44	550	17	390
70	740	43	540	16	390
69	730	42	540	15	380
68	720	41	530	14	370
67	710	40	530	13	360
66	700	39	520	12	360
65	690	38	520	11	350
64	680	37	510	10	340
63	670	36	510	9	330
62	660	35	500	8	320
61	660	34	500	7	310
60	650	33	490	6	300
59	640	32	480	5	290
58	630	31	480	4	280
57	630	30	470	3	270
56	620	29	470	2	260
55	610	28	460	1	240
54	610	27	450	0	230
53	600	26	450	−1	220
52	600	25	440	−2	200
				below	200

B

Word Histories

After completing this lesson, you will be able to

1. use your reading about the etymology of words from ancient Greece to define 12 key words.

2. use your reading about the etymology of words from ancient Rome to define 13 key words.

Every Word Has a History

In 1922 British archaeologist Howard Carter amazed the world by discovering Pharaoh Tutankhamon's tomb. Each of the dazzling artifacts that he unearthed yielded new insights into Egyptian history.

Although we usually don't think of them in this way, words are like artifacts. Like the precious jewels Carter found, words also have fascinating histories. *Etymology* is a branch of linguistics that specializes in digging up the origins of words.

Each word in our language has a unique history. Even our names have fascinating origins. For example, the name John (and its forms Joan, Jack, Janet, and Jane) is derived from a Hebrew word meaning "God is gracious." The African name Rashida means "righteous." And Linda is from a Spanish word meaning "pretty." You can become an amateur etymologist by looking up your name in a book of name origins.

The English language contains an especially rich collection of words derived from legends, places, customs, and names. These "history-based" words are frequently used by SAT writers.

Our etymological tour will begin in ancient Greece. Greek customs, rulers, myths, and philosophies have generated a number of high-frequency SAT words.

Words from Everyday Life in Ancient Greece

Draconian

Draco was an ancient Athenian ruler. Before he came to power, Athens had a chaotic system of justice in which most punishments were based upon personal revenge. Draco believed that this haphazard judicial system had to be reformed. In 621 B.C., he issued a new code of laws. Draco's code was comprehensive, but it was also very severe. Whether trivial or serious, most criminal offenses called for the death penalty. Draco's laws were so severe that they were said to be written not in ink, but in blood. Today, the word *Draconian* refers to a law, measure, or rule of authority that is notably harsh or cruel.

Ostracism

Each year the citizens of Athens gathered in the agora, or marketplace, to decide who, if anyone, should be temporarily banished from the city. The Athenians voted by writing someone's name on an *ostraka*, or oyster shell. After the vote, the ostraka were counted. Provided that there was a total of at least 6,000 shells, the man whose name appeared on the largest number was *ostracized*, or banished, for ten years. However, the man ostracized did not forfeit his citizenship or property and could return to live in Athens without any disgrace. Today *ostracism* is the exclusion of someone from the favor or fellowship of a group.

Laconic

The ancient Greek city-state of Sparta was located in a region called Laconia. The Spartans were fearless warriors who had no patience for long speeches. As a result, they were noted for their sparing use of words. For example, when King Philip of Macedonia invaded Greece, he sent this message to the Spartan king: "If we capture your city, we will burn it to the ground." The Spartans upheld their reputation of not wasting words when they replied with one word: "If." Today the word *laconic* means "terse, concise, and succinct." A laconic reply is thus direct and to the point.

Spartan

The Spartans were more than just laconic. They also prided themselves on being tough warriors who avoided luxuries and led hardy lives. For example, Spartan soldiers lived in army barracks and ate meager servings of a coarse black porridge. Today the word *Spartan* describes a plain life without luxuries.

Meander

The Meander River twists and turns as it wends its way through the plains of western Turkey. Frustrated Greek travelers counted over 600 trip-delaying turns. The Greeks soon applied the river's name to anything that followed an especially twisted path. Today *meander* still means "to wander aimlessly." If you write a paper that rambles from one point to another for no apparent reason, a reader might tell you that your thoughts seem to meander on the page.

Words from Greek Mythology

Iridescent

Have you ever seen a rainbow? What words would you use to describe it? According to modern scientists, a rainbow is an arc of color formed by the refraction, reflection, and dispersion of the sun's rays in the falling rain or mist.

The ancient Greeks had a far more poetic way of describing rainbows. For them a rainbow was a trail of color left by Iris, the goddess of the rainbow. Iris was a lovely maiden who left a trail of dazzling colors as she carried the gods' messages to earth.

While we no longer speak much of Iris, her name still lives on in our language. Iris is the name of a beautiful flower that has many colors. The word *iris* is also used to refer to the pigmented (colored) membrane surrounding the pupil of the eye. The goddess Iris is reflected in the word *iridescent*, meaning a "rainbow-like display of colors."

Herculean

Hercules was the son of Zeus and Alomene. He was renowned for his feats of strength. For example, King Augeas owned twelve white bulls sacred to Apollo. However, their stables had not been cleaned in thirty years! As one of his twelve labors, Hercules was ordered to clean up the stables in one day. Undaunted by this seemingly impossible task, the mighty Hercules devised a clever plan. Using his great strength, he diverted the course of a river so that it ran through the stables and washed away the filth. Today a *herculean* task is one that is very difficult and requires great strength.

Tantalize

Tantalus was a Greek king much favored by the gods. On one occasion the gods invited Tantalus to a special feast where he could eat ambrosia and nectar, their special food and drink. But Tantalus stole the gods' delicacies and gave them to the mortals.

When the gods discovered what Tantalus had done, they all agreed that he had to be severely punished. But since Tantalus had eaten divine food, he was now immortal and could not be killed.

The gods solved this problem by conceiving an everlasting punishment. Tantalus' punishment was to stand in water up to his chin. Branches bearing delicious fruits hung just over his head. When he tried to pick some fruit, the branches withdrew until they were just beyond his outstretched hands. Each time Tantalus tried to drink, the water receded just beyond his parched lips. In other words, Tantalus was continually *tantalized*. Today *tantalize* means "to tease or entice," usually by making something appear so attractive that it is hard or impossible to resist. Advertisers are constantly trying to tantalize you into purchasing their products or services.

Words from Greek Philosophy

Cynic

Antisthenes was a Greek philosopher who taught that self-control and independence are the highest virtues. Antisthenes urged his followers to lead simple lives and reject material possessions. His most famous student, Diogenes, showed his contempt for wealth and pleasure by sleeping in a large tub. During the day, he would startle strangers by shining a lamp in their faces and declaring that he was looking for an honest person.

Diogenes' unorthodox lifestyle and critical attitude offended many Athenians. His excessive faultfinding and snarling verbal barbs reminded them of a surly dog. They therefore ridiculed Diogenes and his followers by calling them *cynikos*, the Greek word for "dog-like." Later Cynics did little to change public attitudes as they continued to criticize social customs and beliefs. As a result, the word *cynic* entered the English language with negative connotations. Today *cynic* refers to someone who distrusts human actions, believing that even good deeds are motivated by self-interest.

Stoic

Zeno was a fourth-century Greek philosopher who taught that wise people should strive to free themselves from intense emotions and calmly accept all occurrences as the unavoidable result of divine will. Since Zeno taught at a site called Stoa Poikile (Painted Portico), his philosophy became known as *Stoicism* and his followers were called *Stoics*. The Stoic philosophy later spread to the Roman Empire, where statesmen such as Seneca and Marcus Aurelius admired its emphasis on self-discipline. Today the word *stoic* refers to someone who is indifferent to pain or pleasure.

Hedonist

Aristippus was a fourth-century Greek philosopher who taught that there was no life after death. Given this belief, Aristippus and his followers concluded that since there was no hope for happiness in the afterlife, the primary goal of living should be to have pleasure. This creed was called *hedonism*, since *hedone* was the Greek word for *pleasure*. Today *hedonism* refers to a way of life devoted to the pursuit of physical pleasure.

Eclectic

Alexandria was a thriving center of Hellenistic civilization. The city's famous museum and library buzzed with excitement as philosophers debated ideas from Greece, Rome, Egypt, and Persia. A philosopher named Potamon hoped to select the best ideas from a variety of philosophical systems. Since the Greek word for selecting is *eklektikos*, Potamon's technique was called *eclectic*. Today *eclectic* still means to select what appears to be best from diverse sources, systems, and styles.

Using Your VOCABULARY

ODD WORD OUT

DIRECTIONS: Each question below consists of four words. Three of them are related in meaning. Circle the word that does not fit.

1. Draconian — (lenient) — severe — harsh
2. (embrace) — exclude — shun — ostracize
3. (luxurious) — plain — stark — Spartan
4. aimless — meander — (straight) — wander
5. laconic — succinct — concise — (wordy)
6. tempt — (gratify) — entice — tantalize
7. (optimistic) — skeptic — cynic — pessimistic
8. weak — feeble — frail — (Herculean)
9. iridescent — (dingy) — colorful — rainbow-like
10. uncontrolled — undisciplined — (stoic) — emotional

RELATIONSHIPS

DIRECTIONS: For each question below, decide whether the pair of words are synonyms (S), antonyms (A), or unrelated (U) to each other.

___U___   1. Herculean . . . . homogeneous

___A___   2. tantalize . . . . repulse

___U___   3. iridescent . . . . effervescent

___A___   4. stoic . . . . ebullient

___U___   5. hedonist . . . . savory

___U___   6. cynic . . . . skeptical

___S___   7. laconic . . . . succinct

___S___   8. meander . . . . circuitous

___U___   9. Spartan . . . . subtle

___U___   10. ostracize . . . . rejuvenate

COMPLETE THE HEADLINE

DIRECTIONS: The following headlines are taken from newspaper and magazine articles. Use one of the following five words to complete each headline: Spartan, Draconian, Laconic, Meandering, Ostracized.

1. China Cracks Down on Births: ___Draconian___ Steps Cut Fertility Rates to Lowest Ever

2. Hurricane Emily: ___Meandering___ Path, Destination Unknown

3. ___Laconic___ Loser Has Little to Say

4. Olympic Athletes Enjoy Village Despite ___Spartan___ Living Quarters

5. ___Ostracized___ Worker Wants Back in Union

LESSON
2

Every Word Has a History

In the previous lesson, you learned that etymologists study the origins of words. In this chapter we will continue our etymological tour with words derived from the customs and myths of ancient Rome.

Words from Everyday Life in Ancient Rome

Desultory, Insult, Resilient, Salient

Have you ever been to the circus? What was your favorite act? In ancient Rome, excited spectators packed the Circus Maximus to watch a performer known as a *desultor*. The *desultor* amazed cheering crowds by performing the feat of jumping from one racing horse to another. The performer's name still lives in our language. Today the word *desultory* means "to jump from one idea or topic to another."

Take another look at the word *desultory*. Note that it contains the root SULT, meaning "to jump or leap." Words containing SULT, SAL, and SIL all involve jumping. For example, when you *insult* someone, you verbally "jump" all over him or her. A *resilient* person jumps or bounces back from adversity. A *salient* point is so important that it jumps out at you.

Nefarious

During the Pax Romana, the Latin word *nefarious* referred to a criminal. This unsavory connotation continued over the centuries. Today the word *nefarious* is used to describe someone or something that is extremely wicked or evil. For example, although Brutus and Cassius thought that assassinating Caesar would save the Roman republic, they had in fact committed one of the ancient world's most *nefarious* crimes.

Sinister, Dexterous

The Latin word *sinister* meant "left" or "on the left side." Superstitious Romans believed that omens observed from one's left side were unlucky. In contrast, the Latin word *dexter* meant "right" or "on the right side." Since most people do things better with their right hand, *dexter* gradually came to mean "skillful or agile." Today *dexterous* refers to skillful actions that are performed in a deft or adroit manner.

Impecunious

When the Romans first settled the lands along the Tibia River, they lacked a metal currency. Nonetheless, Roman farmers did have an ample supply of cattle. As a result, cattle were often used as a measure of wealth. In Latin the word for cattle is *pecus*. A Roman without a cow, or *pecus*, was thus *impecunious*, or not wealthy. Today the word *impecunious* means "destitute or without money."

Prolific

Proles is a Latin word for "offspring." Since the poorest Romans had little or no property, they were expected to serve the Empire by having many children. Today the word *prolific* means "to be very productive." *Proliferation* is a related word that means "to multiply rapidly."

Words from Roman Mythology

Jovial

Zeus was the king of the gods who ruled from high atop Mount Olympus. The ancient Greeks believed that he sent the rain and wind and was master of thunder. The Romans called him Zeus, Jupiter, or Jove. Although Jove was a majestic and awe-inspiring god, he was also viewed as fun-loving and the source of joy and happiness. Today the word *jovial* means "jolly and cheerful." *Jocund, jocular,* and *jocose* are three synonyms of *jovial* that are popular with SAT writers.

Mercurial

In Roman mythology Mercury was the god of commerce. However, he is better known for his role as a swift messenger who flew with the aid of his winged sandals. The Romans honored this fleet-footed messenger by naming the fastest moving planet Mercury. Mercury's name also lives in the English word *mercurial*. Today *mercurial* means "swift and fast-changing." It especially refers to a rapidly changing mood. A person with a *mercurial* personality demonstrates unpredictable and rapidly changing moods.

Lethargy

In Roman mythology the river Lethe ran through Hades, the underworld. Anyone who drank from this river forgot his or her past and thus became lethargic. Today the word *lethargic* means "lazy and sluggish."

Somnolent

Somnus was the Roman god of sleep. Somnus lived in a cave beside the river Lethe. The soft sound of the river brought sleep to everything in the cave. Each evening Somnus cast his spell of sleep over the earth so that all living things could rest before beginning a new day. Today the word *somnolent* still means "sleepy, drowsy."

Moribund

Mors was the twin brother of Somnus. His name comes from the Latin word *mors*, or death. Mors' name still lives in the English language in words such as *moribund* (at the point of death), *mortal* (one who is subject to death), and *immortal* (deathless, having eternal life).

Using Your VOCABULARY

MATCHING

DIRECTIONS: Match each word in the first column with its appropriate definition in the second column.

B	1. desultory	A.	destitute, very poor
I	2. prolific	B.	random, erratic
J	3. moribund	C.	sluggish, lazy
D	4. mercurial	D.	changeable, volatile
G	5. jovial	E.	irrepressible, flexible
A	6. impecunious	F.	wicked, evil
H	7. dexterous	G.	cheerful, merry
F	8. nefarious	H.	skillful, agile
E	9. resilient	I.	fruitful, productive
C	10. lethargic	J.	dying

ODD WORD OUT

DIRECTIONS: Each question below consists of four words. Three of them are related in meaning. Circle the word that does not fit.

1. methodical   systematic   orderly   (desultory)
2. inactive   lethargic   (alert)   indolent
3. (mercurial)   unchanging   stable   fixed
4. stiff   rigid   (resilient)   inflexible
5. barren   (prolific)   sterile   arid
6. moribund   waning   stagnating   (rejuvenating)
7. indigent   destitute   (affluent)   impecunious
8. (minor)   salient   obvious   conspicuous
9. jovial   (gloomy)   jocund   jocose
10. active   alert   energetic   (somnolent)

COMPLETE THE HEADLINE

DIRECTIONS: The following headlines are taken from newspaper and magazine articles. Use one of the following five words to complete each headline: Mercurial, Resilient, Lethargic, Proliferate, and Adroit.

1. "Wake Up! Wake Up!" Is the Chant from Fans During a ____Lethargic____ 3 - 3 Tie

2. ____Resilient____ Cowboys Bounce Back to Win Game

3. ____Adroit____ Diplomacy Produces New Mid-East Treaty

4. As Golf's Popularity Increases, New Courses ____Proliferate____

5. John Starks: ____Mercurial____, Moody, and Multi-talented

Subject Area Vocabulary

After completing this lesson, you will be able to

1. use your reading about Social Studies terms to define 20 key words.

2. use your reading about literary terms to define 20 key words.

Subject Area Terms

Social Studies

Your Social Studies courses include Law, Economics, Geography, Government, and History. Each of these subjects has a distinctive vocabulary. Key Social Studies terms regularly appear on the SAT. Here are 20 key vocabulary words drawn from major Social Studies subjects.

Law and the SAT

1. *Perjury* – When witnesses take the stand they first take an oath swearing to "tell the whole truth and nothing but the truth." If a witness violates this oath, he or she is guilty of *perjury*. *Perjury* is the deliberate giving of false, misleading, or incomplete testimony by a witness under oath.

2. *Acquit* – Each juror has the all-important task of voting to convict or *acquit* the defendant. *Acquit* means "to free or clear from a charge or accusation."

3. *Injunction* – Our laws give judges great power. One of their most important powers is the ability to issue an *injunction*. An *injunction* is a court order requiring or prohibiting an action.

4. *Codicil* – At some point in life most people have a will drawn up. But what if you change your mind and want to add someone to your will? No problem. You simply add a *codicil*, or supplement, to your will.

Economics and the SAT

5. *Duty* – Have you ever been in a duty-free shop in an airport or a foreign country? Why are these shops so popular? The answer lies in the meaning of the term *duty*. A *duty* is a tax on imports. A duty-free shop contains goods whose price does not include a *duty*, or tax. These goods are less expensive than in other shops.

6. *Depreciate/Appreciate* – Is it better for your house to depreciate or appreciate in value? *Depreciate* means "to fall in value." *Appreciate* means "to rise in value." Needless to say, homeowners hope their property *appreciates* in value.

7. *Dearth* – If an automobile dealer had a *dearth* of a popular new model, would you expect the price to go up or down? *Dearth* means "an inadequate supply, scarcity." The price of this popular car would go up, since demand would be greater than supply.

Geography and the SAT

8. *Arid* – What does it mean when a region has an *arid* climate? *Arid* means "dry, lacking moisture." A region with an arid climate suffers from a lack of rain.

9. *Desiccate* – Many regions in Africa are suffering from a severe drought. As a result, the land has become *desiccated*. *Desiccate* means "to become thoroughly dry."

10. *Archipelago* – Suppose your teacher concluded his or her lesson by saying that tomorrow's class would examine the Japanese *archipelago*. What would you study the next day? An *archipelago* is a large group of islands. Your lesson would therefore focus on the unique geography of the islands comprising the Japanese archipelago.

Government and the SAT

11. *Tyrant* – Is it a compliment for a ruler to be called a *tyrant*? In most cases, probably not. A *tyrant* is a ruler who exercises power in a harsh, cruel manner. Can you name a *tyrant* who was overthrown?

12. *Enlightened Despotism* – Many rulers in eighteenth-century Europe were called "enlightened despots." A *despot* is an absolute ruler and *enlightened* means "to become acquainted with information, to be informed." According to eighteenth-century political philosophers, an enlightened despot would be an absolute ruler who used his or her power for the good of the people.

13. *Constituent* – Are you a subject or a *constituent* of the governor of your state? A subject is under the power or authority of a ruler. In contrast, a *constituent* is someone represented by an elected official. In a democracy, citizens are *constituents*, not subjects.

14. *Consensus* – Politicians often say that they want to govern by *consensus*. But, what does this mean? A *consensus* is a general agreement. Governing by *consensus* means trying to find a collective opinion on public issues.

History and the SAT

15. *Line of Demarcation* – Most students know about lines of latitude and longitude. But can you recall what the *Line of Demarcation* was? As the early leaders in the Age of Exploration, Spanish and Portuguese explorers often claimed the same land. In order to prevent disputes, the two Catholic powers agreed to divide control over any newly discovered lands. Under the terms of the Treaty of Tordesillas of 1494, they drew an imaginary line, or *demarcation,* around the world. Territory explored west of the line would belong to Spain, east of the line to Portugal. *Demarcation* means "to set or mark the boundaries or limits of something."

16. *The Coercive Acts* – Following the Boston Tea Party, an outraged Parliament passed a series of punitive laws known in Britain as the Coercive Acts. *Coerce* means "to compel by pressure or threat." The Coercive Acts helped spark the American Revolution. Can you recall what these acts did?

17. *The Sedition Act* – Have you ever been stung by what you consider unfair criticism? If so, you can empathize with leading Federalists in the late 1700's. At that time Jefferson and his supporters bitterly criticized Federalist policies. In an effort to gag their foes, the Federalists passed the Sedition Act, which provided that anyone who falsely defamed government officials would be liable to a heavy fine and imprisonment. *Sedition* means "conduct or language inciting rebellion against the authority of the state."

18. *Secede* – In December 1860, a special convention meeting in Charleston, South Carolina, unanimously voted to *secede* from the Union. *Secede* means "to formally withdraw from membership in an organization. How many states ultimately *seceded* from the Union?

19. *Containment* – During the Cold War, most Americans agreed that the Soviet Union posed a serious threat to the American way of life. In an effort to prevent the extension of Soviet influence, the United States adopted a foreign policy known as *containment. Containment* means "to restrain, hold within." Can you name a war that America fought to contain Soviet expansion? Is *containment* still America's foreign policy?

20. *Dissolution* – On December 25, 1991, Mikhail Gorbachev officially resigned his office as president of the Soviet Union. Gorbachev's resignation marked the final *dissolution,* or breakup, of the Soviet Union. How many new countries were formed as a result of the *dissolution* of the Soviet Union?

MATCHING

DIRECTIONS: Match each word in the first column with its appropriate definition in the second column.

C	1. dissolution	A.	cruel, unjust ruler
J	2. perjury	B.	general agreement
D	3. arid	C.	break-up
B	4. consensus	D.	very dry
I	5. demarcation	E.	court order
H	6. containment	F.	to find innocent
E	7. injunction	G.	addition to a will
G	8. codicil	H.	restrainment
A	9. tyrant	I.	to establish a boundary
F	10. acquit	J.	false testimony

ODD WORD OUT

DIRECTIONS: Each question below consists of four words. Three of them are related in meaning. Circle the word that does not fit.

1. indict   convict   (acquit)   condemn

2. consensus   (discord)   concord   accord

3. force   compel   coerce   (permit)

4. (join)   leave   withdraw   secede

5. scarcity   (abundance)   dearth   shortage

APPLYING YOUR KNOWLEDGE

DIRECTIONS: Use your knowledge of the terms in this chapter to respond to the following.

1. The dissolution of the Soviet Union marked a watershed (turning point) event in the twentieth century. Give one other example of a country or empire that experienced a dissolution.

   the United States during the Civil War

   the Austro-Hungarian Empire after World War I

2. What famous doctrine first declared America's intention to contain Soviet expansion?

   Truman Doctrine

3. The Tariff of Abominations established a duty of nearly 40 percent on imported goods. Was this duty popular or unpopular in the South? Explain your answer.

   Unpopular. The South imported many goods from Great Britain. The high tariff

   forced Southerners to pay more for the imported goods.

4. Which American state is an archipelago?

   Hawaii

5. South Carolina was the first state to secede from the Union. Which state was the second to secede?

   Mississippi

6. If a defendant is acquitted, is he or she also exonerated?

Yes. Exonerate means to free from blame.

7. Name two enlightened despots who ruled during the 18th century.

Frederick the Great and Catherine the Great

8. Was what is now the United States east or west of the Line of Demarcation?

west

9. Was anyone ever convicted of violating the Sedition Act?

Yes. Suits were initiated against the editors of eight major newspapers. The principal target was the Philadelphia *Aurora*, long a thorn in the side of the Federalists, whose editor William Duane was prosecuted under the act.

10. What were the Coercive Acts called in the 13 colonies?

Intolerable Acts

Subject Area Terms

Literature

Your American, British, and World literature courses include a number of important literary terms. Here are 20 key terms that regularly appear on the SAT.

1. *Protagonist* – What do Beowulf and Macbeth have in common? Both are *protagonists*. A *protagonist* is the central character of a drama, short story, or narrative poem.

2. *Antagonist* – What do the monster Grendel and the evil villain Professor Moriarty have in common? Both are *antagonists*. An *antagonist* is a person or force opposing the *protagonist*. Grendel was Beowulf's *antagonist* and Professor Moriarty was Sherlock Holmes' *antagonist*.

3. *Elegy* – An *elegy* is a poem of mourning, usually over the death of an individual. Gray's *Elegy Written in a Country Church* and Tennyson's *In Memoriam* are two of the best known *elegies* in British Literature.

4. *Anecdote* – An *anecdote* is a brief story about an interesting, amusing, or strange event. *Anecdotes* are told to illustrate a point.

5. *Parody* – Have you ever done a humorous imitation of one of your teachers or coaches? If so, you have created a *parody*, or humorous imitation. In literature a *parody* can be made of a plot, a character, a writing style, or a theme.

6. *Polemic* – A *polemic* is an aggressive attack on or a refutation of the opinions or principles of another. For example, *Common Sense* by Thomas Paine was a *polemic* designed to convince the colonists to reject the king and declare independence from Great Britain.

7. *Raconteur* – A *raconteur* is a person who excels in telling stories. For example, Abraham Lincoln was a renowned *raconteur* who amused audiences with his witty stories.

8. *Aphorism* – An *aphorism* is a concise, pointed statement expressing a wise or clever observation about life. For example, "To err is human, to forgive divine," is a famous *aphorism* by Alexander Pope.

9. *Epic* – An *epic* is a long narrative poem telling about the deeds of a great hero and reflecting the values of the society from which it originated. For example, John Milton's *Paradise Lost* is one of the most famous epics in British literature.

10. *Satire* – A *satire* is a kind of writing that ridicules or holds up to contempt the weaknesses and wrongdoings of individuals, groups, institutions, or humanity in general. Jonathan Swift's *Gulliver's Travels* is a famous *satirical* work.

11. *Stereotype* – A *stereotype* is an oversimplified mental picture of a person, a group, or an institution. Sweeping generalizations about "mad scientists," "crafty used-car dealers," and "absent-minded professors" are *stereotypes*.

12. *Oratory* – *Oratory* is the art of public speaking. An *oration* is a formal address given on a special occasion, such as a holiday. An *orator* is a person who delivers an oration.

13. *Parable* – A *parable* is a short story that teaches a lesson or illustrates a moral truth. For example, both Jesus and Confucius used *parables* to instruct their followers.

14. *Paradox* – A *paradox* is a statement that seems to be contradictory but is nevertheless true. For example, the following verses from "To Althea from Prison" by Richard Lovelace are a famous example of a *paradox*.

> "Stone walls do not a prison make,
> Nor iron bars a cage;
> Minds innocent and quiet take
> That for an hermitage."

15. *Irony* – *Irony* is a contrast between what is stated and what is really meant, or between what is expected to happen and what actually happens. Verbal *irony* occurs when a writer or speaker says one thing and means something entirely different. For example, in Shakespeare's play *Julius Caesar*, Marc Antony keeps repeating, "For Brutus is an honorable man." In reality, Antony despises Brutus and is trying to convince his listeners that Brutus is a liar who can't be trusted.

16. *Vernacular* – *Vernacular* is the ordinary language of the people living in a particular region or with a particular group.

17. *Fable* – A *fable* is a brief story, usually with animal characters, that teaches a moral lesson.

18. *Eulogy* – A *eulogy* is a statement or speech praising someone or something.

19. *Foil* – A *foil* is a person or thing that, by strong contrast, underscores or enhances the distinctive characteristics of another person or thing. For example, the antagonist usually serves as a *foil* to highlight the hero's virtues.

20. *Skit* – A *skit* is a short humorous or satirical play or piece of writing.

Using Your
VOCABULARY

MATCHING

DIRECTIONS: Match each word in the first column with its appropriate definition in the second column.

H	1. irony	A.	long narrative poem
D	2. fable	B.	storyteller
G	3. skit	C.	a self-contradiction, but true
F	4. parable	D.	brief story with animal characters
M	5. parody	E.	opposes the protagonist
N	6. stereotype	F.	illustrative moral story
E	7. antagonist	G.	short humorous piece of writing
B	8. raconteur	H.	contrast between what is said and what is meant
I	9. polemic	I.	aggressive attack on or refutation of something
A	10. epic	J.	speech praising someone
S	11. aphorism	K.	very short story meant to illustrate a point
K	12. anecdote	L.	story written to ridicule human weaknesses
O	13. oratory	M.	funny imitation
L	14. satire	N.	oversimplified image of a person
C	15. paradox	O.	art of speaking in public
R	16. vernacular	P.	poem of mourning
Q	17. protagonist	Q.	central figure of a story, hero
J	18. eulogy	R.	ordinary language used in a region
T	19. foil	S.	wise, witty saying
P	20. elegy	T.	used to underscore a contrast

ODD WORD OUT

DIRECTIONS: Each question below consists of four words. Three of them are related in meaning. Circle the word that does not fit.

1. hero   star   protagonist   (adversary)

2. adage   truism   (banality)   aphorism

3. criticism   (eulogy)   slander   vilification

4. (ally)   opponent   rival   antagonist

5. praise   acclaim   laud   (satirize)

Reader's Guide to the SAT I

Becoming a skilled critical reader is essential to doing well on the SAT I and in preparing for college work. There is no substitute for reading a wide variety of well-chosen books. Sampling the 45 books listed in this section will make you a better reader and test-taker as you prepare for the SAT I.

Reader's Guide to the SAT I

Contrary to popular belief, SAT writers do not choose the most obscure sources they can find. The passages selected for the SAT I come from highly regarded books that are appropriate for college freshman and sophomores. Many of the books currently used can be found in a good community library or college book store. The following 45 books have been carefully chosen to provide you with a representative list of books that have recently been used by SAT writers. We strongly recommend that you read portions of a variety of these books. They will help enhance your critical reading skills, strengthen your vocabulary, and broaden your general knowledge.

American Studies

James Lincoln Collier, *The Making of Jazz*

Charles Dickens, *American Notes*

S.I. Hayakawa, *Language and Thought in Action*

Irving Howe, *World of Our Fathers*

H.L. Mencken, *A Gang of Pecksniffs*

David Protess, *Journalism of Outrage*

Ronald Takaki, *Strangers From a Different Shore*

Gore Vidal, *United States: Essays 1952–1992*

Howard Zinn, *A People's History of the United States, 1492–Present*

Fiction

Abraham Cahan, *The Rise of David Levinsky*

Rebecca Harding Davis, *Life in the Iron-Mills*

E.M. Forster, *Howards End*

Zeno-Gandia, *La Charco*

Kazuo Ishiguro, *An Artist of the Floating World*

Paule Marshall, *Reena and Other Stories*

Terry McMillan, *Breaking Ice*

Toni Morrison, *Sula*

Gloria Naylor, *The Women of Brewster Place*

Gender Studies

Anne Fausto-Sterling, *Myths of Gender: Biological Theories About Men and Women*

Paula Giddings, *When and Where I Enter: The Impact of Black Women on Race and Sex in America*

Glazer and Slater, *Unequal Colleagues: The Entrance of Women into the Professions*

Literary Criticism

Nicolas Kanellos, *Mexican-American Theatre Then and Now*

Arnold Kettle, *An Introduction to the English Novel*

James Sutherland, *Daniel Defoe: A Critical Study*

Ian Watt, *The Rise of the Novel*

Personal Narrative

William Beebe, *Edge of the Jungle*

Elizabeth Bishop, *Efforts of Affection: A Memoir of Marianne Moore*

Jill Ker Conway, *The Road from Coorain*

Eva Hoffman, *Lost in Translation*

Tillie Olsen, *Silences*

Patricia J. Williams, *The Alchemy of Race and Rights*

Science

George and Muriel Beadle, *The Language of Life: An Introduction to the Science of Genetics*

William Beck, *Modern Science and the Nature of Life*

Hsu, *The Great Dying*

Evelyn Fox Keller, *A Feeling For The Organism: The Life and Work of Barbara McClintock*

T.R. LeMaire, *Stones From the Stars*

Barry Lopez, *Arctic Dreams*

David Quammen, *Natural Acts: A Sidelong View of Science and Nature*

William W. Warner, *Beautiful Swimmers*

World History

William Y. Elliott and Neil A. McDonald, *Western Political Heritage*

Ann Sutherland Harris, *Women Artists: 1550–1950*

Robert L. Heilbroner, *The Making of Economic Society*

Ralph Linton, *Tree of Culture*

Jerrold Seigel, *Bohemian Paris: Culture, Politics and the Boundaries of Bourgeois Life, 1830–1930*

Thucydides, *The Peloponnesian War,* Crawley Translation

Mastering the PSAT Writing Test

After completing this section, you will be able to

1. identify the three types of questions on the PSAT writing test.

2. apply your grammar skills to *Identifying Sentence Errors*.

3. apply appropriate strategies for *Improving Sentences*.

4. adjust your test-taking strategies for *Improving Paragraphs*.

5. identify your personal starting score range on the PSAT writing test.

INTRODUCTION TO THE PSAT WRITING TEST

This new section of the test will be quite different from anything you have seen before. Almost every student is familiar with reading comprehension tests. Analogies and sentence completions might be strange to you, but it's not too hard to get the hang of attacking these questions. The writing test, on the other hand, will take some getting used to. It shows up on the SATII and on the PSAT, but it's not on the SATI. The test presents an interesting challenge for students with a knack for language. Unfortunately, if you're not prepared, the format can be quite confusing.

The writing test includes questions found in the following sections: *Identifying Sentence Errors, Improving Sentences,* and *Improving Paragraphs.*

Strategies for Identifying Sentence Errors

This section of the test, *Identifying Sentence Errors,* will test your knowledge of grammar, usage, and structure. You'll read 19 sentences, looking for an error in each sentence. About one in five sentences contains no error (always choice (E)). The other four out of five sentences have something wrong with them. Your mission is to identify the part of each sentence that contains an error. You don't need to correct the mistake, you need only to find it.

To do well on this test, you need to keep track of things such as subject-verb agreement, pronoun/noun-antecedent agreement, and verb tense. This lesson includes a number of tips to help you keep track when you're attacking these sentences.

TIP **Carefully read the entire sentence.**

Quickly, but *carefully,* read the whole sentence. By reading the entire sentence before thinking about the underlines, you should be able to see it as a unit with connecting parts that must be compatible. In other words, everything should fit together. This is another way of looking at the tracking issue. In order to keep track of everything, you need to start by reading the entire sentence.

TIP **2**   ## Say the sentence out loud (to yourself).

Don't mindlessly read the sentence—verbalize it! Imagine that you are listening to it being read by an English teacher. Or imagine that you're reading it to your class. If you can hear the difference between proper and improper English, you don't need to know a lot of rules. If it sounds wrong, it probably is.

Don't assume that something has to be wrong with every sentence. About one in five sentences will be correct as written. Out of 19 sentences, you should find about 4 that contain no error. If a sentence sounds OK, it probably is. Mark answer (E) and move on.

TIP **3**   ## Don't dilly-dally.

A big part of taking control of the test is to keep your pace in mind. The sections in which you will be asked to improve sentences and paragraphs (editing) will probably take more time for each question, so keep moving on these sentences. You will probably want to spend about 30 seconds on each item.

TIP **4**   ## Keep in mind *that/which* is not human.

You'll be presented a couple of sentences where you need to choose *that*, *which*, *who*, or *whom*. For this tricky usage issue, remember these easy rules:

- Use *that* to introduce clauses with no commas (restrictive clauses).
- Use *which* to introduce clauses with commas (nonrestrictive clauses).
- Use *who* or *whom* when introducing relative clauses referring to humans.

For example:

> Political cartoons *that* make fun of lawmakers can be useful tools in a democratic society.
>
> Political cartoons, *which* make fun of lawmakers, can be useful tools in a democratic society.
>
> Political cartoonists *who* draw cartoons can be useful tools in a democratic society.

TIP **5**

When is it *better* and when is it *best?*

Some sentences may make you choose between *better* or *best*. Remember this easy guideline: *Between two choices pick the better, among three or more choices pick the best.* To pick the best choice, simply track the number of things being compared.

For example:

> Director Milos Forman received Academy Awards for *One Flew Over the Cuckoo's Nest* and *Amadeus;* it is difficult to say which is the *better* of the two films.
>
> Out of all five of Milos Forman's films, the critics liked *One Flew Over the Cuckoo's Nest* best.

TIP **6**

Are you tracking *among* choices or *between* choices?

Look for sentences that force you to choose between *among* and *between*. If your eighth-grade English teacher taught you to remember "between two and among three," then she gave you a simple rule for a complex grammatical issue. Although many textbooks agree with the simple rule, the most authoritative source for correct English, *The Oxford English Dictionary,* states:

> "In all senses *between* has been, from its earliest appearance, extended to more than two . . . It is still the only word available to express the relation of a thing to many surrounding things severally and individually." (*The Rhinehart Guide to Grammar,* page 380)

For example:

> Sparta, the fiercest of the ancient Greek city-states, imposed rigorous military training upon every male between the ages of seven and sixty.

> The treaty between France, Italy and Russia was ill-fated from its conception due to outside pressures from the Germans.

So when can you use *between?* Pretty much whenever it sounds OK. The people who write the SAT would have a hard time refusing an answer that is supported by *The Oxford English Dictionary.*

But what about *among?* The use of this word is much more restricted. For this reason, therefore, it is more likely to be tested. *Among* is best used when it suggests a relationship of someone or something to a surrounding group. It is NOT a good word to use when comparing only two things.

For example:

> In an effort to learn about South American gold mining practices, the anthropologist lived among the miners for five years.

T I P ## Sentences run parallel, just like railroad tracks.

Many sentences on the PSAT will contain lists or sequences, including noun and verb clauses and phrases. Whenever a list is included in a sentence, each thing on the list must have the same (parallel) grammatical construction. If you master parallelism, you can turn hard questions into easy ones. If a sentence presents a sequence of any kind, everything listed must have parallel structure.

It is especially important to track parallelism when listing prepositional phrases. A sequence of phrases must have the same basic grammatical structure. Conjunctions of all kinds are red flags signaling the need to track parallel structure.

and   but   for   either, or   not, only   but, also

For example:

Parallel Prepositional Phrase: Aretha Franklin's longevity as a successful performing artist has depended *on the superb quality of her singing voice and on her ability to adapt the trends of popular music* to her own creative style.

Parallel Verb Phrase: In order to prepare for the symposium, Sandy organized the lecture, picked up the posters, and rearranged the room.

Parallelism with Correlative Conjunction: Signed into law in 1972, Title IX not only expanded women's opportunities in sports, but it also made academic gains for women possible.

TIP **8** ## Take a break at Coordinating Conjunction Junction.

Coordinating conjunctions connect two parts of a sentence. They can also play a very important role in relating the logic of a sentence. Pay close attention to reversal and supporting words such as *and* and *but* that connect two parts of a sentence. Remember, *and* is a supporting word that indicates no change in the tone of the sentence. *But* is a reversal word and, therefore, will indicate a change in the tone of a sentence.

For example:

Reversal: The price of petroleum products remains affordable, but the price does not reflect the long term cost of depleting a non-renewable resource.

Supportive: The price of petroleum products does not reflect the long term cost of depleting a non-renewable resource, and that should be one of the most important factors considered when evaluating the cost of a natural resource.

TIP **9**

Follow those hard-to-track pronouns.

Whenever you see a pronoun, be sure to track its antecedent. The antecedent is the noun or subject to which the pronoun refers. For example, in the sentence "Joe went to the store because he needed some milk," the pronoun is *he* and the antecedent is *Joe.* When the antecedent appears in an earlier sentence, sometimes it's difficult to keep track of the noun or subject to which the pronoun refers. This is another case where verbalizing each sentence will help you. Many times you will hear whether or not a pronoun matches its antecedent in number and case (singular or plural).

> *For example:*
>
> **Incorrect pronoun-antecedent disagreement:** Marketing studies show that when people see an attractive person using a product, you identify with the person and may consequently purchase the advertised item.
>
> **Correct pronoun-antecedent agreement:** Marketing studies show that when people see an attractive person using a product, they identify with the person and may consequently purchase the advertised item.

The first sentence begins with *people* as the subject, then shifts incorrectly to *you* to indicate the same entity. It is incorrect to rename the same noun within a sentence. The pronoun used in the sentence should be the same throughout, and every pronoun must have a clearly stated referent, or antecedent.

TIP **10**

The Sentence Error Grammar Review

The *Identifying Sentence Errors* section will test a variety of skills, including some fairly picky grammatical concepts. Since you probably haven't seen some of these rules in print since the eighth grade, use the following Grammar Review section to refresh your memory.

Grammar Review

Periods   A period ends a complete sentence. A complete sentence contains both a *subject* (who or what is doing the action) and a *predicate* (the action). If one of these is missing, you have a *sentence fragment.*

> **The moldy sandwich, a fuzzy-green and smelly entity.**

There is no predicate. What is the moldy sandwich *doing?*

> **Lives in the fridge and continues to grow.**

There is no subject. We don't know *what* "lives and continues to grow."

> **The moldy sandwich, a fuzzy-green and smelly entity, lives in the fridge and continues to grow.**

The sentence has both subject and predicate. We know what's doing the action ("the moldy sandwich") and we know what the action is ("lives . . . and continues to grow").

Commas   A comma is simply a signal to the reader to pause. There are many rules for the use of commas, but most situations are covered by the "Fab Four" comma rules below.

1. **Commas after items in a series**—If you list three or more items in a row, you need a comma after each item in the series except the last one.

> **John, Paul, George, and Ringo first recorded together in 1962.**

2. **Commas after an introductory phrase**—An introductory phrase is a short phrase at the beginning of a sentence that introduces the main idea of the sentence. An introductory phrase is followed by a comma.

> **By the end of 1964, the Beatles had several number one records in England.**

> **Though it may not have seemed overly important at the time, the "British Invasion" marked the beginning of a new era in rock-n-roll history.**

3. **Commas to set off material that's not essential to the meaning of the sentence.**

   • Parenthetical expressions—A parenthetical expression is a phrase that modifies the entire sentence. These are common parenthetical expressions: "as a matter of fact," "believe me," "I am sure," "to tell the truth," and "it seems to me." Parenthetical expressions need to be set off by commas.

The Beatles' most experimental album, in my opinion, is *Sgt. Pepper's Lonely Hearts Club Band.*

A parenthetical expression is not necessary to the meaning of the sentence; it's almost like an aside. As a matter of fact, you could remove it altogether and the sentence would still be acceptable.

The Beatles' most experimental album is *Sgt. Pepper's Lonely Hearts Club Band.*

   • Appositives—An appositive is a group of words that describe a noun or a pronoun. Appositives can appear at the beginning, middle, or end of a sentence. An appositive is set off by commas.

Paul McCartney, perhaps the most musically proficient of the Fab Four, played bass guitar.

An appositive is also not essential to the meaning of the sentence. What would happen if we just took it out? The sentence would still be acceptable.

Paul McCartney played bass guitar.

Examples of comma misuse:

The Beatle, who played the drums, was the last to join the group.

The words "who played the drums" are necessary for the reader to know which Beatle is being discussed; DO NOT set off with commas.

The album, recorded just before the band's breakup, was *Abbey Road.*

The words "recorded just before the band's breakup" is necessary for the reader to know which album is being talked about; DO NOT set off with commas.

4. **Commas to separate independent clauses**—An independent clause is a string of words that can stand alone as a sentence; it contains both a subject and a predicate. When two independent clauses are joined by a comma and a *conjunction* (and, but, or, nor, for), you have a *compound sentence.*

> **John, Paul, and George all played guitar, Ringo played the drums.**

> This sentence needs a conjunction.

> **John, Paul, and George all played guitar but Ringo played the drums.**

> This sentence needs a comma.

> **John, Paul, and George all played guitar, but Ringo played the drums.**

> This sentence has both a comma and a conjunction and is correct.

Semicolons

Semicolons are also used to link independent clauses, only *without* the use of a conjunction. A semicolon acts much like a period; everything on both sides of the semicolon must be able to stand alone as a sentence. A semicolon links two ideas more closely than a period does.

> **Shaquille is a powerful player; his size and strength make him a formidable obstacle on the court.**

> Everything on both sides of the semicolon can stand alone as a sentence.

A semicolon also separates items in a list, much like a comma does. Use semicolons to make a list less confusing when there are already commas separating things within the list.

> **Please find the following items for the party: a stereo with both a cassette and a CD player; a birthday cake, but not the kind with icky-sweet icing; a location that has a kitchen, folding tables and chairs, and air conditioning; and plenty of invitations.**

A semicolon is never interchangeable with a colon or a dash.

Colons   A colon causes a break in a sentence and calls the reader's attention to what follows. Use a colon in the following ways:

1. To explain or add emphasis to the first clause in a sentence:

   David Letterman did something no other late-night talk show host had done: he hired his own mom as a correspondent.

2. To introduce a list following an independent clause:

   I have three simple wishes for my birthday: a year's supply of CDs, a summer vacation in Europe, and a guest appearance on *Friends*.

3. To introduce a quotation that relates strongly to the clause before it:

   In the midst of her most pressing problems, she comforted herself with a saying she'd heard since childhood: "This is a job for Kool-Aid!"

Dashes   Dashes are used to set off information that is not necessary to the meaning of the sentence, somewhat like commas do.

   The Woodstock II concert—a pale imitation of the original—was an overpriced fiasco.

   Today I went to Jeans World—the one in the mall next to the music store— to shop for a new pair of jeans and a belt.

Dashes are also used to emphasize sentence elements, somewhat like colons do.

   A new scientific study has indicated a characteristic consistent in highly successful people—a love for chocolate.

Apostrophes   An apostrophe indicates possession. The apostrophe comes before the *s* when the noun is singular and after the *s* when the noun is plural.

Dave's mom	**the girls' books**
Spike's camera	**the doctors' opinions**

The possessive can also be stated as follows:

   the mother of Dave

but never:

   the mother of Dave's

When a plural noun does not already end in *s*, add an apostrophe + *s*.

the children's toys

the mice's cheese

With indefinite pronouns, the apostrophe always comes before the *s*.

Everyone's **expectation was that Michael would eventually return to basketball. When that might happen was** *anyone's* **guess.**

Parentheses

Parentheses are used to set off information that is not essential to the meaning of the sentence.

Who would have thought that Superman (he calls himself the "man of steel") would wear tights made by his mom?

Whether you use commas, dashes, or parentheses to set off information that is not essential to the meaning of the sentence is often an editorial choice. The PSAT will not ask you to make arbitrary decisions.

They will, however, ask you to be consistent, at least within the same sentence. The sentences below are all acceptable.

Students often differ from their parents and teachers, and among themselves, on many issues.

Students often differ from their parents and teachers—and among themselves—on many issues.

Students often differ from their parents and teachers (and among themselves) on many issues.

Inconsistent punctuation in the following sentences makes them unacceptable.

Students often differ from their parents and teachers—and among themselves, on many issues.

Students often differ from their parents and teachers, and among themselves—on many issues.

Don't mismatch them!

Common Usage Mistakes

What's wrong with this sentence?

Everyone here should have their books.

It sounds okay to most people, but in formal speech and in writing it is more acceptable to say:

Everyone here should have *his* book.

Since many people prefer to avoid the generic pronoun *he* when talking about a male or female, *his or her* is commonly used:

Everyone here should have *his or her* book.

Of course, if you know the gender of the person, you would say so:

Somebody on the girls' basketball team forgot *her* gym bag.

Watch for pronouns on the PSAT Writing Test. Whenever a pronoun is underlined, quickly check for its antecedent (what it is refering to).

The possibilities for interacting with art, rather than gazing mutely at *them*, are endless.

In the sentence above, *them* refers to *art* and should be changed to *it*. Other cases of pronoun-antecedent agreement are more subtle:

The team pays *their* own travel expenses.

Team is a collective noun, requiring a singular verb (*pays*) and a singular pronoun. Hence, *their* would change to *its*.

The following pronouns require singular verbs and antecedents:

anybody, anyone, each, either, everybody, everyone, everything, neither, nobody, no one, one, somebody, someone, something

The following pronouns always take a plural verb and antecedent:

both, many, several, all

These pronouns can be plural or singular, depending on how they are used:

all, any, none, some

For example:

All of you are fine students.	Plural—"All of you"
All of my soup is ruined.	Singular—"All of my soup"

It is easy to become confused when choosing between singular and plural forms. That's why you're likely to see a few agreement questions on the Writing Test. Here are two other ways that the PSAT makes it hard to know whether to use a singular or plural verb:

1. Fake compound subject:

   The list of repairs and hours of labor *is/are* too large.

   This sentence sounds like the list of repairs and the hours of labor are both too large.

   The only thing that is too large is the list, which happens to contain repairs and hours of labor. You wouldn't say that the hours of labor are too large, so you could tell that *list* is the subject. The correct verb would be *is.*

2. Reversed order of subject and verb. What is the subject in this sentence?

   In the middle of the park *stand/stands* two fine statues.

   Statues is the subject, so the verb should be *stand:*

   Two fine statues stand in the park.

   Be careful when the normal order of the sentence is reversed.

Verb Check for the PSAT Writing Test

Regular Verbs   A regular verb is one that forms its past and past participle by adding "*-ed*" or "*-d*" to the infinitive form.

Infinitive	Past	Past Participle
kick	kicked	(have) kicked

Irregular Verbs   An irregular verb is one that forms its past and past participle in some way other than a regular verb. Some irregular verbs form the past and past participle forms by changing the vowels, some by changing the consonants, and others by making no change at all. The following is a list of common irregular verbs.

Infinitive	Past	Past Participle	Infinitive	Past	Past Participle
begin	began	(have) begun	give	gave	(have) given
blow	blew	(have) blown	go	went	(have) gone
break	broke	(have) broken	ring	rang	(have) rung
bring	brought	(have) brought	run	ran	(have) run
burst	burst	(have) burst	see	saw	(have) seen
choose	chose	(have) chosen	shrink	shrank	(have) shrunk
come	came	(have) come	speak	spoke	(have) spoken
do	did	(have) done	steal	stole	(have) stolen
drink	drank	(have) drunk	swim	swam	(have) swum
drive	drove	(have) driven	take	took	(have) taken
fall	fell	(have) fallen	throw	threw	(have) thrown
freeze	froze	(have) frozen	write	wrote	(have) written

LESSON 2

Strategies for Improving Sentences

This section of the test, *Improving Sentences,* checks your ability to edit a sentence. You will read 14 sentences and decide whether you could improve the underlined portion. About one in five sentences are best with no changes (always choice A). The other four out of five sentences need a correction. Your mission is to identify the best choice for stating the underlined portion of the sentence.

 TIP 1

Carefully read the entire sentence, not just the underlined part.

You need to establish a context for the underlined part of the sentence. To do that, you need to read every word. The questions in this section are asking you to look at the sentences as a whole. Although you may change only the underlined part, the parts that are NOT underlined will usually determine the correct answer.

TIP **2**

To get started, cover the choices until you get the feel of the sentence.

As you first read each sentence, cover the choices and try to get a feel for what the sentence needs. If you go straight to the choices without thinking, you can get very confused. Say the sentence out loud to yourself and listen to whether it *sounds* right. Listen for anything that seems awkward or too long. Then go to the choices.

TIP **3**

Focus your edit on the underlined portion.

Even though you need to read the entire sentence, your editorial attention must focus on the underlined portion. Remember that the portion without underlining must stay the same. You are not at liberty to change anything except what is underlined. Do not waste time considering how the part of the sentence without underlining might be better written.

TIP **4**

If the sentence sounds correct as is, pick (A).

About one out of five sentences will be fine just the way it is. Choice (A) exactly repeats the underlined portion. Always pick (A) if the sentence sounds OK as is. Trust yourself. If English is your first language, you are probably better at hearing the correct expression than you think you are.

On the other hand, as soon as you realize that a change is needed, don't bother rereading choice (A). Simply *ZAP* it.

TIP **5**

Consider the best fix, then check the choices.

When you read the sentence without looking at the choices, you should get some idea of what it will take to fix it. If you have already isolated the problem, finding your preconceived solution among the four remaining choices will be much easier.

If you don't immediately recognize the solution you had in mind, quickly plug in each choice to see which one works best. If nothing works, you may want to reconsider choice (A). Don't take too long on any one sentence. If you don't keep moving, your frustration level will start to build. First think about the sentence, quickly check out the choices, then pick an answer and move on.

 TIP 6

Before you commit to an answer, plug it in and say the sentence again out loud to yourself.

This strategy is worth the extra time. It is a safety step to avoid making stupid mistakes. Before committing to an answer, verbalize the choices in order to hear which one sounds correct. Reading your answer back into the sentence will help you to see if it fits into the context of the whole sentence. Otherwise, you may frequently introduce an error where there was none before, or you may exchange one error for another.

 TIP 7

Keep an eye on the parallel bars.

Everything about parallelism in the first writing section, *Identifying Sentence Errors,* also applies to *Improving Sentences.* Whenever you see a sequence, make sure the format of the wording is the same. Remember, parallel structure applies whenever any part of speech, clause, or phrase is used in a list format.

> *For example:*
>
> Set in the American southwest, Tony Hillerman's mystery novels offer the reader details about Navajo and Hopi culture as well as *having suspenseful plots.*
>
> (A) having suspenseful plots
> (B) the suspenseful plots they offer
> (C) have suspenseful plots
> (D) they offer suspenseful plots
> (E) suspenseful plots
>
> Choice (E) is correct because the structure of the two things the author offers needs to be as parallel as possible. To see what structure is needed, simplify the sentence to its core elements: *The novels offer details and plots.*

TIP **8** # Watch out for sentence fragments.

Incomplete sentences (fragments) are a frequent occurrence in student writing, so the problem is likely to appear on this part of the test. A fragment is a group of words that does not express a complete thought. A complete sentence requires both a subject and a verb. If either part is missing, the sentence is incomplete and must be corrected. This can happen with a lot of words as easily as with only a few. In other words, you might come across long sentence fragments, not just short ones. Whenever you find a fragment, something must change, so *ZAP* (A) immediately.

For example:

Running and jumping in new *sneakers, and kicking* at an anthill to see what we could stir up.

- (A) sneakers, and kicking at
- (B) sneakers and kicking at
- (C) sneakers; and kicking at
- (D) sneakers, we would kick at
- (E) sneakers, and kick at

The given sentence is a fragment because it lacks a subject. Choice (D) corrects the problem.

TIP **9** # Avoid wordiness—shorter is better.

The test is after clear, concise language. If a sentence is grammatically correct, then leave it alone. Additional information, in order to be relevant, must either add new information or clarify existing information. Do not fall into the trap of picking longer, wordier choices just because you think they sound more intelligent. Make sure the additional wording serves a purpose. In the following example, answer choices (C), (D), (E) offer "wordier" solutions to a sentence that is correct as is.

Cockroaches were the predominant insects 300 million years *ago and are likely to survive* into the next era of geologic time.

(A) ago and are likely to survive

(B) ago; and they are more than likely to survive

(C) ago, and it is still likely they could survive

(D) ago; still, they would be likely to survive

(E) ago, they will be likely to survive

In situations where you are guessing between three or four choices, your best bet is to choose the shortest option. Choice (A) is the correct answer.

TIP 10   Study proper use of semicolons, commas, and conjunctions.

As many as one-third of these questions will be involved with commas, semi-colons, and conjunctions. Each of these three serves a very different purpose, and they are not interchangeable. If this is a weak area for you, get help from a tutor or English teacher.

Strategies for Improving Paragraphs

This section of the test, *Improving Paragraphs*, switches focus from a nit-picking grammar edit to taking a look at the bigger picture. You read a passage and answer six questions about how it might be improved. The first two parts of the writing test checked on your ability to catch specific grammar errors. This part of the test is looking at logic, coherence, and organization.

TIP 1   Imagine the passage was written by a friend.

It's hard for most people to edit a passage that they think was written by an expert. Instead, to get you into the right frame of mind, imagine that this passage is the first draft of a friend's paper. Your friend has done poorly in English class and has come to you for help with an assignment. You need to help with the big picture, so ignore grammar issues as you consider this first draft.

TIP **2** ## Get the main gist, as in *F - L - O - W.*

Read each passage carefully, but don't try to memorize it. You're going after the big picture. As you read, focus on the FLOW.

F— Feel. What is the general feel of the passage? Is it an informal passage written to inform? Is it a formal essay written to persuade you to reconsider an important issue?

L— Logic. Follow the logic of the passage. Is it well organized as is, or will it need to be reorganized later? Is the author leading you to a logical conclusion?

O—Overall picture. Read the passage carefully enough to be able to sum it up into one sentence. What's the big idea? Think of yourself as an editor looking at a rough draft for the first time.

W—Writing style. What is the tone? Understanding the tone will help you to understand the writer. Get a feel for what type of language will be appropriate when you begin to correct errors.

TIP **3** ## Quickly read the whole passage from start to finish.

Before making your first comment on your friend's paper, you need to read it from start to finish. Don't bother with editorial notes in the places where you notice small grammar mistakes. Look for The Big Three: logic, coherence, and organization. Ask yourself, "Does this passage make sense?"

TIP **4** ## Look for clarity, conciseness, and directness.

In order to be effective, each paragraph needs to have these three qualities. Like the *Improving Sentences* section, the simplest, most direct way to present information is usually best. It is your job as editor to make sure each paragraph states its information in the most concise manner possible.

TIP

Paragraph by paragraph—consider the organization.

One of the most important aspects of paragraph development is its organization. This is not an issue of right and wrong so much as an issue of clarity and artistry. Many well-developed paragraphs follow a general format that includes three parts:

The topic sentence—This sentence often comes first. It introduces the subject of the paragraph and gives the reader a hint of what will be discussed in the sentences to follow. It is the most general of the sentences listed because its purpose is simply to introduce what is to come.

The middle—These sentences will explain and illustrate the topic of the paragraph that was introduced by the topic sentence. These will be detail sentences that offer specific information.

Concluding Sentence—In a free standing paragraph, the concluding sentence will tie things up, usually by drawing some conclusion from what has been said in the paragraph's middle. In a collection of paragraphs, the conclusion often includes a transition into the upcoming paragraph.

TIP

Refrain from wide-open editing.

If you're good with language, you might have an editorial idea for greatly improving one of the paragraphs. This is a trap for high-scoring students. You're not at liberty to create new ideas or make open-ended improvements. If you want a high score, consider the choices and pick the best choice offered. Don't waste any energy formulating a better idea than those presented in the choices. You might exhibit brilliant insight, but the only way to grab a point is to pick the right choice from those offered.

TIP **7**

An entire paragraph provides the context for each question.

Even though a question may refer to only one or two sentences, the answer will depend on the context created by the whole paragraph. You not only need to read the whole paragraph, you need to consider it as an entity when you select an answer.

TIP ## Read each question carefully.

When you read the question, cover up the choices with your hand. Look for clues to the answer as you reread the section to which the question refers. Try to formulate an idea of what the correct answer might look like. This strategy will be more difficult here than it was with the *Improving Sentences* questions, but it will save you time by helping you to *ZAP* out obviously wrong choices.

TIP ## Decide what the question is addressing.

Each question on this subtest is going to address a certain issue. First, figure out what editorial problem the question is addressing. Look inside the question for clues. Most questions will refer to one of five areas:

- a particular part of a sentence
- an individual sentence
- a group of sentences
- an entire paragraph
- the passage as a whole

Focus primarily on the area to which the question refers, but keep in mind that the context, or the bigger picture, must be considered for every question.

TIP ## Finally, look at the choices.

After reading the passage and figuring out what the question is really asking, you should have a pretty good idea of what the correct answer is. Remember your time constraints—about one minute per question. If you don't see the correct answer immediately, begin to look for the wrong choices and *ZAP* from there.

TIP 11 ## Plug your choice into the paragraph and reread it.

Developing and improving paragraphs is a skill that you can work on and refine. Practice will help you to take this test more quickly and effectively. After just a few practice tests, you should be moving quickly enough to read through the paragraph after plugging in your answer choices.

Writing Practice Test

Administer

Take the practice test on the following pages. Set up a situation that is as close as possible to the actual testing situation. Use an accurate clock or timer. Do not allow interruptions. Attack the test under timed conditions and with no extra assistance.

If you violate any of the normal rules of administration, your estimated score will be less accurate.

Pacing

Keep in mind that each question is worth only a single raw score point, whether it eats 10 seconds or 2 minutes of your time. Your best bet is to attack with a clear strategy. Focus on the sections from which you can get the most amount of points in the least amount of time: *Identifying Sentence Errors* and *Improving Sentences.*

The *Identifying Sentence Errors* section is a gold mine of points. This section allows you to score the most amount of points (19) in the least amount of time. You'll probably spend about 10 minutes working these problems.

The *Improving Sentences* section provides the possibility of 14 points, but each question requires considerable time. Your target should be a little less than a minute for each question. Spend about 12 minutes on this section.

Save the *Improving Paragraphs* section for last—it requires the most amount of time per question, with the least amount of points (6) possible. Many students consider this section the most difficult. Spending only 8 minutes on this section is your best strategic bet. Remember that all of the questions are worth 1 point; don't get trapped in this section.

Time–30 Minutes   For each question in this section, circle the best answer from among the choices
39 Questions   given.

Directions: The following sentences test your knowledge of grammar, usage, diction (choice of words), and idiom.

Some sentences are correct.
No sentence contains more than one error.

You will find that the error, if there is one, is underlined and lettered. Elements of the sentence that are not underlined will not be changed. In choosing answers, follow the requirements of standard written English.

If there is an error, select the one underlined part that must be changed to make the sentence correct and circle the letter under that part.

EXAMPLE:

The other delegates and him immediately
   A   B   C
accepted the resolution drafted by the
                              D
neutral states. No error
                    E

---

1   Sparta, the much fiercer of the ancient Greek
                 A
city-states, imposed rigorous military

training upon every male between the ages
        B   C   D
of seven and sixty. No error
                        E

2   Although dogs demand considerable care,
             A
it invariably rewards the caregiver with
B   C   D
boundless loyalty and affection. No error
                                    E

3   The researchers, having discovered the gene
                     A
for baldness in humans, speculated with the
                         B
possible implications of their findings.
                       C   D
No error
   E

4   After eight rounds of boxing, the besieged

veteran conceded that it was his age and not
        A   B
in his experience that would determine the
        C   D
bout's outcome. No error
                    E

5   Tecumseh was a Shawnee leader that
                                   A
encouraged Native Americans to eschew
                              B
white customs, advocating an economy
                C
based on hunting and trading rather than
D
agriculture. No error
                E

6   Television stations are now equipped with

computers that monitor barely perceptible
           A   B   C
nuances in meteorological phenomenon.
                           D
No error
   E

GO ON TO THE NEXT PAGE ⇨

7 Laura Esquivel's novel *Like Water for Chocolate* <u>includes</u> recipes <u>for</u> dishes that
          A   B
<u>determines</u> the twists and turns of <u>its</u> plot.
●   D
<u>No error</u>
E

8 After 155 years of <u>being</u> a British
       A
dependency, Hong Kong returned <u>to</u>
           B
Chinese rule in 1997, <u>as stipulated</u> <u>by</u> an
       C   D
agreement signed by the two countries in
1984. <u>No error</u>
   ●

9 Among the many uses of holograms <u>are</u> the
              ●
condensation of digital data bases <u>when</u>
             B
information <u>is recorded</u> at different angles
      C
<u>relative</u> to the holographic plate. <u>No error</u>
D   E

10 Turn-of-the-century Swedish author Selma
Lagerlöf wrote romantic fiction, <u>whereby</u>
           ●
other European novelists <u>of the time</u> <u>tended</u>
         B   C
to focus on the gritty <u>realities</u> of life.
         D
<u>No error</u>
E

11 Aretha Franklin's longevity <u>as</u> a successful
           A
performing artist <u>has depended</u> on the
       B
superb quality of her singing voice <u>and on</u>
             C
her ability to adapt the trends of popular
music <u>to her own creative expression</u>.
      D
<u>No error</u>
●

12 Political theorist Benjamin Barber argues
<u>that paying taxes</u> and <u>obeying</u> the law are
    A   B
not the same thing <u>to taking</u> responsibility
        ●
for <u>one's self</u> as a member of society.
   D
<u>No error</u>
E

13 While some claim <u>that</u> information-age
        A
technology is a democratizing force, <u>neither</u>
             B
the equipment nor the dial-up Internet
access <u>are</u> readily available <u>to</u> low-income
  ●   D
and rural citizens. <u>No error</u>
        E

14 The Viceroy butterfly's black and orange
markings <u>mimic</u> <u>the Monarch butterflies</u> and
    A   ●
repel birds and other predators <u>that know of</u>
           C
the Monarch <u>as toxic</u>. <u>No error</u>
     D   E

15 A casual inventory of services available <u>to</u>
            A
individuals willing to pay for <u>them</u> <u>suggests</u>
         B   C
an <u>increasing</u> specialization in today's work
  D
force. <u>No error</u>
   ●

16 Eating <u>healthy</u> is the only way for animals to
   ●
obtain the "essential" eight <u>of the twenty</u>
          B
amino acids <u>comprising</u> the proteins that
      C
make up <u>our</u> cells. <u>No error</u>
    D   E

GO ON TO THE NEXT PAGE

17 <u>Hardly none</u> of our representatives attend
    ●

    <u>those</u> sessions <u>in which</u> <u>the least contro-</u>
    B   C   D

    versial legislation is proposed. <u>No error</u>
                                      E

18 Marketing studies show <u>that when</u> people
                            A

    see an attractive person using a product,

    <u>you</u> <u>identify with</u> the person and may
    ●   C

    <u>consequently</u> purchase the item. <u>No error.</u>
    D   E

19 <u>At the 1972 Olympic games</u>, American
    A
    swimmer Mark Spitz not only <u>won</u> gold
                                B

    medals in 4 individual and 3 relay races, <u>but</u>

    <u>he also</u> set <u>world records</u> in each of them.
    C   ●
    <u>No error</u>
    E

Directions: The following sentences test correctness and effectiveness of expression. In choosing answers, follow the requirements of standard written English; that is, pay attention to grammar, choice of words, sentence construction, and punctuation.

In each of the following sentences, part of the sentence or the entire sentence is underlined. Beneath each sentence you will find five ways of phrasing the underlined part. Choice A repeats the original; the other four are different.

Choose the answer that best expresses the meaning of the original sentence. If you think the original is better than any of the alternatives, choose it; otherwise choose one of the others. Your choice should produce the most effective sentence—clear and precise, without awkwardness or ambiguity.

EXAMPLE:

Laura Ingalls Wilder published her first book
<u>and she was sixty-five years old then</u>.

(A) and she was sixty-five years old then
(B) when she was sixty-five
(C) at age sixty-five years old
(D) upon the reaching of sixty-five years
(E) at the time when she was sixty-five

---

20 Available to residents free of charge in racks
    at several central locations, <u>the city has an
    alternative newspaper publishing</u> in-depth
    articles, concert reviews, and weekly listings
    of events.

    (A) the city has an alternative newspaper
         publishing
    (B) the city publishes an alternative
         newspaper with
    (C) the city's newspaper is an alternative,
         publishing
    (D) the city's alternative newspaper is
         published with
    (E) the city's alternative newspaper
         publishes

21 The students insisted that they learn more
    words reading well-written books than
    <u>learning by memorizing</u> vocabulary lists.

    (A) learning by memorizing
    (B) they learn memorizing
    (C) if they learn by memorizing
    (D) they learn when memorizing
    (E) are learned by memorizing

GO ON TO THE NEXT PAGE ⟩

22 Social scientists continue to debate whether types of behavior such as risk-taking <u>is an inherited trait, or if it is learned</u>.

(A) is an inherited trait, or if it is learned
(B) is an inherited or learned trait
(C) is inherited or a learned trait
(D) are inherited traits, or it is learned
(E) are inherited or learned traits

23 Hundreds of different books about gardening, <u>each having their own</u> particular angle, are released every year by the major publishing houses.

(A) each having their own
(B) they each have their own
(C) which all have their own
(D) each with its own
(E) with each of them having its own

24 <u>It was less than a year after the first manned Soviet spacecraft orbited the earth, that John Glenn made three orbits of the earth, being an American astronaut.</u>

(A) It was less than a year after the first manned Soviet spacecraft orbited the earth, that John Glenn made three orbits of the earth, being an American astronaut.
(B) Less than one year after the first manned Soviet spacecraft orbited the earth, American astronaut John Glenn made three orbits of the earth.
(C) First the manned Soviet spacecraft orbited the earth, then less than one year later American astronaut John Glenn made three orbits of the earth.
(D) Less than one year after the first manned Soviet spacecraft having orbited the earth, American astronaut John Glenn made three orbits of the earth.
(E) John Glenn, being an American astronaut, made three orbits of the earth less than one year after the first manned Soviet spacecraft's having orbited the earth.

25 The causes of the Seminole Wars include the Seminoles' occupation of coveted land <u>and that they were giving refuge</u> to runaway slaves.

(A) and that they were giving refuge
(B) and also they gave refuge
(C) and the given refuge
(D) and their giving refuge
(E) in addition to giving refuge

26 In order to limit the grain surpluses of the early 80s, the government offered farmers per-acre stipends for idled fields, <u>thereby aiding</u> efforts to reduce soil erosion, as well.

(A) thereby aiding
(B) and so it had aided
(C) this aided
(D) whereby they have aided
(E) they having aided

27 When Mrs. Sebring teaches a novel or a play, <u>its central themes are illuminated, but they are not belabored</u>.
(A) its central themes are illuminated, but they are not belabored
(B) their central themes are illuminated without being belabored
(C) their central themes are illuminated, but she does not belabor them
(D) she illuminates, but does not belabor, its central themes
(E) she illuminates its central themes without their being belabored

28 While celebrities of the 70s and 80s championed liberal causes, today's celebrities use their influence <u>to promote expensive brand-name products</u>.

(A) to promote expensive brand-name products
(B) in the promotion of brand-name products that are expensive
(C) by promoting expensive, brand-name products
(D) through the promotion of expensive, brand-name products
(E) promoting brand-name products they are expensive

GO ON TO THE NEXT PAGE

29   The Renaissance Period in Europe witnessed a burst of discoveries and inventions, <u>and in return these</u> achievements stimulated visual and literary arts such as painting and poetry.
(A) and in return these
(B) therefore
(C) in which
(D) these
(●) and these

30   The Supreme Court appointee was rejected not so much for his record of inappropriate behavior, <u>but for his being lacking in</u> the usual qualifications for the post.
(A) but for his being lacking in
(B) but for his lacking of
(C) as for his lacking of
(●) as for his lack of
(E) the reason being his lack of

31   Juliana's research proved more intriguing than she had <u>imagined; when she found</u> a love letter in her boyfriend's handwriting tucked inside a library book.
(A) imagined; when she found
(B) imagined, finding
(●) imagined: she found
(D) imagined, among which she found
(E) imagined and thus found

32   Known to reach 23 feet in length <u>and there are rumors of their reaching</u> up to 30 feet, Indo-Pacific crocodiles are possibly the largest living reptiles in the world.

(A) and there are rumors of their reaching
(●) and rumored to reach
(C) they are rumored to reach
(D) with rumors about their having reached
(E) having reached, according to rumor,

33   The horns commonly shown on Viking helmets are a modern <u>invention, however excavations of Viking settlements have brought to light many helmets, but none with horns.</u>

(A) invention, however excavations of Viking settlements have brought to light many helmets, but none with horns.
(B) invention; excavations of Viking settlements have brought to light many helmets, but none with horns, however.
(●) invention; excavations of Viking settlements have brought to light many helmets, but none with horns.
(D) invention, because, excavations of Viking settlements have brought to light many helmets, but none with horns.
(E) invention, therefore excavations of Viking settlements have brought to light many helmets, but none with horns.

GO ON TO THE NEXT PAGE

Directions: The following passage is an early draft of an essay. Some parts of the passage need to be rewritten. Read the passage and answer the questions that follow. Some questions are about particular sentences or parts of sentences and ask you to improve sentence structure and word choice. Other questions refer to parts of the essay or the entire essay and ask you to consider organization and development. In making your decisions, follow the conventions of standard written English.

Questions 34-39 are based on the following essay.

(1) My favorite television shows are nature documentaries. (2) I wish I were one of those people who study animals and photograph them in their habitats. (3) They have an important job. (4) Without them we would never know about exotic animals. (5) Some of the animals they have documented include the arctic fox, African elephant, and wooly kangaroo.

(6) I may never see these animals in the wild. (7) I feel good just knowing they are out there. (8) The nature shows bring you so close to the animals. (9) Viewers can relate to the animals. (10) They scratch when they have an itch, yawn when they're bored, and demonstrate surprise, curiosity, contentment, and fear.

(11) The documentaries about plants can be just as interesting, especially the time-lapse photography sequences showing how plants move across the forest floor or wrap themselves around insects. (12) Time-lapse photography is part of the "magic" of television. (13) I know it sounds crazy. (14) I sometimes imagine I can ride the light beams coming from the TV back inside it to find myself in one of the unique habitats I've seen there.

34 Which of the following is the best way to revise the underlined portions of sentences 4 and 5 (reproduced below) in order to combine the two sentences?

Without them we would never know about exotic <u>animals</u>. <u>Some of the animals they have documented include</u> the arctic fox, African elephant, and wooly kangaroo.

(A) animals, animals like
(B) animals, some of them being
(C) animals such as
(D   animals: including
(E) animals; documenting

35 In context, which of the following should be inserted at the beginning of sentence 7?

(A) Even though
(B) Basically,
(C) As a result,
(D) For example,
(E) Still,

36 Which of the following sentences, if added after sentence 7, would link it to sentence 8?

(A) In one sense they are far away, but in another they are not.
(B) Sometime I will take a trip to see them all.
(C) It is better that they are there than confined inside the zoo.
(D) Usually I think about the arctic fox, but I like all of the canids.
(E) There are a lot of other television programs that don't interest me at all.

37 Which of the following would be the best way to combine sentences 8 and 9 (reproduced below)?

The nature shows bring you so close to the animals. Viewers can relate to the animals.

(A) The nature shows bring you viewers so close to the animals that you can relate to them.
(B) The nature shows bring you so close to the animals that viewers can relate to them.
(C) The nature shows bring animals so close to viewers, who can relate to them.
(D) The nature shows bring viewers so close to the animals that they can relate to them.
(E) On the nature shows, animals is brought so close to you, that viewers can relate to it.

GO ON TO THE NEXT PAGE

38 In context, what is the best way to revise the underlined portion of sentence 10 (reproduced below)?

They scratch when they have an itch, yawn when they're bored, and demonstrate surprise, curiosity, contentment, and fear.

(A) They also
(B) In addition, they
(C) Like humans, the animals
(D) Humans, as well as animals,
(E) The animals

39 To conclude the final paragraph in the best way, which of the following sentences should be added after sentence 14?

(A) Just as long as I can return.
(B) Then I could be one with the arctic fox.
(C) I would take photographs of all of the animals.
(D) That would truly be magic.
(E) Hopefully, some day I'll be able to do that.

Calculating Your Score on the Writing Test

S T E P **1**   **Count**

Total Number of Blanks: _____ + _____ + _____ = _____
                            Sec. 1   Sec. 2   Sec. 3

Total Number Correct: _____ + _____ + _____ = _____
                            Sec. 1   Sec. 2   Sec. 3

Total Number Incorrect: _____ + _____ + _____ = _____
                            Sec. 1   Sec. 2   Sec. 3

ADD to CHECK YOUR COUNTING. The Sum should be 39: _____

S T E P **2**   **Determine Your Score Adjustment**

The Score Adjustment is:

Total Number Incorrect x .25 = _____

S T E P **3**   **Determine Your Writing Test SCORE**

Your Writing Test SCORE is the Total Number Correct minus the Adjustment:

Total Correct: _____

Minus Adjustment: – _____

Writing Test SCORE   = _____

WRITING SKILLS	
Points	PSAT Range
39	80
35	66–76
30	58–68
25	52–62
20	46–56
15	40–50
10	36–46
5	30–40

Preparing for the Big Day

You've done your best to prepare for the test. Now comes the Big Day. To get the most out of all the time and effort you have put into studying for the SAT, you will want to make sure that the Big Day is also a good day for you. On the next two pages are a few tips for taking the test under the best possible conditions.

The Day Before

1. **Know the directions.** If you are taking the SAT at a high school you don't attend or at some other location with which you are unfamiliar, make sure you know the directions to your test center.

2. **Avoid stress.** The day before the SAT is not a good time to have an argument with your boyfriend or girlfriend. Avoid stressful situations. Try to participate in relaxing activities. For example, many students find it relaxing to watch a movie or favorite TV program.

3. **Have your test material ready.** Before going to sleep, gather all the items you will need for the SAT and put them all in one place. Here is a checklist of the materials you will need:
   - admission ticket
   - driver's license or picture I.D.
   - four sharpened No. 2 lead pencils with erasers
   - a wristwatch
   - a calculator

4. **Get a good night's sleep.** The SAT is a long test. Don't stay out late. Save your celebrations for after the test. Go to bed early and get a good night's sleep.

The Morning of the Test

1. **Wake up early.** Be sure to set your alarm clock to avoid oversleeping. You don't want to wake up late and then have to rush to the test center.

2. **Have a good breakfast.** Eat plenty of food, but don't overeat. Opt for healthy, high-energy foods. Remember, you'll be at the test center from 8:00 a.m. until noon. You will not be allowed to snack during the test, and you might not have access to snack machines during the break.

3. **Dress comfortably.** Room temperatures at testing centers can vary. Dress in layers—an extra sweater or sweatshirt is a good idea. If the room is too cold, you can keep your top layer; if it's too hot, you can take it off.

4. **Don't forget your materials.** Don't leave home without your admission ticket, driver's license or picture I.D., sharpened pencils, wristwatch, and calculator.

5. **Arrive early.** Plan to arrive at the test center no later than 8:00 a.m. This will allow time for you to collect your thoughts and relax before the test. It will also spare you the anxiety that comes with being late. Remember, no one will be allowed into the test center after the test has begun.

Taking the Test

1. **Be comfortable.** You have the right to take the SAT under the best possible conditions. If you are left handed, for example, insist on a left-handed desk. If the sun is in your eyes, close the curtains. If you are distracted by something in the room, do not be afraid to tell the proctors. Most proctors will be glad to help you if you let them know that you have a problem with the test-taking conditions.

2. **Don't be distracted by other students.** Each SAT test booklet contains seven sections. Since the sections are scrambled, the students seated around you will NOT have the same sequence of sections as you. If a student turns a page before you, don't be distracted. Your job is to focus on your test.

3. **Use the breaks.** You will receive a five-minute break after the first hour. If you need to use the restroom, this is the best time. Actually, it's the only time. Your final break will be a one-minute stretch break after the second hour. It is a good idea to stand up and stretch a little. Remember, you've still go another hour to go.

4. **Remember your indomitable will.** The SAT is a long and demanding test. Many students experience a moment of doubt when they lose their focus and want to give up. Recognize that this can happen. If a question is really tough, don't fixate on it. Skip the question and go on to the next one. Always stay focused and remember your indomitable will!

GOOD LUCK!

Acknowledgments, continued from page iv

From LOST IN TRANSLATION by Eva Hoffman. Copyright © 1989 by Eva Hoffman. Used by permission of Dutton, a division of Penguin Putnam Inc.

From YOUNG HEARTS CRYING by Richard Yates. Copyright © 1984 by Richard Yates. Used by permission of Delacorte Press, a division of Bantam Doubleday Dell Publishing Group, Inc.

From ARCTIC DREAMS by Barry Holstun Lopez. Reprinted by permission of Sterling Lord Literistic, Inc. Copyright © 1986 by Barry Holstun Lopez.

From "Economic Priorities and the Environmentalist" by Richard McGuire. Copyright © 1992 by Vital Speeches of the Day. Reprinted by permission of Vital Speeches of the Day.

"Media Meltdown" by Scott Menchin. Reprinted with permission from the April/May 1993 issue of GARBAGE the Independent Environmental Quarterly, 2 Main Street, Gloucester MA 01930.

From WOMEN ARTISTS 1550-1950 by Ann Sutherland Harris and Linda Nochlin. Copyright © 1976 by Museum Associates of the Los Angeles County Museum of Art. Reprinted by permission of Alfred A. Knopf, Inc.

Abraham Maslow, TOWARD A PSYCHOLOGY OF BEING. Copyright © 1968 by John Wiley & Sons, Inc. Reprinted by permission of John Wiley & Sons, Inc.

From Modern Science and the Nature of Life by William S. Beck. Copyright © 1957 by William S. Beck. Published by Harcourt, Brace and Company. Reprinted by permission of William S. Beck, M.D.

From "The Boundaries of Bohemia," from BOHEMIAN PARIS by Jerrold Seigel. Copyright © 1986 by Jerrold Seigel. Used by permission of Viking Penguin, a division of Penguin Books USA Inc.

From NATURAL ACTS by David Quammen. Reprinted by permission of David Quammen. All rights reserved. Copyright © 1983 by David Quammen.

From "Mastering the Writing Test," from INSIDE THE NEW SAT. Reprinted by permission of Profiles Corporation, © 1998 by Profiles Corporation. All rights reserved.

From THE UPROOTED by Oscar Handlin. Copyright © 1973 by Oscar Handlin. By permission of Little, Brown and Company.

From Rob Swigart's "Introduction" to the section "Japan," from WOMEN POETS OF THE WORLD by Joanna Bankier and Deirdre Lashgari. Copyright © 1983, Joanna Bankier and Deirdre Lashgari. Reprinted by permission.

"Etta Mae Johnson," from THE WOMEN OF BREWSTER PLACE by Gloria Naylor. Copyright © 1980, 1982 by Gloria Naylor. Used by permission of Viking Penguin, a division of Penguin Putnam Inc.

Excerpt from CAMPING WITH THE PRINCE. Copyright © 1990 by Thomas A. Bass. Reprinted by permission of Houghton Mifflin Co. All rights reserved.

ZAPS is a registered trademark of Profiles Corporation. The terms *ZAP, ZAPS,* and *ZAPPING,* as well as the methodology of *ZAPPING,* are used by permission throughout this book.

SAT/PSAT test questions selected from the following College Entrance Examination Board sources:

SAT Form Codes		PSAT/NMSQT Forms	
RL/RV	May 1995	T	October 1993
RB/RW	May 1995	S	October 1991
RE/RV	November 1995	10 SATs 1983 Edition	
QA/QN	March 1994	Real SAT	
8S	March 1993	PSAT	
8R	March 1993		
3W	May 1993		
2L	November 1992		

Reprinted by permission of Educational Testing Service and the College Entrance Examination Board, the copyright owners. Permission to reprint SAT test questions does not constitute review or endorsement by Educational Testing Service or the College Board of this publication as a whole or of any other questions or testing information it may contain.

SAT Words You Absolutely Need to Learn

The following pages contain flash cards for 355 words that frequently occur on the SAT and PSAT. Two additional word lists will supplement your study of the flash cards. Below are a few tips for incorporating these words, 400 in all, into your vocabulary.

- **Sort 'em.** Separate the cards and sort into three piles: words you know well, words you do not know at all, and words you are somewhat familiar with but still need to review. You may also wish to sort words by meaning or topic clusters, parts of speech, or word parts (prefixes, roots, or suffixes).

- **Take it personally.** Relate the word to something in your experience. Write a sentence with the word, relating it to the thing it reminds you of.

- **Be a show off.** Write a letter to a friend using as many of the words as you can, then have him or her respond with an equally verbose letter to you.

- **Think back.** The order of the 400 words in this list is based on the vocabulary-building system used in this book. Refer back to previous chapters to review words you find particularly perplexing.

- **Stack the deck.** As you encounter unfamiliar words in your everyday reading, make new word cards and add them to your deck.

Begin your word study by writing a sentence using each of the following words. Then make note cards to help you practice the words that are unfamiliar to you.

Twenty-three Four-letter Words You Can Use in Class

1. **Arid** – very dry

   _____

2. **Balk** – to stop short and refuse to proceed

   _____

3. **Bard** – a composer or singer in epic verse

   _____

4. **Bask** – to lie in or expose oneself to a pleasant warmth

   _____

5. **Bilk** – to cheat out of something valuable

   _____

6. **Boor** – a person known for rude or insincere behavior, someone who lacks refinement

   _____

7. **Dolt** – a person known for stupidity

   _____

8. **Dupe** – to trick or deceive by underhanded means

   _____

9. **Flag** – to lose energy or enthusiasm

   _____

10. **Foil** – someone or something that serves as a contrast to another

    _____

11. **Gait** – a manner of walking

    _____

12. **Hail** – to praise, acclaim; to call out to

    _____

13. **Lull** – temporary period of calm, as a lull before a storm

    _____

14. **Mute** – to muffle the sound, to tone down

    _____

15. **Plod** – to walk slowly or tediously

16. **Quip** – a clever witty remark

17. **Rend** – to tear apart or split, as to rend a fabric

18. **Ruse** – a wily or clever trick, stratagem

19. **Seer** – someone who predicts the future

20. **Stem** – to restrain, check

21. **Tiff** – a petty quarrel

22. **Vain** – marked by futility, as a vain effort

23. **Wary** – cautious, careful

Twenty-two Words Off the Beaten Path

1. **Calumny** – a misrepresentation intended to damage another's reputation

2. **Cathartic** – an emotional cleansing, purging

3. **Caustic** – sarcastic, biting; a caustic remark

4. **Conspicuous** – very visible, standing out

5. **Entourage** – attendants or associates surrounding a monarch or celebrity

6. **Epistolary** – a collection or series of letters

7. **Ethos** – a collection or set of values

_____

8. **Grovel** – to act in a servile or excessively subservient manner

_____

9. **Hermetic** – airtight, impervious to external influences

_____

10. **Imbroglio** – an intricate or complicated situation

_____

11. **Ire** – intense and usually open display of anger

_____

12. **Lampoon** – to ridicule, satirize

_____

13. **Maxim** – a proverb expressing a general truth of life

_____

14. **Melange** – a mixture, often of incongruous elements

_____

15. **Repartee** – an exchange of clever, witty remarks

_____

16. **Salvo** – a spirited attack, often verbal

_____

17. **Shroud** – to obscure the view of, veil

_____

18. **Superficial** – just above the surface, shallow, lacking in depth

_____

19. **Vapid** – flat, dull, lacking taste

_____

20. **Vignette** – a short descriptive literary sketch

_____

21. **Viscous** – thick and thus having the property of resistance to flow

_____

22. **Whelp** – a young dog

_____

1. **Eccentric**

2. **Elusive**

3. **Eminent**

4. **Exorbitant**

5. **Expound**

6. **Extricate**

7. **Extrovert**

8. **Amorphous**

9. **Anarchy**

10. **Anomaly**

11. **Atheist**

12. **Redundant**

13. **Refurbish**

14. **Rejuvenate**

15. **Repatriate**

16. **Resilient**

17. **Revitalize**

18. **Revoke**

PREFIXES – RE (back, again) 13.

to make new again, renovate

PREFIXES – the BIG E (out) 7.

an outgoing personality

PREFIXES – the BIG E (out) 1.

off center, hence a bit odd, weird, peculiar

PREFIXES – RE (back, again) 14.

to feel young again

PREFIXES – A (no, not) 8.

having no form or shape

PREFIXES – the BIG E (out) 2.

out of reach, hard to catch, evasive

PREFIXES – RE (back, again) 15.

to return to one's country of origin

PREFIXES – A (no, not) 9.

having no government, hence great disorder, chaos

PREFIXES – the BIG E (out) 3.

outstanding, illustrious, very prominent, notable

PREFIXES – RE (back, again) 16.

to bounce back from adversity or change

PREFIXES – A (no, not) 10.

not following the norm, hence an exception to a rule

PREFIXES – the BIG E (out) 4.

literally out of orbit, hence unreasonable

PREFIXES – RE (back, again) 17.

to regain energy

PREFIXES – A (no, not) 11.

person who does not believe in God

PREFIXES – the BIG E (out) 5.

to elaborate, to explain in great detail

PREFIXES – RE (back, again) 18.

to take back

PREFIXES – RE (back, again) 12.

to repeat something over and over again

PREFIXES – the BIG E (out) 6.

to get out of an entanglement or difficulty

Fold along perforation before detaching cards.

19.

Immutable

20.

Impartial

21.

Impious

22.

Inauspicious

23.

Incorporeal

24.

Incorrigible

25.

Indefatigable

26.

Insatiable

27.

Intrepid

28.

Inviolable

29.

(a) Unfazed
(b) Unflappable

30.

Unfettered

31.

Unfounded

32.

Unorthodox

33.

Unparalleled

34.

Unremitting

35.

Unscathed

36.

(a) Unsubstantiated
(b) Unwarranted

PREFIXES — UN (not) 31.

groundless, without substance, false

PREFIXES — IN/IM (not) 25.

incapable of being fatigued, having great stamina

PREFIXES — IN/IM (not) 19.

unchanging

PREFIXES — UN (not) 32.

not following established ways of thinking

PREFIXES — IN/IM (not) 26.

incapable of being satisfied

PREFIXES — IN/IM (not) 20.

unbiased, treating all equally

PREFIXES — UN (not) 33.

having no parallel, hence unequaled

PREFIXES — IN/IM (not) 27.

having no fear, dauntless

PREFIXES — IN/IM (not) 21.

lacking reverence, disrespectful

PREFIXES — UN (not) 34.

unrelieved, relentless, ceaseless

PREFIXES — IN/IM (not) 28.

secure and thus cannot be violated

PREFIXES — IN/IM (not) 22.

not favorable

PREFIXES — UN (not) 35.

unhurt, unharmed

PREFIXES — UN (not) 29.

(a) calm, not disturbed

(b) not easily upset, calm

PREFIXES — IN/IM (not) 23.

without material form or substance

PREFIXES — UN (not) 36.

(a) not proven

(b) lacking justification

PREFIXES — UN (not) 30.

free from restraints, liberated

PREFIXES — IN/IM (not) 24.

incapable of being reformed

37.

Untenable

38.

Abdicate

39.

Aberration

40.

Abhor

41.

Benediction

42.

Benefactor

43.

Benevolent

44.

Benign

45.

(a) Malefactor
(b) Malignant

46.

(a) Malediction
(b) Malevolent
(c) Malicious

47.

Supercilious

48.

Supersede

49.

Misanthrope

50.

Miscreant

51.

Misnomer

52.

(a) Amicable
(b) Amity
(c) Amiable

53.

Gregarious

54.

Segregate

PREFIXES — MIS (wrong/bad)   49.

a person who hates or distrusts mankind

PREFIXES — BENE (good/well)   43.

an inclination to do good, kindliness

PREFIXES — UN (not)   37.

that which cannot be defended

PREFIXES — MIS (wrong/bad)   50.

one who behaves criminally, an evildoer, a malefactor

PREFIXES — BENE (good/well)   44.

good natured, kindly, favorable, not malignant

PREFIXES — AB (away from/off)   38.

give up, resign, as to abdicate a throne

PREFIXES — MIS (wrong/bad)   51.

wrong name

PREFIXES — MAL (bad)   45.

(a) an evildoer or criminal

(b) having an evil influence, very harmful

PREFIXES — AB (away from/off)   39.

a departure from what is normal or typical

ROOTS — AMI (friend)   52.

(a) pleasant, friendly

(b) peaceful, friendly relations

(c) friendly, affable

PREFIXES — MAL (bad)   46.

(a) to say bad things, a curse

(b) wishing evil or harm to others

(c) to cause pain, injury, or distress to another

PREFIXES — AB (away from/off)   40.

to dislike intensely, loathe, despise

ROOTS — GREG (group)   53.

enjoying the company of groups, affable

PREFIXES — SUPER (above)   47.

thinking you are above others, arrogant, haughty

PREFIXES — BENE (good/well)   41.

to say or speak well of, hence a blessing

ROOTS — GREG (group)   54.

separating into different groups

PREFIXES — SUPER (above)   48.

replace, take the place of

PREFIXES — BENE (good/well)   42.

one who has given help, especially financial

Fold along perforation before detaching cards.

55.

Egregious

56.

(a) Antipathy
(b) Empathy

57.

Diffident

58.

(a) Fidelity
(b) Infidelity

59.

Perfidious

60.

(a) Elucidate
(b) Lucid

61.

(a) Pellucid
(b) Translucent

62.

Acrid

63.

Acrimonious

64.

(a) Acuity
(b) Acumen

65.

Acute

66.

Exacerbate

67.

Affluent

68.

Confluence

69.

Superfluous

70.

Complacent

71.

Implacable

72.

Placate

ROOTS – FLU (flow)   67.

to flow in abundance, wealthy

ROOTS – LUC (light)   61.

(a) very clear, transparent

(b) permitting the passage of light

ROOTS – GREG (group)   55.

out of the group, outstandingly bad

ROOTS – FLU (flow)   68.

to flow together, convergence

ROOTS – ACRI/ACER (very sharp)   62.

unpleasantly pungent in taste or odor

ROOTS – PATHOS (feeling)   56.

(a) feeling against someone or something, dislike

(b) feeling the same thing as someone else

ROOTS – FLU (flow)   69.

to flow above, hence exceeding what is necessary

ROOTS – ACRI/ACER (very sharp)   63.

full of spite, bitter, nasty

ROOTS – FID (faith)   57.

lack of faith in oneself, lack of confidence

ROOTS – PLAC (calm)   70.

to be so calm as to be self-satisfied, smug

ROOTS – ACRI/ACER (very sharp)   64.

(a) keenness of perception

(b) mental sharpness

ROOTS – FID (faith)   58.

(a) loyalty, faithfulness

(b) unfaithfulness

ROOTS – PLAC (calm)   71.

incapable of being calmed, relentless

ROOTS – ACRI/ACER (very sharp)   65.

a sharp angle, very keen

ROOTS – FID (faith)   59.

treacherous, untrustworthy

ROOTS – PLAC (calm)   72.

to calm the anger of

ROOTS – ACRI/ACER (very sharp)   66.

to sharpen or aggravate a conflict, inflame

ROOTS – LUC (light)   60.

(a) to make clear, clarify

(b) clear, readily understood

Fold along perforation before detaching cards.

73.

Placid

74.

Anachronism

75.

Chronological

76.

Synchronize

77.

Circumspect

78.

Perspicacity

79.

Specious

80.

Impugn

81.

Pugnacious

82.

Repugnant

83.

**Ecstatic
Exultant**

84.

**Elated
Exhilarated
Exuberant**

85.

**Despondent
Dejected**

86.

**Disconsolate
Dispirited**

87.

**Dogged
Obdurate
Recalcitrant**

88.

**Intractable
Intransigent
Obstinate**

89.

**Clandestine
Furtive**

90.

**Covert
Stealthy
Surreptitious**

85.

SO SAD CLUSTER – The Agony of Defeat

disconsolate, dispirited

86.

SO SAD CLUSTER – The Agony of Defeat

despondent, dejected

87.

STUBBORN CLUSTER – Stubborn, Inflexible, Hard to Budge

intractable, intransigent, obstinate

88.

STUBBORN CLUSTER – Stubborn, Inflexible, Hard to Budge

dogged, obdurate, recalcitrant

89.

SNEAKY CLUSTER – We've Got a Secret!

covert, stealthy, surreptitious

90.

SNEAKY CLUSTER – We've Got a Secret!

clandestine, furtive

79.

ROOTS – SPEC/SPIC (see)

seemingly fair or true, but actually not so, deceptive

80.

ROOTS – PUG (fist, fight)

to challenge the accuracy or honesty of something

81.

ROOTS – PUG (fist, fight)

combative, quick to fight

82.

ROOTS – PUG (fist, fight)

offensive, very distasteful, repulsive

83.

SO HAPPY CLUSTER – The Thrill of Victory

elated, exhilarated, exuberant

84.

SO HAPPY CLUSTER – The Thrill of Victory

ecstatic, exultant

73.

ROOTS – PLAC (calm)

to be outwardly calm, composed

74.

ROOTS – CHRON (time)

something that is not happening in its proper time

75.

ROOTS – CHRON (time)

arranged in the order of occurrence

76.

ROOTS – CHRON (time)

to occur at the same time, simultaneous

77.

ROOTS – SPEC/SPIC (see)

to look around and thus be cautious

78.

ROOTS – SPEC/SPIC (see)

having keen vision, as in being perceptive, astute

Fold along perforation before detaching cards.

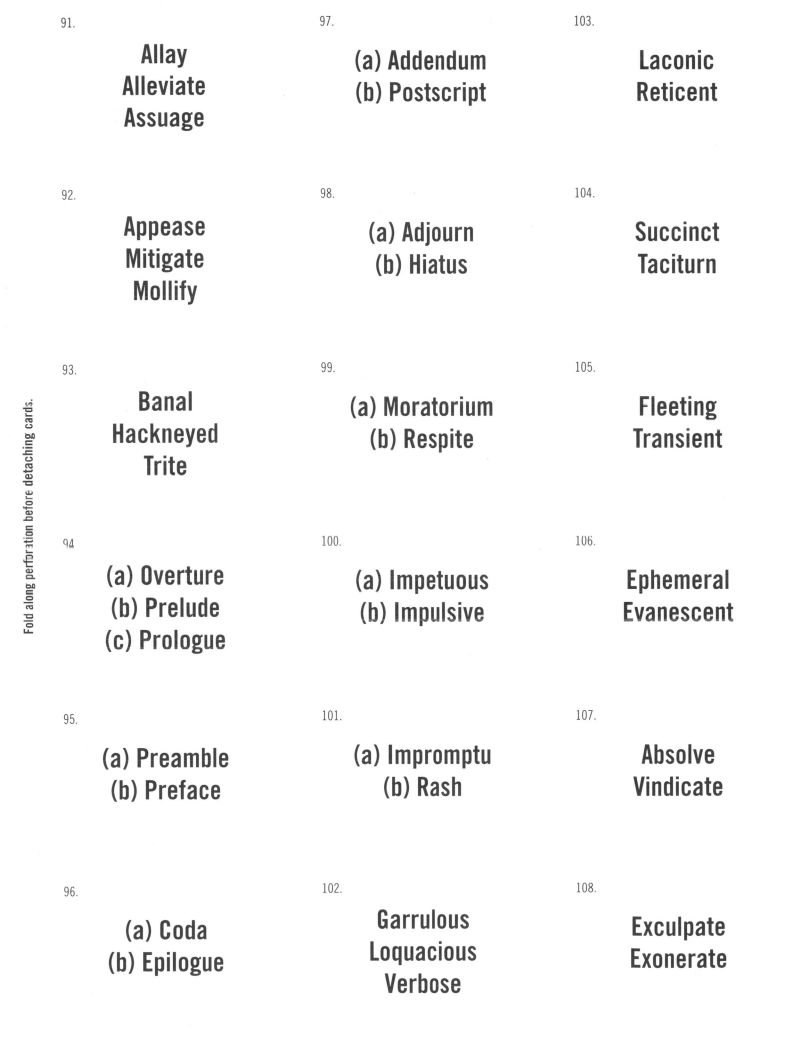

91.

**Allay
Alleviate
Assuage**

92.

**Appease
Mitigate
Mollify**

93.

**Banal
Hackneyed
Trite**

94.

**(a) Overture
(b) Prelude
(c) Prologue**

95.

**(a) Preamble
(b) Preface**

96.

**(a) Coda
(b) Epilogue**

97.

**(a) Addendum
(b) Postscript**

98.

**(a) Adjourn
(b) Hiatus**

99.

**(a) Moratorium
(b) Respite**

100.

**(a) Impetuous
(b) Impulsive**

101.

**(a) Impromptu
(b) Rash**

102.

**Garrulous
Loquacious
Verbose**

103.

**Laconic
Reticent**

104.

**Succinct
Taciturn**

105.

**Fleeting
Transient**

106.

**Ephemeral
Evanescent**

107.

**Absolve
Vindicate**

108.

**Exculpate
Exonerate**

TO the POINT CLUSTER — 103.

succinct, taciturn

saying little, keeping brief and to the point

TO the POINT CLUSTER — 104.

laconic, reticent

saying little, keeping brief and to the point

SHORT-LIVED CLUSTER — 105.

temporary, ephemeral, evanescent

SHORT-LIVED CLUSTER — 106.

temporary, fleeting, transient

PROVING BLAMELESS CLUSTER — 107.

exculpate, exonerate

to free from blame, prove guiltless

PROVING BLAMELESS CLUSTER — 108.

absolve, vindicate

to free from blame, prove guiltless

AT the END CLUSTER — 97.

(a) an addition or supplement to a book

(b) a note or series of notes appended to a completed letter; abbreviated P.S.

TAKE a BREAK CLUSTER — 98.

(a) to suspend until a later time

(b) a temporary gap, break in continuity, moratorium, respite

TAKE a BREAK CLUSTER — 99.

(a) a temporary pause, suspension of activity

(b) a temporary pause, adjournment, hiatus

HASTY CLUSTER — 100.

impromptu, rash

(a) done on the spur of the moment

(b) done on first impulse, without careful thought

HASTY CLUSTER — 101.

impetuous, impulsive

(a) done on the spur of the moment

(b) done on first impulse, without careful thought

YACK YACK CLUSTER — 102.

overly talkative

SOOTHING CLUSTER – Soothe, Calm, Relieve — 91.

appease, mitigate, mollify

SOOTHING CLUSTER – Soothe, Calm, Relieve — 92.

allay, alleviate, assuage

COMMONPLACE CLUSTER – Cliches/Commonplace — 93.

commonplace, trivial or made common and worn out by overuse

IN the BEGINNING CLUSTER — 94.

(a) an introduction to a musical

(b) an introduction to a performance

(c) an introduction to a poem, play, etc.

IN the BEGINNING CLUSTER — 95.

(a) an introduction to a constitution or legal document

(b) an introductory statement to a book, article, or speech

AT the END CLUSTER — 96.

(a) a concluding musical section

(b) a concluding section of a literary work

109.

**Abhorrent
Appalling
Despicable**

110.

**Heinous
Repulsive**

111.

**Apprehension
Foreboding
Premonition**

112.

**Enervated
Languid
Wan**

113.

**Indolent
Phlegmatic**

114.

**Lethargic
Listless**

115.

**Diatribe
Harangue
Tirade**

116.

Braggart

117.

Brigand

118.

Chauvinist

119.

Cynic

120.

Debunker

121.

Demagogue

122.

Egoist

123.

Glutton

124.

Hedonist

125.

Hypocrite

126.

Iconoclast

121.

A PERSON

known for using popular prejudices and false claims to gain power

122.

A PERSON

known for being excessively concerned with himself/herself, conceited

123.

A PERSON

known for having a huge, insatiable appetite for food and drink

124.

A PERSON

known for seeking pleasure

125.

A PERSON

known for saying one thing and doing another, insincere

126.

A PERSON

known for attacking settled beliefs

115.

NASTY LECTURE CLUSTER

a long abusive speech or lecture

116.

A PERSON

known for bragging

117.

A PERSON

known for living by plunder, a bandit

118.

A PERSON

known for excessive nationalism, a jingoist

119.

A PERSON

known for distrusting human nature

120.

A PERSON

known for exposing falsehoods

109.

DISGUSTING CLUSTER

heinous, repulsive

horrible in an extreme way

110.

DISGUSTING CLUSTER

abhorrent, appalling, despicable

horrible in an extreme way

111.

FUTURE WORRIES CLUSTER

uneasy feeling about the future

112.

OUT OF GAS CLUSTER

indolent, phlegmatic, lethargic, listless

exhausted and lacking energy

113.

OUT of GAS CLUSTER

enervated, languid, wan, lethargic, listless

exhausted and lacking energy

114.

OUT of GAS CLUSTER

enervated, languid, wan, indolent, phlegmatic

exhausted and lacking energy

Fold along perforation before detaching cards.

127.

Laggard

128.

(a) Loafer
(b) Loiterer

129.

Magnate

130.

Malingerer

131.

Martinet

132.

(a) Miser
(b) Skinflint

133.

Optimist

134.

Pacifist

135.

Pessimist

136.

Philanthropist

137.

Pragmatist

138.

Quack

139.

Raconteur

140.

Renegade

141.

Reprobate

142.

Rogue

143.

Sage

144.

Spendthrift

139.

A PERSON

known for telling witty stories
and anecdotes

140.

A PERSON

known for rejecting lawful or
conventional behavior

141.

A PERSON

known for being morally corrupt,
depraved

142.

A PERSON

known for being mischievous

143.

A PERSON

known for wisdom

144.

A PERSON

known for spending money
unwisely

133.

A PERSON

known for having a hopeful
outlook on life

134.

A PERSON

known for opposing war and
violence

135.

A PERSON

known for having a gloomy
outlook on life

136.

A PERSON

known for generosity, a
humanitarian

137.

A PERSON

known for using a practical
approach to solving problems

138.

A PERSON

who pretends to have skill or
knowledge he/she does not have;
charlatan

127.

A PERSON

known for being habitually tardy,
dilatory

128.

A PERSON

(a) known for being habitually
   lazy

(b) known for idleness

129.

A PERSON

known for having great power

130.

A PERSON

who pretends illness so as to
avoid work

131.

A PERSON

known as a strict disciplinarian

132.

A PERSON

(a) known for being stingy, a
   skinflint

(b) known for excessive thrift, a
   miser

Fold along perforation before detaching cards.

145.

Stalwart

151.

Bequest

157.

Perjury

146.

Stickler

152.

Codicil

158.

Deify

147.

Virtuoso

153.

Embezzlement

159.

Devout

148.

Zealot

154

Heir

160.

Heretical

149.

Acquit

155.

Injunction

161.

Orthodox

150.

Alias

156.

Jurisprudence

162.

Sanctimonious

LAW and the SAT 157.	**LAW and the SAT** 151.	**A PERSON** 145.
to give false testimony	something left to an heir in a will	known for being very loyal to a cause
RELIGION and the SAT 158.	**LAW and the SAT** 152.	**A PERSON** 146.
to worship as a god, to show great respect	an addition to a will	known for insisting on exact standards
RELIGION and the SAT 159.	**LAW and the SAT** 153.	**A PERSON** 147.
very religious	to illegally take another's property	known for excelling in the technique of an art
RELIGION and the SAT 160.	**LAW and the SAT** 154.	**A PERSON** 148.
holding an opinion opposed to official or established beliefs	a person who inherits another's property or title	known for excessive loyalty to a cause
RELIGION and the SAT 161.	**LAW and the SAT** 155.	**LAW and the SAT** 149.
conforming to established beliefs, conventional	a court order requiring or prohibiting an action	to clear of a charge
RELIGION and the SAT 162.	**LAW and the SAT** 156.	**LAW and the SAT** 150.
pretending to be pious and devout, false piety	the science of law	an assumed name, a false name or pseudonym

Fold along perforation before detaching cards.

163.

(a) Appreciate
(b) Depreciate

164.

(a) Dearth
(b) Duty
(c) Remuneration

165.

Belligerent

166.

Coerce

167.

Covenant

168.

Demarcation

169.

Dissolution

170.

Dominion

171.

Mandate

172.

Sedition

173.

Olfactory

174.

Palatable

175.

Savory

176.

Tactile

177.

Unpalatable

178.

Unsavory

179.

Abstruse

180.

Aesthetics

FIVE SENSES and the SAT   175.

appetizing to the taste or smell

FIVE SENSES and the SAT   176.

connected with the sense of touch

FIVE SENSES and the SAT   177.

not agreeable to the taste, hence
unacceptable

FIVE SENSES and the SAT   178.

distasteful, disagreeable

---

110 TOUGHEST WORDS on the SAT   179.

difficult to understand, very
abstract

---

110 TOUGHEST WORDS on the SAT   180.

the study of beauty

HISTORY and the SAT   169.

to dissolve, fall apart

HISTORY and the SAT   170.

to have supreme authority over

HISTORY and the SAT   171.

an authoritative command
requiring someone to do
something

HISTORY and the SAT   172.

to incite resistance against lawful
authority

FIVE SENSES and the SAT   173.

connected with the sense of smell

FIVE SENSES and the SAT   174.

agreeable to the taste, hence
acceptable

ECONOMICS and the SAT   163.

(a) to rise in value

(b) to fall in value

ECONOMICS and the SAT   164.

(a) an inadequate supply, scarcity

(b) a tax on imports

(c) payment due for a service

HISTORY and the SAT   165.

at war, engaging in hostilities

HISTORY and the SAT   166.

to compel, to use force to achieve
one's goals

HISTORY and the SAT   167.

a solemn and binding agreement

HISTORY and the SAT   168.

the settling or making of
boundaries or limits

Fold along perforation before detaching cards.

181.

Affable

182.

Ameliorate

183.

Amenable

184.

Approbation

185.

Appropriated

186.

Arduous

187.

Audacious

188.

Blanch

189.

Bombastic

190.

Brandish

191.

Brusque

192.

Burgeon

193.

Cantankerous

194.

Capacious

195.

Circuitous

196.

Circumscribe

197.

Compendium

198.

Consensus

193.

110 TOUGHEST WORDS on the SAT

difficult or irritating to deal with

187.

110 TOUGHEST WORDS on the SAT

very bold

181.

110 TOUGHEST WORDS on the SAT

pleasant, friendly

194.

110 TOUGHEST WORDS on the SAT

spacious, roomy

188.

110 TOUGHEST WORDS on the SAT

to drain of color, become pale

182.

110 TOUGHEST WORDS on the SAT

to make better, improve

195.

110 TOUGHEST WORDS on the SAT

following a circular or winding path, indirect

189.

110 TOUGHEST WORDS on the SAT

pretentious, inflated speech or writing, lacking in humility

183.

110 TOUGHEST WORDS on the SAT

willing to agree, responsive, cooperative

196.

110 TOUGHEST WORDS on the SAT

to draw a line around, hence to restrict or limit

190.

110 TOUGHEST WORDS on the SAT

to shake or wave in a menacing manner

184.

110 TOUGHEST WORDS on the SAT

approval

197.

110 TOUGHEST WORDS on the SAT

a concise list or summary

191.

110 TOUGHEST WORDS on the SAT

rough and abrupt in manner or speech, curt

185.

110 TOUGHEST WORDS on the SAT

to take or make use of without authority or right

198.

110 TOUGHEST WORDS on the SAT

a general agreement, common consent

192.

110 TOUGHEST WORDS on the SAT

to grow rapidly

186.

110 TOUGHEST WORDS on the SAT

long and difficult and thus hard to accomplish

199.

Corroborate

200.

Decorum

201.

Defile

202.

Demonstrative

203.

Demystify

204.

Desolate

205.

Desultory

206.

Dilatory

207.

Disabuse

208.

Disdain

209.

Disingenuous

210.

Disparage

211.

Diversion

212.

Divulge

213.

Docile

214.

Dogmatic

215.

Eclectic

216.

Effervescent

110 TOUGHEST WORDS on the SAT 211.	**110 TOUGHEST WORDS on the SAT** 205.	**110 TOUGHEST WORDS on the SAT** 199.
something that diverts or amuses	marked by a lack of a plan or purpose, lacking direction	to support with evidence, confirm a claim
110 TOUGHEST WORDS on the SAT 212.	**110 TOUGHEST WORDS on the SAT** 206.	**110 TOUGHEST WORDS on the SAT** 200.
to make known, reveal	tending to delay or procrastinate	conformity to accepted norms of behavior
110 TOUGHEST WORDS on the SAT 213.	**110 TOUGHEST WORDS on the SAT** 207.	**110 TOUGHEST WORDS on the SAT** 201.
easy to manage, malleable	to rid of false ideas, enlighten, free from error	to make unclear or impure, desecrate
110 TOUGHEST WORDS on the SAT 214.	**110 TOUGHEST WORDS on the SAT** 208.	**110 TOUGHEST WORDS on the SAT** 202.
very stubborn adherence to beliefs	to look on with scorn	an open display of feelings
110 TOUGHEST WORDS on the SAT 215.	**110 TOUGHEST WORDS on the SAT** 209.	**110 TOUGHEST WORDS on the SAT** 203.
selecting from a wide variety of sources, methods, or styles	giving a false appearance of simple frankness, hence calculating and crafty	to make clear and thus less baffling
110 TOUGHEST WORDS on the SAT 216.	**110 TOUGHEST WORDS on the SAT** 210.	**110 TOUGHEST WORDS on the SAT** 204.
to give off bubbles and thus be bubbly, exuberant	to run down, belittle, speak poorly of	lonely, uninhabited

Fold along perforation before detaching cards.

217.

Emulate

218.

Enamor

219.

Equanimity

220.

Espouse

221.

Exasperate

222.

Exigency

223.

Fallible

224.

Fastidious

225.

Fathom

226.

Feasible

227.

Fervor

228.

Flaunt

229.

Garish

230.

Gingerly

231.

Gratuitous

232.

Gullible

233.

Hubris

234.

Idiosyncrasy

110 TOUGHEST WORDS on the SAT

229.

excessively vivid colors

110 TOUGHEST WORDS on the SAT

223.

prone to making errors

110 TOUGHEST WORDS on the SAT

217.

to imitate, copy

110 TOUGHEST WORDS on the SAT

230.

very cautious, careful

110 TOUGHEST WORDS on the SAT

224.

exacting, meticulous, hard to please

110 TOUGHEST WORDS on the SAT

218.

fill with love

110 TOUGHEST WORDS on the SAT

231.

not called for by the circumstances, as a gratuitous insult

110 TOUGHEST WORDS on the SAT

225.

figure out, comprehend, probe the depth of

110 TOUGHEST WORDS on the SAT

219.

evenness of mind, especially under stress

110 TOUGHEST WORDS on the SAT

232.

easily fooled or duped

110 TOUGHEST WORDS on the SAT

226.

possible

110 TOUGHEST WORDS on the SAT

220.

to give support to

110 TOUGHEST WORDS on the SAT

233.

excessive pride, arrogance

110 TOUGHEST WORDS on the SAT

227.

intense feelings, great passion

110 TOUGHEST WORDS on the SAT

221.

to cause irritation or annoyance

110 TOUGHEST WORDS on the SAT

234.

any personal peculiarity, eccentricity

110 TOUGHEST WORDS on the SAT

228.

to violate conventions, treat with contempt

110 TOUGHEST WORDS on the SAT

222.

great urgency, requiring immediate attention

Fold along perforation before detaching cards.

235.

Incandescent

236.

Incantation

237.

Incipient

238.

Incontrovertible

239.

Indelicate

240.

Indiscreet

241.

Indomitable

242.

Ineffable

243.

Innate

244.

Insipid

245.

Insolent

246.

Insuperable

247.

Irrevocable

248.

Legion

249.

Levity

250.

Limpid

251.

Linchpin

252.

Machinations

110 TOUGHEST WORDS on the SAT

not possible to revoke, unalterable, unable to be called back

110 TOUGHEST WORDS on the SAT

incapable of being subdued, unconquerable

110 TOUGHEST WORDS on the SAT

giving off light, gleaming, brilliantly shining

110 TOUGHEST WORDS on the SAT

a very large number

110 TOUGHEST WORDS on the SAT

incapable of being expressed, indescribable

110 TOUGHEST WORDS on the SAT

use of spells or verbal charms spoken as part of a magical ritual

110 TOUGHEST WORDS on the SAT

light-hearted humor

110 TOUGHEST WORDS on the SAT

present in an individual from birth

110 TOUGHEST WORDS on the SAT

in the early stages, just beginning, embryonic

110 TOUGHEST WORDS on the SAT

transparent, perfectly clear

110 TOUGHEST WORDS on the SAT

without flavor, tasteless, not exciting, dull

110 TOUGHEST WORDS on the SAT

cannot be disproved

110 TOUGHEST WORDS on the SAT

the key element in something

110 TOUGHEST WORDS on the SAT

disrespectful in speech or conduct, haughty

110 TOUGHEST WORDS on the SAT

lacking a sensitivity for the feelings of others, tactless

110 TOUGHEST WORDS on the SAT

scheming or crafty actions intended to accomplish an evil end

110 TOUGHEST WORDS on the SAT

something incapable of being overcome

110 TOUGHEST WORDS on the SAT

an action marked by a lack of decorum, hence tasteless

Fold along perforation before detaching cards.

253.

Mercurial

259.

Paragon

265.

Predilection

254.

Milestone

260.

Paramount

266.

Quixotic

255.

Munificent

261.

Patronizing

267.

Ransack

256.

Nuance

262.

Perfunctory

268.

Raucous

257.

Ominous

263.

Polemic

269.

Rebuke

258.

Ostentatious

264.

Precipitous

270.

Rectitude

110 TOUGHEST WORDS on the SAT

a liking or preference for
something

110 TOUGHEST WORDS on the SAT

a model of excellence

110 TOUGHEST WORDS on the SAT

rapid and unpredictable changes
in mood

110 TOUGHEST WORDS on the SAT

idealistic in an impractical way

110 TOUGHEST WORDS on the SAT

of supreme importance

110 TOUGHEST WORDS on the SAT

a significant or important turning
point

110 TOUGHEST WORDS on the SAT

to search closely and carefully, to
turn upside down

110 TOUGHEST WORDS on the SAT

to act superior toward, to adopt
an air of condescension

110 TOUGHEST WORDS on the SAT

very generous

110 TOUGHEST WORDS on the SAT

harsh, jarring sound, blaring

110 TOUGHEST WORDS on the SAT

done in a routine manner

110 TOUGHEST WORDS on the SAT

a subtle distinction or shade of
difference

110 TOUGHEST WORDS on the SAT

to criticize sharply, reprimand,
berate

110 TOUGHEST WORDS on the SAT

involving a dispute, very
argumentative

110 TOUGHEST WORDS on the SAT

threatening evil or disaster,
inauspicious

110 TOUGHEST WORDS on the SAT

great integrity, moral uprightness,
honesty

110 TOUGHEST WORDS on the SAT

acting with undue haste

110 TOUGHEST WORDS on the SAT

fond of conspicuous display,
pompous, pretentious

Fold along perforation before detaching cards.

271.

Redoubtable

272.

Reprehensible

273.

Skulk

274.

Specious

275.

Sporadic

276.

Spurious

277.

Staid

278.

Stanch

279.

Strident

280.

Suffuse

281.

Talisman

282.

Torpor

283.

Ubiquitous

284.

Usurp

285.

Vacuous

286.

Venal

287.

Wan

288.

Watershed

110 TOUGHEST WORDS on the SAT 283.	**110 TOUGHEST WORDS** on the SAT 277.	**110 TOUGHEST WORDS** on the SAT 271.
present everywhere, pervasive	marked by self-restraint, sober, grave	formidable, worthy of respect

110 TOUGHEST WORDS on the SAT 284.	**110 TOUGHEST WORDS** on the SAT 278.	**110 TOUGHEST WORDS** on the SAT 272.
to illegally seize power, property, or position	to stop the flow of blood from a wound	conduct deserving criticism or censure

110 TOUGHEST WORDS on the SAT 285.	**110 TOUGHEST WORDS** on the SAT 279.	**110 TOUGHEST WORDS** on the SAT 273.
empty, having or showing a lack of intelligence or insight	loud, harsh sound	to move in a stealthy or furtive manner

110 TOUGHEST WORDS on the SAT 286.	**110 TOUGHEST WORDS** on the SAT 280.	**110 TOUGHEST WORDS** on the SAT 274.
capable of being bought or influenced by money, corrupt	to spread over or through, to diffuse	tempting but false, untrue, spurious

110 TOUGHEST WORDS on the SAT 287.	**110 TOUGHEST WORDS** on the SAT 281.	**110 TOUGHEST WORDS** on the SAT 275.
lacking vitality	an object held to act as a charm to avert evil and bring good fortune	occurring occasionally, infrequently, not regular

110 TOUGHEST WORDS on the SAT 288.	**110 TOUGHEST WORDS** on the SAT 282.	**110 TOUGHEST WORDS** on the SAT 276.
a very important event	a lack of energy, lethargy	falsified, fake, and thus not genuine

Fold along perforation before detaching cards.